DIFFICULT & DANGEROUS ROADS

Hugh Clapperton's Travels
in Sahara and Fezzan
(1822-25)

DIFFICULT & DANGEROUS ROADS

Hugh Clapperton's Travels in Sahara and Fezzan (1822-25)

Edited by
Jamie Bruce-Lockhart and John Wright

Published by Sickle Moon Books
in association with The Society for Libyan Studies

First published in 2000 by Sickle Moon Books,

3, Inglebert Street, Clerkenwell, London EC1R 1XR

in association with The Society of Libyan Studies

The Society for Libyan Studies, founded in 1969, is established as a British Institute Abroad and funded by the British Academy. Its aims are to encourage and co-ordinate the activities of British scholars in Libya covering as wide a range of interests as possible including the natural sciences, linguistics and history as well as archaeology, and to foster and develop relations between British and Libyan scholars.

Since its foundation the Society has sponsored many differing projects in Libya within the subject areas of archaeology, education, geography, geology, history and Islamic law. Its resources to date have been concentrated on supporting long term archaeological projects and their subsequent publication, including excavations in Benghazi, Tolmeita, Ajdabiyah and Germa in the Fezzan; and more recently the multi-disciplinary survey in the pre-desert valleys of Tripolitania, the Islamic excavation at Medinet Sultan and the publication of the postwar excavations at Sabratha.

For details of membership, subscriptions, lecture meetings, use of the library, the annual *Libyan Studies* journal or grants in aid of research write to the General Secretary, The Society for Libyan Studies, c/o The Institute of Archaeology, 31-34 Gordon Square, London WC1H OPY.

ISBN 1-900209-06 3

The cover shows a portrait of Hugh Clapperton by Gildon Manton, c.1826 by courtesy of the MOD Art Collection.

Designed by Mick Keates

Formatting and typesetting by Mike Miles

Printed by Anthony Rowe Ltd

CONTENTS

ILLUSTRATIONS

MAPS

FOREWORD

Hugh Clapperton's Libyan travels form part of an extraordinary and gripping "exploration narrative" of the early nineteenth century. This was one of the earliest European missions seeking to reach Central Africa from the north across the Sahara. The fascination of the story, and what still gives it an universal appeal, lies in what it reveals of the reality of the African exploration business and the psychology of those who undertook it. When I first read the published account of the Oudney, Denham and Clapperton expedition I was completely gripped by the dramatic events and intense personality clashes that their expedition got caught up in. Faced with extraordinary dangers on a largely uncharted route, often enduring deprivations and beset with debilitating illnesses, their response was all too humanly flawed. A simmering dispute about the leadership of the expedition erupted into a bitter and dangerous rift between the two members who survived, Dixon Denham and Hugh Clapperton. The hardships endured by Clapperton and his fellow travellers are clear from the account, but there is also a great deal of acute observation of the people of southern Libya and the Saharan caravan routes, not least the slaves who were a major item of traffic.

I had always assumed that the full story of the expedition was told in Bovill's excellent re-edition of the Mission papers in 1966, with his painstaking examination of the disintegration of personal relationships. I was thus very surprised and excited when Jamie Bruce-Lockhart first made contact informing me that he had transcribed an unpublished diary of Clapperton and was interested in publishing the Libyan sections. Since Denham had managed to suppress much of this material at the time of its first publication, in favour of his own narrative, it was clear that this was indeed a major addition to our knowledge of the activities of the mission and of southern Libya in the early nineteenth century.

The diary also sheds further light on Clapperton as a person. In his sometimes terse shorthand he speaks to us in a modest factual voice: a man of his time, but an acute observer. The "Difficult and Dangerous Roads" are vividly depicted for the reader, even in the fractured and abrupt entries put down (at who knows what cost) during the ravages of malaria. The acid test of such a narrative is its readability for people who know little of the background. Field-testing of the typescript on numerous participants on my current archaeological project in southern Libya, based in Germa – one of the settlements described by Clapperton – has been uniformly enthusiastic.

The Clapperton diary adds to our knowledge of Libyan history, society, geography and antiquity, reflecting the broad research mandate of the Society of Libyan Studies. I am personally delighted that the Society has been involved in bringing this important work to press and would like to acknowledge the British Academy's support in this. The project owes everything to the dedication and enthusiasm of the editors, Jamie Bruce-Lockhart and John Wright, and our publisher, Barnaby Rogerson, who have produced an accessible and attractive book, which will also have lasting scholarly value.

Professor David Mattingly
Chairman of the Society for Libyan Studies
University of Leicester, July 1999

ACKNOWLEDGEMENTS

The editors wish to thank the Brenthurst Library, Johannesburg, for their kind permission to publish these journals from their collection of manuscripts (library reference ms. 171). They have also prepared (and in some cases donated) the fascimiles for all the text and illustrations that appear in this volume. In particular Mrs Diana Madden, the Manuscript Librarian, has proved unfailingly helpful and sympathetic to the project. The Ministry of Defence Art Collection have kindly given us permission to reproduce the portrait of Hugh Clapperton by Gildon Manton that appears in the biographical introduction. The Royal Geographical Society have also kindly given their permission for us to reproduce those letters that appear in appendix 1. We were also fortunate to have been able to make use of the expertise of Simon Pressey, an archaeologist familiar with the Fezzan, who has drawn up all the maps.

Amongst the many specialists and academics who have freely given of their advice and time we would especially like to mention Professor H.T. Norris, of the School of Oriental and African Studies (SOAS) for his commentaries on Clapperton's observations on the Tuareg and his Tamasheq word list which appears in Appendix 2. Other invaluable assistance was received from Dr R. Blench of the Overseas Development Institute, Dr G. Clifton of the National Maritime Museum, Dr G. Crook, editor of the 20th edition of Manson's Tropical Diseases, Professor N. Cyffer of the University of Vienna, Professor W. M. Edmunds of the British Hydrological Survey, Mr O. M. Gaasholt of SOAS, Mr C. Gardiner at Sotheby's, Professor P. Lovejoy, York University, Ontario, Professor N. Petit-Maire of the Centre de Recherches Sahariennes, Aix en Provence and Brigadier K. A. Timbers of the Royal Artillery Historical Trust.

They would also wish to express their deep gratitude to the British Academy and the Society of Libyan Studies who have provided generous and consistent financial support for the project. In particular the Chairman of the Society of Libyan Studies, Professor David Mattingly, must be credited for his personal interest and enthusiastic commitment.

Special thanks are due to Flip Bruce-Lockhart for her painstaking and expert help with the transcription of the manuscripts.

TRANSCRIPTION OF THE TEXT

In order to retain the flavour of the original the following devices have been used.

[   ]   indicates a space left in the journal

italics   signifies "looks like"

[=   ]   suggested replacement of erroneous word

Elsewhere, abbreviated forms have been expanded if there was a danger of ambiguity, some spelling corrected (such as 'there' for 'their') and the minor omission of letters filled (such as 'off' from of). Any elucidation of words that are now uncommon is based on the *Shorter Oxford English Dictionary*, 2 Vols, London, 1983, cited in the text as [ShOED]. Otherwise the editors have taken great delight in retaining Hugh Clapperton's own idiosyncratic orthography.

Those interested in a full account of the problems encountered and the practices adopted in transcribing Clapperton's manuscript will find it in Appendix 6. An account of the cartographic basis for the present maps, and the transliteration of place-names from the original Arabic and Saharan languages is given in Appendix 5.

INTRODUCTION

Fezzan and Sahara in the early 19th century

To Europeans of the 18th-century enlightenment, Africa was the Dark Continent. There was darkness in its people's colour; in their unbaptised souls and unenlightened minds; in their societies lacking civil "politeness"; in the evils of their enslavement by fellow-Africans; and in Europe's own ignorance of the inner continent. Since first arriving in West Africa in the 15th century, Europeans had been all but confined to small trading settlements and forts on the coastlines. Access to the interior was barred by hostile natives, tropical diseases and poor communications; rivers were unnavigable where falls marked their descent from interior uplands. So long as African middlemen enslaved their fellows for the Atlantic triangular trade linking Africa, the Americas and Europe[1], there seemed few rewards in opening up the inner continent. European understanding of Africa – and thus in effect the sum of knowledge in the wider world – drew on Classical sources at least 1,500 years old, on sketchy and mostly outdated medieval Arab accounts, and on contemporary European familiarity with the coasts and their immediate hinterlands.

Then in 1788, the curiosity of the age, the fresh vigour of British intellectual inquiry, prompted the first concerted efforts to explore Africa. Aware that the contemporary map of the continent was "still but a wide extended blank" and "desirous of rescuing the age from a charge of ignorance", a dozen wealthy and influential gentlemen agreed to found an "Association for Promoting the Discovery of the Interior Parts of

---

[1]E. Williams, *Capitalism and Slavery* (London, 1964) pp. 51 et seq.; A. G. Hopkins, *An Economic History of West Africa* (London, 1973) Map on p.100: "Atlantic Commerce in the Eighteenth Century".

1

Africa" (commonly known as the African Association)². They were prompted by curiosity – "a curiosity controlled by rational minds and directed to practical ends"³, and in particular to the problem of the rise, course and outlet of West Africa's greatest river, the Niger.

Not one of the ten explorers sponsored by the African Association between 1788 and 1830 penetrated Africa easily. The most successful was Mungo Park who, on his first journey from the west coast (1795-97), reached the Niger at Segu and at least established its direction of flow.⁴ Among those who approached from the north was Simon Lucas. In 1788-89 he travelled only from Tripoli to Misurata, there being deterred by tribal unrest on the road from visiting Tripoli's tributary province of Fezzan and countries beyond. But he used his fluent Arabic to gain from merchants in Misurata a mass of new and valuable information on the interior⁵. Ten years later a young German sponsored by the African Association, Friedrich Hornemann, travelled from Cairo through Awjila to Murzuq, the oasis-capital of Fezzan, and hub of central Saharan trade and communications. In 1799 he went to Tripoli, forwarded a valuable report to London, and in 1800 left for the interior, where he disappeared⁶.

By the beginning of the 19th century Europe was still sadly ignorant about the interior of Africa, although much had been learned since the travels of James Bruce in 1768-73. When in 1798 the African Association's cartographer, Major James Rennell, drew his map "showing the progress of discovery and improvement in the geography of North Africa", his heavy reliance on Classical and medieval Arab sources led him into many errors that not even his amendments of 1802 could correct⁷.

---

²*Plan of the Association*, reproduced in *Proceedings of the Association for Promoting the Discovery of the Interior Parts of Africa* (2 vols., London, 1810) Vol. I, pp. 3-11; R. Hallett (ed.), *Records of the African Association, 1788-1831* (London, 1964) pp. 42-7; see also R. Hallett, *The Penetration of Africa, etc.* (London, 1965) pp. 193-8.

³Hallett, *Records*, p. 15; A Mori, *L'esplorazione geografica della Libia* (Florence, 1927) p. 5.

⁴For all relevant routes, see Hallett, *Records*, loose map: "The Association's Explorers".

⁵Hallett, *The Penetration*, p. 208. For Lucas's report, see *Proceedings*, Vol. I, pp. 47-205.

⁶His travel journal covering Egypt and Libya is published in *Proceedings*, Vol. II, pp. 39-208 and in E. W. Bovill (ed.) *Missions to the Niger* (4 Vols., Cambridge, 1964-66) Vol. I, pp. 3-122. Captain George Lyon, R.N. [*A Narrative of Travels in Northern Africa in the Years 1818, 1819 and 1820* (London, 1821) p. 132] received news in 1819 of Hornemann's death in Nupe. Major Dixon Denham [unpublished notebook, 1821-2, in Royal Geographical Society, *Denham Collection*, DD 22/1] records the remarks of a merchant encountered in Tripoli who had a similar report:

Hadje Smaene... remembered Hornemann, whose travelling name was Yussuff, at Kashna and

The Sahara is a formidable natural barrier because it is mostly barren and waterless and often hostile, but above all because it is so vast. This largest of the world's hot deserts is continental in scale, reaching almost without a break from the Atlantic coast of Mauritania to the Red Sea, and from the Libyan Sirtica to Lake Chad and the River Niger. Its area is rather larger than the continental United States of America, so that Tripoli is almost as far from Lake Chad as from London.

The great desert's emergence in its present form about 4,000 years ago marked the division of Africa between the "white" north, linked by geography, race, culture and history to the civilisations of the Mediterranean and the Near East, and the sub-Saharan "black" continent – remote, introverted and culturally isolated. That isolation might have been deeper had the Sahara been an absolute natural barrier, instead of allowing selective access to inner Africa from the north[8]. Men have travelled the Sahara for short- or long-range seasonal pasturing, for petty commerce, or to raid others. Only traders have usally made the full crossing from the north to the sub-Saharan Sudan[9]. For, with few exceptions, North Africa and the Sahara have themselves never been prime sources of raw materials or manufactures. Rather, they have always been places of exchange, of import and re-export, between other centres of supply and demand. In broad terms, manufactured goods from Europe were exchanged for African gold, while those sent from Egypt and the Levant were traded for black slaves brought from inner Africa. Thus Saharan trade routes ended at suitable northern oases or at the few safe anchorages on North Africa's exposed and surprisingly inhospitable Mediterranean coast, and at the corresponding location of

saw him frequently. He was much respected & considered a good Mussulman and a Fighi. Hornemann went to Nyffe while Hadje Asmaene remained at Kashna. Some months later he also went to Nyffe on his way to Raka. Here on inquiring he found that Yussuff had died in the house of Abrahim ben Haji Ali. Haji Asmaene went to the house of Ibrahim and heard from him that what money Hornemann had, he gave him on his death; the other property & papers, which Ibrahim said was in two trunks, the Sultan of Nyffe took possession of & he never heard what became of them.

Clapperton obtained another, substantively similar, account in Kano in 1824 [*Missions*, Vol. IV, pp. 657-8]; and on his second expedition to the interior attempted, but without success, to retrieve Hornemann's papers.

[7]For reproduction of Rennell's 1798 map, see M. Park, *Travels in the Interior Districts of Africa* (London, 1799), tipped in at end; for the amended version of 1802, see *Proceedings*, Vol. I, opposite p. 209; see also Hallett, *Records*, end pocket.

[8]J. D. Fage, *A History of Africa* (London, 1978) pp. 12-16; J. Wright, *Libya, Chad and the Central Sahara* (London, 1989) pp. 1-3.

[9]Ar., *Bilad al-Sudan*, the land of the blacks, applied broadly to all the country immediately to the south of the Sahara.

markets and raw materials entrepots in Sudanic Africa.

Such routes were not roads or even tracks in any recognised sense, but rather a general line of travel between two points[10]. They were tried and proven over centuries for the relative ease of travel they offered; for their greater security from marauders; for the location of intermediate oases with their fresh supplies, transport animals, guides and markets; and for the whereabouts of pasture. But vital to any route was the availability of water at suitable intervals, and enough of it, to slake the urgent, sometimes desperate thirst of an arriving caravan, possibly of many hundreds of people (including slaves) and animals[11]. Depending on changing political, economic, security and environmental conditions, different Saharan roads predominated at different times. But the peculiar advantages of Tripoli's position on the central Mediterranean narrows, close to Malta and Sicily, and on the very edge of the central Sahara, ensured its survival as an essential entrepot on the maritime-desert trading frontier. As the trading Phoenicians recognised more than 2,500 years ago, Tripolitania is closer than any other part of North Africa to the Sudan, and three main Saharan roads start at Tripoli. Two take advantage of the natural corridor of the Fezzanese oases, about one-third of the way between the Mediterranean at Tripoli and the southern edge of the Sahara at the edge of Lake Chad. They also lie about mid-way between the Niger Bend to the south-west and Egypt to the north-east. The Fezzanese oases thus provide the essential halting places on the long desert journeys between "white" and "black" Africa[12].

Possibly the oldest and easiest Saharan crossing was by the so-called Garamantian road, named after the Garamantes people of Fezzan mentioned by Herodotus in the fifth century BC[13]. This passed from Tripoli through the Jofra oases and the Jabal

---

[10]J. Chapelle, *Nomades noirs du Sahara: les Toubous* (Paris, 1982), p. 31.

[11]L. C. Briggs, *Tribes of the Sahara* (Cambridge, Mass., 1960) pp. 9, 28-30; R. Mauny, *Les navigations médiévales sur les côtes sahariennes antérieures à la découverte portugaise (1434)* (Lisbon 1960) p.21; I. Droandi, *Notizie sul cammello* (Tripoli, 1915) pp. 107-8; R. Bulliet, *The Camel and the Wheel* (Cambridge, Mass., 1975) pp. 31, 35. For the horrors of waterless caravan travel in the desert, see R. Caillié, *Travels through Central Africa to Timbuctu, etc.*, (2 Vols., London, 1830) Vol. II, pp. 108-19.

[12]E. F. Gautier, *Sahara: The Great Desert* (New York, 1987) pp. 173-5; D. E. L. Haynes, *The Antiquities of Tripolitania* (Tripoli, 1965) p. 17; see also R. Herzog, "Ein Beitrag zur Geschichte des nordafrikanischen Karavanenhandels" in *Die Welt des Islams*, Vol. VI, 1959-1961, pp. 255-6.

[13]Herodotus, *The Histories* (trans. De Selincourt, Harmondsworth, 1954) Book IV, 183, pp. 303-4; see also A. Merighi, *La Tripolitania antica* (2 Vols., Intra, Verbania 1940) Vol. II, pp. 200-3; C. Daniels, *The Garamantes of Southern Libya* (Stoughton, Wis., 1970).

as-Sawda to the Fezzanese wadis; with plentiful water and supplies, it offered relatively easy travelling. The second track from Tripoli to Fezzan across the Hamada al-Hamra plateau was more direct but more difficult, unsuitable for large caravans. From the Fezzanese oases (and different ones predominated at different times) a single road led to Lake Chad. This passed between the central Saharan massifs of Hoggar and Tibesti and then through the natural north-south corridor of the Kawar oases to the Chadian *sahel*[14]. The full distance from Tripoli to Lake Chad is about 1,500 miles, or two to three months' travel for large caravans, not including long halts. Tripoli's third road to Black Africa exploited the phenomenon of the small and isolated oases of Ghadamis, with its direct links to the rich sub-Saharan markets of the Hausa states and, further west, the Niger Bend, some 2,000 miles off, or three to four months' travel[15].

These central routes were part of a complex, Sahara-wide trading system that had linked North Africa with the Sudan from at least the first Millennium BC. Goods in transit had to withstand dust, heat, cold, rough handling and the high costs and losses of long and dangerous desert journeys: this was essentially a trade in luxuries with a high value-to-weight ratio. It is assumed that before the introduction of the Arabian camel into North Africa at about the time of Christ, the trade of the central Sahara was controlled by the Garamantes of Fezzan. It is said that their patterns of trade, using carts drawn by horses or oxen, may be traced along two series of Saharan rock-art sites showing such vehicles (although it is hard to understand how they could have been practical transport for such a purpose)[16]. The trans-Saharan trade of Cyrenaica's Greek colonies is assumed to have passed through the oasis of Awjila and then by the agency of the Garamantes. The Romans, who conquered and ruled

[14]Sahel – Arabic for "coast", but applied also to the pre-desert lands both north and south of the Sahara.

[15]For some maps of the Saharan trade routes at various periods, see E. W. Bovill, *The Golden Trade of the Moors* (London, 1958) Map VII, p. 234, "The Principal Caravan routes of the Nineteenth Century"; A.A. Boahen, *Britain, the Sahara and the Western Sudan, 1788-1861* (Oxford, 1964) Map 3, p. 103; "The Caravan and Sudan Trade Routes of the Nineteenth Century"; Hopkins, *An Economic History*, Map 7, p. 84, "Saharan Trade Routes in the Pre-Colonial period"; J. Thiry, *Le Sahara Libyen dans: L'Afrique du Nord Médiévale* (Leuven, 1995) loose Map V, "Les voies transsahariennes" and loose Map VI, "Les voies translibyennes".

[16]For map, see R. Oliver and J. D. Fage, *A Short History of Africa* (Harmondsworth, 1962) p. 55; see also Daniels, *The Garamantes*, pp.12-3; H. Lhote, *The Search for the Tassili Frescoes* (London, 1959) map facing p. 22; *Les Chars rupestres sahariens des Syrtes au Niger par les pays des Garamantes et des Atlantes* (Toulouse, 1982) pp. 155-6; Bulliet, *The Camel and the Wheel*, pp. 17-19.

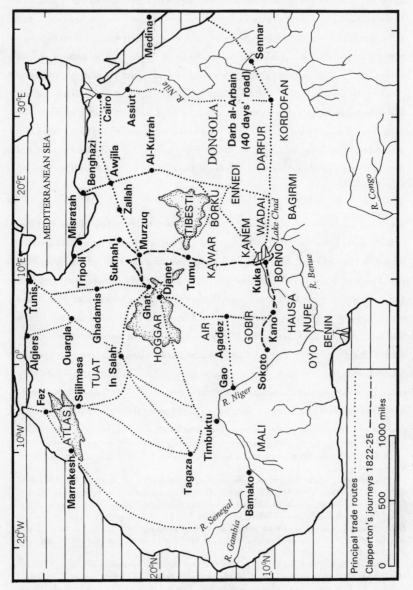

Map 1. Trade Routes of the Sahara in the early 19th century

both Tripolitania and Cyrenaica but, despite punitive expeditions, never controlled Fezzan, carried on an arrangement confirmed by modern archaeological evidence from Fezzan. So did the Romans' Byzantine successors. But it is not wholly clear what was traded across the Sahara in pre-Islamic times. Gold dust, animal skins, ivory, gemstones, perfumes, black slaves – the attested staples of the medieval export trade of inner Africa – are assumed also in earlier centuries to have been exchanged across the desert for the cheap manufactures and trinkets of the Roman world. But a *regular* trans-Saharan trade in black slaves probably only developed after the rise of the Islamic caliphal empire in the seventh century AD[17]. The scale and scope of trans-Saharan trade had by then been transformed by the rise of the long-range camel-mounted Saharan nomad, and the corresponding decline of first Roman and then Byzantine power in the northern coastlands[18]. Thus the coming of the Muslim Arabs in two main waves in the seventh and eleventh centuries, and the rise of a succession of Sudanese states with a surplus of slaves or gold, or both, for export prompted North Africa's commercial, religious and cultural penetration of inner Africa: for the first time, West Africa was in permanent contact with Mediterranean civilisation[19]. The obligation of Black Africa's new Muslims to make the *haj* pilgrimage also stimulated trans-Saharan trade and travel[20].

It is now evident, however, that not Arabs but Berber merchants of the heretical Ibadi sect carried on the medieval trans-Saharan trade in black slaves, either because they started it in the first place, or because they took over, expanded and regularised an existing but random traffic. From about the eighth century on, the small Ibadi centre at Zawila in the eastern Fezzan monopolised the supply of slaves to Egypt and other parts of the greater Islamic world, eventually giving its name to Fezzan as a whole[21].

---

[17]O. Bates, *The Eastern Libyans: An Essay* (London, 1914) pp.101-5; Merighi, *La Tripolitania antica*, Vol. II, pp. 116-7; M. Wheeler, *Rome beyond the Imperial Frontiers* (Harmondsworth, 1954) p. 121; Daniels, *The Garamantes*, pp.42-4; R. C. C. Law, "The Garamantes and Trans-Saharan Enterprise in Classical Times", *Journal of African History*, VIII, 2 (1967) pp. 181-200.

[18]This theme is developed at length by E-F. Gautier in his *Passé de l'Afrique du Nord* (Paris, 1952), pp. 188-244; see also Bulliet, *The Camel and the Wheel*, pp.138-40. Bulliet (p. 221) remarks that "the desert never looms in the medieval Muslim mentality as the formidable barrier it had been in pre-Islamic times".

[19]J. S. Trimingham, *A History of Islam in West Africa* (Oxford, 1970) p. 20; P. B. Clarke, *West Africa and Islam* (London, 1982) pp. 8-12.

[20]U. Al-Naqar, *The Pilgrimage Tradition in West Africa*, etc. (Khartum, 1972) map on p. 113.

[21]J. Wright, *"Nothing Else but Slaves": Britain and the Central Saharan Slave Trade in the Nineteenth Century* (unpub. Ph.D. Thesis, London, 1998) pp. 45-7.

In the early middle ages, the peoples and tribes of the Sahara and its fringes began to fall into the broad distribution patterns that still endure. Although a nomadic tribe is a political rather than a territorial organisation, both in relation to other nomads and settled society[22], in the Sahara distinct nomadic peoples came to be associated with their respective quarters of the desert. Tensions were obviously greatest along tribal and ethnic boundaries, including the southern stages of the Garamantian road that divided the Tubu and Tuareg peoples. In such a troubled environment, outsiders risked life and property unless they duly acknowledged this local ascendancy by paying for guides and suitable "protection". Thus the central Sahara between Sirtica and Fezzan, including the main Tripoli-Fezzan road, came under the control of Arab or arabized Berbers, notably the Awlad Slaiman and their allies, yearly migrants between the northern steppe pastures and the rich date groves of the southern wadis[23].

South-western Tripolitania and western Fezzan were dominated by the veiled, Berber-speaking Tuareg nomads, and also by various small Tuareg communities long settled in the Fezzanese wadis. The main tribes of the Tuareg Ajjer confederation found in western Fezzan are the Imaghassaten (in Wadi al-Ajal and western Wadi Shati) and the Ouraghen, with smaller sub-groups (between Ghat and Wadi al-Ajal)[24]. Each of the four great Tuareg confederations was associated with a Saharan upland: the Ajjer and Hoggar mountains; the highlands of Air; and the Adrar of the Iforas[25]. The Tuareg thus bestrode the south-western routes through Ghadames and Ghat to Hausaland, the Niger Bend and beyond, while control of the main road through southern Fezzan to Lake Chad was constantly contested with the Tubu of Tibesti and other peoples who, if they could not control its trade, would surely disrupt it.[26] The

---

[22]A. M. Khazanov, *Nomads and the Outside World* (Cambridge, 1983) p.151.

[23]A. Cauneille, "Le semi-nomadisme dans l'Ouest Libyen (Fezzan, Tripolitaine)" in *Nomades et nomadisme du Sahara* (Paris, 1963) pp. 104-6; D. Cordell, "The Awlad Sulayman of Libya and Chad: Power and Adaptation in the Sahara and Sahel" in *Canadian Journal of African Studies*, 19, 2 (1985), pp. 319-43.

[24]Cauneille, "Le semi-nomadisme", p. 105.

[25]For the Tuareg, see H. Duveyrier, *Les Touaregs du Nord* (Paris, 1864) passim; F. Rodd, *People of the Veil*, etc.(London 1926), *passim*; J. Nicolaisen, *Ecology and Culture of the Pastoral Tuareg* (Copenhagen, 1963); Briggs, *Tribes of the Sahara*, pp. 124-66.

[26]For the Tubu (or Teda) in general, see W. Cline, "The Teda of Tibesti, Borku and Kawar in the Eastern Sahara" in *General Series in Anthropology No. 12* (Menasha, Wis., 1950); Briggs, *Tribes of the Sahara*, pp.167-89; A. Le Rouvreur, *Sahéliens et sahariens du Tchad* (Paris, 1963); Chapelle, *Nomades noirs*; H. Capot-Rey, "Le nomadisme des Toubous" in *Recherche sur la zone aride, XIX: Nomades et nomadisme du Sahara* (Paris, 1963) pp. 81-92.

Tubu, known by many different names, are aboriginal Saharans, few in number but extraordinarily diffuse, lacking political or social coherence – "the principle of freedom raised almost to the level of anarchy".[27] They have a constant and often malign influence on Saharan trade. Tubu were perhaps more common in the northern Sahara in the early 19th century than they are today. There are small communities in southern Fezzan, at al-Qatrun, al-Bakki, Madrusa, Tajarhi and in Murzuq[28].

Different races, confederations and tribes of Saharan nomads were thus the essential middlemen of desert trade. They exploited their geographical location and local strategic superiority, their mobility, and above all their ownership of the transport camels that were both the essential components of any caravan and the main capital input of the whole trading system. Regarding trade as a prestigious calling, they had a positive attitude towards "travelling, migration and movement beyond the boundaries of territory they traditionally occupied"[29].

By about the year 1000, Tripoli had achieved a pivotal role in the intercontinental trade between sub-Saharan Africa and southern Europe; but even more important at the time was the traffic with Egypt and the Middle East[30]. The 10th-century geographer Ibn Hawkal called Tripoli a most wealthy and powerful city with a vast market and busy port[31]. Its trans-Saharan business with Fezzan was mostly with the large, powerful and slaving kingdoms of Kanem and Borno, respectively east and west of Lake Chad. There, as elsewhere in medieval Sudan, regular trade and communications with North Africa and the wider Islamic world ensured the prestige and the political and economic health of the ruling dynasties[32]. These states were entrepots, drawing the trade slaves that were the mainstay of the Saharan traffic from peoples deeper into the African interior (gold was mostly exported along the western routes to Morocco). Recent estimates of numbers of black slaves marched across the Sahara suggest that from the 7th century to the end of the 19th, between 9.4 and

---

[27]Briggs, *Tribes of the Sahara*, p. 170.

[28]Chapelle, *Nomades noirs*, pp. 98-9.

[29]Khazanov, *Nomades and the Outside World*, p. 209.

[30]H. J. Fisher, "The Eastern Maghreb and the Central Sudan" in R. Oliver (ed.), *Cambridge History of Africa, Vol.3. 1050-1600* (Cambridge, 1977) p. 253.

[31]G. Wiet, *Configuration de la Terre* (Beirut and Paris, 1964) p. 129.

[32]Oliver and Fage, *A Short History of Africa*, pp. 86-8.

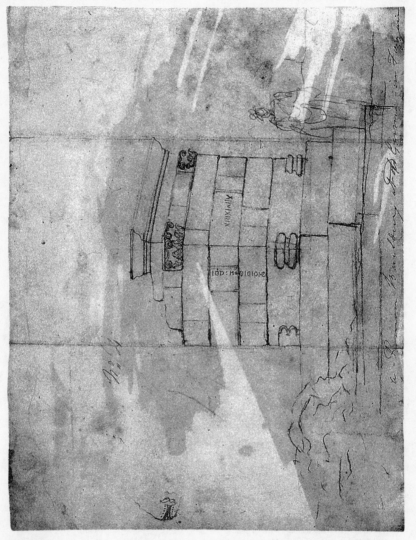

Figure 1. A Roman Mausoleum, Garma

13.7 million may have made the crossing – figures comparable to the estimated total shipped during the four centuries of the Atlantic slave trade[33].

Tripoli's role as political capital and port inevitably involved it in the rising hostility between European Christendom and Afro-Asian Islam. Between the 12th and 16th centuries, the town was contested by a succession of Christian and Muslim powers, finally falling in 1551 to the Ottoman Turks. While trans-Saharan trade continued to bring some prosperity to a town and dependent region of generally poor natural resources, an additional source of income was developed in state-sponsored Mediterranean piracy, or corsairing, that continued until the early 19th century. The Turks never established direct, lasting authority over Tripoli's Saharan hinterland. Even in Fezzan they had to rely on the dubious allegiance and irregular tribute of the Awlad Mohammad dynasty which ruled at Murzuq from the early 16th century until 1813[34].

In 1711 Tripoli itself became semi-independent under the dynasty of Karamanli pashas who ruled (more often in name than in actual practice) the Regency of Tripoli (roughly modern Libya) until 1835. For most of that period they relied for their revenues on the two parasitic activities of trans-Saharan slave trade and on corsairing against the smaller Mediterranean powers unable to protect their shipping or to buy immunity from attacks, or both[35]. But by the time Yusuf Pasha Karamanli came to the throne in 1795, it was becoming clear that corsairing was no longer a politically acceptable or economically viable activity. Moreover, Saharan trade in general and the slave trade in particular – inefficient, under-capitalised and under-developed for over a thousand years – were not contributing as much as they might have done to the revenues of a ruler with greater domestic and international ambitions than his predecesors.

---

[33]See Wright, *"Nothing Else but Slaves"*, Table 2. 1, p. 64: "Some Estimates of Saharan Slave Transits: Average Yearly Numbers".

[34]Most historians put the fall of this dynasty in 1811; El-Hesnawi, however, has 1813 [H. W. El-Hesnawi, *Fezzan under the rule of the Awlad Muhammad*, etc., (Sebha, 1990) pp. 135-154.]

[35]S. Dearden, *A Nest of Corsairs: The Fighting Karamanlis of the Barbary Coast* (London, 1976), *passim*; C. R. Pennell (ed.), *Piracy and Diplomacy in Seventeenth Century North Africa*, etc. (London, 1989) pp. 45-52.

At the end of the Napoleonic Wars, British African exploration, and in particular the Niger quest, remained where Mungo Park had left them on his fatal second expedition in 1805. But as peace returned, a conjunction of circumstances and personalities for a few brief years brought together the interests and ambitions of Tripoli, Great Britian and a revitalised Sultanate of Borno, making Tripoli and central Sahara appear as Britain's most promising approach to the inner continent.

Yusuf Pasha Karamanli – "a cruel and unprincipled tyrant who never honoured his engagements unless it suited him[36]" – had usurped the throne of Tripoli in 1795. Within twenty years he had consolidated his political and military power in the capital and had then "pacified" the rebellious provinces of his regency. This was the beginning of a process of sedentarising the pastoral nomads of the central Sahara that was to continue throughout the 19th century and for most of the 20th. Yusuf Pasha first put down the revolt of the Awlad Sulayman tribe that dominated Tripoli's main road to Fezzan, and that had disrupted trade for many years. In 1810 he sent troops to Ghadamis to secure the nearest stages of the south-westerly road to the Hausa states and the Niger Bend. And in 1813, with the Awlad Sulayman temporarily pacified and the road to Fezzan open, he overthrew the Awlad Mohammad dynasty that had been precariously independent at Murzuq for the past three centuries[37]. He thereby achieved his long-standing objective of tighter control over and further stimulation of Fezzan's traffic in the black slaves and gold that had always underpinned the province's role as a semi-independent but tribute paying fief of Tripoli (in obligation, if not always in practice).

In the 1790s he had appointed an old supporter and favourite, Mohammad al-Mukni, as collector (Bey al-Nawbah) of Fezzan's yearly tribute of slaves and gold and other trade goods. But Al-Mukni soon realised that the amounts forwarded to Tripoli were only a small part of the Sultan of Fezzan's takings. He accordingly persuaded Yusuf Pasha that, as vice-regent of Fezzan, he could triple the province's

[36]Bovill, *Missions*, Vol. I, p. 150; Dearden, *A Nest of Corsairs*, p. 141; E. Rossi, *Storia di Tripoli e della Tripolitania dalla conquista Araba al 1911* (Rome, 1968) p. 260.

[37]M.Morsy, *North Africa 1800-1900: A Survey from the Nile Valley to the Atlantic* (London, 1984) p. 100; El-Hesnawi, *Fezzan under the Rule*, pp. 135-54.

yearly tribute to 15,000 dollars[38]. Al-Mukni was duly appointed Bey of Fezzan when the Awlad Mohammad were overthrown, and for the next few years he ruthlessly exploited the province and its trade. But it was not enough to rely solely on the arrival of commercial caravans with variable numbers of trade slaves and packets of gold dust to determine the value of his own revenues, his own profit and – most important of all – the greatly increased tribute he had promised to Yusuf Pasha. Instead he had to speed up and expand the whole slaving business by raiding and enslaving pagans from neighbouring communities and countries. As these yearly raids brought in between 1,000 and 1,500 *surviving* slaves (perhaps only a quarter of those originally captured) he effectively doubled Fezzan's slave traffic and the shares and revenues he claimed from it[39]. But he did so at enormous cost to Tripoli's reputation and standing in those countries already raided for slaves, or expecting to be.

In 1817 Yusuf Pasha was ready to project Tripoli's power, influence and lust for slaves fully across the Sahara to Sudan to satisfy what has rightly been called "an imperial ambition"[40]. This ambition was driven by an urgent need for more money. It has been estimated that by 1820, two-thirds of the regency's yearly revenues were spent on keeping the Pasha and his court; paying the regular troops; maintaining Tripoli's fortifications; and on acts of public generosity expected from such a ruler. The remaining third had to meet all other expenses of government[41]. But the fact was that Yusuf Pasha had never come to terms with the greater political and economic obligations that the European powers and the United States of America had imposed on him and his regency during and after the Napoleonic Wars[42]. Under British and French naval pressure, Mediterranean corsairing was no longer a viable source of revenue, and there was little scope for raising taxes from a rural popula-

---

[38]The so-called Spanish Dollar, the English name for the peso or Spanish "piece of eight" (8 reales) was in wide circulation in Africa, the Mediterranean and in Tripoli's external trade. Its value varied between four and five to the Pound Sterling, depending on location.

[39]G. Lyon, *A Narrative*, pp. 3-4, 189, 268.

[40]K. Folayan, *Tripoli during the Reign of Yusuf Pasha Karamanli* (Ife Ife, 1979) pp. 25-77.

[41]R. Micacchi, *La Tripolitania sotto il dominio dei Caramanli* (Intra, 1936) pp. 224-34; see also Public Record Office, Kew, London, Foreign Office Papers: FO 76/16 [Consul General Tripoli, Hanmer] Warrington to [Colonial Secretary Lord] Bathurst, 6th July 1822, enclosed *An Account of the Annual Revenues of Tripoli*.

[42]L. J. Hume, "Preparation for Civil War in Tripoli in the 1820s: Ali Karamanli, Hassuna D'Ghies and Jeremy Bentham" in *Journal of African History*, 21. 3 (1980) p. 311. For the Pasha's general financial difficulties, see Micacchi, *Tripolitania sotto il dominio*, pp. 224-32.

tion reduced by drought to the very margins of survival for an average of two years out of every ten. There was even less hope of raising more from nomadic tribespeople always jealous of such perceived threats to their freedom as paying taxes. The trans-Saharan slave trade thus seemed to offer the only means of increasing the Pasha's income from taxes levied on the sale of all slaves in Fezzan, and again at Tripoli. In addition, the Pasha stood to gain indirectly from the sale of the share of slaves (usually one quarter) claimed by his tributary, the Bey of Fezzan, from the regular trade caravans and also from the large numbers then being captured on raids and brought up to Fezzan and Tripoli[43].

At the end of the Napoleonic Wars, Great Britain's naval, industrial and commercial-financial supremacy was beyond doubt. The implications of the Battle of the Nile (1798) which stranded Napoleon's punitive expedition in Egypt; the capture and occupation of Malta (1800); and the Battle of Trafalgar (1805) were not lost on Yusuf Pasha Karamanli, whose Mediterranean interests and relationships were still at least as important as those in and beyond the Sahara. The possession of Malta, less than 200 miles north of Tripoli, made the British close neighbours of the Pasha, as well as ready customers for meat and grain from his regency for naval and garrison victualling. The rulers of Tripoli could henceforth never forget that British warships, if not the assembled Mediterranean fleet, were always close at hand: behind the diplomacy and negotiating position of every British consul general in Tripoli in the 19th century (and earlier ones had extraordinary autonomy) was the reality of overwhelming naval might.

Thus by the beginning of the century, Britain had a two-fold interest in the Regency of Tripoli: one as a close neighbour of Malta, the other as a base for African exploration. Frustrated curiosity about the interior of Africa, and especially the question of the Niger, was still the main driving force behind three British expeditions of exploration that set out from Tripoli between 1819 and 1825. Little had been added to knowledge of the interior continent since the publication of the reports of Lucas and Hornemann and the account of Mungo Park's first expedition. Secondary to these new expeditions' geographical and scientific objectives were interest in diplo-

---

[43]Morsy, *North Africa*, p. 63.

matic ties with the larger states and more important rulers of inner Africa, and the promotion of British business, trade and finance in the widest sense.

British explorers in the 19th century – including vicarious and arm-chair travellers – were in their own eyes enlightened in their penetration of the mysteries of the so-called Dark Continent. They were confident that in so doing they had a moral duty to put an imperfect world to rights: to implement indeed what became the Palmerstonian grand agenda "intended to regenerate the fallen nations of the world, and to uplift those who had never risen"[44]. Although the British slave trade was declared illegal in 1807, Britain's growing obsession with African slave trade abolition (which was to assume almost the character of an official ideology) was not yet considered a moral objective of African explorers, and certainly not of those approaching the interior across the Sahara. This was largely because British official and abolitionist opinion was to all practical purposes, at least up to the 1840s, hardly aware of the existence of the ancient trans-Saharan slave trade. In the minds of the abolitionists, the Atlantic trade was the only one that mattered[45].

Britain's short-lived attempts to open up inner Africa through Tripoli and the good offices of Yusuf Pasha Karamanli were prompted and nurtured by a remarkable consul general, Colonel Hanmer Warrington, who held the post from 1814 to 1846. He did more than anyone to make the central Saharan routes Britain's exclusive highway into Africa[46]. His long exile in Tripoli seems to have been due to youthful money troubles; yet despite some grave diplomatic and other blunders during his time there, he probably held on to his post because of superlative, possibly royal, patronage at home[47]. Warrington had the great good fortune, for his career and his standing in Tripoli, in arriving there just as victorious Britain's prestige was reaching new heights. If Warrington himself had no doubts about his country's foremost place in the world now that France was defeated, nor did Yusuf Pasha Karamanli. An appar-

---

[44]P. J. Cain and A. G. Hopkins, *British Imperialism: Innovation and Expansion, 1688-1914* (London, 1993) p. 398.

[45]Wright, *"Nothing Else but Slaves"*, pp. 88-9.

[46]For biographical material on Warrington, see Bovill, *Missions*, Vol. I, pp. 151-61 and many other entries in Vols. I-IV; *The Niger Explored* (London, 1968) pp. 41-53 and other entries; "Colonel Warrington" in *The Geographical Journal*, Vol. 131, Part 2, June 1965, pp. 161-5; Dearden, *A Nest of Corsairs*, pp. 223 *et seq.*

[47]Wright, *"Nothing Else but Slaves"*, p. 104.

ent coincidence of views with the Pasha, and seemingly shared interests beyond the Sahara, enabled the consul to establish a close and even dominating rapport with the despot to whom he was accredited. At least until the relationship deteriorated in the mid-1820s, Warrington wielded unusual influence over him with "abrupt and hectoring tactics"[48]. Contemporary witnesses confirm this extraordinary relationship.

Stout, uncompromising patriotism seems to have been Warrington's greatest virtue. His very real desire to forward Britain's interests promoted an expansive vision that often overlooked the practical and wider implications of the plans and projects of this not particularly intelligent man. Thus, despite the evidence of those who had actually tried it, he never really lost the belief that crossing the Sahara was no more difficult or dangerous than a journey through contemporary England. He believed that it was simply enough to abolish the Saharan slave trade to open up the continent to "legitimate" commerce, enlightenment and "civilisation" – processes from which Britian naturally stood to gain more than any other power: he had already found that "the flag could not be more respected"[49].

In 1816 and 1817, Commander W. H. Smyth, RN, visited Tripoli to salvage Roman remains for the Prince Regent. He was hugely impressed by Warrington's relationship with the Pasha. After one particularly fruitful audience, Smyth reported to Malta and London the Pasha's standing offer to protect any British travellers in his territory and beyond:-

> I am becoming still more convinced that here – through this place
> and by means of these people – is an open gateway into the interior
> of Africa. By striking south from Tripoli, a traveller will reach Bornu
> before he is out of Yusuf's influence; and wherever his power reach-
> es, the protecting virtues of the British flag are known... I think this
> ought to be the chosen route, because practicable into the very heart
> of the most benighted quarter of the globe[50].

---

[48]Dearden, *A Nest of Corsairs*, p. 241.
[49]FO 76/11, Warrington to [Secretary of State, Foreign Office, Henry] Goulbourn, 15th April 1817.
[50]W. H. Smyth, *The Mediterranean: A Memoir Physical, Historical and Nautical* (London, 1854) p. 487; see also Colonial Office Papers: CO 2/9, Smyth to [Admiral Sir Charles] Penrose (Malta), 26th November 1817.

Smyth was not aware that the Pasha's real influence reached little beyond Murzuq; while Warrington's duty was to be better informed, it was also in his interests to exaggerate the Pasha's power and influence in his official correspondence with London.

Warrington believed that British interests in the interior would be best promoted by a vice consul at Murzuq, as the hub of the trade and communications of the central Sahara in general and the black slave trade in particular. As far back as August 1817, as part of wider proposals for the development of British trade with Tripoli and the far side of the Sahara, he had suggested the establishment of such a post, which would of course come under his own authority and report to London through him.[51] Warrington's enthusiasm brought a ready official response from John Barrow, Second Secretary to the Admiralty, who was then becoming "the dominant personality in the field of African exploration", enjoying the confidence and support of the Colonial Secretary, Earl Bathurst.[52] The apparent meeting of British and Tripoline interests was thus officially recognised as a chance too good to miss. The decision of January 1818 to appoint a 29 year-old Scottish surgeon, Joseph Ritchie, as temporary vice consul in Murzuq[53] was a reflection of Commander Smyth's timely intervention, and a broad endorsement of the course Warrington had been proposing.

This was in many ways a far-reaching decision: Murzuq had been visited by only one European traveller (Friedrich Hornemann, some twenty years earlier) and even its position was not exactly known. In opening a diplomatic post there, Britain was declaring interests far deeper into Africa than any other European power had at that time, and was establishing an official presence at a centre of transcontinental trade and communications.[54]

Joseph Ritchie may, according to his travelling companion, George Lyon, have been a "gentleman of great science", but he was not a happy choice for the Murzuk post. He was more interested in natural history than exploration: his baggage included a

---

[51]FO 76/11, Warrington to Bathurst, 24th August 1817.
[52]Bovill, *The Niger Explored*, p. 40.
[53]CO 2/8, Bathurst to Ritchie, 1st January 1818. Warrington had of course hoped that the post would be permanent.
[54]Wright, *"Nothing else but Slaves"*, p. 134.

camel-load of corks for preserving insect specimens, and his financial management of the expedition was inept.[55]

In his instructions to Ritchie in January 1818, Earl Bathurst wrote that the purpose of opening a vice consulate in Fezzan was to facilitate "the discoveries now attempting in the Interior of Africa". Ritchie was to learn local languages, gather information of every kind, and was authorised to accompany any southbound "expedition" under the authority of Yusuf Pasha Karamanli. For the "grand object" of the appointment was "to proceed under proper protection to Tomboctoo", or to any other city or country in the interior. If he reached Timbuctu, Ritchie was to gather information about the course of the Niger, and then sail downstream to its outlet.[56] Timbuctu was the chosen goal because it was assumed still to be the great city of trade and learning that it had been at least three centuries earlier. Significantly, Ritchie's instructions made no mention of trade, trade promotion or slavery abolition. Later in 1818, Consul Warrington was instructed that on arrival in Tripoli, Ritchie was to be presented to Yusuf Pasha simply as a traveller in search of geographical knowledge: the Pasha was to be told that in sending this mission, Britain had no political, commercial or colonial ambitions.[57]

Ritchie's travelling companions – the young naval officer George Lyon, and John Belford, a shipwright from the Malta dockyard – arrived in Tripoli in October 1818. Belford had been appointed because John Barrow at the Admiralty wanted, in addition to Lyon's presence, to ensure a naval "interest" in African exploration and retain Admiralty control of the results of those "surveys", even so far inland. The mission's objective also reflected Barrow's personal conviction that the Niger and the Nile were one river.

But in a series of audiences with the Pasha, the travellers learned that Commander Smyth had been quite misled over the ruler's claimed influence in countries beyond the Sahara; relations were indeed so poor that he was unable even to send an

---

[55]Boahen, *Britain, the Sahara*, pp. 49-52.
[56]CO 2/8, Bathurst to Ritchie, 1st January 1818.
[57]CO 2/9, Penrose to Warrington, 24th September 1818.

embassy to any of them.[58] The Pasha did however arrange for the travellers to go to Murzuq under the protection of the Bey of Fezzan, Mohammad al-Mukni, who was then in Tripoli, preparing another great slave raid, this time into Wadai, far to the east of Lake Chad. By accepting the Bey's protection, the travellers seemed to be associating themselves with one of these "predatory excursions" which, as Ritchie had already learned from black slaves in Tripoli, were causing deep hatred of Tripoli in sub-Saharan countries, making the Bey's name "the terror of those regions". But, apparently misunderstanding the essential purpose of slave raiding, Ritchie suggested to Bathurst that Britain might become a mediator between the Pasha of Tripoli and the peoples of the interior persecuted by the raiders and so "advance under the safeguard of such a title to the very heart of Africa".[59] Putting aside obvious misgivings about the character of the travellers' protector, Bathurst merely warned Ritchie against showing any approval of Al-Mukni's mission. He then also ordered him to find out all he could about the Saharan slave trade and prospects for its abolition.[60] This additional order is almost certainly the first official, ministerial notice of the trans-Saharan slave trade and slave raiding as evils that Britain, having learned of them, was morally bound to try to end. It also gave what was originally intended as a mission of exploration the further important and highly sensitive moral duty of investigating the whole complex, inter-regional system of slave raiding, enslavement and slave trading. Ritchie indeed took up the abolitionist issue even before he left for Fezzan in late March 1819, when he raised with Bathurst the possibility of persuading the Pasha of Tripoli and the Bey of Fezzan to give up the slave trade in return for "some pecuniary compensation".[61]

When the Ritchie-Lyon mission at last left Tripoli, the caravan of that great slaver and the mission's protector, Mohammad al-Mukni, was also accompanied by many freed black slaves. They had gathered in Tripoli from as far off as Constantinople and the Levant, hoping to return to families, homes and communities that probably still existed only in the returnees' imaginations.[62] The mission followed the relatively

---

[58]CO 2/9, Ritchie to Bathurst, 28th October 1818.
[59]CO 2/9, Ritchie to Bathurst, 29th November 1818.
[60]CO 2/9, Bathurst to Ritchie, 19th January 1819.
[61]CO 2/9, Ritchie to Bathurst, 24th March 1819.
[62]CO 2/8, Ritchie, *Journal of my Journey to Fezzan*.

easy road through Bani Ulid and the Jofra oases, reaching Murzuq in early May. Due largely to Ritchie's mismanagement, the travellers were by then very short of funds, and they missed good chances of penetrating the interior – one by accompanying the great slave raid that left Murzuq in July, and the other in the company with an envoy sent to Borno four months later. The travellers were in effect marooned in Murzuq, one of the unhealthiest places in the Sahara, thoughout the summer of 1819. (As caravans usually broke up and dispersed on arrival at Murzuq, onward travellers, including impatient European explorers, might have to wait many months before the merchants and all the necessary guides, servants, equipment for the journey and, most particularly, the necessary camels were all brought together to form the new caravan.) Unable even to afford proper food, Ritchie sickened, and died in November. George Lyon then remained the sole source of information on the central Sahara and its trading and raiding links with the Sudan. He added to his findings by making a five-week journey with shipwright Belford into southern Fezzan in the winter of 1819-20. They visited Traghan, Zawila and Al-Qatrun, beyond which they fell in with the raiders whom Al-Mukni had sent out in July, now returning to Murzuq with the slave booty – "800 lean cripples, clad in skins and rags".[63] After returning to Murzuq, Lyon and Belford travelled back to Tripoli in March, in company with a caravan of trade slaves. They thus witnessed at first hand the slave drivers' general treatment of their mainly female charges. Lyon's despatches, and especially the prompt publication by John Murray of his eminently readable *Narrative of Travels*,[64] made the London abolitionists at least aware of the Saharan slave trade as a potential issue. Lyon greatly expanded existing knowledge of Fezzan, and Attilio Mori singles out the information he gathered in southern Fezzan on Ghat and on the routes across the Tibesti Mountains as particularly valuable.[65]

Back in Tripoli, Lyon wrote a long despatch to Bathurst on slave raiding and the slave trade, suggesting (quite unrealistically) that the abolition of raiding from Fezzan would end slave trading in general, and that this in turn would encourage a substitute "legitimate" trade in the produce of Sudan – gold, ivory, senna, fine cloth

---

[63]Lyon, *A Narrative*, p. 249-50.
[64]The first English edition was published by John Murray in 1821; a French edition was published in Paris in 1822.
[65]Mori, *L'esplorazione geografica della Libia*, p. 20.

and "excellently prepared leather".[66] He concluded that he intended to devote his life to the cause of abolition: in the event, he did no such thing, turning instead to Arctic exploration[67].

But most attention seems to have been given in London to Lyon's remarks on the course of the Niger after it left Timbuctu, as he had learned it second-hand from Borno traders in Fezzan. According to his informants, the river flowed through Lake Chad in Borno and then through Bagirmi: "all agree... that by one route or other, these waters join the great Nile of Egypt to the southward of Dongola"[68]. As soon as this was learned from Lyon's despatches in London early in 1820, Borno replaced Timbuctu as the main focus of interest in the Niger quest. Fresh instructions to Lyon to make straight for Borno were sent when he had already started for home. But John Barrow at the Admiralty, ever eager to have his belief in the unity of the Niger and Nile proved beyond doubt, was already preparing a new expedition by the time Lyon reached London in July.[69] It is with this great and eminently successful expedition of exploration, the Borno Mission, that this study is concerned.

The Empire of Borno was then also an obvious objective for British explorers because it was the nearest Sudanic state to Tripoli and – despite the vagaries of Yusuf Pasha Karamanli's diplomacy – the most readily approachable. Moreover, by 1820 Borno had recovered from recent disasters brought by the expansion of the Sultanate of Wadai in the east and, in 1808, defeat by the forces of the Fulani *jihad*, the militant Islamic revival that carried war and chaos across most of the Sudan after 1804. Out of these setbacks arose a truly remarkable leader, Shaikh al-Amin al-Kanami, who rallied Borno's political, religious and military resistance and over the next 25 years revived and restored the empire. At the same time, Borno's commercial attraction was ensured by the large surpluses of exportable trade slaves that many nearby communities had accumulated through the *jihad*.[70]

---

[66]CO 2/9, Lyon to Bathurst, 26th March 1820.

[67]Not least because he was denied the naval promotion he believed his travels had earned him. [CO 2/9, Lyon to Bathurst, 26th March 1820; *Dictionary of National Biography* (Oxford, 1921-22) Vol. XII, p. 346.]

[68]Lyon, *A Narrative*, p. 148.

[69]Bovill, *The Niger Explored*, p. 71.

[70]A. Mahadi, "The Aftermath of the *Jihad* in the Central Sahara as a Major Factor in the Trans-Saharan Slave Trade in the Nineteenth Century" in E. Savage (ed.) *The Human Commodity: Perspectives on the Trans-Saharan Slave Trade* (London, 1992) pp. 114 *et seq..*

Al-Kanami was born in Fezzan of Arab and Kanemi descent and, after education in Egypt, he settled in Kanem. Once in power, he sought help from Tripoli against the threats to Borno from Wadai and Bagirmi to the east and the jihadists to the west. Tripoli was already the source of the guns and ammunition that gave Borno some local military superiority. But Al-Kanami's proposal of 1817 to Yusuf Pasha for a joint assault on Bagirmi had the unforeseen outcome of further encouraging the Pasha's own designs on Borno as an apparently limitless reservoir of trade slaves.[71]

The British government's decision of 1820 to mount a new mission of exploration again tested Yusuf Pasha's claims to influence in and beyond the Sahara, and his ability to guarantee the safety of travellers to and from Borno. Anglo-Tripolitan cooperation and mutual trust were clearly essential: the difficulty was that the two parties' objectives in Borno were not at all the same. While Tripoli sought the empire's military conquest and enslavement, British interests there were geographical, scientific, diplomatic, commercial and potentially abolitionist.

These incompatible interests and the very real limits to the Pasha's influence became much more apparent in August 1820. Consul Warrington again reported that Yusuf Pasha could guarantee travellers' safety to and from Borno, but only so long as they were accompanied by an armed escort of 1,000 men (a fair army by Saharan standards), available at the enormous charge of £5,000. Of course, Warrington innocently added, "that force would be employed as a Safe conduct and not any Hostility would be resorted to in the Capture of Slaves". Warrington's despatch also made it clear that Yusuf Pasha's plans to annex Borno, as well as "Sudan" (the name by which the people of Fezzan and Tripoli called Hausaland, by then part of the Caliphate of Sokoto), had matured, for he was in addition asking the British government to lend the estimated cost of sending a force of 6,000 men to take and hold both places, presumably relying on their superiority in firearms to do so. He baited his proposal through Consul Warrington with the prospect of ending the slave trade, arguing that once under his rule, his new possessions would provide quite enough alternative "legitimate" trade, especially in gold dust.[72] This prospect was, of course,

---

[71]Folayan, *Tripoli during the Reign*, p. 85.
[72]FO 76/14, Warrington to Bathurst, 5th August 1820.

quite unrealistic. Consul Warrington, at least, should have known that without its main prop of the black slave traffic, the whole antiquated and fragile Saharan trade system would collapse, as indeed it did under European abolitionist and other pressures at the century's end.[73] While the British government declined to finance the Pasha's imperial ambitions, the conviction nevertheless remained that British travellers could only reach Borno if the government paid for a large armed escort.

Originally, Consul Warrington had offered to go to Borno himself. John Barrow had accordingly found a suitable assistant, a 31 year-old Edinburgh doctor and former naval surgeon, Walter Oudney. Bovill records that Oudney was

> ...a quiet, self-effacing little man, with a weakly constitution, he was ill-equipped for the physical and mental hardships which he would shortly have to endure... but he was to prove himself a brave and resolute man.[74]

Warrington then changed his mind about going to Borno and Oudney needed another travelling companion. The choice was a young naval lieutenant, Hugh Clapperton, who Barrow expected would possess "resources of a superior kind, more especially if the party should get afloat on the Niger".[75] But then an army lieutenant, Dixon Denham, put in a strong claim to join the mission. Bovill judges that Denham was "a man of no consequence and would certainly have been turned down but for his having the backing of someone who the Colonial Secretary had no wish to offend", possibly the Duke of Wellington.[76] Denham's appointment as the mission's leader on its arrival in Borno was plainly made at the expense of Oudney's and Clapperton's interests. Once in Borno, Oudney was merely to establish himself as consul and promote trade, instead of exploring, as he had hoped to do. Clapperton, despite his service seniority and earlier appointment to the mission, was expected to travel in Borno as Denham's assistant, or to explore on his own in another direction. As the Niger was believed to run through Borno, Denham's main duty was to trace its course to its mouth, a journey expected by some to take him to the

---

[73]For fuller discussion of this development, see Wright, *"Nothing Else but Slaves"*, especially Chapter Eleven "The Delusions of Abolition".

[74]Bovill, *The Niger Explored*, p. 72.

[75]CO 2/14, John Barrow (Admiralty) to Goulbourn, 14th July 1821.

[76]Bovill, *Missions*, Vol. II, p. 16; *The Niger Explored*, pp. 72-3.

Nile, and so to Egypt. These unfair and ambiguous instructions, particularly concerning the mission's leadership, were to cause much trouble and unhappiness between the three travellers.

Because Denham was not ready to travel, Oudney and Clapperton started for Malta in early September 1821 and were in Tripoli by late October. Denham arrived a month later with a shipwright, William Hillman, whom he had engaged at the Malta dockyard to build a boat to sail the Niger and the "Great Lake" (Lake Chad)[77]. Here again was evidence of John Barrow's concern to uphold the "naval interest" in these inland journeys, and of his special Niger theory.

Yusuf Pasha had in the meantime joined in another enterprise that left no doubt as to his real interests in the Sudan. In mid-1821 Shaikh al-Kanami invited him to join in an attack on Borno's rebellious neighbour, Bagirmi. The Shaikh's motives for an initiative apparently so hazardous for Borno's own security are not really clear.[78] In the event, Yusuf Pasha agreed to support what promised to be a massive slave raid, sending 450 cavalry and 1,300 infantry under the command of the new Bey of Fezzan, Mustafa al-Ahmar, who had recently replaced Mohammad al-Mukni.[79] The assault on Bagirmi was indecisive, but Yusuf Pasha's men had advanced further south than ever before, had gained the military and logistical experience for an eventual attack on Borno, and had seized a huge booty in slaves.[80] North African slave raiding into the Sudan was by then becoming more commonplace: in July 1820 the semi-independent ruler of Egypt, Mohammad Ali, invaded the Nilotic Sudan, mounting what was in effect a massive hunt for slave-recruits for his new army. News from Egypt may have prompted Ottoman pressure on Yusuf Pasha to supply 1,000 male slaves as tribute from his own successful Sudanese forays.[81]

---

[77]The character of 'Old Chips', a typical old salt, emerges in correspondence collected by Benton, P.A., *Languages and People of Bornu* (2 Vols., London, 1912), Appendix XV, Unpublished Correspondence, pp. 368-373.

[78]See Bovill, *Missions*, Vol. III, pp. 540-1.

[79]Mustafa al-Ahmar (Mustafa the Red) was a Georgian renegade who had probably arrived in North Africa as a prized slave. He found service with Yusuf Pasha Karamanli, eventually marrying one of his daughters and becoming Bey of Fezzan.

[80]Folayan, *Tripoli during the Reign*, p.89; Bovill, *Missions*, Vol. III, pp. 539-54; F. Rodd, "A Fezzani Military Expedition to Kanem and Bagirmi in 1821" in *Journal of the Royal African Society*, Vol.XXXV, No. 139 (April 1936) pp. 153-68.

[81]See Diary entry for Friday 3rd May 1823, Chapter One & n.13. Mohammad Ali's need for black

With the Borno Mission in Tripoli, Consul Warrington reopened with the Colonial Office the question of the Murzuq vice consulate, vacant since Ritchie's death two years before. Warrington had already decided that John Tyrrwhit, son of a friend and creditor, should fill the post. London had made no decision by the time the mission left Tripoli, but Tyrrwhit went with it anyway.

There were the usual inevitable delays in the mission's departure, and many audiences with the Pasha during the three or four months its members spent in Tripoli as guests of the hospitable Consul Warrington. Although the Colonial Office had forwarded funds to Warrington to pay the Pasha for the mission's armed escort, the consul wisely advanced only part of them. For it was soon clear that the Pasha planned to send the travellers (at no expense to himself) with the Bey of Fezzan when he returned south after his yearly visit to Tripoli. But by the spring of 1822, with still no sign of the Bey, the travellers decided to go to Murzuq alone. They set out in early March: five Europeans (Oudney, Clapperton, Denham, Tyrrwhit and Hillman), dressed as Europeans – "to give a degree of consequence to the Mission", as Warrington had put it – and therefore obviously alien and Christian. They arrived in Murzuq without incident in early April, finding there that the Bey had not even left for Tripoli and that when he did, he would be away for months, gathering men, camels and supplies for the escort that was supposed to take them to Borno. They were unable to go further because, as Oudney had already explained to the Colonial Secretary, "we all wished to proceed to our destination direct, but being under the protection of the Bashaw [Pasha], it is our duty to conform to his wishes".[82] Besides, there were no camels to be had, hardly surprising at a time of year when no large caravans were planned. The travellers were rightly worried by the expense of staying in Murzuq – their funds were hardly enough for their plans – and the notorious unhealthiness and boredom of the place.[83] Denham tried without success to put pres-

---

recruits may also have inspired the Pasha's attempt of 1823 to meet his Egyptian debts by delivering 2,000 male slaves to Mohammad Ali's agents on the coast at 100 dollars each. See FO 76/17, Warrington to [Under Secretary, Colonial Office, Wilmot] Horton, 16th November 1823.

[82]CO 2/13, Oudney (Tripoli) to Bathurst, 21st January 1822.

[83]For Murzuq's unhealthiness, see Duveyrier, *Les Touareg du Nord*, p. 282; G. Nachtigal, *Sahara and Sudan* (Trans. and ed. A. G. B. Fisher and H. J. Fisher, 4 Vols., London, 1971-88) Vol. I, pp. 84, 131; Bovill, *Missions*, Vol. II, p. 283; for its boredom, see Hallett, *The Penetration*, p. 260, quoting Friedrich Hornemann in a letter to his mother: "after the caravan had left, the most disinteresting town I ever saw".

sure on the Bey, and then began exploring another option, of travelling with an escort offered by Abu Bakr bu Khallum, an influential Arab merchant and notable originally from Awjila, who was seeking Yusuf Pasha's favour. In the meantime, Oudney and Clapperton made a short journey into eastern Fezzan, following Lyon's route to the ancient capitals of Traghan and Zawila (see Chapter One).

Desperate to do something rather than spend the best part of a year in Murzuq, the party agreed that Denham would return to Tripoli, where he and Warrington would together put renewed pressure on Yusuf Pasha.[84] Denham appears to have been particularly alarmed by Murzuq's summer sicknesses, and the others were not sorry to see him go. "His absence," wrote Clapperton, "will be no loss to the mission." Denham was back in Tripoli by mid-June. But when the Pasha admitted that the mission was likely to be delayed at Murzuq until at least the following spring, he decided to return at once to London to make representations to the Colonial Secretary. He boarded a ship for Marseilles the following morning, later claiming that his hasty action had been intended to scare the Pasha to action. But self-interest, and especially hopes of promotion and full confirmation of his leadership of the mission, seem to have been his main motive.[85]

At this juncture, the Pasha proposed a solution that Denham had been pursuing weeks before in Murzuq. This was to send Abu Bakr bu Khallum, then in Tripoli, to Murzuq and Borno with a smaller escort for the mission of 100 each of cavalry and infantry. For a fee of 10,000 dollars, to be shared equally with the Pasha, Bu Khallum agreed to leave Tripoli within 15 days of payment, and Murzuq two months later. Warrington wrote accordingly to Denham, then in quarantine in Marseilles (and where he also received a letter of severe rebuke from Earl Bathurst for leaving Tripoli and the mission). By late September Denham had hurried back to Tripoli and joined Bu Khallum's southbound caravan. But his adventure had further harmed his already strained relations with the mission's other members, leaving them bitter about what was seen as Denham's desertion.[86] Yet Warrington, who had done more than anyone to help and promote the mission through all its difficulties,

---

[84]See correspondence in Appendix I.
[85]Bovill, *Missions*, Vol. II, pp. 40-1; *The Niger Explored*, pp. 81, 84-5.
[86]FO 76/16, Oudney to Warrington, 17th September 1822.

was still quite right when he reminded the Foreign Office that such a time and opportunity for exploring had "never before offered and probably may never again, therefore the most ought to be made of such favourable circumstances".[87]

During Denham's absence from Murzuq in the summer of 1822, Oudney and Clapperton escaped from that depressing place by making an enterprising secondary expedition to Ghat (see Chapters Three to Seven). This remote and ancient trading oasis, dominating the routes from Tripoli and Fezzan to the Hausa States and the Niger Bend, was not then as important as it was to become later in the century with the decline first of Ghadamis and then of Murzuq as the Saharan slave trade came under increasing abolitionist and other pressures. When Denham rejoined his companions at Murzuq at the end of October, he was not at all pleased that they had gone to Ghat without him and, according to Bovill, "he later succeeded in preventing the publication of much of what Oudney had written about the expedition".[88] Clapperton's travel diary of course remained wholly unpublished. This act of mischief by Denham, which has denied Oudney and Clapperton full recognition of their achievements and enterprise as travellers in unknown Fezzan, is at last put right in the present publication. For Clapperton's travel diary reveals just how much original and valuable material was left out of the official account of the mission, first published in London in 1826, and thus out of all subsequent editions, including the three Bovill volumes of 1966[89]. In western Fezzan the travellers crossed territories quite unknown to the outside world, and they literally put Ghat itself on the map, for it is shown neither in Rennell's map of 1802 nor on the one Lyon published to accompany his *Narrative of Travels*. Although both Friedrich Hornemann and George Lyon had travelled in different parts of Fezzan before then, Clapperton and Oudney saw much more of the country and its people; they seem to have had the time and the inclination to be more observant and, in Clapperton's case at least, more conscientious in recording what they saw.

When they travelled, Fezzan was about to be troubled by the intrusive and irresistible forces of the 19th century. Because of lack of reliable statistics, it is difficult

---

[87]FO 76/16, Warrington to Wilmot, 4th November 1822.
[88]Bovill, *The Niger Explored*, p. 88.
[89]See pages 35-6 notes 1 & 2 below.

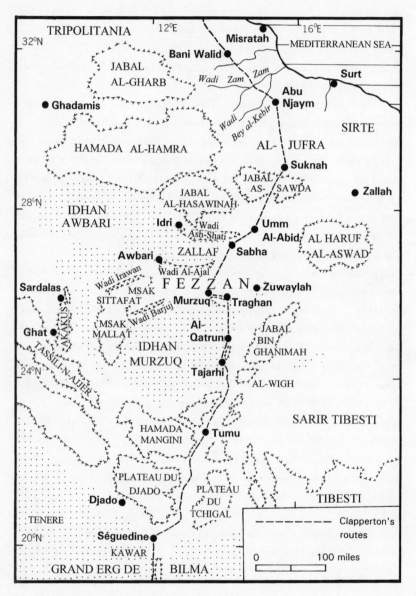

Map 2. Fezzan

to judge whether Saharan trade, and particularly the slave trade, as the mainstays of the Fezzanese economy, had by the 1820s fallen off in comparison with the previous century. The few random slave trade figures available from European consular sources suggest that the number of trade slaves passing through Fezzan may have nearly doubled, and in some years tripled, between the mid-18th and the mid-19th centuries. In the four years 1753-56, a total of 3,280 slaves passed through Fezzan, a yearly average of 820. In the 1840s, slaves were being traded through Murzuq alone at an average rate of nearly 1,400/year; in 1852-54, the traffic had risen to an average of over 2,650/year.[90] Such figures suggest that the province, relying as it did on the slave trade to make the difference between almost unrelieved destitution and some modest wellbeing, should have become more, not less prosperous in the 19th century than it had been in the 18th. But Clapperton's daily diary accounts of central and western Fezzan, as he witnessed them in the summer of 1822, do give an overall impression of material and social decay, of people then suffering greater hardships and leaner times than even they were used to, living as most of them normally did near the very margin of survival. Clapperton's account of Fezzan, as it emerges plain and unadorned from his daily, immediate jottings, is thus essential raw material for a fuller understanding of the country and its people as yet hardly changed by such unfamiliar outside influences and intrusions as the British travellers themselves represented. For Fezzan, as Clapperton saw it on his travels of 1822, and again on his return home across the Sahara in 1824-25, was on the threshold of interesting times. These had perhaps already started with Yusuf Pasha Karamanli's suppression of the long-established and semi-autonomous Awlad Mohammad dynasty a decade before the Borno Mission's arrival. For Fezzan, the rest of the 19th century was to be marked by a series of political, economic and social upheavals that were to leave the province destitute and its people practically without purpose by that century's end.

Major Denham returned to Murzuq on 30th October with Bu Khallum and the escort of over 200 Arabs, wild men drawn mainly from the tribes of the Sirtica and Wadi Shatti. Although Clapperton had earlier expressed misgivings about such an escort of trouble-makers, Denham now judged that they were "a great and most nec-

---

[90]Wright, *"Nothing Else but Slaves"*, Table 2. 2 "Slave Arrivals in Tripoli, 1753-56" and Table 7.1 "Slaves Arriving in Murzuk from 1843 to 1854".

essary protection to us".[91] Yet there was still no disguising the fact that the escort, if not a reconnnaissance for Borno's future conquest, was at least bent on large-scale slave raiding there. As for Bu Khallum, however, the travellers were agreed that he was an excellent conductor – "I verily believe that no better man could have been found," Oudney wrote.[92]

When it at last assembled at Murzuq, the mission consisted of Denham, Oudney and Clapperton, as well as shipwright Hillman. (Young Tyrrwhit, whose Murzuq appointment London had not approved, had returned to Tripoli.) There were five servants – freed slaves as personal servants for the three officers, and two others, both remarkable men. One was Jacob Deloyice, a Gibraltar Jew who became the mission's mess-steward and store-keeper. The other was a West Indian named Adolphus Sympkins [Simkins], so widely travelled that he was known as Columbus, and whose languages included excellent Arabic. He became the mission's general guide and interpreter. There were also four drivers for the 33 transport camels hired at Murzuq, as well as three horses for the British officers and a mule for Hillman.[93]

The mission carried firearms for hunting and protection; navigation and scientific instruments; writing materials; many medecines; common trade goods for barter; and rich presents for rulers and their greater officials. The caravan was swelled by a dozen merchants from Tripoli and Murzuq who valued the escort's protection, as well as 30 freed slaves returning home. In all, the caravan was a large one, at around 300 people.

Unwilling to face any further delays in Murzuq, Oudney, Clapperton and Hillman set out on 19th November 1822, while Denham followed with the main caravan on the 29th. From Fezzan to Lake Chad the caravan used the ancient Garamantian road, probably still the easiest Saharan crossing. Despite sickness and the very real hardships of desert travel, they made good time. They reached Lari, on the northern

---

[91]Bovill, *Missions*, Vol. II, p. 162.
[92]Bovill, *The Niger Explored*, p. 88
[93]Horses and mules were luxurious mounts in the desert, since several camels were neeed to carry their fodder and *daily* water needs.

shore of Lake Chad, on 4th February. There the present diary leaves Clapperton and his companions.[94]

As a group, explorers of Africa who travelled inland from the Mediterranean coast are less well known than those who penetrated the continent from other directions. No Park or Burton, Speke or Livingstone, entered Africa at Tripoli and achieved lasting and popular fame by crossing the Sahara as a prelude to celebrated adventures and discoveries deep into the unknown.[95] The names of Denham, Oudney and Clapperton are undeservedly obscure, their achievements and explorations now little known, even in their own country. This is perhaps largely because they travelled deep into Africa from the "wrong" direction. For by 1860, when Britain at last had the medical and technical knowledge to exploit the Niger rivers system as a safe, swift and reliable highway to the central Sudan (leading to the eventual creation of modern Nigeria), the Saharan approach was recognised as a dead end for British African interests. It was accordingly abandoned to any other powers that cared to make use of it – eventually France and, to a lesser extent, Italy.

Yet the fact remains that the Borno Mission of 1822-25 was the most dramatically successful expedition of exploration that the British government had up to then sent into inner Africa. Even if they did not solve the problem of the Niger, its three members explored much of Lake Chad; they travelled widely in Borno and other parts of the central Sudan; and after Oudney's death on the road in January 1824, Clapperton reached the great trading city of Kano and the Fulani capital at Sokoto. By the time Denham and Clapperton returned to Murzuq and Tripoli in early 1825 (see Chapters Fourteen to Sixteen), the central Sahara, Lake Chad, and the central Sudan had all been charted, and were soon revealed to the British public and the outside world. The mission was "one of the greatest achievements in African discovery" and had "flooded with light areas which till then had been merely a subject of speculation".[96] It had shown that the Sahara was not as formidable a barrier as had been supposed, and that Europeans could safely travel the ancient Garamantian

---

[94]The text of Clapperton's recently-discovered diary of travels in Borno and other parts of the Sudan is published by Jamie Bruce Lockhart (ed.) *Clapperton in Borno* (Cologne, 1996).

[95]Wright, *"Nothing Else but Slaves"*, p. 101.

[96]Bovill, *The Niger Explored*, pp. 145-6

road from Tripoli to Fezzan and Lake Chad. Contrary to common belief, it was now known that there were beyond the Sahara large and wealthy countries, great trading cities and welcoming and sophisticated peoples. Promising preliminary contacts had been made with the outstanding leaders of two of contemporary Africa's greatest states: Shaikh Al-Kanami of Borno and Sultan Mohammad Bello of Sokoto.

The fact that successive British governments did not follow up the Borno Mission, that no further official expedition of exploration crossed the Sahara from Tripoli to the Sudan until the Central African Mission of 1849-55 (James Richardson, Heinrich Barth and Adolf Overweg),[97] does not really detract from the earlier and pioneering work and achievements of Hugh Clapperton and his colleagues in the central Sahara and Sudan.

John Wright
Richmond, May 1999

---

[97]James Richardson, *Narrative of a Mission to Central Africa*, etc. (2 Vols., London, 1853); Heinrich Barth, *Travels and Discoveries in North and Central Africa*, (3 Vols., New York, 1857-59, reproduced by Frank Cass of London in 1965).

Figure 2. Portrait of Lieutenant Hugh Clapperton

Lieutenant Hugh Clapperton, R.N.

An account of the Mission was first published by John Murray in 1826[1] followed quickly by two further editions by Murray in England, a reprint in New York and a translation into French, published in Paris. In 1831 Murray brought out a new version in 16° as part of a newly launched popular series entitled 'Family Editions'. Extracts of the *Narrative* were included in other compendiums of travel published in the 1830s. By the early 1840s, however, British public interest in the interior of Africa had waned following the costly failure of the attempt to penetrate the lower Niger by steamers, and against a background of colonial retrenchment. By the second half of the nineteenth century the work of Clapperton, Denham and Oudney had been overtaken by the achievements of a new generation of explorers and travelling scholars in other parts of Africa.

The high empire mood and European "scramble" for Africa of the last years of the century renewed public interest in the feats of earlier travellers, and the *Narrative* again featured in anthologies. Another half century was to pass however before the work of the Borno Mission came to notice again – when the independence movement in Africa at the turn of the 1960s inspired a new interest in the continent's pre-colonial past. The second (1826) edition of the *Narrative* was republished in facsimile in 1965 by Frank Cass & Co. of London, as part of a high quality series of reprints of early writings on Africa. In 1966 E.W. Bovill edited a definitive version for the

---

[1]Major Denham, Captain Clapperton and the late Dr. Oudney, *Narrrative of Travels and Discoveries in Northern and Central Africa in the Years 1822,1823 and 1824* (London, 1826); referred to below as the *Narrative*.

Hakluyt Society in his four volume work, *Missions to the Niger²*. This was founded on a detailed review of Denham's papers, which are available in full³, and also incorporated the official correspondence of the Mission, the Colonial Office and the Consulate General in Tripoli.

Modern research on pre-colonial central Sudan has drawn extensively on the *Narrative*, which is a first and seminal European account of the region and its people before exposure to western influences. Extracts from the text of the *Narrative* have reappeared at various lengths and for differing reasons. The value or otherwise of these works has largely depended on the accompanying editorial setting and comment. References, both by later travellers and subsequent commentators, to the published material of the Borno Mission are thus numerous, but are necessarily one dimensional.

With the exception of one chapter drawn from Oudney's diaries and one written by Clapperton relating his journey from Borno to Sokoto and back in 1823, the record was Denham's. When the travellers handed their journals to the Mission's Colonial Office sponsors in June 1825, John Barrow took charge of the material, forwarding it to John Murray, a personal friend and a leading publisher of the day. Denham's writings formed the basis of the published account. His literary skills were considerable and he collaborated closely with Murray. When, by contrast, Clapperton left on his second expedition into the interior, Barrow edited his contribution. Denham tried to suppress any reference to achievements in which he himself had had no part⁴, but Barrow was able to some extent to see fair play and he excised Denham's more critical comments on his companions. He failed, however, to make full use of all the manuscript material available to him. The bulk of Oudney's manuscripts had unfortunately disappeared after his death on the road to Kano, but Barrow had all Clapperton's papers to hand. However, either for reasons of space, or because he found the manuscripts rather too difficult to deal with – or both – Barrow did not

²E. W. Bovill, *Missions to the Niger*, (4 Vols., Cambridge, 1964-66), Vols. II – IV. (Vol. I contains the journals and letters of the Saharan travellers Friedrich Hornemann and Major Alexander Gordon Laing.)

³Royal Geographical Society, London, Manuscript Collection AR64, Dixon Denham Collection.

⁴In his Preface to the *Narrative*, for example, Denham alleges that Clapperton had not kept a journal regularly until after Oudney's death [*Missions*, Vol. II, p. 131].

draw on any of Clapperton's material other than the commissioned chapter[5]. Within three months of his return to London, Clapperton had set off to Africa again, this time as leader of a new expedition into the interior, where he died in April 1827. His journals of the Borno mission were thus put aside and became lost to public view for over a century and a half[6].

The journals which Clapperton kept in Borno in 1823 and on his outward journey to Sokoto in 1824 are held in the Public Record Office, London (Admiralty Series 55 – Vol 10 – a volume which contains miscellaneous logs of personnel serving on HMS *Brazen*, the ship on which Clapperton sailed to the Guinea Coast in August 1825). The rest of his known papers from the Borno Mission remained in the John Murray archives until 1945 when they were acquired at auction, along with other Africana, by Sir Ernest Oppenheimer, who in turn presented them to the Brenthurst Library, Johannesburg in South Africa (Clapperton,H., Papers, MS 171/1-4). These are the records with which we are concerned in the present work. They comprise the following:

MS 171/1 journal 18 November 1822 to 10 February 1823: southward Saharan journey (Chapters Nine to Thirteen of the present text).

MS 171/2 fair copy journal 14 December1823 to 21 January 1824: journey from Kukawa to Kano (published in *Journal of an Excursion etc.*, as a supplementary Chapter of the *Narrative*).

MS 171/3 journal May 1822 to October 1822: a) journals kept in Fezzan (Chapters One to Eight of the present text).

b) charts and courses in Fezzan and Sahara.

MS 171/4 27 February 1824 to 25 January 1825:

a) journey from Kano to Sokoto – February to May 1824.

b) return journey to Kukawa – May to July 1824.

c) return desert journey – July 1824 to January 1825

(Chapters Fourteen to Sixteen of the present text).

---

[5]He may also have been concerned to suppress material which conflicted with his own cherished theories about the course of the Niger.

[6]An edited transcription of Clapperton's journals of his travels in Borno in 1823-4 is presented in Lockhart (ed.), *Clapperton in Borno*.

No previous record has been published of Clapperton and Oudney's sortie east-wards from Murzuq in May 1822; nor of their short stay in Ghat and return journey to Murzuq, nor of their second stay in Murzuq in the summer months of 1822. And Clapperton's account of their travels in Wadi Gharbi and Wadi Shati adds significantly to the published account by Oudney. With regard to the two Saharan journeys, Clapperton sheds new light on life in two, markedly different, caravans, adding to Denham's accounts carried in the *Narrative*.

Hugh Clapperton was born in May 1788 in Annan, a small town in Dumfriesshire in south-west Scotland, and brought up in what was essentially a community of agricultural small-holders and a handful of merchants in a region well outside the mainstream of the early industrial development of the eighteenth century[7].

His father and grandfather were town surgeons; his mother came from a yeoman farming family. He was the seventh surviving child of his father's first marriage. When Hugh was four years old his mother died and his father married a woman twenty years his junior. It is unlikely that Hugh was given much time and attention either by his step-mother, soon pre-occupied with her own many children, or by his father, who by this time reputedly had become a hard drinker and something of a wastrel. Older brothers had left home to go into the armed services or medicine.

After a modest but sound education at a village dame school, Hugh left at around the age of thirteen to go to sea, as a ship's boy on a 258-ton schooner trading out of Maryport on the Solway Firth on regular passages to the Baltic states and across the Atlantic to North America. Aged seventeen, he was press-ganged into the Royal Navy. He started at the bottom – as a cook's mate on a 600-crew man-of-war. After six months he ran to serve in a privateer, only to rejoin the Royal Navy in Gibraltar a few months later, this time as a volunteer. He started again before the mast; but by

---

[7]Sources include: memoirs by Rev T. Nelson [*A Biographical Memoir of the late Dr. Walter Oudney, Captain Hugh Clapperton and Major Gordon Laing* (Edinburgh, 1830)] and Clapperton's uncle, Lt. Col Samuel Clapperton, in the Preface to *Journal of a Second Expedition*; contemporary Dumfriesshire accounts; Clapperton's Royal Navy Record of Service [ADM 9], Ships' Musters [ADM 36, 37] and Captains' Logs [ADM 51], etc., in the Public Record Office, Kew, London; and archival material in the Huronia Historical Resource Centre, Wyebridge, Ontario, Canada.

seeking out an uncle who was a Major of Marines also serving on the Mediterranean station, Hugh Clapperton finally joined the ranks of officers and non-commisioned officers whose naval careers could be developed by connection as well as ability.

Two years' service in the Mediterranean, now as a midshipman, saw Clapperton involved in cutting-out actions off the coasts of Spain. He joined his next station, the East Indies, after a voyage which took him to South America as well as to South Africa and during which he survived capsize in a ship's boat deployed in a mid-ocean rescue operation in a storm. He participated in the capture of Réunion from the French in 1810 and was among the first through the breach in the shore action. There followed two years on patrols around the East Indies and the China seas, now acting as Master's Mate (responsible for the actual sailing of the ship), on ill-supplied and badly-maintained ships, and in harsh conditions in which numerous shipmates died of disease and fever. On return to England in early 1814 he was one of a number of officers selected to train to instruct in a newly-introduced system of cutlass fighting.

Sent next to the Great Lakes of Canada in the war against the United States (1812-14), Clapperton obtained a number of acting commands afloat. Finally, in 1816, he gained a Lieutenant's commission and command of his own schooner. He undertook pioneering and hydrological survey work in remote outposts on Lake Huron – a frontier existence that put a premium on qualities of toughness and self-reliance and demanded a considerable degree of tolerance of unfamiliar cultures and customs. Clapperton was well suited to this life. Indeed, frustrated at one time by delays in obtaining promotion, he is alleged to have considered staying on and turning backwoodsman.

Demobilised on half pay in 1817, Clapperton returned to Scotland but could not settle back easily into life in Dumfriesshire, where he drifted into a round of rural sports and drink, and had an affair with a local girl who bore his illegitimate son. Growing impatient with provincial life, he moved back to Edinburgh and the more stimulating, rowdy company of a circle of former naval friends. It was here that he met Walter Oudney who subsequently recruited him into the Borno Mission.

Clapperton was physically tough, self-reliant and independent – a down-to-earth type but with a certain prickliness of character. We have various accounts of him. Oudney always referred to him as 'stout' in the sense of strong and steadfast. Consul Warrington saw him as 'uncomplicated', but was also a little wary of his rough and ready manner. Denham considered him 'vulgar, conceited, quarrelsome', obstinate and quick to take offence, 'this Son of War, or rather, of Bluster'[8]. On the other hand, the posthumous eulogy by Richard Lander, his servant on his second expedition into the interior of Africa (1825-27), is no doubt over-romanticised[9]. The truth probably lies somewhere in between. Oudney, recommending Clapperton for preferment, highlights a key point:

"He possesses spirit and enterprize. He has good sense and has several acquirements usefull for a traveller. He has not the faculty of making trifles appear as matters of great moment and clothing in fine words what ought to be plain language. Caution is very well but it is unbecoming a traveller to have too much of it...[10]"

Clapperton held strong views on right and wrong, rooted in a Christian upbringing. He was essentially a tolerant man, with a gift for integration, and considerable empathy for the populations he encountered on his travels. His natural instinct was to support the underdog. In his references to slavery, for example, Clapperton's objections are not to the system itself but to its abuses.

Clapperton's literary experience and interests were limited. While his grandfather, Dr. Robert Clapperton, an antiquarian and man of wide literary interests, may have had a positive influence during the dame school days, Clapperton's own further educational studies were limited to midshipman's examinations in the Royal Navy. Subsequent writing experience was essentially utilitarian: keeping the ship's log and writing up logistical or technical reports, for instance on hydrological survey work on the Great Lakes. On return to his native Scotland he had an opportunity to meet the literary elite of Edinburgh through a would-be patron, the dowager Countess Seaforth, whose son he had befriended some years earlier. The evidence is however

---

[8]Denham to his brother Charles, 11th April 1822 [RGS], quoted in *Missions*, Vol. II, p. 37
[9]Richard Lander, *Clapperton's Last Expedition* (2 Vols., London, 1830) Vol. II, pp. 78-80.
[10]Oudney letter to John Barrow, 4th November 1822; see Appendix 1. iv.

that he rejected anything more than passing contact with these circles. Clapperton was also among the founding subscribers to a new library in his Dumfriesshire home, but this may reflect the social position of his family rather than personal literary interest.

There is no reason to think that Clapperton had any particular difficulty in expressing himself in writing, but his interests were not intellectual. His recourse to cliché and the multiple alterations in the fair copy version of his journal indicate that trying to write well might have been hard work. On the other hand, his official correspondence and a handful of private letters written on his two journeys to Africa show a considerable vocabulary, an articulate phraseology and competence in grammar, and a practical, somewhat terse, down-to-earth style. There are no literary flourishes nor emotional outpourings. His natural authorial habitat remained the log or report rather than the essay.

Clapperton's enquiries into more intellectual subjects – traditions, history, politics, etc. – are ad hoc rather than sustained. His thought processes tend to be somewhat disorganised – attempts at summaries of information, for instance, indicate neither a very methodical mind nor a naturally systematic approach. But when he does not know, or if he feels unqualified to comment, he says so.

The pressure of expectations, official and private, on a mission of this kind were considerable; but Clapperton did not bow to them in writing his journals. The Borno Mission's official purpose was threefold: scientific, diplomatic and commercial. Its primary task was to acquire information on the countries of the interior, their geography, natural history, commercial and military capability, and their languages – everything in fact that was needed to prepare the way for future extended contact, alliance, trade and further exploration. This process entailed the establishment of lines of communication and forward bases manned by vice consulates. Clapperton's duties in the Royal Navy on the Lake Huron frontier had already equipped him to cope with the organisational and logistical problems of African travel and he was diligent in solving them. He established latitudes and longitudes, learned the languages, brought back 'specimens and objects' of natural history and notes and samples of commercial interest; he established promising contact with the Sultanate of Sokoto. This kind of work was his preferred métier, and his diaries represent a competent report of his activities, challenges and achievements.

On the other hand, the private interests of the men of learning and letters in Britain were both more extensive and more varied. They were fired with a passion for intel-lectual-philosphical enquiry and evangelical fervour. They wanted to know every-thing there was to know about the unexplored regions of the world. Notions of the wider public about the interior of Africa were stamped with mystery and miscon-ceptions – lost kingdoms, exotic fauna and flora, unspeakable Moors, innocent sav-ages waiting to be saved – and, frankly, arrogance. Reviews and accounts of the Borno Mission's work carried in the literary journals of the day reflect this curiosi-ty and these passions: the people of Britain wanted to be shocked and thrilled. The pressure on explorers to respond to these interests must have been considerable.

Clapperton's accounts of Fezzan and the Sahara are of course euro-centric, but they do not pander to these perceptions and pre-occupations and are less coloured by the fashions and prejudices of the day than the writings of many other travellers of the early 19th century – Richardson or Denham, for example[11]. He certainly took pride in Britain and in the contemporary achievements of the western world, but he had also a genuine personal interest in how others behaved and obtained a living. What most mattered to Clapperton on the Borno expedition was the business of getting there: the logistics and security of the mission; the daily routines and disciplines of travel; the geographical features of the road; the welfare of the mission's servants; its relations with its hosts, escorts and guides; the care of its animals. He was always interested in things military, the weaponry of others and how it was used. He enjoyed all opportunities for sports.

He had two particular preoccupations where the Borno Mission's objectives were concerned. He felt he could make a genuine contribution to its scientific work through his cartographic reports – a casus belli with Denham. And he and Oudney

---

[11]As Paul Curtin [*Image of Africa* (Madison, Wisc. 1975) p. 207.] observes: "More important (and unfortunately more rare among his colleagues) he portrayed the culture of the Western Sudan with sympathy and an unusual degree of modesty."

were determined to prove their own preferred theory about the final course and termination of the Niger, to which they believed the key lay in Nupe, south of Hausaland. In the course of the journey, it also became important to Clapperton to prove his precept that travel in small groups, without the panoply and support of local rulers, was the right and best way to explore.

Changes in Clapperton's attitude and character over the course of the Borno mission are also detetectable. At the outset, there was both the challenge of adventure and the familiarity of a practical role in command of the organisation, the security and logistics of the Mission. Three wearying and frustrating years in the field, however, created psychological as well as physical strain. In Borno during the rains of 1823 Clapperton suffered six weeks of fever and nearly died. He came near to physical collapse again the following season – and was so haggard upon return to Kukawa that Denham barely recognised him. This grave debilitation, from which he had still not completely recovered in September 1825, must have affected particularly deeply a man who had taken pride in, and always been able to count on, his own physical strength.

Constant wrangling and one severe altercation with Denham which could neither be resolved nor put to one side for three years may well have left a psychological mark. In addition Clapperton found himself confronting new and unsought challenges and responsibilities after the death of his friend Oudney. On return to Borno in June 1824 he faced a fundamental dilemma: should he remain in Borno through another season of rains and then make an immediate second attempt to reach the Niger – which, on the basis of information obtained on his journey to Sokoto, he was confident he could do with success – or should he return to Tripoli and London with the others and try to mount a new expedition? Each course of action offered its prize, but each contained its uncertainties. The difficult choice left him depressed, and once he had made the decision to return to Tripoli, his need to get back to London and set off again to the Niger before anyone else, acquired an almost obsessional urgency.

Clapperton's notion of the purpose of his written records underwent corresponding changes. Journals of the months exploring Fezzan with Oudney, or hunting antelope and shooting game on the plains of Lake Chad, tell of halcyon days. The account of the outward journey to Sokoto, however, with Oudney close to death, shows Clapperton to be aware of new responsibilities and is more rounded, more careful and more detailed. By the time of the return journey to Borno, Clapperton felt responsibility only to himself: he had achieved all his own (and Oudney's) objectives for the expedition and his mind was already turning to possible future travels; he cared little about the other aims of the current mission; and even less about Denham. It is of course a general truism that outward and return journeys have a very different character. For Clapperton too, on an outward journey, travelling into unkown territory, everything was new and merited recording. On a return journey there was no need for the same care. Returning from Sokoto to Kukawa he had been very ill, weary and exhausted. Furthermore, the Sahara and its people were by then familiar – there was little he felt like adding.

For much of the expedition, Clapperton kept two separate sets of journals – a normal practice for the security of documents[12], which naturally involved much writing. One was a 'remark book', sometimes written up in the course of the day, for example at the noon halts, in which he entered course details and brief jottings by which to recall encounters and incidents for writing up later. The second was a journal proper, in which he re-wrote these jottings in an expanded and more organised form. In addition, Clapperton kept other notes of a general nature, in separate remark books or occasionally on loose paper, such as second copies of correspondence, navigational calculations, language notes, sketches, or financial accounts[13].

In any event, Clapperton's practice was to keep a journal only when on the road. The exceptions were when he took time to assemble what information he could about places visited for longer periods (Ghat, Bilma)[14]. Clapperton may have reasoned that there was less obligation to keep a systematic journal himself when all members of the Mission were together. In sum, the indication is that Clapperton regarded his journal entries as a form of survey reports, essentially practical

---

[12]On Clapperton's second Mission to Africa, the single copy of one diary was stolen and never recovered, leaving a hiatus of six weeks in his records [*Journal of a Second Expedition*, p. 178].

[13]Any remark books with regular daily entries which Clapperton may have kept during the southbound journey across the Sahara appear to have been lost.

[14]These passages of commentary may have been modelled on Lyon's *Narrative of Travels*, a copy of which the Mission had taken with them.

accounts. Publication, if any, would be a quite separate excercise – and one which for most of the journey he was probably not anticipating.

The remark books represent the raw log of the journey[15]. From an editorial point of view, the evolution of Clapperton's diary from log to journal is straight-forward. New information is added, but there are few changes of any substance to existing information. Jottings in the log become sentences in the journal, but language change is minor, with Clapperton employing the same private style in both log and journal. One or two corrections were made, after reflection or perhaps after consultation with others, but Clapperton's approach remains essentially unaltered. On the other hand, passages summarising observations or information received were attempted in the journal but not in the log. Records of conversations were also normally reserved for the journal[16].

At the same time, however, the log contains more cartographic information than the journal, serving as a note book from which Clapperton could draft maps and charts of routes. While some notes and scribblings in the remark books, for example, the name of a guide, or lists of food or presents received, are of only minor interest today, other entries – such as landscape sketches or weather records, notes of expenses, jottings of names in Arabic script, detail of navigational calculations or of medicines and instructions in their use – can provide valuable data today or shed interesting light on the conditions of travel and the temper of the traveller.

As the present text shows, Clapperton also made a number of changes within the journal itself. It is probably safe to say, however, that the few deletions and insertions in question need give us little if any cause for concern today. Most are merely reorganisation of information, and the self-editorial quotient is low[17]. The matter of lit-

---

[15]Clapperton's remark books from his travels in Fezzan cover the period from 8th June to 18th October 1822. References to them in the footnotes to the present text are made under the annotation "Log".

[16]And, especially, for the fair copy version when he made one – see note 17 below.

[17]This spontaneous, natural approach to diary-keeping can be compared with Clapperton's more careful approach when writing a fair copy journal – an official account for publication – of his journey from Borno to Sokoto and back in December 1823 to July 1824. This version [Brenthurst Library, MS 171/2] reveals a higher degree of self-awareness and audience-awareness, and the changes from the original journals to the fair copy are substantial and significant throughout.

eracy is relevant here: some writers constantly have second thoughts while drafting: Clapperton did not.

The insertions in the journals are for the most part routine additions or completions, made in the process of recalling, reflecting and writing in order to improve accuracy, rather than embellishments. Most deletions are equally normal corrections of grammar or slips of writing. Some may be amendments after a pause for reflection; others relate to turns in thought for a variety of unexceptionable reasons.

The style and content of the journals is sometimes also affected by other factors which cannot easily be reflected in a printed transcription of the text, such as the pressures of time, illness or poor writing conditions. Passages written when Clapperton was ill are notably terser and rarely contain alterations. Accidental factors, such as shortage of space on a page already crammed with writing or a natural reluctance to embark on a new page for a short entry, may also have played a role. On occasion, a different handwriting or strength of ink indicates a change or addition made at some later time. While such changes could, in theory, have editorial significance, there is no way of identifying the period of delay, and, fortunately, the instances are few.

A number of factors temper the journals' value as historical source material today. For example, Clapperton had learned to speak reasonable working Arabic, but had no knowledge of the other vernacular languages. His method of collection of information was rarely systematic ; and the possible motives of his interlocuteurs or influence of discussion of a topic with other members of the mission are not always easy to gauge. The strength of the diaries, however, lies in their immediacy and in the manifest objectiveness of Clappperton's visual observations. Here we are on strong, safe ground. There is nothing prejudiced or slanted in his account, for example, of the reactions of the townspeople of Murzuq to a threatened rebel attack, or of attempting to help a camel up a difficult rocky pass. Compared with other journals of travel, Clapperton's journals may be naive in both preparation and style, but his observations on life around him and comments on the incidents of travel make a spontaneous, modest and uncomplicated record: a solid benchmark against which to measure other accounts of early 19th-century Fezzan and the Sahara, oral and written, indigenous and external.

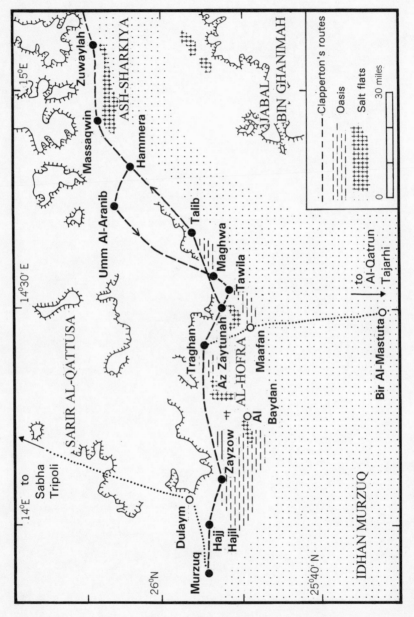

Map 3. Central and Eastern Fezzan

48

CHAPTER

1

Eastward excursion

[Wednesday 1ˢᵗ May 1822]

in which[1] were a number of people gathering in the harvest – they cut the grain off near the head with a small sickle in the form of those used in Great Britian it has also small teeth – the grain is trodden out in the fields with asses – & the straw left to rot what the asses do not eat – in the date trees were a number of wild pigeons

At 2-30 saw Treghan[2] to the Eastᵈ disᵗ about ¾ of a mile standing on a little rising ground clear of Trees it had rather a pleasant appearance the walls appearing new & of a greenish colour – we entred the town by the Western gate & proceeded to the house of [   ][3] Maraboot who is the principal person in the town & has a great character for holiness   we

---

[1]Clapperton and Oudney left Murzuq on 30th April. Clapperton had evidently not taken a fresh journal with him on this, his first, excursion from Murzuq, but began making entries on loose pages – of which those for the previous day and the start of 1st May have become lost. He then went on to use a small pocket notebook, leaving the first pages blank, which later served as a remark book.

[2]In the late 1250s, *mai* (King) Dunama of Kanem (1221-59) annexed all Fezzan as far north as the Jofra oases, thus for the first time bringing all the central Saharan trade route under one political authority. He made a new provincial capital at Traghan, where he installed a viceroy, possibly a Tubu. This man soon rebelled and established the independent black Banu Nasr dynasty that lasted until the 14th century. [G. Nachtigal, *Sahara and Sudan*, Vol. I, p. 150 &n.; J. Lethielleux, *Le Fezzan; ses jardins, ses palmiers* (Tunis, 1948), p. 16; Chapelle, *Nomades noirs*, p. 50.] At the lowest point of the Murzuq depression, Traghan is particularly rich in date palms. In December 1819 Lyon found Traghan "nearly in ruins" with only 5-600 inhabitants [*A Narrative*, pp. 205-8].

[3]Left blank; Clapperton presumably intended to fill in the name later – in this case, 'Hassun', see same day's entry below. There are a number of such blank spaces in the text.

found him sitting in a porch before his house where there was a fine cool current of air   he was surr^d by a number of people of different discriptions – who arose from their seats at our entery & At his invitation we alighted & waited untill the camels came up   he offered us a house to stop in while we remained in the town   which we would not accept – prefering a tent   & when the camels came up he sent a person to show us the best spot where to pitch them   which was on the N.E side of the town –

After the tents were pitched we went & visited the springs which are about a mile & a quarter to S.W. of the town amongst the date groves & Gumah^4 fields to which they give an abundant supply of water   There were a number of frogs hopping in & out & the sides were covered with their spawn –   the D^r collected a number of plants & the sides of the channels were covered with fine grass   The temperature of the water in the resauvoir was 78° of Farnheit ["though exposed to the Sun all day & the Therm on the shore was 92°'" inserted]   the people of Mourzuk told us they were hot springs   they are but 500 or 600 y^{ds} north of the great Salt plain that comes from Zezou to the East –   the water is sweet and Good   there are three spring[s] –   The largest of which is called the Sultan's   allways full   the other two some times dry up in the hot months – we did not leave this pleasant spot untill nearly dusk –   when we returned to our tents we had our mats spread out in the open air to enjoy the cool of the evening   when we were visited by the Maraboot whose name is *Sa Hassun*^{5} he appeared to be a good & generous hearted man

---

^{4}The staple grains of Fezzan are the northern grains – wheat (*gummah*) and barley (*shair*), grown as winter cereals, sown with litttle preparation of the ground in November or December and harvested around April – and the summer-sown cereals of southern origin, sorghum and millet. Barley grows well on sandy soil and can withstand brackish water. Wheat, on the other hand, requiring a soil that is not uniquely sandy and more irrigation, is less common and is principally grown in the oases of Sharkiya and on the steppes of northern Fezzan, particularly Wadi ash-Shati. The rate of exchange between the two cereals in the mid-twentieth century was approximately two kilos of barley to one of wheat. Of the summer-sown cereals, sorghum (*gafuli*) is the preferred grain after wheat; millet (*gussub*, or *dhourra*) is used for couscous and occasionally (poor quality) bread, and is frequently cut green and used for animal fodder. [J. Despois, *Mission Scientifique du Fezzan 1944-45: Géographie Humaine* (Algiers, 1946), pp. 147-153; see also Nachtigal's inventory of agriculture in Fezzan [Nachtigal, *Sahara and Sudan*, Vol. I, pp. 109-118.]

^{5}"The Maraboot, the principal man here ... very fat, greasy and consequential" [Lyon, *A Narrative*, pp. 205-8].

he drank tea with us & was attended by a number of the towns people who treated him with the greatest respect – he is about 65 years of age a tall venerable looking man with a thin white beard   he applied to the Dr for some medecine being much troubled with the rehumatism   & when we return from Zuela[6] he accompanies us back to Morzuk   We were sent an abundant supply of provisions for ourselves servants & Animals   & Showse[7] Ranaime was not forgot for he had an abundance of Lackbi[8] –

Treghan is a neat little town for Fezan   the houses appear to be much cleaner – & the walls are in better repair than any we have seen   on the East side are the ruins of a Castle[9] which appear to have been built by the early Arabs –   the town is of square form having round flanking towers   a small gate in the South & two large ones in the North & West

Thursday 2nd

Started before Sunrise & crossed a plain covered with fine sand & gravel bounded on the North by low hills & on the South by a stripe of date groves running between the plain & the Salt plain   to the South[d] of which were high sand hills – we rode up & examined the hills to the north which

---

[6]It is uncertain whether Zawila is a pre-Islamic foundation. By the 10th century it was the capital of a small Ibadi Berber (Bani Khattab) state renowned in the Islamic world for its trade in slaves, and particularly eunuchs. Al-Biruni in the 11th century called Zawila "the gateway for imported slaves" [N. Levtzion and J. F. Hopkins (eds.), *Corpus of early Arabic sources for West African History*, (Cambridge, 1981) p. 57]. It gave its name to all medieval Fezzan and the Fezzan caravans assembled at Bab Zawila in Cairo (still standing). Zawila declined with the political and commercial ascendacy of Traghan [see n. 2. above].

[7]Ar., *shawsh*, (sarjent), an officer appointed by the Sultan with the role of superintendent [Lyon, *A Narrative*, p. 279] – here as an official escort officer. "Our establishment is large and supported at no inconsiderable expence, for to ourselves, servants and horses, was added a kaid and chouse of the Bashaw and their horses…" [CO 2/13, Oudney to Bathurst, 11th April 1822].

[8]Ar., *laqbi*, a drink fermented from the juice of date palms which is good when fresh but becomes strong and acrid and increasingly alcholic as it continues fermenting.

[9]Gasr Hamadi [Lyon, *A Narrative*, p. 207] – a castle, 120 metres in diameter, similar in construction – large blocks of pise tassé (compressed earth) on wooden frames – to that of Zawila but round. According to local tradition the castle is attributed to ancient ancestors. It is reminiscent of Roman and Byzantine styles and different from more recent gsars which are irregular in form and of a much lighter construction [Despois, *Mission Scientifique*, 57-9].

we found to be composed of a clay stone containing a considerable quantity of iron and sand stone   about 6 miles from Treghan we came to the Well of Bendelmas where our servants had lighted a fire & were cooking breakfast   the Well was 6 feet deep & the water sweet & good –

After breakfast we went into Zetowna where there are the remains of An Arab castle having square towers at each angle   the first of the kind I have seen built in the manner since I came to the country   it is built of mud and close to it are the remains of a large mosque in which are buried some pious maraboots   by the flags that are hanging over the graves   the houses of Zetowna are mostly ["composed" deleted] built of date tree branches –   the inhabitants appear very poor though surrounded with fine date trees & Gumah fields – in which the people were at work   the women seem very loqacious and some of them were not bad looking – to the north^d of the town at a little distance is the ruins of a n° of another castles of Mud about 60 feet high & surrounded with trees   ¼ of a mile E.S.E is Tawela to which we proceeded & arrived at 10 oClock   the Sheikh had prepared a house for us in which we lay down for some time untill a dinner was prepared for us   in the Mean time our horses & the camels were well supplied   & Showse Ranaime behaving with a great deal of state & dignity   so much from his usual manner that two or 3 times I could not help bursting out into a laugh at him for his self importance –   however when the dinner was brought in   which consisted of a plentiful supply of fowels & bazeen[10] &^c   he carefully examined every dish   turnd the towns people out of the house & shut the door –   he then was himself again   after we had finished our meal we asked him his reason for behaving in the manner he had done

he said that 18 Months or 2 years ago (for he is like the rest by no means particular with respect to time) he was sent up from Tripoli by the

---

[10]A porridge of grain flour; in Fezzan and the Sahara normally made of barley, rather than of soft wheat as is more generally the case in north Africa [Despois, *Ibid.*, p. 190]. Boiled in water and stirred into a thick paste, it is then beaten into a circular shape and eaten with gravy, oil, butter or grease poured on it [Lyon, *A Narrative*, p. 49].

Basha[w] to arrest 18 of the inhabitants & send them to Mourzuk where the unfortunate people were all strangled in prison & their goods confiscated   their only crime was that they were going to leave the country without his permission – after dinner – the showse threw of[f] his gravity – & said he could not help it as the Bashaw had ordred him – & indeed people are not thought the worse for having stood executioner two or three times in their lives – & our worthy friend showse R– is amongst the best natured fellowes I have seen amongst them being a plain downright fellow – & however much he might regret to take men['s] heads of[f] were he ordred by the Bashaw – he would do it & with all the good nature in the World

a man came & brought us a second dinner he said he had taken protection in the house of the English Consul for 2 years at Tripoli[11] & we must eat some of his fowels & Cuscassou which was the only thing he had to give so we to oblige this gratefull man eat a second dinner after which we accompanied the Sheikh of the town a black man to the ruins of a Castle which he said was built by the romes[12] to whom they ascribe all the old building – We had the greater part of the inhabitants of the town accompany us – we found only a mound of loose stones – such as would be used by the Arabs in their building   however there were a number of wells which the people had opened running in a line East & West about 20 or 30 feet distant from each other some of them of a great depth & built up with stone from bottom to top which is not the case with most of the wells in this country   some of them are of an oval

---

[11]Consul General Hanmer Warrington [see Introduction]; a man noted for his open-handed hospitality – but also acting under the terms of the Ottoman Capitulations – often gave protection and welfare at his country estate (the English Garden) outside Tripoli to slaves seeking their freedom, and others in trouble. Sometimes, he claimed, he had up to 25 slaves under his care. In September 1828 he reported that he had given hospitality to over 700 people seeking refuge during the Neapolitan assault on Tripoli the previous month. See Clapperton's drawing of "A Maraboot or priest under the protection of the English Consul", Illustration...

[12]Ar., *rumi*, Roman or Byzantine; a term used loosely in North Africa for local pre-Islamic peoples. Despois [*Mission Scientifique*, pp: 57-9] concludes that the earliest gsars were built at the end of the Roman period or a little later, of which some were ruined by the Arab invasions.

Figure 3. A Maraboot

shape[13] – we here took leave of our friends – who appear to be a cheerful sort but poor ragged in their appearance   the place is surrounded with Gumah fields & date trees   the town is small & built of mud walled round like all the rest of the towns in this country   to the South of the Town the salt plain ends about a mile to the south of this place

we   after leaving the ruins of this castle   ascended a stoney plain having low hills to the North   high sand hills to the South   the face of the plain covered with loose pieces of clay iron stone   our course E.N.E 8 Miles then we descended into a bay formed by the stony plain   crossing which for a Mile we arrived at Mughwa at 6   it is a town built altogether of Branches of the date tree   The Sheikh of the town is a negro of which the D^{rs} serv^t & mine were not a little proud[14] – there is very little Gumah here but plenty of food for goats & Camels   the inhabitants subsisting principally upon their milk & dates   we got plenty of food for ourselves & horses &c with Lackbi for Showse Ranaime – it blew a sand storm during the night – with some little rain[15]

Friday 3rd

at Day light the Gale moderated – & sunrise it blew a light air from the North^d our road lay along a beautiful wady covered with date trees & bushes of the agool[16] which is a favourite food of the camels sheep

---

[13]The remains of a *foggara* : a specialised irrigation technique, using an almost horizontal tunnel (1:1,000 or less) from an aquifer to an outlet where the water is needed, a few hundred metres or many kilometers away. The tunnel's course is marked by a series of vertical shafts sunk to allow ventilation and soil disposal. The technique, known also in Iran (*qanat*) and in Oman (*falaj*) and Spain, is clearly of considerable antiquity, but it is not known when, or by whom, it was brought to Fezzan and other parts of the Sahara. [A.Y. Al-Hassan and D.R. Hill, *Islamic Technology: An Illustrated History*, (Cambridge, 1987) pp. 84-5; Briggs, *Tribes of the Sahara*, pp. 10-12.]

[14]See Introduction. Fezzan has always had a certain "Sudanic" character, being in some respects closer to Black Africa than the Maghreb, with ethnic and cultural characteristics reinforced by the 13th century domination of Kanem and by the steady contributions of the black slave trade. In the 11th century Al-Bakri called the Fezzanese capital, Zawila, "the first point of the land of the Sudan" [Levtzion and Hopkins, *Corpus.*, p. 63].

[15]Parts of Fezzan get 4" to 6" of rain a year compared with a Saharan average of about 2".

[16]Ar., *aghul, Alhagi maurorum*, a prickly desert scrub [Bovill, *Missions*, Vol. II, p. 195].

& goats – at 7 we ascended a stoney plain covered with sharp pieces of quartz & Clay iron stone   course E.N.E. –

at 9 we arrived at Taleb where we had break fast in the Mosque no other door being open to receive us   we would not have been guilty of this piece of sacrilege but for Showse Ranaime whom faith sits very easy upon & he says that only for the Bashaw he would become like one of us – When we had finished our break fast the Sheikh came & invited us to his house to remain for the heat of the day – he brought us a dinner of Fowels and fatat[17] a kind of paste like pancakes half boiled half roasted – There are but few houses in Taleb the greater number of which are built of the branches of the date tree   the people supplied our horses and camels with great cheerfulness

At 3 P.M left Taleb   our road lay over a plain E.N.E – to the North of which are a range of low hills running to the N.W.   upon examination we found them to be composed of Sand stone & Clay Iron stone   the outer surface of All the sandstone we have seen in the country whither on the plain or the Mountain has the outer surface quite black at first sight looking like basalt –

at Sunset we arrived at Hamera which stands on a little rising ground surrounded by Gumah fields & date trees – the Wells are about 30 feet in depth – the water excellent running below a stratum of red sand stone about 8 feet thick –

we pitched our tent on the east side of the town   we were immediately [waited] on by the Gayde[18] who happened to be the same that accompanied Captᵃ Lyon to Gatrone & Zuela   he brought a plentiful supply of provisions for man & beast & *stocks* of Lackbi for Rainaime –

---

[17]Thin, sourish pancakes of unleavened bread.

[18]Ar., *kaid*, a district governor – an administrative appointment by the Sultan. Some kaids were ignored by the population, while others enjoyed considerable local power, largely depending on the authority of the local Shaikh. Clapperton also writes the word as *Gayeda*.

We were also visited by Shereef Ali with whom we had got acquainted at Morzuk & who had given us an invitation to Zuela over which & the neighbouring district he was Gayde   he said that he had been collecting the male slaves for Constantinople[19] – & that he was sorry that he could not accompany us to Zuela as they were all in very low spirits at the loss of their slaves whom they had brought up more as their children than slaves – but that he would send a letter to his brother[20] to show us every kindness – & as he had to be back in Morzuk ["to morrow" deleted] in two days but he would endeavour to get back before we left Zuela   he and the Gayde then left us & we went to bed but had scarcely fallen asleep when we were awoke by the – Bagpiper[21] of the town accompanied by two others playing on tambourine – with a crowd at their heels holloaing & dancing – we gave them a dollar & told them to be gone but the Lackbi having bigun to operate upon Showse Rainaime – he the camel men & our servants with some of the inhabitants of the town kept dancing untill day light

Noon Lat^{de} by Mn Alt^{de} of Dubhe 26°-6'-3" N –

Saturday 4th
we left Hamera at Sunrise   our Course was E. by N. ½N over a plain covered with sand & gravel   about 6 Miles from Hamera we came to a salt plain of about ¾ of a mile in breadth from E to W – & about 6 miles from North to South   it is lower than the surrounding plain about 40 feet particularly the North & West sides – and appears like broken ice

---

[19]As suggested in the Introduction, the slave-raiding expeditions of Mohammad Ali's Egypt into the Nilotic Sudan may have stimulated Ottoman demands for a tribute of male slaves from the central Saharan trade. But the fact that most slaves brought through Fezzan were women and young girls would have caused considerable difficulty in finding as many as 1,000 male trade slaves: hence the need to seize established household slaves to make up the number.

[20]Shereef Hamed of Zawila; see Saturday 4th and Sunday 5th May.

[21]The bagpipe was one of the most common wind instruments of Tripoli, Fezzan and the Sahara. An inflatable goatskin was fitted with a wooden mouth-piece and two horn-like pipes, "playing melodies unknown in the west" [M.L. Todd, *Tripoli the Mysterious*, (Boston, Mass., 1912) p. 142 & plate opposite. See also Lyon, *A Narrative*, at front, lithograph of a piper-dancer of Tripoli.]

frozen together again covered in most places with sand there are air holes in it but more numerous than in ice & in the morning a number of places are quite wet with the exhalations – it crisps under the feet like wet ground nearly frozen when walking over it[22] –

at 10 we arrived at Massaguin where we were taken to the house of Shereef Ali by his servant who had accompanied us from Hamera we had lief cooked but found the house in such bad condit[n] it being only used by Shereef Ali when collecting the tribute – Showse Ranaimi swore by the head of the prophet if they did not find a better instantly he would send the Sheikh's head to Morzuk the poor Sheikh begged we would go to his house saying that as we asked for the house of Ali when we came he did not think of offring his own we accordingly accompanied him to his house w[h]ere we lay down to sleep & [arose] at 2 oClock when we were going to set of[f] for Zuela but the Sheikh who was a very talkative fellow amused us untill our Cuscassou & fowels were cooked & brought in & after eating a little of which – we at 3 P.M. left Massaguin traveling in a direction E. by N. ½ N. over a gravelly plain having date trees & sand hills on the South & a range of low hills on the north –

at Sunset we arrived at Zuela and riding into the town we enquired for the brother of Shereef Ali – we thought it rather strange that no one had come out to meet us Showse Ranaime was in high dudgeon he having dressed himself as gay as he was able – & when he found there was no house prepared for us ["him" inserted] for our part we never expected such a thing & were going out to have the tents pitched – The people begged we would go into their houses untill the return of the Shereef Ali's brother – he was at the gardens they had sent a messenger for him

---

[22]Typical features of the Saharan salt plains. Clapperton's diary distinguishes the principal desert forms: *hamada*, the rocky desert – a table-land of rock denuded by wind erosion; *serir*, an older formation of stony desert consisting of pebbles and rounded stones; *reg*, beds of pure gravel of alluvial origin from which the sand has been removed by wind; *sebkha* or *shott*, the terminal basin of a desert wadi where salt is deposited by evaporation; *erg*, a region covered deeply with pure sand and occupied by dunes. The *bahr* or *Bir* is a deep natural spring, often giving rise to reedy lakes shaped by water. [E-F. Gautier, *Sahara : The Great Desert*, (New York, 1987), pp. 202-3].

– but no – Ranaime would not permit us to stop saying that he had sent forward a letter to inform them of our coming & it was their duty to him as a servant of the Bashaw to have come out & show him their respect & still more so to us who were very great men & friends of the Bashaw – in spite of all their solicitations he took us out side & we sat down on a mat to wait untill the camels came up   a number of the respectable persons of the town accom^{pd} us to try & prevail upon Ranaimi to return & we would not interfere but remained perfectly passive to see how he would conduct himself

at last the brother of Shereef Ali arrived but he [Ranaimi] was still imovable though they profferd him money to return at last we were getting tired of his obstinate consequence and made some inquiries when we found that the letter he had sent said that we would not arrive untill to morrow & they read the letter over   the worthy Showse's secretary had made a slight mistake for Ranaimi cannot write himself   we then asked him to come in   & then the brother of Shereef Ali & another taking hold of his hands raised him from the ground with as much respect as if he had been the Sultan of Constantinople   we then went to the house which we found a very good one & the same that Capt Lyons had accepted when he was here   we had an excellent supper of fowel & Cuscassou sent us by Shereef Hamed the brother of Shereef Ali

Sunday 5th
morning hot with a strong gale from the East^d we were waited upon by Shereef Hamed before we got out of bed & in about an hour after^{ds} he returned & we went with him to visit the remains of the castle which has been the largest in this country that we have seen but is now in ruins it is built of clay & gravel being placed in large wooden frames & beat down with *ramers* at first sight they look like immense stones and are mostly as hard it has flanking towers of a square form about 20 paces distant from one another – the north end which is compleate & joins part of the Town wall is 200 paces in length & the height of what remains

may be about 35 feet & is nearly 25 feet thick at the base decreasing in thickness as it goes up – the greater part of the town is built within the square of the castle   the houses are the best I have seen in Fezan & the streets are much broader than in Moorish towns in general

from the Castle we went to the ruins of a Mosque about a ¼ of a mile to the East^d of the town   the walled part of the Mouaden[23] & most of the Arches that supported the domed roof yet remain   they are formed much like the gothic arch but the pillars are very rude – the whole is built of sun dried bricks & morterd   it has been white washed & plasterd inside   from the church we went to their tombs[24] which they say were built by the Romes but they *were* Mislem   each tomb may be about 30 feet high having small window[s] near the top covered with [a] dome at top containing one grave each the bodies lying north & south like all true believers who are buried with their right arm under their head & their faces looking to towards Mecca   they are built of sun dried bricks faced over with flags of sand stone & round the tops below the dome has been a cornice with ornaments & arabic inscriptions only two or three of which now remain – There are two windows at the [top] & one at the bottom of each of the buildings those at the top being longer & broader & arched over

it was cloudy all night so that I could not take my observations to obtain Lat^de Long^de of this place – which is the easternmost town in Fezan but one[25] & on account of the Shereefs residing in it it is allways spoke of by the Fezaneers with a great deal of respect & indeed it deserves it for the Shereefs are certainly the best people we have met with – & have treated·us with a great deal of hospitality & kindness & feed both ourselves &

---

[23]Ar., *madhana*, minaret – from which the muezzin (Ar., *muadhdhin*) calls the faithful to prayer.

[24]In the middle ages, Zawila's buildings impressed visitors. The 11th-century geographer Al-Bakri recorded that Zawila had a cathedral mosque, a bath and markets [Levtzion and Hopkins, *Corpus*, p. 63]. The Bani Khattab rulers were buried in two-storey domed tombs built of sun-dried bricks and at least partly faced with stone. [See *Il Sahara Italiano, Parte Prima: Fezzan e oasi di Ghat* (Rome, 1937) plate opposite p. 629 for appearance in the 1930s.]

[25]viz, Tmassah, 70 km further east.

our horses in the best manner the country could afford – we were to night visited to night [*sic*] by the Bagpiper & his spouse playing on the tamborine who came kapering into the house with a mob at their heels just as we were laying down   we rose up to see these worthies   making it a point never to treat the musicians or Maraboots with disregard   the pipers wife was a compleate Meg Merrilees[26] & when we gave her a dollar she cast forth such unearthly yells &   waived the remains of her ragged barrican[27] over our heads – that we begged Ranaime to get the old dame to take the mob out of the house   which she did but not before she had shown us all the different dances of the country & then they only went out side to dance & yell at the door untill day light

Monday 6th

we left Zuela at day light & were acc[d] outside the gates by Shereefs Ismaia & *Hiade* & one or two more of the descendants of the Prophet & given what little we saw I think they are very great people   they are a fine looking set of men   mild & obliging in their manner   have the true arab countenance & have been settled in Zuela for 100 years –   their ancestors come from Wadun near Sockna[28] –

at 6 we passed out side Massaguin   not wishing to stop   we watered our horses & eat a few dried dates – at 10 we arrived at Hamera   I being ½ a mile ahead of the party entred by a hole in the wall that was large

---

[26]   Old Meg was brave as Margaret Queen
And tall as Amazon;
An old red blanket coat she wore;
A chip hat she had on.

John Keats (1795-1821), *Meg Merrilies*.

[27]The baraccan is the all-enveloping, usually off-white, woollen outer garment of Libya, worn by both sexes. It is tied, toga-fashion, over one shoulder and wrapped more or less tidily around the body and head, as required. Women cover the face, except one eye, with a loose end of their barracans.

[28]Two of the Jofra oases (Ar., *jufra*, a pit or hollow), the third being Hon. They lie in a depression on the main Tripoli-Fezzan road. Although separated from Fezzan proper by the Jabal as-Sawda, they are still considered its threshold. In the early 19th century, Arabs of Sockna were active central Saharan traders and financiers, especially in Murzuq, inevitably in close association with the war-like Awlad Sulayman and the Gadadfa tribes who had proprietorial interests in the oases' economic life.

enough to admit me & my horse when I had dismouted as soon as I had entred I was surrounded by women amongst whom was one that had got some medecine from the D^r at Morzuk from the D^r [sic] for an erruption on the skin & as she was now perfectly well she had spread his fame amongst the rest of the towns people and as the men were all at work in the fields the women came out without fear & all were wanting some thing or other but a stop was soon put to their clamour by the arrival of the D^r & Showse Ranaime at the hole in the wall when the young ones took to their heels   the D^r dismounted & entred as I had done but Rainaime would not he began tearing down the wall swearing he would represent to the Bashaw What gates they had in Hamera that would not admit a man & horse – however he was at last obliged to dismount finding that it would cost him a great deal of trouble to enlarge the ["north" inserted] Gates of Hamera –

we then took shelter from the heat of the sun in the first house we saw open which happened to belong to an old woman – we had mats spread & the mule arriving with the canteen we had tea – after which we went to the house of the Sheikh where the D^r was surrounded with patients but fortunately the camels had not arrived so he dismissed them & told them to come when our camels arrived as all the medecine was with our baggage – when they arrived the house was soon full of people with sore eyes consumptions & liver complaints & a n^o of women wanting medecine to make them bear male children & amongst the rest was one of the Sheikhs wives the same woman that applied to Captn Lyons when he was here   she has now been according to her servant with child 5 years the D^r gave her two very strong doses of Jalap[29] if one did not take effect she was to take the other she then took the D^r to one side out of hearing of the rest of the people & begged he would give her a little dose to poison the other wife of the Sheikh saying he had no use for more than her the D^r gave her a very severe lecture – & as for the other

---

[29] A purgative drug [ShOED].

ladies we said the Medecine for getting boys was all at Morzuk if they come there we should serve them – Two sons of Sheikh Barood[30] Came & invited us to visit Omlaraneb a town that belongs to their father

at 4 P.M. we left Hamera in company with these young men our road lying over a gravelly plain having in the Sth a stoney plain & on the N.E covered with bushes of the agool in which they say there are plenty of hares – the agool much resemble the furze but does not grow such large [ ] Course N.W. 2

At Sun set arrived at Omlaraneb[31] the eldest of the young men had rode on before to acquaint the inhabitants of our comming & who had come out of the gates to receive us we were welcomed to the town by all the Elders of the people who conducted us through the different streets which are very narrow & crooked – the town is small & has not been [built] above 7 or 8 years – we after riding through the diffrent streets returned to our tents which had been pitched outside we were accompanied by the young men to the tents who saw our horses & Camels provided with barley grass & dates & in a short time a sheep *dressed* with plenty of soup bread & Cuscassou was brought us –

Sheikh Barood is the richest Arab in Fezan possessing nearly a 1,000 camels & several thousand sheep that feed between this & the gulph of Sirtis he has a great number of Arabs of different tribes in his employ who tend his flocks in peace and with those he is at war fight for this he protects them feeds & cloaths them pays all taxes to the Bashaw which is mostly done by service and one of his sons is on the point of going down to Tripoli with 200 camels ["belonging to his father" deleted] laden with the Sultans merchandise – in this way was the Tribe

---

[30]A wealthy Bu Wadi Arab, who was a particular friend and supporter of Al-Mukni, and manager of the latter's affairs [Lyon, *A Narrative*, pp.168 & 211].

[31]Ar., *Umm Al-Aranib*, mother of hares – so-called because of the reputed abundance of hares thereabouts. As Clapperton remarks, it was a new place. Settled mainly by Orfilla Arabs from south-east Tripolitania, it was already an important sub-centre of the caravan trading system.

Walid Suliman they were from all the different tribes of the regency all those who were too brave to starve & too idle to work joined the Walid Suliman who's Tribe & family occupy Tooat[32]

the Sheikh is at present in Morzuk awaiting the Sultan's departure[33] – he is possessed of a great number of slaves who have a little town to themselves outside of Omlaraneb

Thursday 7th

we started 30' before one & traveled S.W by W over a plain composed of sharp flat stones at day light we entred the plain a mile to the Eastd of Morzuk[34] – we waterd our horses and had a drink of sour Milk & proceeded on to Towela & Zetaona & took up our quarters at the house of the Sheikh who rules over both Zetaona & Towela he was out in the field at work when we arrived but he soon made his appearance & provided both ourselves & horses with food – ["we thanked" deleted] for which the Dr paid[35] & in addition gave his daughters 3 in number a pair of scissors a string of beads & a thimble each – with which the Sheikh was much pleased –

at 4 we left Zetaona for Treghain riding over the same road at sunset we arrived & pitched our tents – sent the Showse in to acquaint the Maraboot of our arrival – but he had been gone for two days to Morzuk to wait on the Sultan before he went to Tripoli – however we were as well supplied by his servants as if he had been present – for before he

---

[32]At the time of the Bornu Mission, the Awlad Sulayman tribe was still recovering from a series of defeats at the hands of Yusuf Pasha Karamanli in the previous decades [see Introduction]. Remnants of the tribe were still widely dispersed and recuperating in other parts of the Sahara. The tribe's paramount family, the Saif al-Nassr, had traditional marriage alliances with the Sultan of Morocco's family. The Tuat oases-complex, then owing allegiance to Morocco, was one such refuge.

[33]For Tripoli, with the tribute from the booty captured in the 1821 raid on Bagirmi.

[34]A slip by Clapperton, who means Maghwa, not Murzuq.

[35]*Teskera*, lit., an Imperial decree; a binding and enforceable order from the Sultan. Armed with the Bey's *teskera*, the travellers could have demanded supplies – an imposition normally accepted stoically by the populations concerned. Richardson [*Travels*, Vol. I, p. 187] commented, however, that the generosity of the Bornu Mission had spoiled things in Fezzan "as Englishmen have spoiled the routes of the Continent of Europe".

left his house he had given orders that on our arrival we were to be supplied with every thing that was to be got – we could not get this man to take any money for the provisions sent us but we *always* made a present of the value to his servants – This being the feast of the old *Men*[36] the townspeople were dancing & feasting all night

Wednesday 8<u>th</u>

we arose at 3 A.M. & left Treghain for Zezau traveling over the same road & at 10 we arrived at that place famous for Lackbi & the drunkness of the inhabitants   however we had the good fortune to find the Sheikh's brother sober who invited us into what had once been a good house where we breakfasted after which Ranaimie & our servants went & visited their friends the Sheikh & all got beastly drunk but fortunately they had seen the horses well fed before they began – & the Sheikhs wife supplied the D<u>r</u> & I who were left alone with good cuscassou & fowels – They told us the Sheikh had once a very good property which he had sold & is now drinking Lackbi with the money There is the remains of a ruined Castle here & the houses of the town are mostly in the same condition to[o]   the place is surround[ed] with fields & date trees every house has got a lackbi tree near to the door to supply the wants of the drunken inhabitants who have by their drunkness been obliged to sell their fields & Gardens – so that most part now belongs to the Sultan & a few of the inhabitants of Morzuk

at 4 we got our servants sober enough (for the effects of Sour Lackbi appears sooner to work off than rum or wine) to proceed & we arrived at Haje Hajill[37] at Sunset where we pitched our tent – the Ther<u>m</u> in the shade at Zezau was 106° of Farnheit –

---

[36]Ar., *id al-kabir*, the festival marking the pilgrim rites in Mecca. Clapperton was here confusing different possible meanings of the root-word *kabir*, 'great' or 'old man'.

[37]The principal gathering place for caravans on the southern and eastern approaches of Murzuq, one half day's journey from the city.

Figure 4. The Gildon Manton portrait of Clapperton

CHAPTER

2

Planning in Murzuq

Thursday 9th
Arose before day light and went into Morzuk   we found on our arrival
M[r] Tirwhit laid up with inflamed eyes M[r] Hillman looking very ill & the
Major as usual – during our absence the Ther. in the shade in the heat
of the day was very regular from 102° to 106° – at night & in the morning 76° – the Sultan had sent 1,000 slaves to Tripoli during the Time we
were away[1]

Friday 10th
Clear & fine

Saturday 11th
M[r] Hillman & Major D[s] per[sonal] servant taken ill with inflamation of
the eyes

Sunday 12th
Clear & warm

---

[1]Black trade slaves from the Sudan usually arrived in Murzuq early in the year and made the final
Murzuq-Tripoli journey in May-June, at the latest. This timing was determined by the main slave
raiding and trading dry season in Sudan (October to April) and by the need to move slave caravans
across the Sahara before the hottest months.

Monday 13th

Clear & warm   Major D– having heard from some of the inhabitants of the town when we were absent that the Sultan had said he would allow us to go to Bornow if we would give him 2000$ we accordingly waited upon [him] after send[ing] to say we wished a private audience – & made him the minded proposition –   he said if we were to give him 20,000$ he could not send us without the Bashaw's permission

Tuesday 14th

Clear & Warm   the D^r & Major & Mr Tirwhit have had applications from the different Mamalukes to lend them money

Wednesday 15th

Clear & Warm

Thursday 16th

Clear & Warm

Friday 17th

Clear & Cool   the Sultan attended the Mosque & at 2.30 he left the Town his band playing before him   he was attended by [a] few horse viz Lizari Mohamed Baba our Mamaluke[2] & one or two others – & the flags of Tripoli & the Green Flag of the Prophet were carried before him he had not got outside the gate before old Hadje M^d[3] & some others

---

[2]"In Morzouk there are some white families who are called Mamluks, being descended from Renegades, whom the Bashaw had presented to former Sultans." [Lyon, *A Narrative*, p. 279]. Denham reports that there were traditionally about a dozen, residing in the Castle, assisting in government, and all extensive and wealthy dealers in merchandise and slaves [*Missions*, Vol. II, p. 277-8].

[3]Hajj Muhammad bin Ab-dun was a leading Mamluk of Murzuq who took charge of and befriended Ritchie and Lyon and then the Borno Mission both in Murzuq and later on their travels to Borno when he acted as the kadi to Bu Khulum's caravan.

came & began to abuse him saying that they never had had such a *bad* Sultan in Fezan that he had taken all the money out of the country & left them nothing in fact that he was every thing that was bad Mukni they said was a kind & munificent prince compared to him that he used to swear at & abuse them with his tongue but let their money alone – They allow that this man says little & never spoke ill to anyone – from the character we had of him in Tripoli – from people of all classes he is a good & just man & during his stay here he has ever treated us with kindness – & when we went to make him that indiscrete offer of 2,000$ to forward us to Bornou he told us the people of Fezan were on no account to be believed – & that he had ever found them cheats & liars – Mustapha a[l] Ahmer – or the Red from his beard is a Circassian by birth[4] – between 30 & 40 years of age above the Midle size about 5ᶠ 10ⁱ black eyes rather long face with an expressive countenance writes & reads Arabic & Italian[5] – & from the conversations that we have had with him I should think he was a sensible man – he has got the reputation of being a very brave one in the late expedition to Bagermie – but the Murder of so many unfortunate people in cold blood can not be justified even by neccessity –

Mohamed Baba our Mamaluke having no further occasion for his service – we had paid him *120$* with which he appeared contented – & if we judge by the number of his applications to supply his place the people here think so too – He is a Georgian was born at Teffiles & taken from his own country at 13 years of age he has a laughing round face fair hair and blue eyes stout make & about 5 feet 6 inches high according to the account he gave me he first served under *Diguerron* Pasha of Acre

[4]The Turks had long imported "white" slaves across the Black Sea from Georgia, other parts of the Caucasus, southern Russia and the Crimea, collectively calling them "Circassians". The women were noted for their beauty and the men for their skills and intelligence. Circassian slaves usually fetched the highest prices, and some gained high places in the Ottoman Empire. Suleyman the Magnificent (1520-66) was, for instance, of Circassian descent on his mother's side.

[5]Italian was for centuries the commercial and diplomatic language of the central and eastern Mediterranean and has long been understood in Tripoli and other parts of Libya. Yusuf Pasha Karamanli spoke Italian badly, and his Ottoman Turkish successors continued to use Italian in official correspondence with foreign officials and consuls in Tripoli until the later 19th century.

from thence he went on to Egypt where he remained untill the quarells with the Pasha & the Mamalukes[6] when he came to Tripoli where he has remained in the service of the Basha[w] ever since

he was at the taking of this place by Mukni – & was the person who strangled Hadje Osman[7] & his two sons – & he used to sit & converse with one of that person's sons who had the good fortune to be out of the way at that time – with as much ease & freedom as if nothing had ever been done to his unfortunate father & brothers – who they say were good & aimeable men – & gave a great deal away in charity   the Father I believe was upwards of 80 years of age & his only crime was being rich Mohamed when you ask him about it laughs & says what could he do as it was the Bashaw's orders & you know says he they must be obeyed he had a scarlet Bornous[8] trimmed with broad gold lace which belonged to Hadje Osman which he used to wear & offred for sale to us – during the time he was on the above expedition they said his wife played the truant for which he cut her throat – I shuddered when he told me this, and asked him if he had no other proofs than people saying so – no says he that was enough damn her father he was hung by the Bashaw for being rich

such was our country conductor & protector who allways showed a great deal of friend ship for me though some times I have threatened him roundly   he ever spoke to the Arabs in the Mildest manner even when they deserved curses was carefull & attentive to all our wants   he showed us every attention in his power   he was a regular man at his prayers but was very fond of wine – as the whole of the Mamalukes are

---

[6]In 1811 the Governor of Egypt, Mohammad Ali, liquidated the last of the ruling class of Mamluks (originally Circassian slave-soldiers). Many took refuge in the Nilotic sudan, but fled again in the face of the Egyptian invasion of 1820. Some who survived a dangerous journey across hostile countries sought refuge in Borno and Fezzan.

[7]The principal Mamluk of Sultan Muntasar, who after a dispute with Al-Mukni was murdered, together with his two sons, on the latter's orders [Lyon, *A Narrative*, p. 295].

[8]Ar., *burnus*, a cloak of wool or wool and camel hair, with a hood, worn by both sexes, and most common from Tunisia westwards.

& when they can get drunk every night they do not like Europeans get drunk in company but drink for the express pleasure of getting drunk or as they say making their head go round beautifully

This evening the Dr Major D– & myself having agreed that it would be better for one of the party to go down & lay before the Consul General at Tripoli the real state of our Situation as we saw no probability of the Army going down to Bornou for 18 months at least that there was nothing ready for such a thing in Fezan that nothing was preparing for such a thing & that ["nothing" deleted] should an opportunity arise of a Kaffle[9] going there we in all likely hood would not be allowed to accompany it – – & the Sultan had expressly said that he was not allowed to provide us with an escort how ever small to conduct us there – It being Major D^s particular wish to go down to Tripoli for this purpose it was ["proposed" deleted] agreed that he should set of[f] on the 20th & return in 3 Months if nothing was done before that time & in the mean time the D^r & I were going to attempt to get to Ghaat – with Hatita[10] to employ the time who had to remain in Fezan as usefully as possible

Saturday 18th
Cool & clear with wind from the North

Sunday 19th
Cloudy & cool at 4 oClock P.M. three camels with the Majors baggage set forward it consisted of three camels & his mule his black servant Angelo the servant of Mr Tirwhit who wanted to go & see his mother Abshom the Jew who had disposed of all his goods & wanted to see his

---

[9]Ar., *qafila*, a caravan or convoy. Clapperton's spelling varies: gaffle, kaffle and kafila.

[10]Hatita ag Khuden, of the Imaghasseten noble clan of the Ajjer Tuaregs, befriended first Ritchie and Lyon, whom he offered to accompany to Sudan [*A Narrative*, p. 293], and, later, the British explorer Alexander Gordon Laing, whom he accompanied from Ghadamis to Tuat in 1825. Richardson subsequently encountered him in 1845 – "Consul of the Europeans, as the Moors call him. Hatita himself assumes the distinction of "Friend" or consul of the English" [*Travels*, Vol. II, p. 10].

mother also   this rascal has behaved with the greatest ingratitude to the
D^r   Jacob the Majors other servant is very ill with a fever & unable to
go with his master — what has sickened all these fellows of this place I
cannot say — for they lived better & been better paid since they have been
with us than ever they did before — all the Tripolines appear to fear Fezan[11]

Monday 20th

Cloudy & cool   at day light the Major set out   Mr Hillman & myself
accompanied him as far as Deleegen[12] where he stoped for the heat of the
day — he is accompanied by showse Ranaimee

Sunday 21st

Cool & cloudy   this afternoon Hadje Mohamed & Abderassoul wanted
to know if we would see the Moon to ["day" deleted] night as the fast of the
Ramadam commences when it is seen but fortunately it was cloudy so
they will have another day of joy & bliss for eating & wommen [sic] all that
they hold dear in this World & the next with the addition of fine cloaths

Wednesday 22nd

Clear & fine   this evening the New Moon was seen   a few Musquets
were fired and old Hadje Mohamed repeated a prayer looking at the
Moon — when this was ended the[y] went to the Mosque

Thursday 23rd

Clear & cool

---

[11]All the Tripolines appear to fear Fezzan: the German traveller and medical doctor, Gustav
Nachtigal, who was in Fezzan in 1869-70, found it generally healthy, being largely desert. But the frequent *sebkhas* (salt marshes) bred malaria, especially in Murzuq and in the oasis-villages of the well-
watered Wadi ash-Shati. Murzuq was known as one of the Sahara's unhealthiest places, especially for
outsiders in summer, and Nachtigal complained that he had suffered more from fever there than in
the well-watered regions south of the Sahara. [*Sahara and Sudan*, Vol. I, p. 131]. Slave caravans imported smallpox into Murzuq [*Ibid.*, p. 133] and syphilis was common [*Ibid.*, p. 137].

[12]Dulaym, gathering place of caravans for the north and the east, 9 miles east of Murzuq.

Friday 24ᵗʰ

Clear & cool   we heard to day that the Tuaricks of Ghaat & Tuat were at war[13] – this we take to be raised to prevent us going there

Saturday 25ᵗʰ

Clear & fine

Sunday 26ᵗʰ

Clear & warm   a report was brought us that 4 Arabs had returned after attempting for 2 Months to get to Soudan – being prevented by the war between the black & white Tuaricks[14] – this is another maneauvre

Monday 27ᵗʰ

Clear & warm   this morning a man came to beg of Mᵣ Tirwhit to intrete to Hadje Mohamed who was beating his eldest son (a man between 30 & 40 years of age) most unmercifully for getting drunk –   when Mᵣ T went in he found him in irons & two of his brothers & [had] just given him 200 bastinados on the feet with date sticks[15] & were going [to] repeat this dose when fortunately for him Mᵣ T arrived & begged him off

---

[13]Even if it was a manouevre to dissuade the Mission from travelling to Ajjer Tuareg country, where the Murzuq authorities feared for its safety, for which they were responsible, there was quite possibly some substance behind the fabrication or exaggeration. Tuat, of course, was not permanently populated by Tuaregs [see Chapter Five, n. 32], but the latter controlled the roads to Tuat from Ghat, and there might have been an increase in plunder, ransom and blackmail against Ghatian traders and travellers.

[14]'Black' would denote slaves, of whom there were two classes: the *Ighawalen* (stock-herders of mixed negroid-Tuareg descent) and the *Iklan* (household slaves, in origin blacks captured in the Sudan). The latter were of an altogether lower status and represented no threat to the noble 'white' classes. The *Ighawalen* however, some of whom could obtain employment in a military capacity, were often armed. [See H. Norris, *The Tuaregs: Their Islamic Legacy and its Diffusion in the Sahel* (Warminster, 1975) pp. 4-5.] Thus, while war might be too strong a word, this was perhaps a reference to a, recent or potential, state of social upheaval involving armed conflict.

[15]Sp., *bastinado*, punishment by beating on the soles of the feet with a stick; 200 strokes could well be fatal.

Tuesday 28ᵗʰ
Clear & warm

Wednesday 29ᵗʰ
Fresh breezes & clear   to day our neighbours Hadje Mohamed & Abderassoul came with some scraps of paper with words from the Koran written on them to stick in the holes of the Walls & prevent the scorpions[16]   Jacob Major Dʳˢ Servant is getting better   Mʳ Tirwhit is a little unwell with a bowel complaint

Thursday 30ᵗʰ
Clear & Warm with a Strong Northerly Wind

Friday 31ˢᵗ
we engaged a man belonging to Sockna & his 4 Camels to take us to Ghaat & Mohamed the Neapolitan Renegado[17] volunteered to accompany us & we engaged the son of Hadje Mohamed – as a showse

Saturday June 1ˢᵗ
This morning when we were packing up our things for our journey to Ghaat the Mamaluke came & told us that there was a great disturbance

---

[16]Common in Murzuq, especially in the late summer, and much feared [Lyon, *A Narrative*, p. 184]. For the menace of Saharan scorpions (particularly in oases) and myths about them see G. Scortecci, *Sahara* (Milan, 1945), pp. 163-8; Briggs, *Tribes of the Sahara*, pp. 260-1. Some Arabs and Tuareg are said to be immune from scorpion-stings, as were, allegedly, the Psylli people of ancient Libya. [O.Bates, *The Eastern Libyans: an Essay* (London, 1914) pp. 179-80].

[17]At the age of eight, this son of a Neapolitan corporal had been captured by corsairs and sold as a slave in Tripoli, where there were at any time several hundred enslaved Christians. He had there gained local freedom and bettered his prospects by accepting Islam. He spent about ten years in service at the Castle in Tripoli, the seat of government and the Pasha's residence. Yusuf Pasha Karamanli gave him to Al-Mukni, who used him to spy on Ritchie and Lyon in Murzuq in 1819 but, Lyon says, "we employed many tricks to deceive him" [*A Narrative*, pp. 104-5]. By December 1822 he had been appointed kaid of the district of Al Qatrun and Tajarhi [Friday 6th December].

at that place   one fighting against the other – & that the man whose camels we had hired was affraid to go with us – & several other tricks & stories they are playing of[f] to prevent our going to Ghatt– telling the Arabs they will steal their camels & us that the Tuaricks are a treacherous people

Sunday 2<u>nd</u>
Clear & fine   we had today some more maneauvering about the camels[18] – we told them there was no truth to be placed in what they said

Monday 3<u>rd</u>
clear & fine   the Mamaluke Renegado brought us a Tuarick who agreed ["to take us to Ghaat for 40$ there and back" deleted] to bring 5 Camels in 2 days time with which he would take us & our baggage to Ghaat & back for 40$[19]

Tuesday 4<u>th</u>
Clear & fine   we were this morning agreeably surprised by the arrival of a Courier from Tripoli bringing us letters & some of the things we had ordred in England for presents in the interior – We bought some very fine Apples & peaches   the first we have seen here

Wednesday 5<u>th</u>
Clear & warm   a Tuarick came from Wady Gharby from Hatita who has

---

[18]Hiring camels was not easy. Despite Murzuq's role as a centre of Saharan trade and communications, camels suitable for long Saharan journeys were not necessarily readily available, and particularly not in early summer. Even if owners were prepared to hire them out, camels had to be rounded up and brought in from pastures to the west and south, many days away. Impatient European travellers often unfairly blamed delays in acquiring camels, and the high prices asked for them, on locals' malice and greed.

[19]See Introduction, n. 38.

been there for this some time sick with a Guinea Worm[20] in his knee

Thursday 6th
Warm & Cloudy   no camels as yet   we had strong arguments against going to Ghaat to day from a number of the inhabitants – but they lie so abominably there is no putting any trust in what they say – they thieve

Friday 7th
Warm & Clear   in the after noon we agreed with a Tuarick to bring 5 Camels in the morning to convey our baggage to Ghaat

---

[20]Guinea worm, *Dracunculus medinensis*, is endemic in central and west Africa today but was probably more wide-spread in the early nineteenth century. The infection is spread by contaminated drinking water, and its most serious complications tend to arise through secondary infections leading to severe joint problems and crippling [G. Cook, Editor, *Manson's Tropical Diseases* (20th edition), personal communication].

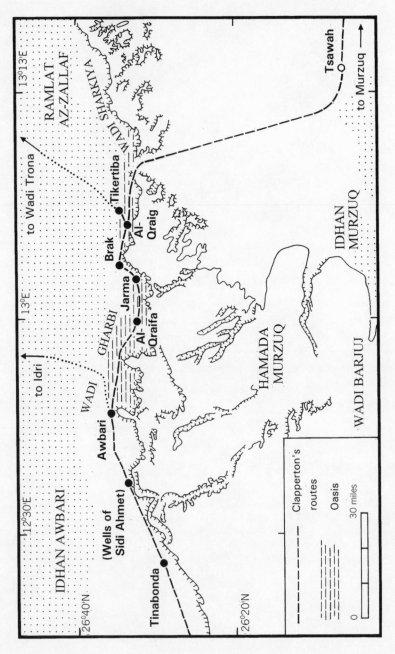

Map 4. Wadi Gharbi in the Wadi Al-Ajal

CHAPTER

3

Wadi Gharbi

Saturday 8ᵗʰ

Clear & warm   at 6 A.M. left Morzuk acc^{pd} by Mohamed Ben Abdullah the Neapolitan ["Mamaluke", deleted] Renegado who had volunteered his services – Mohamed the Son of Hadje Mohamed our neighbour Hadje Ali the brother of Bukaloom – we rode in a direction W.N.W. 12 Miles to Humum so called from its heat & not from its baths for there is no such *a thing* in Fezzan   our road was level all the way   having high sand hills to the south & a stripe of Gumah fields to the north   we staid in the house of a friend of Hadje Ali's untill the heat of the day was over (we having arrived at noon [)] – we were presented with some very fine figs & peaches   the houses are mostly built of date branches   the inhabitants being poor and employed in taking care of the fields & date trees which mostly belong to the inhabitants of Morzuk[1]

at 4 P.M. we started and rode over a gravelly desert in [ ] direction having the date trees and gumah fields on the south   about ¼ of an hour after sunset we came up with the camels who had started before us & at 8.40 P.M– we arrived at Tezawa & pitched our tents outside the gate   had our tea & went to sleep very tired

---

[1]Much of Fezzan's cultivated land was owned by absentee landlords, and worked by servile labour; see n. 25 below.

to Humum W.NW 12 Miles – from H[umum] to Tezawa N.W 15 Miles

Sunday 9th

Tezawa is a small town walled round & the inhabitants are a mixed race like the rest of Fezzan it is governed by a Maraboot who is a young man and half a Tuarick his mother being one of that nation and in consequence of which a n° of the Tuaricks have settled here and in its neighbourhood[2] it is surrounded by fields gardens date trees & the best grapes & peaches in Fezzan they say are produced here – the Maraboot was very civil to us and the D[r] as usual had a great no. of patients amongst the extrodinary cases was a Tuarick who was sick for money[3]

at 8 A.M– we left Tezawa and traveled N by W over a gravelly desert level as a Sea – at 2 arrived at a well Called the Tallah tree well where we halted untill the Camels came up which the[y] did at 3 P.M. – when we pitched our tent as there was no water to be got between this well & Tickerteba – Hadje Said the owner of our camels wet his body & Cloaths with water it being the Rhamadam & he a Tuarick who are strict Mohamedans it would not do for him to take a drink of water till after Sunset – it came to blow very hard from the E.N.E bring[ing] clouds of sand along with it which was more painful than hail beating on our legs & faces – & it soon laid our tent low which we did not pitch again untill it had moderated which was at 6 oClock   our Course N. by W 18 Miles

---

[2] The *Tanalkum*, semi-nomadic Tuareg of the vassal class who over the centuries had become progressively fezzanized, pasturing in and near the great wadis of western Fezzan and participating directly in the economic life of Fezzan, husbanding and hiring camels, selling the produce of their flocks, and trading products from Aïr and Sudan in exchange for dates and cereals. "The Azkar-Tawarek, who, leaving their miserable abodes, migrate to those more fertile districts, where they build themselves light cottages of palm branches, and indulge in a patriarchal life, breeding camels and rearing sheep ... but nevertheless they keep up their family ties with their brethren near Ghat and respect in some degree the authority of the chief ..." [Barth, *Travels*, Vol. I, p. 142].

[3] Log: "one of them asked the D[r] for a Dollar for the diarea".

Monday 10th

At day light left our encampment & traveled in a direction North 8 Miles to some Tallah trees at the foot of the Mountains which were in a direction East & West   entred the pass   went 2 Miles N.W by N 2 and then entred a narrow ravine – having stripey hills of sand stone on each side containing a great quantity of iron on the outside   quite black like lava or green stone[4] – we also saw a no. of petrified trees lying in the pass having the trunks and part of the branches complete[5]

North 8 Miles   N.W by N 2 – North 6 –

at 10 we descended into wady Gharby[6] by a narrow steep winding rocky pass where the least false step would have hurled us into eternity – the view was one of the finest that is to be seen in the country having to the North high black sand hills & the Wady lying ["as it seemed", deleted] at a great depth below – studded with little black hills like Isld[s] & here and there a grove of date trees scattred on the level bosom of the Wady   at 1.30 arrived at Teckerteba[7] after having travled North 8 Miles   N.W. by N 2 Miles   North 6 Miles   We found a great deal of trouble in getting any thing to eat – at last by the exertions of Hadje Ali we got some fow-

---

[4]A wide term, usually comprising the greenish-coloured eruptive rocks containing feldspar and horneblend (or augite) (1805) [ShOED].

[5]The petrified tree trunks could be cretaceous – i.e. mesozoic, from the period when the equator crossed Africa between, roughly, the Gulf of Guinea and Cairo – or, perhaps more likely, originate from the Late Pleistocene or Holocene. The petrification results from rather specific climatic and geo-chemical conditions, the trees having to imbibe solutions containing silica – which could only come from saturation with alkaline water. Most likely the area was inundated by waters from an alkaline lake after some catastrophic event. This is one speculation but there may be other specific conditions that could lead to the petrification. [Professor M. Edmunds, personal communication.]

[6]A valley some 60km long and 2 to 12km wide, it is the western extension of Wadi al-Ajal, and one of Fezzan's main centres of amenity and ancient human settlement, as well as an axis of communications. As water lies only 3 to 9 metres below the wadi, palms flourish unirrigated, other crops being watered from shallow wells or *foggaras* (see n.13, Chapter One). There is good grazing for Tuareg camels. Inhabited oases include Jarma, the ancient Garamantian capital of Garama (see Introduction) and there are ancient cemeteries and other sites nearby. [Daniels, *The Garamantes*; P. Ward, *Touring Libya: The Southern Provinces* (London, 1968) plans on pp. 70-1.]

[7]The division between Wadi al-Garbi (the western part of Wadi al-Ajal) and Wadi ash-Sharkiya (the eastern part) falls at Tikertiba, where the escarpment swings north and meets the sand sea, providing a narrow 'passage obligé' for movement along Wadi al-Ajal. Tikertiba is the first village in al-Garbi and controls the defile [Dr. D. Mattingly, personal communication].

els &c & My servant Madie going out to look for some straw for the horses the Gayeda of the town and some of his servants set upon him & gave him a beating – we were under the necessity of threatening them with the vengeance of the Bashaw which produced us some grain & straw – and a mess for ourselves which we would not accept

Lat^{de} by Mn. Alt^{de} of Spica 26°–33'–55" N

Tuesday 11th
Fresh breezes & Clear at 8 A.M. our friend Hatita arrived and the people of Tickerteba got him to intercede for their Gayde[8] they brought a ragged young fellow who they said had been guilty of thrashing Madie and as Madie was contented to be imposed upon we let it pass without any further notice not wishing to give the inhabitants a bad opinion of our Mercy[9] – We had Hatita & two of his men to breakfast as also old Hadje Said the owner of our camels who is a very decent man the[y] were very inquisitive about England whether we put our enemies to death When we took them in battle or whether we made slaves of them or not they were quite surprised when we told them the contrary – Hatita promised to bring us camels in two days to take us to Ghaat for some reason best known to himself Hadje Said cannot go to Gaat

At dinner we were visited by another Tuarick called Ager Sheikh who Hatita [says] is one of their great men – we got a mess of meat from the town which we gave to the Tuaricks who went outside & eat it

Young Hadje Ali would not eat his dinner as the parsons nose of the fowels we had for dinner was not cut in the name of God which it seems

---

[8]Log: "they said the Bashaw would take his head off." The reference to Hatita's apparent authority indicates that he may have had some responsibility for dealings with foreigners and foreign trade in the Ghat heirarchy; cf. observations by Rodd [*People of the Veil*, p.106] on comparable functions of the 'Sultan Turawa' in Aïr.

[9]Log: "we said he must come & beg Madies pardon".

must be done the same as the throat – but he got muzzy on a bottle of rum which requires no ceremony to go through in drawing the cork – however it loosened his tounge and he recommended us strongly to the Tuaricks

The D^r & I ascended the Mountains on the south side of the Wady which are composed of Strat[a] of Sand stone alternating with blue clay about 600 to 700 feet high conical table & rugged tops and on the north side in most places inacc^{ble} the Wady appears like the dry bed of a large river the north side bounded by high sand hills from 300 to 400 feet in height –

Wednesday 12th

at 8 struck our tents and went West 4 Miles along the Wady to Kharafa we passed through 4 small towns the largest of which is called *Grajia* the wady is well cultivated here the road lying through date groves Gardens and Gummah fields the Whole way there is abundance of water the Wells about 12 feet deep & the water sweet & good – we sat down under the spreading branches of an Atilla[10] tree which served to shade the Tomb of some pious Maraboot[11] who rest[s] here outside the town with his face to the East untill his 500 years are expired when he will be called amongst the faithfull[12] to enjoy those delights which the faithful appear to reserve their share of in this world to themselves alone – it came on to blow very hard from the ENE at Noon so that every thing was covered with sand – at 4 we pitched our tent –

an hour after sunset Sheikh Aga sheikh left us for his country which is 5 days S$^{t[h]}$ of Ghaat[13] he said he would not inform the inhabitants of

---

[10]Ar., *atil*, tamarind tree, *Tamarix orientalis*.

[11]Many graves of pious men (marabut) are in Libya protected and given prominence by a small domed structure (Ar., *qubba*), sometimes decorated with flags and bright stuffs. Such tombs may be centres of pilgimage [see Thursday 20th June].

[12]Possibly an indirect reference to the traditions allowing the peripatetic nature of the spirit of marabuts, whose graves, for example, are to be found in several places [Professor H. T. Norris, personal communication].

[13]Log: "South^d & West^d of Ghaat"; i.e. Djanet, the capital of the Ajjer Tuaregs.

our intended visit as the road would be beset with people wishing us to make them presents – He nor Hatita or any of the Tuaricks will not eat fowels or their eggs or any thing that fowels have been cooked with[14] – since they have been with us they have all ways eat alone going outside their tents after sunset – Hatita would some times take a cup of tea when he does it is after a great deal of pressing and he laughs and says what should the sons of Adam drink warm water for – We had a visit from the Gayde of the wady[15] a black man – who pays 600$ for this wady & 800 for the other

Thursday 13<u>th</u>
Clear & warm at 3 A.M. Hadje Ali the brother of Bukaloom left us to return to Morzuk

The D<u>r</u> has been much troubled with people wanting medecine to day and indeed every day since we have been here he mixed up salt & sugar for those who wanted children &c[16] –

in the evening we heard a pair of Bagpipes playing and occasionaly guns firing to the West<u>d</u> the music and firing drawing near we went out to see what it was when we found it to be a party of young men and women accompanied by a pair of Bagpipes and a sort [of] drum they were dancing in a circle having a woman inside with a basket on her head in to which every one was solicited to put some thing in to assist 2 young poor people that were going to be married – the young man belonged to

---

[14]The refusal of Tuareg, nobles in particular, to eat fish, fowls or their eggs is attested by Duveyrier [*Les Touareg du Nord*, pp. 401-2]; but slaves and marabuts did not abstain. The Tuareg were unable to give Duveyrier any reason for their abstention. [See also Bates, *The Eastern Libyans*, pp. 176-7.]

[15]Log has: "Wady *Shirgi*". The kaid apparently had responsibility for all of Wadi al-Ajal.

[16]Log: "some without any complaint whatever to these the Dr gave salt & sugar mixed ... the most common complaints are consumption Direa and Liver & sore eyes – & the ladies as usual wanting boys"

[17]Log [15th June]: "a town about 2 Miles to the West<u>d</u> of this place ..."

Kharifa & the woman to Tawiwa[17] – and this was her party – when they came near the former place they were met by a no. of people with Music &c and the Mouadun ascended the Minaret and called all the generous to come and contribute to the wedding   we gave them a dollar

Friday 14th

Clear & warm   the Dr had to tell the people to day that he could give them no more Medecine as Hatita said there were a no. of sick at Ghaat but on his return to Morzuk if they would come or send they should have all their wants supplied – we examined the hills on the south side of the Wady which we found composed of Sandstone alternating with pipe clay[18] & Iron stone at the line of junction of the Sandstone –

Saturday 15th

Clear & warm   after breakfast we shifted our tent a little further from the tomb of the Maraboot as we found that we were in a bad neighbourhood or perhaps the scorpions ants beetiles and other ["reptiles", deleted] insects that guarded the pious remains of this worthy Moslem were unwilling that such Kaffirs[19] as we were should lodge so near – or what was more likely they found better fare with us fat Englishmen than with his old dry bones   however we put to death a no. of young scorpions that we found after removing the mats – & the Maraboot of the town sitting down on the place we had moved from   the mother of the brood very quietly crawled up his leg in search of her young but his reverence not liking such company without regard to the pious predess [= predecessor] put her to death –

---

[18]A fine white clay, which forms a ductible paste with water, used for making tobacco-pipes, and whitening fabric [ShOED].

[19]Ar., *kafir*, an unbeliever, infidel; applied primarily to pagans and thus to enslaveable black pagans. The term "kaffer" passed into English as a (now) derogatory term for blacks in general regardless of religion.

[20]Log: "Ali Tibbo a black man.."

The Sheikh of Kharifa Ali Tibbo[20] told us that once in a term of years
the rains fell in torrents   the torrents from the hills fill the wady below
and it then looks like a sea that the Town of Tiwiwa was washed down
in this manner (for like Morzuk the houses are built of mud) which took
place about 8 years ago[21] – the sand hills on the north side of the wady
are then covered with fine grass & the Wady yields abundant crops – but
every winter the[y] have some rain less or more –

the inhabitants of Kharifa appear to be very poor though surroun[d]ed
with fine fields gardens & date groves   the Wells are plentiful and the
water good   it appears that most of the land belongs to the Sultan and
other people who reside in Morzuk – the Sheikh Ali Tibbo was in rags
and we through the Meanness of the government at Morzuk can hardly get anything to buy for ourselves or horses as they want us not to go
to Ghaat   this afternoon a fellow pestered us very much by wishing us
to repeat the Fatha[22]   we were at last under the necessity of turning him
out though we thought it a trick to get us into a scrape

Sunday 16th
Warm & Clear   no camels arriving we hired 2 from a man that had
encamped near us & who came from Oubari – to take us to Germa for
we could get nothing to eat neither for man or beast – at 8 A.M. we left
Kharifa which by a Mn Alt[de] of Spica is in Lat[de] 26°–33'–30" N   our
road lay through date groves fields & gardens and we passed the Towns
of Tiwiwa 2 miles to the West and El Fougar where there is the foundation of some ancient stone building – Braik which is 4 Miles to the West

---

[21]As European travellers experienced, the traditional buildings of Fezzan, being built largely of
sun-dried brick and mud containing much salt, and inadequately roofed with palm beams and fronds,
were liable to rapid dissolution and collapse in the rare but heavy rain storms. [See Nachtigal, *Sahara
and Sudan*, Vol. I, p. 73; P. Gladstone, *Travels of Alexine* (London, 1970), p. 205.]

[22]Ar., *Al-fatiha*, "the opening"; the first *sura* (chapter) of the Holy Koran, recited at the start of
public or private muslim worship.

[23]For an account of the irrigation systems tapping the aquifers in the alluvium at the foot of the
hamada escarpment and associated water levels in Wadi al-Ajal, see A. I. Wilson and D. Mattingly *et
al.* " The Fezzan Project 1998" in *Libyan Studies*, Vol. 29, 1998, pp. 137-142.

– here the Wells are about 3 or 4 feet deep[23] & the Wady narrows at this point then Tewish about 2 Miles from Braik to the S.W. at 11 we arrived at Germa we were accompanied by Hatita who appeared much anoyed at the camels not coming as he had promised – but to his great joy we met them on the road We pitched our tent outside the town amongst some Tallah trees – We were visited by the Sheikh who is an old man called Mustapha who brought some fowels which we ordred and paid for W. by N ½ N 8 Miles

Monday 17<u>th</u>

clear & warm went this morning accomp<u>d</u> by the Sheikh & Mamaluke to visit the ruins of Old Germa [which] is about 2 Miles S.S.W. of the new town – by the Mud ruins it appears to have been of considerable extent[24] – the houses much larger and of a more solid construction than any now existing in Fezzan – on the south Side of it and near the foot of the Mountains – by the side of the road leading to Morzuk stands a Roman building perfect on two of its sides – wither it has been an Altar or a place where a Statue has stood I cannot pretend to guage there are some of the stones pulled down on the Eastn side – the westn appears more worn by the weather – there are no inscription[s] that we could find the whole solidly built with the sandstone of the neighbouring mountains – being about 12 feet high and 8 feet square with a cornice at top and pilasters, at the corners whose capitals are very bad Corinthean

---

[24]Log: "... appears to have been much larger than any town in Fezzan". The site of the extensive abandoned settlement which Clapperton calls 'Old Germa' appears to lie in an almost direct line between the site known today as Old Germa (but in Clapperton's time, still occupied and known as New Germa) and the Roman period mausoleum – Clapperton's 'Altar'. Barth (*Travels*, Vol. I, p. 144) also mentions the ruins of 'Old Germa' – a long-deserted mud-brick town with a circumference of 5,000 paces – on the southern fringe of the oasis. This site is also almost certainly that of a mud brick castle visited by Duveyrier [*Exploration du Sahara*, Vol. I, Pl. XV, fig. 1, facing p. 279] in 1861 and at that time known as the Qasr al-Uatuat (Castle of the Bats). The settlement is represented today by a prominent mud-brick tower by the main Sabha – Awbari road. [D. Mattingly, personal communication.]

[25]"by far the most southerly momument of Roman type in Africa..." [Wheeler, *Rome*, p. 101], the mausoleum was restored in the 1960s. [See C. M. Daniels "The Garamantes of Fezzan" in F.F. Gadallah (ed.), *Libyan History. Proceedings of a conference held at the Faculty of Arts, University of Libya*, 1968 (Benghazi, 1971) pp. 267-268, figs. 11-12, Plates VI & IX, showing the composite Ionic-Corinthian pilaster capitals.] The mausoleum is today known as the Qasr al- Uatuat – the name having

the whole is cemented with lime[25] – & I may safely say it is a Roman building its being very like their buildings that I have seen in the Regency of Tripoli where they are in great no– and some in very good preservation[26]

We could get no fowls or any other kind of provisions to purchase as the people said they had got orders not to sell any though they came in crowds to get Medecine –

in the after noon our camel driver and a young Tuarick quarreled about their dinner the old camel driver threw a stick at the Targie[27] who instantly returned his spear and [had] not the former been very quick in jumping out of the way it would have gone through his body – another Tuarick who happened to be at the Tent Seized the spear and was on the point of returning it with all his force at the young fellow who he said ought to have returned the stick instead of the Spear – but the Mamaluke interfered[28] & took the spear away and threatned to beat them both – in the evening the young fellow who had got his spear again brought it in to the Mamaluke with the staff broke as a sign of his repentance and gave him the pieces to take care of for the night.

---

been transferred, probably in recent times, from the now derelict mud-brick castle visited by Duveyrier [see n. 23 above]. Clapperton's sketch, the first known drawing of the mausoleum, shows Tifinagh inscriptions on its walls which have since eroded [Illustration p.93].

[26]The Roman buildings Clapperton and his companions are likely to have seen on their travels up to that time included the half-buried, four-sided Arch of Marcus Aurelius in Tripoli. [For contemporary views, see R. Tully, *Narrative of Ten Years' Residence at Tripoli in Africa*, etc. (London, 1817) coloured aquatint opposite p. 8, and Lyon (*A Narrative*), lithograph.] They might have seen other small remnants in and around the town, including pieces dug up in Consul Warrington's English Garden, and possibly also on the road through Bani Walid to Bu Njaym. At Bu Njaym they would no doubt have seen the great Roman fortress gateway described and drawn by Lyon in 1819 [*Ibid.*, pp. 65-6 and lithograph] but not mentioned in the Bornu Mission's *Narrative*.

[27]Correctly, *Targee* (sing.), *Tuareg* (pl.), as Clapperton points out in his passage of commentary on Ghat [Wednesday 31st July]; see Rodd [*People of the Veil*, pp. 273-4] for an account of some supposed origins of the name. The name the Tuaregs use themselves is *Imashaghen*, 'the noble and the free'. [Norris: *The Tuaregs*, p. 12].

[28]Clapperton's log records that "the whole party were much against Mohamed [the young Tuareg] for throwing the spear" and that the Mamluke "got up and beat them both".

Tuesday 18th

Warm & Clear   New Germa is in Lat^{de} 26°–32′–45″ N by a Mn Alt^{de} of Spica   it [is] situated nearly in the middle line between the Mountains on the south and the Sand hills on the north surrounded by date trees gardens and fields which they say belong all to the Sultan   the soil appears much better here than in most parts of Fezzan consisting mostly of a black mould but on the north side of the Town is a considerable salt marsh the salt of which looks like a mighty hard frost after a day of rain and tastes very bitter – The town is surrounded by a high Wall of mud and flanking towers and there is the remains of a wet ditch which surrounded the town now nearly filled up – the castle is inside the Walls but no[w] serves to keep the Sultans dates in only and a very poor place it is for that – The inhabitants are miserably poor in their appearance and the houses are most all in ruins[29] – the Waters in most of the wells are sweet & good and we have in various places in Fezzan found wells of excellent water within a few feet of a salt Marshes

the Maraboot of Braik brought a sheep for sale which after a good deal of maneauvering we got for three dollars and then he begged very hard for the head but we refered him to our Mahometan servants who have allways considered this part as their perquisate but his reverance was sent of[f] from there with very little ceremony –

Mr Hillmans Mule having a very bad sore back we considered it necessary to have something done for it we there fore by the Advice of the Mamaluke and the rest of our party who pretended to be judges – had it burnt round the sore which appears to be the favourite remedy for all sores or diseases in man or beast[30] – they did it in the following manner

---

[29]See Daniels' plan of 'Old Germa' [*Garamantes*, p. 35 & fig. 8]; and account of current archaeological work in D. Mattingly *et al.* "The Fezzan Project 1997: methodologies and results of the first season" in *Libyan Studies* Vol. 28, 1997, pp. 11-25; and "The Fezzan Project 1998: preliminary report on the second season of work" in *Libyan Studies* Vol. 29, 1998, pp. 115-144.

[30]According to Lyon, curing animals by burning with a hot iron was usual in Fezzan [*A Narrative*, p. 301]; such was also the treatment of common human complaints, including asthma, consumption, blindness and ruptures [*Ibid.*, pp. 106-7; see also 30th December 1824]. Sick trade slaves on the

the animals legs were secured and when the iron (a sickle) was red hot the mule was thrown down and the red hot iron passed rund the sore untill the flesh was well scorched –

Hatita arrived to day and in the evening he had a very severe fit of the ague or Homa[31] as it is called in the country – and Germa is considered by the people of the country as more sickly than any other and indeed it has the appearance of it but the people of the Wady are as drunken a set as are to be met with in any part of the world –

Wednesday 19th
Arose before day light & struck our tents as it appeard our friends were very loth to proceed and as we could [get] no provisions for ourselves and horses here it was nec[sy] to go on or return so we determined on the latter [sic] and being informed that there was no food to be procured for the horses on the road to Ghaat we determined upon sending them back keeping only the D[rs] mule as Hatita said they had never seen such an animal at Ghaat and that they would like to see it we accordingly sent our horses and Mr Hillmans mule back to Morzuk under the charge of the D[rs] servant Adam –

When Hatita and his friends saw this determination in us not to return they began slowly to load the camels at 6.40 we started traveling to the Westd along the south side of the wady having the mountains about 5 miles on our left and the sand hills 8 or 9 on our right at 8 we passed the Town of Gharfa which is inhab[t] principally by arabs[32] who live in the town built of Mud & walled around and the houses of date tree

---

march were burned on the belly with a red-hot iron, apparently more as a punishment for malingering than as an effective cure [*Ibid.*, p. 343]. Perhaps more sensibly, scorpion stings were also treated by burning [Scortecci, *Sahara*, p. 166].

[31] Ar., *hamah*, fever. Log: "We pitched the small tent for him but he slept outside".

[32] Presumably either Magarha or Al-Hasauna.

branches are inhabited by poor people and slaves[33] who cultivate the fields and gardens and take care of the date trees

at 2–30 P.M– we arrived at Oubari[34] having traveled through the heat of the day which was very disagreable – When we arrived we made a dinner of part of our Sheep that remained – and the Sheikh of the town and some of the principal persons visited us from whom we bought another[35] –

Our road to Oubari lay principally through date groves & Gumah fields except for about 4 Miles which was a gravelly desert but not incapable of being planted with date trees like the rest as the water is only 4 feet below the surface upon a clay soil & very good – In the evening Hatita arrived very ill[36] – My servant Madie without our knowledge went into the town to the Sheikh and asked him if he was not going to make the servants a present   the Sheikh replied that he had nothing And pointing to a flock of sheep said would one of these do   Madie wanted no more & hove of[f] his prize in triumph to the tent – after this the Sheikh brought us a dish of Fatat some bread and Sour milk – our course from Germa to Oubari W. by N. 18 Miles

Thursday 20th

Arose before day light   found that neither the camels or their owners had made their appearance – we went up to the nearest mountain which

---

[33]Most work in the small gardens and plantations of Fezzan was (at least up to the 1960s) done by economically and socially debased, mostly negroid, labourers of mixed racial origins. A share-cropping cultivator (*jibbad*) usually had as helper a child or teenaged water-drawer and distributor (*saggay*) [see Chapter Four, n. 11]. They usually worked on yearly contracts for a "white" nomadic overlord (*sharik*), keeping one-quarter or more of the produce for themselves. [J. Lethielleux, *Le Fezzan*, pp.73-6, 241-9; Briggs, *Tribes*, pp. 66-8.] In other parts of the Sahara these people were known as Harratin.

[34]Log: "this town appears to be the strongest in Fezan ... it being the westermost town in Fezan – and kept in repair through fear of the Tuaricks".

[35]Log: "We were visited by the Sheikh & some of the inhabitants who wanted medecine – as also a no- of Tuaricks. The Tuaricks brought us a Guana or lizard a very fine one". (Probably the waran lizard; common in Fezzan, where it is kept in the house to keep away scorpions and vipers [Nachtigal, *Sahara and Sudan*, Vol. I, p. 141].)

[36]Log: "with the ague   the Dr offred him an emetic but he would not take it   he kept drinking bruized dates – & water".

is Sth of the town about 4 Miles[37] and on which they said there were a no— of inscriptions written by the Romes — we ascended at the north end and about halfway up where the sandstone rock was bare for about 50 feet long and 30 high ["forming a precepice" inserted] we found it nearly covered with inscriptions in the Tuarick characters — one of the most perfect was as follows

[drawing of inscriptions[38] as illustrated opposite]

Our ascent after going round the precepice on which the characters were set out was both attended with difficulty and danger as the side of the mountain was composed of large blocks that had been loosened by the rains and had but a very infirm hold so that a sudden grasp at any of them in the chance of slipping a foot would have broken it from its hold and it and the person who might be so unfortunate would have been ground to pieces long ere the[y] crashed [to] the bottom — however we got to the top in safety though very much fatigued & out of wind — but the coolness of the breeze and the extensive view repaid richly for all our troubles   The Wady beneath appeared like a plain of great extent the cultivated parts of which winding through [the] centre from West to East like a river and where the face of the plain was clear of sand the clay soil reflected back the suns rays and made it appear like small lakes on the north at the distance of about 20 miles the view was bounded by distant sand hills — but on turning to the south the Tops of the Mountains to the south appeared like a baren black and stoney plain without a break in it to relieve the view and looking near you were convinced there was neither food for man or beast —

on the top lies buried a pious Shireef whose mortal remains The Tuaricks hold in great veneration and when ever they camp near Oubari

---

[37]The Garamantian site of Tinda lies on the lower northern slopes of the escarpment below the point where most of the inscribed rocks are found. [See C. M. Daniels, "Excavation and fieldwork amongst the Garamantes" in *Libyan Studies*, Vol. 20, 1989 pp. 48-9, 51.]

[38]The Tifinagh inscription is legible and probably dates between the 4th and 14th centuries [Professor N. Petit-Maire, Aix-en-Provence, personal communication].

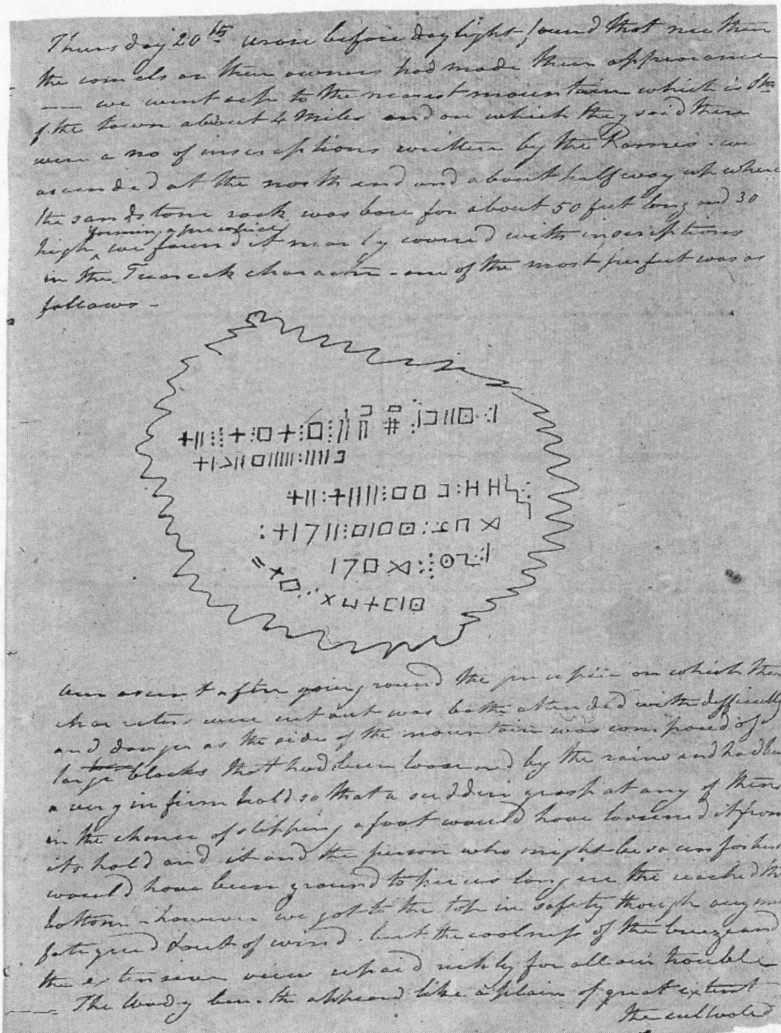

Figure 5. Inscription in the Tuarick characters

they come up here to pray for which purpose they have cleared several places on the top of the [ ] large enough for a man to say his prayers in which places are allways of the same form being an Oblong square the shortest side presented towards the holy city of Mecca — however we were not troubled with any inclination to follow the example of the faithful in praying either to the prophet or to his pious descendant and I suppose he out of spite or fear ["that we should say a christian pray[er]" inserted] inspired Mʳ Hillman to sing God save the King in which the Dʳ & I joined

We found the mountain like all the rest composed of Sandstone & a beautiful blue & white Slaty clay stone this forms generally the lower stratum — we descended by a much easier path on the N.E end of the Mountain — on our return to our tent we found our camel men accompanied [by] a Ghadamis merchant — they told us they would not go to Ghaat unless we paid them 12$ for each camel there and back to Morzuk this was just half as much again as we had agreed with them for this they denied & we refered to Hatita who said we were right they then said they would not go but after a great deal of argument on both sides we agreed to give them 10$ for each camel's hire thinking it better to put up with this imposition than give up all hopes of geting to Ghaat — as we well knew if these fellows did not go we would get no others — they then demanded half the money in advance with which we complied then they begged to stop untill the feast after the Rhamadam was over — which we complied with also knowing well it was no use to refuse and besides Hatita was very unwell —

at Sunset the new moon was seen which put an end to the fast of Rhamadam every one that had a musquet or pistol fired it of[f] every face beamed with Joy every one knelt down and repeated a prayer looking at the Moon whither it was addressed to her or Mohamed I know not even — the Neapolitan Renegado had to say a prayer which the cur appeared much ashamed off [sic] which and he allways is of his new faith before the Dʳ & I

at night we were visited by 3 drummers & a Bagpiper with a large mob
at their heels   they continued playing round the tents for some time   we
gave them a dollar and desired them to return as we wished to go to rest
but the drumming piping singing and firing of musquets in the town
which was kept up all night prevented us shutting our eyes

Friday 21ˢᵗ

Hatita a great deal better   this morning all that were able dressed in
their best & went to the Mosque to return thanks for the ending of the
Fast –   they danced drummed & eat all the day

Saturday 22ⁿᵈ

Strong breezes & Clear   the people of the town Still drumming and
drinking – we assistᵈ our servants in repairing and cleaning our water
Gerbas intending to start before day light on the morrow

Sunday 23ʳᵈ

Clear & Warm   we arose before the sun but no camels – the Renegado
praying drunk and the son of Hadje Mohamed little better –   all the
Mohamedans of our party nearly in the same state save the Tuaricks
who were not addicted to drinking sour Lackbi or any intoxicating
licorse – After breakfast the Dʳ was called to visit some Tuarick women
in Hatita's tent who thought they had some complaints – but we thought
it was a plan to see us so I accompanied the Dʳ we found 6 of them 2
of whom were married women –   one said she had lost the use of her
limbs from a paraletic stroke – we found them very free & good looking
women   they do not wear their faces covered like the other women of
Moslem countries we found them [to have] no fear & to behave as any
woman of England[39] –   the young women had their hair hanging in

---

[39]European travellers were always struck by the personal and social freedoms allowed to women
in the semi-matriarchal Tuareg society.

ringlets on each side of the neck the married women had a piece of blue cloth round their heads and Shells in their ears instead of ear rings their dress was otherwise much the same as the – Fezzan women what struck both the D^r & Myself particularly was the likeness between the women and two of [the] Boys that were in the tent to the Egyptian figures in the faces –

Oubari is in Lat^{de} 26°–34'–35" N by a Mn Alt^{de} of Antares it [is] situated amidst well cultivated fields and Gardens surrounded by a higher wall and in better condition than any other town in Fezzan the houses are also in good condition as is the Castle which like all other buildings in this country is built of mud or clay though the foundation of this castle is built of rough stones – the inhabitants appear to be more plentifully supplied with the good things of this world than the rest of their country men – it is governed by 3 Sheikhs who take it 4 months [each] through the year

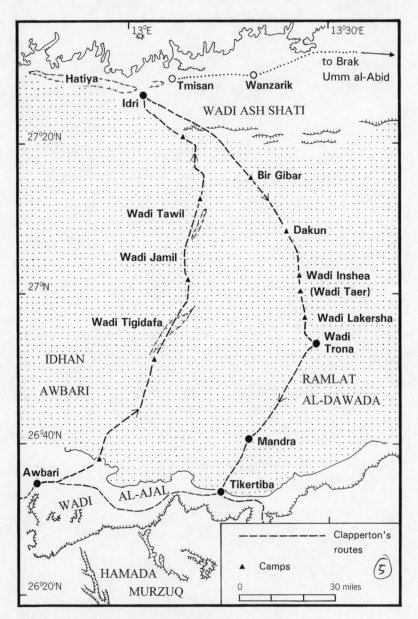

Map 5. Wadi Shiati and the Dawada Sand Sea

CHAPTER
4

Wadi Shiati

Monday 24ᵗʰ
Clear with strong breezes from the Eastᵈ   no appearance of any camels
this morning but a great many frivolus excuses

In the afternoon camels came and we and tho' it was late we packed all
up & struck the tent   then Hatita & his men began to move and at 5.30
P.M. we left the ["Wady" deleted] Oubari traveling along the Wady W
by N. and at 6-25 we halted for the night but did not pitch the tent as we
were told that we would start very early   W by N 5

Tuesday 25ᵗʰ
Clear & Cool   arose an hour before day light but we did not [get] away
through the dilitoriness of the Tuaricks untill 5.40 A.M.   I rode on one
of the camels having hurt my leg but I found it very disagreeable for the
small of the back   the motion was something like that of the jib boom
end of a small ship in a short head sea   W by N 10

at 9.45 A.M. halted and pitched our tent at the well and maraboot of Sidi
Ahmet el Hadje   the wady is here about 15 miles in breadth with a clay
soil having a slight covering of sand and gravel   the Mountains of the
same appearance as to the Eastᵈ   there are a great nᵒ of Tallah trees

growing in the wady on which the Camels sheep and goats of the Tuaricks feed – our Course was W by N 10 Miles

we were visited by a number of the Tuaricks who come here at this time to feed their flocks on the Tallah trees in the wady they were very earnest in their enquiries about England its manners and customs &ᶜ one of them said that we and the Tuaricks must be the same people our manners were so much alike particularly with respect to the women and they say it is very bad in the Turks to confine their women as they do

Wednesday 26ᵗʰ

arose before daylight and got every thing ready but it was 6 oClock before we got the camels ready & just as we were going to mount the Dʳˢ mule being loose set off full Tilt back and all our endeavours to catch it were in vain we then unloaded the camels and sent Abdullah the Dʳˢ servant¹ to Oubari to bring it back if it had stopped there if not to tell the Sheikh to send a letter to Morzuk and acquaint the governor that no bad construction might be put upon the mules arriving back without its rider – However an hour after we had pitched the tent ["we were" deleted] Abdullah and a Tuarick brought the Mule back which they found feeding about 4 miles down the wady – ["here we" deleted] it was now too late to go on and Hatita being taken very ill with the ague we determined not to proceed untill next morning Latᵈᵉ by Mn. Altᵈᵉ of Antares 26°-32'-35" N

Thursday 27ᵗʰ

Morning Calm & Clear Hatita so unwell that we proposed he should remain here & we would make a journey to Wady Shiati for 10 days hoping he would be recovered on our return – in the mean time Mʳ Hillman

---

¹Log: "Abdullah key Gumah". And the log has it differently: "One of the Tuaricks [i.e., not Abdullah] went with a letter to the Sheikh of Oubari to acquaint the Govr. of Morzuk of the circumstances".

was to return to Morzuk to send us a supply of provisions and money and remain & take care of the stores there – we got a good supply of sour milk from the Tuaricks – and a she-goat from Hatita

Friday 28th

arose before day light and prepared every thing for starting but our camel men with their usual song froid kept us untill 6.30 and then they travled along as slowly as possible, and even had the impudence to attempt staying at the place we had halted at when we were comming up here and they would have done it had Mr Hillman not been out of sight a head with the mules – we then moved on at a quicker pace when they found we would not stay – we then at 1 P.M- halted at about a mile S.E of Oubari where we pitched our tent intending to start at 4 PM. or Sunset – at 4 oClock & sunset no camels or the guide we had hired mak-ing their appearance – the Renegado sham[m]ing a fit of the ague on purpose to excite our pity & make us stay that he might have the pleas-ure of getting drunk on sour lackbi but we struck our tent and packed all up determined if the camels should not come untill midnight that we would start we never the less sat down upon our baggage and sent a messenger into the town after them at 9 P.M- they made their appear-ance and we started E.N.E- for the Sand hills & Mr Hillman down the wady for Morzuk – at 1 halted & spread our mats & went to sleep – E.N.E 8 miles

Saturday 29th

at 5 started & entred amongst the sand hills Course E.N.E – the Sand hills forming hill & dales the hills about 300 feet high

at 4 P.M started Course [ ] amongst the sand hills and at 8 after wind-ing amongst the sand hills for an hour before without knowing what way we were going – we halted & scraped a few roots together and made a fire with which we were enabled to make some Kuscassou and a little coffee with out sugar[2].   The D.^r unwell with a cold   his servant with *swelled* legs the Renegado with the ague   N.N.E 4 E by N 6 N.E by E 8[3]

Sunday 30th
at 5.30 Started after taking a cup of Coffee   the road both difficult and dangerous to the camels owing to the steep ness of the sand hills that lay across our path   at 9.10 A.M. arrived at the well and Wady of Tiga Defa where we pitched the tent – there is a well of fine clear sweet water three date trees in this little wady which is about 2 miles in length & one in breadth – surrounded by high sand hills rising above the level of the wady about 400 feet – at 5.20 P.M- Started again our course in a direct line [ ] but crooked & winding amongst the sand hills over which we had to make roads for the camels ["to pass over" inserted] with our hands – at 7-20 P.M. halted in a sandy plain   the D.^r & Mamaluke both unwell – eat some Kuscassou and Coffee – not being able to Sleep I walked about our tents all night N.E 5   N.E by N. 5   North 2

Monday July 1st
Arose before day light had a cup of coffe & Started   at 7 we arrived in Wady Jamia where there were a number of fine date trees loaded with fruit and what made the place appear to us more beautiful was its being so clear & Cool   the wady is crossed by several banks of sand in a zig zag direction like lines of a fortification   they are formed by the eddy wind blowing between the hills – ["the weather looks like" deleted] Sand hills – which makes the hills when it blows a gentle breeze look as if a beautiful cloud were playing on their tops -

at 10-30 A.M- halted & pitched the tent

---

[2]Log: "and some very mouldy biscuits" .

[3]Clapperton kept detailed notes of the courses marched across the Dawada Sand Sea and back to Wadi al-Ajal. His log here has: "N.N.E 4 miles to the Sand hills E by N 6 miles N.E by E 8 miles"; and a bearing "W.^m Ex.^t of Oubari hill – W by S ½ S – 20 Miles".

at 4.30 P.M started   crossed a very difficult sand hill into a wady without a name having a well & date trees   went along it 3 Miles & crossed
into wady Tawel or the long wady[4] – at 7-40 PM- halted for the night
N.E 6 – N.W. by W 1 EN.E 2 N.N.E 2

Tuesday 2nd
at day light clear & Cool   at 5-30 started   our way lay across the sand
hills as before the old guide running before & pointing out the way for
the camels

at 11-5 A.M- arrived at a well & some date trees where we halted for the
heat of the day   the Water in the well was brackish but we fortunaty
had brought 4 Gerbas of sweet water from the last well[5]

at 3.30 P.M. – Started   found the heat very opressive   Abdullah &
Madie went on a head as the old guide told them the town was near –
we lost sight of them in a short time they taking the one side of a sand
hill and we the other gave us no alarm – when we found they did not
make their appearance on the other side of the hill which proved longer
than we expected we hallooed fired guns – but no answer   to go back
and trace them was needless as the wind was blowing strong so that the
print of their feet was not left a minute on the ground[6] –

at 7.30 we halted and lighted a large fire to direct the poor fellows where
we were should they see it but we were put also in great alarm for fear
of their perishing for hunger – or thirst as one sand hill is so alike another that neither of them knew the way to go back to the well we left or
had they ever been in wady Shiati – we also conjured up in our minds
that they might wander about the sand hills untill half dead and then be

---

[4]Ar., *tawil*, long.

[5]Ar., *jirab*, a sack or bag. Water on Saharan journeys was carried in waterproofed goatskin bags
with the hair still on, slung across camels' backs. According to Nachtigal [*Sahara and Sudan*, Vol. I, p.
21] the best bags came from the Hausa states.

[6]Clappperton and Mahomet ben Hadje had also become lost on an excursion into the dunes the
same morning – "the moment was trying" [Oudney, *Missions*, Vol. II, pp. 178-9].

put an end to by the troops of Jackalls[7] that haunt the wady – & the hills in this manner of thinking did we pass away the time on the sand by a well of brackish Water – untill 5 o'Clock A.M – on

Wednesday 3rd

[8]and Strong Sand wind if possible increased our fears   the old guide running before pointing out the best road for our camels   at 5-30 saw the hills on the North side of wady Shiati   the[y] extended from WS.W to E.N.E – we were then for striking directly for the hills and insisted with the old guide that he must be wrong as we could not see the town – but the old man held out that he was right & sat down on the sand and would not follow us – we turned and desired him to get up and go on when after [passing] through 2 very high sand hills we saw Idri rising like a hill of basalt in the midst of a salt plain – and from what we saw on passing between the hills it would have been impossible to have gone with the camels in the way we wished owing to the numerous sand hills & the ruggedness of the salt plain before us

at 8 we descended by a strong narrow rocky pass in to the salt plain – the rocks of the pass are composed for the most part of yellowish feltspar red sandstone strongly impregnated with iron ore – we then crossed the Salt plain from which several conical hills rise having the appearance of islands -

The town had a very striking appearance[9] being built on one of the hills rising out of the salt plain & surrounded by gumah fields Gardens & date trees – which are watred from springs rising out of the rock on which the town is built

---

[7]Asiatic, or Common, jackal, Canis aureus, not uncommon in the northern Sahara today.

[8]Log has the preface here: "at 5 Started".

[9]According to Barth [*Travels*, Vol. I, p. 136], the town which Clapperton and Oudney visited was destroyed by the Awlad Sulayman in 1836.

Figure 6. Idri Town

at 9.30 AM we arrived and pitched our tent in front of the town amidst some date trees and near an abundant spring of beautiful clear Water which was boiling up with great force[10]   we found here to our great satisfaction Abdullah the D[rs] servant who after wandring about all night had arrived about an hour before – and Madie had gone to Timisan a town about 6 miles to the East[d]   we were visited by the Gayde of the town who brought us some of the finest dates I ever saw and a skin of sour milk of which we partook very heartily -

we purchased a Sheep for a dollar & a half and some very fine onions – we had the sheep killed & some of it dressed for dinner – young Ben Hadje got notoriously drunk on Lackbi in the Town where he had left

---

[10]Warm springs with a water temperature of 30°C [Oudney, *Missions*, Vol. II, p. 180]. Idri was most likely the Garamntian site of Dedris or Debris mentioned by Pliny [NH 5. 35-7] and famous for its thermal spring.

his companion the Neapolitan Renegado – who had forgot his ague and his cares outside the town and was beastly drunk and unable to come to his dinner – however we enjoyed our selves on our mutton soup – for we had had but indifferent fare since we left Oubari – the D^r still a little unwell

Lat^{de} of Idri by a Mn. Alt^{de} of Antares 27°-26'-3" N   [Course] N.W. 10

Thursday 4th
Clear & Warm – The fields and gardens are watered from the numerous springs in this extensive wady to all the springs are attached large reservoirs into which the water is allowed to collect from 6 AM. untill 5 P.M. when a slu[i]ce is drawn and the water is allowed to run into the different channels which convey it to the fields and gardens – where a slave attends[11] to see that every part is equally and sufficiently watred – we could not make an experiment with the Ther^m as they are so much exposed to the sun – and of a great depth – so much so that my servant was nearly drowned in bathing in one of them – and only for timely assistance being given him he would have gone -

The D^r had a great many patients amongst the extrordinary cases was one man who offered him 2 good fowels if he would write him a charm that would enable him to get children & a tall buxom widow who wanted medecine to bring her another husband I immediately jumped on my feet & said I was ready for her she looked me in the face – and seeing my red mustachoes[12] oh says she thou art an old man but considering a little she said thou art a strong man wilt thou read the Fatha oh yes

---

[11]Log: "examined the springs which are under the charge of the Sheikh". The young water-drawer (*saggay* – see Chapter Three, n. 32) was responsible for irrigating the small, rectangular plots divided by low earth ridges, from wells, *foggaras* or springs for the correct amount of time. He (occasionally she) did so by opening or closing the appropriate sluices or mud dams, starting with the plots nearest the water source. Plots were watered at least once weekly, vegetable plots daily in summer. [Lethielleux, *Le Fezzan*, pp. 107-12; Briggs, *Tribes*, p. 8.]

[12]Since grey hair was customarily dyed with henna, the buxom widow had taken "my friend Clapperton for an old man ... to my great amusement, and his chagrin. He had prided himself on the strength and bushiness of his beard," [Oudney, *Missions*, Vol. II, p. 181].

I replied oh says she thou art a rogue and thou wilt marry me to day
and leave me on the morrow – I know travlers she replied but if you
stay here all night I shall send you some dates & milk – The doctor
though unwell was troubled with a great number of other patients who
unlike the rest of the people we have met with in this country brought
fowels and vegetables as payment for the medecine -

In the afternoon the Sheikh and Cadi paid us a visit and we accompanied them back to the town – which we ascended by a winding path one
house appearing as it were piled up on another we passed through the
Mosque to the Castle which is the highest building and from which we
had an extensive view to the East & W^d the Salt plain does not surround the hills on which the town is built but stretches to a great distance
from East to West on the south side of the hill

The ["most of the houses" inserted] appear to be falling upon the inhabts
and from the mouldering of the rock on which they stand appear to be
in a very precarious situation – as we ascended we observed several
recesses in the rock which we thought were formed by the people taking
out the pipe clay to wash but when we descended to the south side we
found that these places had been the habitations of the ancient inhabitants of this country – The Sheikh and Cadi conducted us to one of great
extent which the[y] said reached to the opposite side of the Wady – we
got a lighted torch and the D^r and I descended into it and found it to
consist of three very large apartments with smaller ones adjoining which
had apparently been used as sleeping & store rooms we saw the
entrance of a no. of others in the side of the rock but not so well finished
the entrance are in the form of an arch the roof– flat and consisted of a
fine yellow sand stone[13] –

---

[13]"the galleries were high (nearly seven feet), and of considerable length (about 150 feet)"
[Oudney, *Missions*, Vol. II, pp. 181-182.]; but Barth found the caverns "interesting only on account of
the oval shaped form in which they have been excavated" [*Travels*, Vol. I, p. 135-136]. These subter-
ranean tri-lobed chambers were almost certainly ancient tombs [D.Mattingly, personal communication].

none of the present inhabitants of Idri had ever ventured into those houses for fear of evil spirits [n]or would they go down with us and when we came out they cheered as if we had returned from a victory – we strongly recommended them to take possession of them as they were much better than their own – and cooler in summer & warmer in winter than those above ground but they only laughed at our advice -

Idri as I said before is in Lat^{de} 27°-26'-3" N by a Mn Alt^{de} of Antares and is the westermost town in Wady Shiati to the Eastd- of it in the same wady which they say stretches to Zeghen lies Temesan in sight from Idri N.E about 5 miles Fanzirak Bergen Gata – about ½ day dist from one another to the East^d Lazrat half a day to the South of Gata – Meharoog – Agar & Tamzawa to the East^d of Lanzerat – Braik half a day south of Lanzerat & Askad east ½ a days journey East of Braik the Wady as far to the west as they are acquainted with it is as abundant in springs as round Idri though without Inhabitants

That worthless wretch the Neapolitan Mamaluke has been drunk all day and abusing the people of the town and telling us that he had cut two of their throats by Mukni's order

Friday 5th

arose before day light & got every thing ready and hired a guide with a camel to conduct us to the Bahr Tron & Bahr Millah[14] – before starting we got a skin filled with sour milk of which we had got very fond as we found it a very cooling beverage and after taking a cup of it in the morning we required no water through the day – the worthy Sheikh of the town to whom the D^r had given a knife and a pair of scissors – wanted to cheat us out of 6 fowels the D^r had paid for the day before but we made him hand them out –

---

[14]Ar., *natrun*, trona, and *millah*, salt. Bahr 'Millah' is a probable reference to Bahr Mandara (Kanuri: *manda*, salt)– see Tuesday 9th July.

at 6.30 A.M- our Course was S.E by S 8 Miles of a salt plain we then ascended a plain composed of loose pieces of Slatey sandstone over which we travled in a S.E direction untill 1.30 P.M — we halted at Birgebana from an elevated part of the plain saw Idri bearing N.W. ½ N 14 or 15 Miles — we halted for the day amongst the date trees — for the purpose of getting the distance between the Moon & Antares as it was not in distance when at Idri — Latde- of Birgebana by Mn Alt^{de} of Antares 27°-19'-6" N   S.E. ½ S. 12 Miles

Saturday 6$^{\underline{th}}$
at 2-40 A.M- Started with a beautiful Moon light Morning our road lay over a sandy plain   Course S by E — at 6 A.M- we stopped at the well of Dakoon to fill our Gerbas   this well is nearly filled with sand which makes it very brackish — we were detained here 2 hours by one triffling thing and another & at 8 we started   Crossed over sand hills in direction S. by E.   we found our new guide by no means such an exper^{cd} sand pilot as the old Tuarick — & to the amusement of the latter and our mortification we had often to retrace our steps & find out a better passage — at 11-10 A.M- halted as we were all very hungry and fatigued with the heat and long fast having started without any thing at [ ]^{15}15 PM — Started our course the same as before but if any thing more tedious and difficult winding amongst and crossing over the sand hills which are from 300 to 400 feet in height and in traveling over which we had to dismount from our camels & My shoes being worn out I got the upper part of my feet and legs scalded every day — So that I could not Since the day we left Oubari wear my boots the loose sand on the side of the hills facing the suns rays was like hot ashes & we had to run down as fast as our legs would carry us the large blisters did not cause much pain and as the soles of my feet kept sound the blisters did not give me any concern though I nearly lost my toe nails — by my carelessness[16]

---

[15]Log: "4".

[16]Barefooted trade slaves who walked across the Sahara often had their feet badly burned by the hot sands. Many suffered swollen feet and, unable to keep up with the caravan, were simply left

7.40 P.M. halted & slept in the open air in the Wady Bilawagi – it has ever been our custom since we came from Morzuk to have a cup of coffe before we started if possible our tea when we halted in the heat of the day and when we came too at night to have Kuscassou or Bazeen – Since we left Idri we have been supplied with milk from the Naga or She camel belonging to our guide – which serves us instead of coffe
S by E. 7   SW by S ½ S 5

Sunday 7th

at 4 A.M. Started our road difficult and dangerous owing to the sand hills we had to cross – & to the great amusement of the Tuaricks the Idri guide often lost his way   at 5 AM arrived at the Well of Inshea where there is six date trees we filled our Gerbas and moved on at 6 the road no better than before   at 9 A.M. arrived at Wady Taer where we halted for the heat of the day and had tea

at 4 P.M. Started our road difficult as before   at 7.30 Arrived at Wady Lakershea where there is 2 wells and a number of date trees – we found the Water in both the Wells horribly bad brackish and Stinking owing to the quantity of sand that had blown into them[17] being very thirsty when we arrived I had taken two or three very Copious draughts without perceiving any thing very disagreeable but in the night my intes[ts]

---

behind to die. According to the British vice consul in Benghazi, reporting in 1847, this was the chief reason for so many slaves being abandoned on the journey [*British Parliamentary Papers: Correspondence Relative to the Slave Trade*, Class D. 1847-8, Vol. 64, p. 67]. The painful leg-swellings suffered by several European travellers in the Sahara remained something of a medical mystery [Bovill, *Missions*, Vol. IV, p. 751n.]. The illness in question, under-recognised until the past decade or so, is *podo coniosis* caused by particles of silica in sand penetrating, as a result of constant exposure, the feet and lower legs and through the lymphatic vessels causing blockages leading to swellings (as in *elephantiasis*). [G. Crook, personal communication].

[17]Briggs [*Tribes*, pp. 247-248] suggests that water from old-fashioned wells and *foggaras* was seldom suitable for drinking, according to modern hygienic standards. Often it was "unpleasantly rich" in magnesium and various calcium salts and even sulphuric acid, and it was often heavily polluted with animal and even human remains, urine and faeces. "In view of this," says Briggs, "it is easy to understand the high rates of gastro-intestinal disturbances which characterise so many Saharan groups…".

were blown up at a fine rate[18]   the Dr could not drink it & the son of Hadje Mohamed had followed my example and was in the same condition – the 2 Tuaricks were not in the least affected by it – nor are they with any thing however coarse in the way of eating or drinking South 6 – S by W 5

Monday 8th

arose before daylight   I and young ben Hadje had the most abominable smell in the nose & Taste in the mouth that could be well imagined from our drinking so freely the night before of wells of Lakersha – at 4-15 A.M. started – our road was over high sand hills and winding round others – at 7.30 AM – arrived in wady Trona and pitched our tents on the south side of the Bihr Trona amongst the date trees[19] – we were waited on by Hadje Ali who has charge of the lake[20]   he is a stout black man with a hoarse voice and pleasing countenance   above the middle size between 50 & 60 years of age   he was very kind and attentive to us & brought us some good water – which we drank with a greater relish than if it had been the sweetest wine – for the taste of Lakershea's waters was not yet vanished from our remembrance nor the smell from our nostrills S by W ½ W 5   –

we found here a Kaffle of the Walid Busaaf[21] Arabs who had come from Tripoli for Trona[22] for which they pay 2$ or its value for each camel load which is about 4 Cwt or 4 ½ -

---

[18]Log: also suffering "a frequent inclination to make water".

[19]Bahr Trona, or Qabr'un, is the largest of the three inhabited Dawada lake settlements. For a good description, including detailed maps, of the lakes and the Dawada, see G. Göttler's travel guide book, *Libyen von Leptis Magna zum Wau an Namus* (Reise, Frankfurt, 1995) pp. 343-359.

[20]According to Oudney, Hadje Ali, in charge of the lake for nine years, had successfully resisted Al-Mukni's attempts to interfere with production and exports [*Missions*, Vol. I, pp. 183-4].

[21]The Walid Bu Saif based on southern Tripolitania nomadized into northern Fezzan.

[22]The fresh waters derived from the weathering of granitic rocks or sandstones lead naturally to sodium bicarbnonate-rich groundwaters or lakes. From these, trona (hydrous sodium carbonate) or other minerals, can precipitate [M. Edmunds, personal communication]. Trona is used, *inter alia*, in tanning, for baking unleavened bread, as an animal feed and as an admixture for pipe tobacco [Bovill, *Missions*, Vol. I, p. 182n.].

we went and visited the lake accompanied by Hadge Ali   there were
date trees growing to the edge of the lake which we found to be about ½
a mile in length and about 200 y^{ds} in breadth at the broadest part   it is
about 2 feet deep but is much deeper in the spring and at that time the
trona disappears – on the north side there oozes out below the bank a
black substance like mineral tar[23] – there are a number of weeds growing on the sides and if they do not take means to clear it it will not be
long in filling up – there is a crust of salt forms on the top like half
thaw'd ice   the trona forms in cakes at the bottom like sunk ice having
a crust of salt upon the top which is removed with ease by a piece of iron
when taken on shore   the trona is brought by slaves who wade in and
lift it out from the bottom as if they were lifting out flakes of ice

[Sketch map of Wady Trona]

Tuesday 9th
Arose before day light and Started   at 5-30 and after a very fatiguing
journey we halted and pitched the tent   took sights for Nn time here
having taken distances at Bhir Trona -

at 3.30 Started   crossing the plain before us   we ascended some very
high sand hills   when at the top we saw Bahr Mandra which had a very
beautiful and singular appearance[24]   it is surrounded by very high sand
hills – and the date trees and fine fields looks like a beautiful island in
the midst of which is the salt lake which looks as if it were in part frozen
over – it was after sunset before we arrived at the place   we had sent
Abdullah on before to purchase some fowels but he returned saying that
a man had come to the village with a report that Lizhari had given

---

[23]Organic lake sediments. [N. Petit-Maire, personal communication].

[24]A coloured etching made from Clapperton's sketch of this view, drawn "sitting on the top of a
high sand hill" [Oudney, *Missions*, Vol. I, p. 184] was published as an Illustration in the *Narrative*
[reproduced in black and white in *Missions*, Vol. II, Plate VI, facing p. 194].

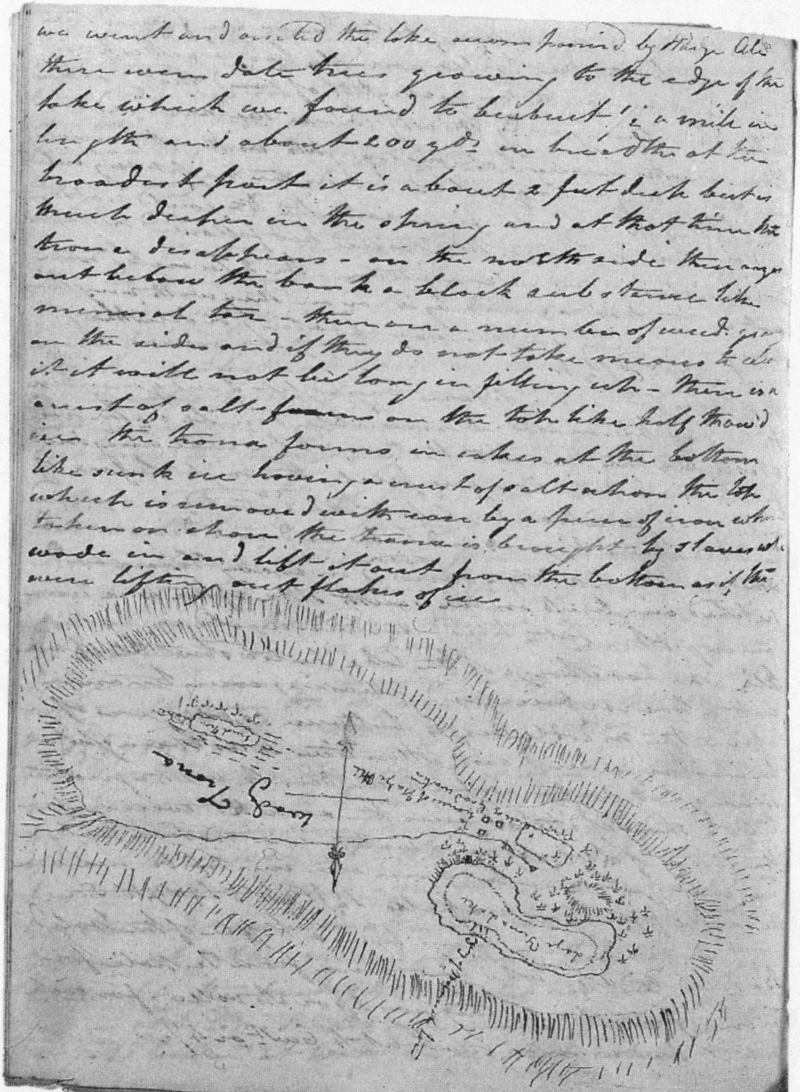

Figure 7. Wady Trona

Orders[25] in Wady Gharbi that any man selling us provisions should be severly punished   we considerd that the contrary was [the] case and tried to find the people as the gyade of the town was not to be found but we managed to get 6 for a Dollar – we engaged a man to bring us some of the Worms[26] alive   S by W ¾ W 8   S by W ¾ W 6

Wednesday 10th

Arose before day and Started at 5 AM – our road lying over a large sandy plain (called Samah[27] as all others are) nearly half way   the rest of the road was both difficult & dangerous – at 10 we arrived at Tikertiba – where we found Mr Tirwhit who had brought a courrier from Tripoli that had arrived at Morzuk and a letter of some importance which was no less than informing us that if we waited to go with the Army we would have to wait till next summer in Morzuk   no very pleasant prospect   however we were not in the least discouraged at the intelligence as we were determined when we came back from Ghaat to make a bold fresh [start] and if we could do no better to go with the Tibbos[28] – it was also as we expectd about Lizhari's letter he had sent Sheikh Busheer with an order upon all the towns in the Wady to have us supplied with whatever we wanted and at the same price as the Sultan or his servants also a severe rebuke to the Sheikh of Garma for his inattention to our wants when we went there before   S byW½ W 10

Thursday 11th

left Tikertiba before day light and arrived at Germa at 10 oClock – we were waited upon by Sheikh Mustafa on our arrival who was as full of

---

[25]Lizhari was Sultan Al-Ahmar's first minister and acting governor, or *Shaikh Al-Balad*, in his absence; see Saturday 13th July.

[26]Ar., *dud* [*Artemia salina*], minute primitive shrimps still harvested today and "pounded with a little salt until the mixture becomes a black paste – rolled into balls about the size of an orange and set in the sun to dry" [Briggs: *Tribes*, pp. 69-70]. There are many accounts, of which Oudney's extensive description [*Missions*, Vol. II, pp. 184-185] is the first.

[27]Ar., *Samah*, a sandy plain.

[28]See correspondence in Appendix I.

promises as before but when he heard the Tiskera read how he stormed & swore calling all the people to witness if he had not done every thing to serve us & then cursed the son of Hadje Mohamed for writing to Lizhari about him

in the evening a bride was led past on a camel   the camel was dressed out very gayly as was also the carriage inside which the bride [was] concealed[29]   an immense concurrence of people was gathered from the different towns to the wedding amongst which we recognised some of our acquaintances from Oubari   the camel with the bride was led round the outside of the town a pair of bagpipes and two drums playing before and every one that had a musquet or pistol kept dancing whooping and hollaoing and firing before the cavalcade   there were also a great number of women who also joined with the marrige cry occasionaly which is lo lo lo lo lo as quick and loud as they can – there were a number of the Tuarick Men & women – but they like ourselves were only lookers on

Friday 12<u>th</u>

at day light left Germa for Oubari the D<u>r</u> & I walked a head to Gharafa where we sat down under the shade of one of the houses untill the camels came up – though a number of the Arabs came out of their houses to converse with us   there was not one who had the good manners to ask us in – and one of them had the modesty to ask for a dollar for a little sour milk which we dispensed with at such a price – the camels we moved on   the Gharafites then asked me to give them some tobaco ah says I you well deserve some you were so kind to us letting us sit outside in the [shade] of your houses and asking a dollar for a little sour milk – oh says he (the one that was spokes man) you will not think ill

---

[29]Oudney [*Missions*, Vol. II, p. 185] records that there were two brides, who shared the "carriage" to save expense. This was not, of course, a wheeled carriage, wheeled vehicles being unknown in the Sahara at that time [for relevant discussion, see R. W. Bulliet, *The Camel*]. The "carriage", or howdah, was no doubt like the large, covered double basket slung across a camel's back, sketched by Lyon at Murzuq and reproduced as a lithograph in his *Narrative of Travels*.

of us for that sour milk is very scarce at this time and if you had wanted to go into the house you ought to have said so – well says I you shall have no tobaco from me though all the camels were loaded with it   and so we parted -

at 1. PM- we arrived at Oubari   I had walked a head of the camels and had fallen asleep under the shade of a date tree when the camels came up – we were waited on by the Sheikh from whom we bought a sheep & had it instantly killed as we had promised our servants a feast at the first opport^y for their privations in the sands which we could not avoid there being nothing to be got on the sands and we were not able to carry any live stock with us -

We were soon waited upon by Hatita who had got better and said he was anxiously waiting our return – he staid with us all the afternoon   we sent part of the sheep home with him to the hills where he was living – the Tuaricks consider the Wady as very unhealthy during the hot season – they that live in and near the towns therefore move to the hills at that time – and indeed we found Mohamed the young Targie who wanted to come as my servant and the one whom we had sent to Morzuk after our stores both very ill with the ague as also a no- of the inhabitants of the town

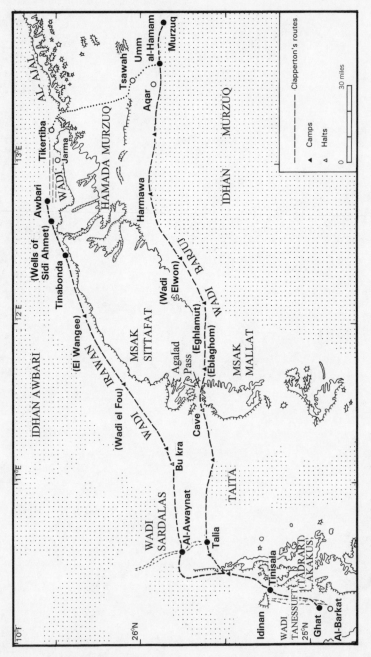

Map 6. Western Fezzan and the roads to Ghat I

5

Journey to Ghat

Saturday 13th

Morning Clear & fine   the camels not coming in time we submited to stay untill next day with a good grace knowing perfectly that we could not better ourselves –

At Midday the Sheikh brought the Kuscassou & bread the Dr had ordered to be prepared before our journey to Shiati & for which he had left money – the bread was short in quantity and very bad as was also the Kuscassou – Sheikh Busheer who had brought the Teskera from Lizhari had the Sheikh who by the by was his namesake seized by the servants & laid on his back and was proceeding to give him the bastinado when the D^r begged he would forgive him and to send the bread & Kuscassou back and make him bring some good and of suficient quantity – Busheer very reluctantly complied, as he had not brought any food for the horses or mules – but he promised to bring all speedily if he was released which was done -

At Sunset no Sheikh appearing with the bread or Kuscassou Sheikh Busheer went into the town with his serv^t to see what he was about – in a short time we heard him returning calling out in a doleful manner that he was no man he was no man – we were at tea when he came in and he kept on singing in the same strain without paying the least attention to our inquiries as to what was the mat[t]er only adding where is my gun I am no man I am no man I could not help laughing at this *worthy* who we learnt from his servant that he had gone into the town to give the Sheikh a drubbing but he was surrounded the sword taken from his *servt* and both soundly beaten – we got him quieted at last and the other two Bindags[1] viz the Renegado and the Son of Hadje Mohamed wished to accompany him into the town with their guns but we advised them to wait untill daylight as the people of the town if they were inclined to fight would have greatly the advantage in a night engagement

we taxed Busheer with ill using the man but he positively denied having done so saying that he had been seized when quietly takling [sic] to him of his neglect and showed two cuts on his arm which had been given with his own sword and his black servant had his shirt nearly torn of[f] his back – we advised him not to meddel in the afair untill he arrived at Morzuk & when there to lay the whole before Lizhari the Governor and have him properly punished – for all Busheer and his servant swearing by the head of the Sultan that they had not ill used the Sheikh we strongly suspected otherwise for on our former visit to Oubari he had been remarkably civil more so than many other in the wady – then we had no Teskera, and he might have done to us as he pleased & we thought it strange he should act in such a contrary way now we had one

Sunday 14th

Clear & fine arose before day light but no camels however they arrived at 7 AM- & we struck the tent and got every thing ready we were told that Busheers sword was lying in a house in the town but we would not allow any one to go and fetch it – We then took leave of M[r] Tirwhit and

---

[1]Marksman [Lyon, *A Narrative*, p. 303]; officially empowered soldiers of the Bey – a role to which some honour attached, but here used ironically. The Arabic word, *bunduqiya*, a rifle or gun, is possibly derived from the Arabic for Venice (*Al-Bunduqiya*), the source of hand-guns transshipped from, principally, Germany and central Europe to Mediterranean Muslim markets.

Busheer – who return to Morzuk   we sent the Neapolitan Renegado Mohamed ben Abdullah back with them as he had been of no service to us   on the contrary we found him a notorious liar constantly drunk when Lackbi was to be got and encouraging our servants to do the same – abusing the people of the towns we visited in a *cowardly* manner and when on the road where there was no Lackbi lazy and sick of the Ague or Hamma as it is called –

At 1.30 P.M- we arrived and pitched our tent at the well and Maraboot of Sidi Ahmet near to the spot we occupied when we were here before – we were soon visited by our old friends the Targies who live in the Mountains near here

Monday 15th

Cloudy   at 8 A.M Hatita arrived and took up his quarters under a Tullah tree near to our tent   he brought us a fine Sheep from Oubari which we had left money with him to purchase – We saw in the Side of the well a snake about 8 feet long[2] lying watching for birds as they come to drink – it looked at us for some time & then went into a hole   I would have shot it but the Tuaricks said it was a Maraboot or holy from its living so near the bones of the saint who built the well[3] -

The Sheikh Maraboot & principal people of Oubari came out to beg that we would forgive the Sheikh & write to Lizhari in his favour   they said that Busheer has behaved very ill and was proceeding to Bastinado the Sheikh in his own house when his relations prevented him & turnd

---

[2] Probably the Striped sand snake [*Psammphis sibbelans*], common in the oases of southern Algeria and western Libya, and less agile but larger (growing to 183 cms) than the Saharan sand snake [*Psammphis aegyptius*]. It is rear-fanged and its poison not serious to humans. [Dr. C. McCarthy, Natural History Museum, London, personal communication.]

[3] A special relationship between holiness and serpents was a common feature of Marabutic Islam, especially of the Isawiyya order which spread south into the Sahara and the Rifa'i Sufi order which was strong in Libya under the Ottomans. The legendary Mauritanian holy man Al-Hanshi, for example, was half Marabut, half serpent. [H. T. Norris, personal communication.]

him out – this was all very natural and the Sheikh had behaved so very well to us when we came without any Teskera we thought in justice we ought to write in his favour & besides it would give the people a good opinion of the English and of their justice and clemency &ᶜ Dʳ Oudney immeadetly wrote a letter to Mʳ T. to interfeer in his behalf with Lizhari – we gave the Sheikh the Letter & desired him to proceed instantly to Morzuk & stay in our house untill it was settled – the poor fellow returned us thanks with tears in his eyes which we would rather have dispensed with -

he brought us the flower & some excellent bread they not having time to make the flower into Kuscassou – washed our Gerbas & filled them in the evening it came on to blow so hard that we struck our tent to prevent it being blown upon us during the night

Tuesday 16ᵗʰ

Strong gales   at day light we had coffe and no camels appearing we thought the old game was going to commence of wearing us out – we went to pitch the tent intending to return to Morzuk – sooner than be humbuged by them any longer as we might lose an opportunity of going to Bornou in the time we were waiting for the Tuar[i]cks at the Wells of Wady Gharbi – when we had nearly finished pitching the tent Hatita came and begged we would stop as the camels would be here instantly we did so but with a bad face not believing a word   however we thought we would go in half an hour and the camels making their appearance at the same time we started at 6.30 A.M- our road lay along the Wady to the Westᵈ which still wears the same appearance – there are great numbers of Tulloh trees growing here which affords food to the sheep goats & camels of the Tuaricks and which they prefer to all others – & they soon fatten where there is plenty of trees   the face of the Wady is a redish clay slightly coverd in some places with a fine gravel   the Mountains on the South wear the same appearance & the Sand hills to the North at the distance of about 20 Miles   after travelling through a very hot sun at

12.15 we arrived at the Well of Tine bonda[4] where we encamped under a beautiful Tallah Tree   after we halted Hatita brought us a dish of Zumita[5] which is made of barley flower pounded dates & cold water   it is just like a pudding before it is boiled and eaten in this state we found it not amiss but it causes a great deal of wind in the bowels   however it is well when you have no fire to cook any thing else – fresh breezes during the Night

Course West 14 Miles

Wednesday 17th

Arose before day light & found the old game playing no camels the water skins being not filled or the camels watred & 2 Kaffles arriving from Ghaat we determined to stop for the day without being obliged to do so -

Hatita and the people of the Kaffle were well acqu[td] and Old Albini who went to Shiati with us & who had by his good temper and inoffensive manners become a great favourite with us came and told us that a few dates would be very acceptable – which the Dr gave them with the addition of some Kuscassou and Albini stood their cook – There were three Hadjes amongst them[6] & they had brought Senna to exchange in the wady for Gumah[7] – we had a long visit from them   they were much concerned about the safety of the Sultan of Cons[le] and asked us several times

---

[4]An important and ancient gathering place of caravans at the extreme western end of Wadi al-Ajal, which also served as a border and customs post [Richardson, *Travels*, Vol. I, p . 290-1].

[5]Zumeta: a paste of flour of wheat, normally of boiled barley, kneaded with oil or dates [Nachtigal, *Sahara and Sudan*, Vol. II, p. 34n].

[6]Apparently Tuareg, in which case, not from the nomadic groups but from the class of middlemen and merchants settled in cities, such as Agadez. This class would have been informed about the affairs of the Porte since they accepted the religious and political authority of the Sultan of Constantinople – whereas in the region of Tuat and further West, nominal allegiance was given to the Sultan of Morocco [H. T. Norris, personal communication].

[7]Senna, obtained from the tropical shrub bearing yellow flowers and flat greenish pods, was noted for its purgative and other medicinal properties. Together with ivory and natron, it became an increasingly important item of "legitimate" trans-Saharan trade in the 19th century. Senna was delivered by 22 of the 57 Saharan caravans that arrived in Tripoli in the first eight months of 1848 [Wright, *"Nothing else but Slaves"*, Table 10.2].

if the russians had not joined the Greeks[8] they made many enquiries
about England said they understood that we were Masters of the sea
and made all other nations behave themselves properly on that element
and called the King of England Sultan el Bh[a]r or Emperor of the Sea
but that the Sultan of Constantinople was Sultan of the Earth – they
made many enquiries after Bonaparte – and Spain calling it Andalusia[9]
and mentioned the circumstance of its once having belonged to the faithful and if it was not mentioned in our books that the Christians were to
conquer all Africa[10] they as usual enquired after our women how they
were treated and how they were dressed &c we told them the truth with
which they were much pleased & said they did the same that it was not
acting like men for the Turks to shut their women up & cover their faces
as they do -

They tried very hard to make me change my faith promising me all the
joys of paradice in the next world & the handsomest girl in their country in this – I told them I should like very much to take a wife amongst
them but that it would be nessassery that she should accompany me to
Bornou and England which I knew they would not agree to – one of the
Hadjes among them giving me a beautiful description of the
Mohamedan Paradice and it[s] never ending joys was watching my
countenance most attentively to see whither I was serious in listening or
inclined to laugh but I instantly saw his aim & I paid as much attention
as if I had heard one of the most sublime and serious discourses for to
have laughed at their paradice would have been a crime for which they
might or would most likely have wet their daggers in the best blood of
my body – even my friend Hatita would have had a dip for he is as

---

[8]In the uprising of 1821 against the Ottoman Turks. See also Chapter Six, n. 4.

[9]Ar., *Al Andalus*, Spain – derived from the various names (*Al-Andalis, Al-Andlish, Al Andlis*) given by
the Arab-Berbers to the German Vandals who briefly dominated northern and southern provinces of
Spain in the early fifth century. [A.D. Taha, *The Muslim Conquest and Settlement of North Africa and Spain*
(London, 1989), p. 31.]

[10]The first reference in the journals to the frequently stated concern of peoples of the interior
about the nature and purpose of British ambitions in Africa – based on accounts received, often in
the course of the Hajj, of British imperialism east of the Ottoman empire, in particular in India.

devout a Moslem as there is in Africa – Hatita or any of the others never attack the D^r about religion[11]

Thursday 18th

Arose at 3 oClock & had coffe & started at 4 AM our road along the Wady the Mountains the same as before Course W ½ S – we are now acquainted that the Tuaricks will not travel in the night unless in casses [sic] of the greatest necessity giving as a reason that the night was given to the sons of men to sleep in not to travel[12] – and as the Tuaricks unlike the Arabs have all their camels tied one to another and following in a line a man leads the headmost camel so that all go at an equal pace[13] – the man who leads our camels is called Mohamed and he is one of those sort of dul[l] personages that speak to him in what manner you may he will not alter his pace nor move to one side though a snake lay across the road – there is this advantage in him that his pace is equal and we can judge pretty correctly of the distance – Course W ½ S 24

at 4.30 P.M- we halted under some Tallah trees at a place called El *Wangee*[14] which afforded food for the camels & wood to boil our kettle

Friday 19th

at 5.40 a.m Started at our usual pace after having a cup of coffe and a little dried bread which is the whole of our sustonance untill we halt at night exept three times in the day that Hatita allows us a drink of water which is at 9 AM – Noon & 3 P.M & when we halt we have Zumeta &

---

[11]Out of a practical concern not to offend a potential provider of help. Such respect, and wariness, was shown to all those with perceived special powers, such as marabuts, and tinkers.

[12]For superstitious reasons – here a belief in the malign spirits and demons, who preyed, more at night than in the day, on travellers at springs and in the deserts; superstitions which are stronger in Fezzan and Eastern Hoggar than in the more Arabized and Islamized Western Sahara with its stricter Ulama presence to suppress pagan traditions. [H. T. Norris, personal communication.]

[13]See Appendix 5: Cartography, n. 4.

[14]Log has *Elewinga*.

tea & then go to rest in the open air and sleep as sound and comfortable as if we were in the best bed in England   at 4 P.M- we saw the Mountains of Ghaat & here the Fezzan Mountains take a turn to the South[d][15]   Hatita say[s] they go in that direction two long days journey when they are joined by the Montains of Ghaat & ["formed" deleted] then run in a S.E direction into the country of the Tibbo that he has 5 times [led] his tribe on plunder parties against the Tibbos[16] and that they allways go allong the Mountains as they find plenty of food for the camels and water

at 8.15 PM we arrived & halted in Wady El Fou or the valley of cool breezes[17] – there were a n⁰ of Tallah trees growing in it – it appears to be the bed of one of the Mountain torrents   had our tea & Zumeta & went to bed   W by S ½ S 29 Miles

Saturday 20th

at 5 A.M- Started our course over a gravelly plain the Mountains of Fezzan to the S.E & the Tuarick mountains to the Westd at 7 P.M- halted on the desert called Taita or a place where there is neither food for man or beast W by S 27 Miles

Sunday 21st

Started at 4.40 A.M- our road lay over wide flats that ended to the West[d] in precipitous descents the strata where exposed was composed of aluminus slate the rest of loose sand gravel &[c]

---

[15]Clapperton uses the term 'Fezzan Mountains' for the Msak Sattafat which, together with the Massak Mallat to the south, forms the western ridge of the plateau of Murzuq.

[16]This distance appears to be outside the normal wandering and raiding area of both Tubu and Tuareg clans. James Richardson learned in Ghat in the winter of 1845-6 that the Ajjer Tuareg of that place had been in the habit of raiding for slaves among the Tubu communities to the southward, some raiders taking up to 20 captives each. But they had recently give up such practices, "considering them inconsistent with their profession of good Musulmans" [FO 97/430, J. Richardson, *Report on the Slave Trade of the Great Desert* (1846)]. The Tubu themselves were also great slavers.

[17]Ar. *fuh*, mouth.

at 8 A.M- passed a small mount composed of Aluminus slate called by the Tuaricks Toskar & by the Arabs Boo kra – or the limping father[18] over this all the young fellows hop on one leg to show their vigor after crossing the desert   after descending a number of steep rocky passes formed by the abrupt termination of the Gravelly plains at 8.30 P.M- we arrived & halted at the spring   castle & Maraboot of Luenat in Wady Sirdiles[19]   our Zumeta being all finished we had tea and all our servants being very tired we would not trouble them to make kuscassou – the camels had had no water for 4 days & no food for 3 so that they were nearly done up[20]   we passed one that had perished for want a few days before we came   W ½ N 30

Monday 22<u>nd</u>

we staid here all day and were visited at an early hour by Sidi Mohamed the Maraboot a Fezzaner who the Tuaricks persuaded to live here to watch and pray over the pious bones of his father[21] who was a Hadje & a Merchant & died on his return from Soudan – the Tuaricks had him buried here & a Small mud edifice raised over his mortal remains which they hold in great veneration   it is also a place of sanctury to those who may comit any crime to fly to[22] – but unfortunately this pious man was not lying here seven years ago when a party of forty Arabs on their return from stealing the camels of the Tuaricks were over taken by Hatita and his men and all put to the sword   their bones were laying strewed about the place where they fell -

---

[18]"small conical hill called Boukra, or Father of the Foot" [Oudney, *Missions*, Vol. II, p.187] – a common place name in North Africa – for example, of the location of the coveted phosphate deposits in the western Sahara today. *Toskar* is probably related to the Berber root word, *sesker*, with the sense of being 'well placed on a base', a pedestal.

[19]"Al Awaynat, the springs from which the whole locality takes its name" [Barth, *Travels*, Vol. I, p. 185]. Sardalas has a thriving agricultural community today [Ward, *Touring Libya*, p. 78].

[20]Camels normally need water every four to five days in the desert in summer, double their winter need. When he does drink, a camel may take up to 40 litres at one fill. [I. Droandi, *Notizie sul cammello* (Tripoli, 1915) pp. 139, 147; Bulliet, *The Camel and the Wheel*, pp. 31, 35. Bulliet suggests that a camel can absorb over 120 litres at a go.]

[21]When Richardson [*Travels*, Vol. II, pp. 261-263] visited the marabet of "Sidi bou Salah, 200 feet from the spring" in 1846, "... the daughter of the Maraboot, aged 70, was still living in the oasis".

[22]An example of the dual, social and religious, role of the rural Marabut.

Wady Sirdalis appears to have been a bed of a large lake at the foot of the Mountains of Ghaat – and its east^{tn} side has been the elevated plains which form the Wady [and] appear like ranges of low hills running from north to south – it is about 20 miles in length and five in breadth covered with a strong rushy grass which harbours a great number of the venomous snakes called Liffa whose bite is considered mortal by the T[u]aricks and Fezzanners^{23} the Wady where cult^d by the Maraboot & his two assistants produces grain in abundance and all other vegetibles common to this country there are several abundant springs of excellent water which would supply the means to irrigate the whole wady if any persons would take the trouble to cultivate it – and by all appearances it seems to be over flowed in the greater part in the winter season – and its outlet to be to the North and then to head to the east^d along the foot of the Sand hills to Wady Gharbi if I may judge by The Tallah trees which run in that direction

The spring at Luenat flows out of a small rock on which there is the ruins of an Arab castle – which the Tuaricks say was built by the Jews^{24} – and is now inhabited by devils so that they will not enter it by night or day – this Spring is very abundant the water clear and good it appears to have been built round by those who built the castle but that would not confine the water for it flows from it in a very large stream so large that I had a very comfortable bath in it and all the trouble they have in irrigating the ground [all] they want is to lead a channel from the Well to the place there being elevation enough at the spring head to conduct it to the Whole of the Wady if necessary -

We bought a very good Sheep from the Maraboot for three dollars and our selves & servants a feast – we were visited by a great number of

---

^{23}The horned asp, *Cerastes cerates*, the most deadly of the Saharan snakes.

^{24}Possibly a phrase loosely used, like Roumi [Chapter One, n. 12], to refer to early and unknown races inhabiting the region. Small Jewish communities still exist, however, in certain parts of the, mostly western, Sahara and this could be a case of a local folk-memory of a specific medieval Jewish community. [H. T. Norris, personal communication.]

Hatita's people who are as fine looking men as I ever saw – and as we had our tent pitched here it often looked like a beautiful war party – the number of Tuaricks sitting around on the ground with every man his spear stuck with point up – & the but[t] in the ground his sword on his back & his dagger at his wrist – the ruins of the old castle within 300 yards and a solitary Tallah tree with a flat top growing near it and the peak'd Mountains of Ghaat appearing blue in the distance   all made the whole look more like enchantment than reality   the Maraboot wrote a number of the Tuaricks charms for which we supplied the paper and on his wanting some medecine for his eyes the D^r said could he not write a charm for them   he laughed and said charms would not do – and he only wrote them because the Tuaricks wished it   Hatita got one for the pain in his head and I gave him a piece of green morroca leather that I cut out of my note book to sew it up in & he placed it in the front of his Turban – the Tuaricks kept us compy the whole day and left us a little before sunset   we gave them some tobaco and other trifles

Made the Lat^{de} by Mn Alt^{de} of Antares 25° 47' [ ]" N & took distances for the Long^{de} from Antares & the Moon

Tuesday 23rd
we were fairly obliged to stay to day by our camel men – who had driven the camels off to feed & made use of the old story said they could not be found -

Wednesday 24th
Arose before day had a cup of coffe & Crossing Wady Sirdilis to the West we passed 4 large Springs   on the banks of one of the drains running to a Gumah field we picked up some fine bog iron ore

after crossing wady Sirdalis to the West,d we entred upon an elevated rocky plain   the rocks appearing like those of a sea beach when left uncovered by the ebbing of the tide as they were all worn & holed as if done by water & the passages between them filled with sand – we then after crossing them entred the pass of the Mountains which is winding narrow and in many places we had to pass down very steep rocks much to the danger of the camels and our baggage – we then entred onto even groun[d] the passage opening amongst the hills which [is] called the Barakat or road[25] the other being the pass which is a very long and strong one and might be deffended with very few men against a great number as the rocks are almost inaccesable on each side – they are composed of Sandstone and layers of blue & white Slate pipe clay and aluminus clay the sand stone forms the upper Stratum – the Slate &c the lower this range of hills is called by the Tuaricks Tadrart[26]   to the North they extend about 10 or 15 Miles – run in a Southly direction two days journey South of the Spring of Luinat then run East join the Fezzan mountains & both take a S.E direction & run through the country of the Tibbo's[27]

the Sandstone contains a great quantity of Iron on appearance the outside like basalt from its exposure to the air but when broke is red – from the decaying of the lower strata & the rains the Westrn sides of the Mountains present a very fantastic appearance – some places like Gothic Cathedrals others like castales [sic] – and in some places oblisks & Monuments appear on the top not like as if they were done by the hand of nature but by art   And – I have remarked that the North and West sides of all the ranges of hills between this & Tripoli are precipices as if they had been the peaks and formed the bold coast of the Sea – the hills on the North side of Wady Shiati excepted – and on the south & east sides the[y] dicline gradualy from this precipice to low hills & gravelly plains

---

[25]Tuareg, *abarekka*, road. A number of roads descend from Wadi Sardalas to the Wadi Tanissuft and Ghat. Baggage trains used the longer but easier northern track, as do vehicles today. On the return journey Clapperton took one of the short-cuts through the escarpment.

[26]Tuareg (and Berber), *tadrart*, mountain.

[27]If the extraordinarily diffuse Tubu have a "country" at all, it has to be the Tibesti massif of the central Sahara. Historically, this has always been less a homeland than a centre of attraction and dispersion of a people thinly but widely spread throughout the central Sahara and its southern fringes, from Kufra to Kawar and from Borku to north-east Nigeria. [Chapelle, *Nomades noirs*, pp. 25-164; A. Le Rouvreur, *Saheliens et sahariens du Tchad* (Paris, 1962), *passim*.]

at 1 PM – it blowing a strong Siroc[28] we cleared the hills & traveled allong their west[rn] side in Wady Ghaat untill 8-30 P.M- when we halted for the night   W by S 2   WN.W 3   W.S.W. 2   S.S.W. 17

Thursday 25th

Arose before day light & had bozeen for break fast – Started at 5-10 A.M – the morning at 8 it came on to blow a strong gale from the East[d]   the Wady & hills wearing the same appearance as before – at 11-30 halted at the well of Tinisala & took up our quarters under an Atilla tree – Mohamed ben Hadje taken ill – we had coffe & it being necessary for the Camels to drink & I & ben Hadje both unwell the D[r] would not go any further to day   S.SW 14

In the afternoon the D[r] took his servant & went to examine the hill of Jinoon or Edinan as it is called by the Tuaricks which in English is the devil's hill[29] Hatita was in the greatest alarm for his safety fearing that the devils that he said inhabited it would run away with him[30] – we had been told many wonderful stories about this hill that there were people with red hair living in it that at night when encamped near it they would hear them beating on their drums see their fires & hear them firing their musquets – that a Kaffle comming from Ghadames had been stoped by one of the people who had demanded a gun which was paid for by a piece of paper with writing upon it that the Merchant did not under-

---

[28]The dust-laden Saharan wind [Ar., *ghibli*] which may blow at any time of the year but is more common in April, May and June and at the end of the summer. According to an old Fezzanese adage, "if the *Ghibli* blows forty days – God preserve us from the evil! – the camel becomes pregnant without the intervention of the male" [Lethellieux, Le *Fezzan*, p.140].

[29]*Kaf Ajnun*, the castle of the jinns [Ward, *Touring Libya*, p. 78].

[30]Oudney, "a good active little walker" [J.R.Scott, letter to John Barrow, 15th November 1820, CO 2/14] achieved the climb – despite his tuberculosis [*Missions*, Vol. II, p.189]; but others failed. Barth collapsed at the foot of the hill, exhausted and in a delirium of fever, remained alone for 27 hours and nearly died. Richardson similarly became lost and wandered for nearly two days dangerously unwell. These superstitions and fears occur throughout the Sahara. Ibn Battuta remarked, for example, of a travelling courrier near Audagusht (in the south-western desert): "That desert is haunted by demons; if the *takshif* be alone, they make sport of him and disorder his mind, so that he loses his way and perishes." [Ibn Battuta, *Travels in Asia and Africa*, 1325-1354, selected and trans. H.A.R. Gibb (London, 1983) p. 319].

stand – this on his arriving at a town in Tuat[31] was to be given to a black
dog that would come out & meet him the Merchant when he got there
received the money from the dog for the letter & has been rich ever since
this story and a hundred other as absurd are firmly believed by the
Tuaricks[32]

Hatita said he would not go up to it for all the dollars in the World that
no Tuarick had ever gone there but that the pious Maraboot Sidi
Mohamed who lives at the spring of Luenat had once gone & seen the
people whom he recounts as having red hair and beards – it is from the
Lies of these pious rascals that the people have such a dread of
Europeans for the T. firmly believed that we were the children of Edinan
or the devil before they saw us in the wady – and this prejudice we have
to remove from those at Ghaat with whom Hatita has had a great deal
of trouble to allow us to come and even now a great many are against it

he has been giving me some very long lectures on the road how to behave
saying I must not laugh sing or play upon the flute but look very grave
& speak little[33] he and I have got very great friends & he has pestered
me not a little to become a Mohamedan promising me a very handsome
wife in this world and all the joys of paradice in the next – and on the
road he would often ride along side of my camel & Say Abdullah Ben
Scotland what do you wish – I knew instantly what he wanted me to say
& I would answer a handsome wife – wife he would say no no – what
do you wish – I would add again a handsome wife of my own country
he would instantly reply quite pettishly say you wish Mohamed the

---

[31]An extended group of oases, now in southern Algeria, about 190 by 100 miles., containing in the
19th century 300 to 400 small settlements inhabited by Berbers, Arabs and Blacks, with its capital at
Ain Salah. Tuat was the main trade and communications centre of the western Sahara (and the mar-
ket-place of the Ahaggar Tuareg) with direct links to Ghat, Ghadamis, Ouargla, the Niger Bend and
the western Sudan. It had obvious strategic significance and, although it always recognised the religious authority of the Moroccan Sultanate, it was annexed to French Algeria in 1900.
[32]Richardson [*Travels*, Vol. I, pp. 436-440] describes some of the legends: the "compact" between
the genii and the Tuaregs; the mountain "hall of council where the genii meet from thousands of
miles round"; and "The Desert Pandemonium ... alive with myriads of spirits".
[33]Rodd [*People of the Veil*, p. 272] writes of 'their grave and dignified demeanour".

prophet of god and you will have everything I used allways to say upon
my word Hatita I do not know about that – and if you saw the women
of my country you would like to have one too – this would make him
shake his head & sa[y] Oh Abdullah Abdullah thou art a great rogue[34] -

during the time the D^r was on the hill we buried our dates & Kuscassou
that was to serve for the journey back[35] as they said the people of Ghaat
were not at all backward in asking for any thing they wanted – at Sunset
the D^r returned much to the satisfaction of Hatita who had given him
up as lost for ever

the hill is the same as those on the South side of the Wady – and form[s]
a part of the same range & runs seven days journey to the N.W. & then
turns to the South   the singular appearance of the whole of the Tadrat
range is caused by the soft Slaty strata forming the lower part giving way
with the rains forms a number of turrets pillars and other figures in the
sandstone Strata above   some parts of which being softer than others
have holes quite through the rocks and this when the wind blows strong
causes a sound or sounds like the Eolian harp which the poor Tuaricks
attribute to the devil and his agents in Edinan – we heard it very dis-
tinctly and I tried to convince them of the cause by placing an empty bottle with the neck out which made a similar sound but I might as well
have saved myself the trouble they all went to prayers except my servant Madie who honest lad is not troubled with any qualms that way[36]
– [n]or is he given to praying at all and Hatita has taken him severly to
task several times for his neglect

---

[34]Hatita, it seems, felt free to enter into a joking relationship with Clapperton, one such as is typ-
ically extended to cross-cousins (*ubajan*), and some outsiders, in contrast to the avoidance relationship towards others, for example, a wife's parents [M. Ole-Nielsen, SOAS, personal communication].
  [35]Leaving depots of food was a common practice in desert travel.
  [36]Clapperton, a man of religious conviction himself, was more cynical of superstition than disre-
spectful towards Islam; see, for example, end of entry for 26th July 1822.

Figure 8. Hills of Jinoon

Friday 26th

at 5-10 AM. Started down the Wady over a fine strong Clay soil thick-
ly interspersed with bushes & Atilla trees having the appearance of being
covered with water at times Hatita says it is over flowed in the winter
& that the water runs down to Ghaat at 10.45 AM – [halted] to dress
ourselves under the beautiful spreading branches of an Atila they are
larger here than any we have seen before – the one whose branches we
are now encamped under is about 9 feet in diameter 6 feet above the
ground – we found shaving a most uneasy task the D^r stood barber for
me & I officiated in that capacity for him & Hatita – when shaving
Hatita he was under a great alarm & kept his hand at his throat all the
time however I finished my task much to his satisfaction & then cut his
hair & trimmed his beard we found our English uniforms which we had
dressed in very hot and uncomfortable but as it was Hatitas wish as well
as our own to show the people of the country our english dress (they
never having seen europeans before) we suffered a good sweating for it[37]

["at – 5-40 P.M" deleted] at 2.30 P.M – we started for Ghaat and at 5.40
we came in sight of the town[38] we wished Hatita joy who was all in raptures for he had not been there for a long time before being detained in
Wady Gharbi by a guinea worm in his leg – he dismounted from his
Mahery and said a short prayer in thanksgiving his manner & the
knowledge of what he was about if possible raised him higher in our esti-
mation – and [made us] think of our own country which at that time was
more dear to our imaginations than paradise

SW 10 S.S.W. 10

---

[37]Some early European travellers in the Sahara (notably Hornemann, Ritchie and Lyon) chose to
go disguised as Muslims. There were obvious risks in doing so and, following Consul Warrington's
advice, the Bornu Mission travelled openly as Christians in European dress, or at least on arrival and
during stays at important places. It thus buried the myth that any European penetrating beyond
Fezzan risked "a cruel death" [Lyon, A *Narrative*, p. 200].

[38]Actually a cluster of small oases, Ghat is a natural hub of Saharan communications and an
ancient trading centre. Effectively a free-trade zone, protected by the Ajjer Tuareg and with access
to Tuareg-dominated roads to the Hausa states and the Niger Bend, by the early 19th century it was
ready to supplant its rivals, Ghadamis and Murzuq.

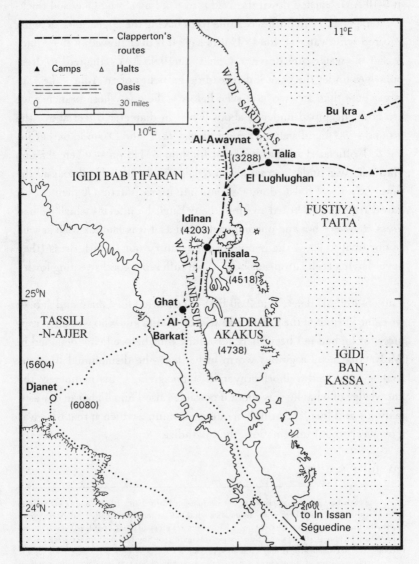

Map 7. Ghat

CHAPTER

6

Ghat

at 7- P.M- we arrived & halted out side the town Hatita thinking it better to pitch the tent than go in side – the spot we chose was about a ¼ of
a Mile to the South^d of the town near a well & garden belonging to one
of Hatita's friends – a number of Hatita's friends came out to see him
amongst them were two of his sisters who hung on his neck & wept as
he had been a long time absent and sick – after they had finished crying
over their brother they called for us   the Change from crying to laughing was not long and the[y] were very much amused with our dress –
but there is one thing they all find fault with – the indecency of our
trowsers   they say all the rest is beautiful but we must wear trousers as
wide as theirs   we soon got as familiar with Hatita's sisters & his female
relatives as if we had been acquainted for a number of years – they staid
with us untill nearly midnight   our seats were on the sand the ladies sitting all around as the[y found it convenient

Sunday 27th
Cool & Clear in the Morning   ["at 8 A.M" deleted] we were early visited by a number of the towns people amongst which were three merchants of Ghadamis[1] – who told us that our friend Mohamed De Ghies[2]
had sent a courier to Ghadamis to request that should any of them fall
in with [us] to show us every attention that lay in their power   Hadje

Ahmet the eldest of the three is one of the most venerable looking men I ever saw – they sent us a mess of Kuscassou for breakfast and some excellent mutton –

at 8 AM- it came on to blow a strong gale accompanied with clouds of sand that darkened the sun – and filled every thing we tried to escape its fury by wrapping ourselves up in our bornouses and laying down under the lee of our baggage – but to no purpose every place was alike so we lay with our backs to the wind – with our faces wrapped up for we could not open our eyes

In the afternoon we went in to the town – accompanied by Hatita to see the Sultan[3] who had sent to say that he was sick or he would come and see us – Hatita led the way to the Sultans house Hatita called it the castle but I saw no difference between it and the other houses in the town – in one of the inner appartments we found the Sultan or Sheikh – seated upon a piece of blue & white striped cotton cloth and a small carpet being spread we were desired to sit down and following the example of Hatita we sat down with as little ceremony as if we had been in our own tent – after we had sat a few minutes the room being crowded with Tuaricks the Sultan asked us a number of questions about our country if we were allways at peace with the Sultan of Constantinople if the war with the Greeks was finished – we told him that we were allways at peace[4] with the Sublime porte that the war with the Greeks was finished

---

[1] Ghadamis in the early 19th century (see Introduction) was still a centre of Saharan trade and finance whose merchant-venturers were known and usually respected throughout northern Africa and the Sudan. The commmercial decline of Ghadamis was accelerated by the abolition of the black slave trade, first in Tunis and then in French Algeria, in the 1840s.

[2] Sidi Mohammed D'Ghies, of Turkish origin, was a merchant, widely travelled in Europe, who became Yusuf Pasha's foreign minister earlier in the century. He had to give up office on account of his blindness, and in 1822 was living in Tripoli.

[3] Sultan Bal Kassim, see below. Before its first occupation by the Ottoman Turks in 1875, Ghat had its own special, complex and hazardous relationship with the surrounding Ajjer Tuareg, while keeping its own precarious political and economic autonomy. The Sultan of Ghat, hereditary through the female line, was nominally responsible for the external relations of the oasis, a role owing more to his personal prestige than any actual powers.

[4] Not quite true, but Clapperton would not of been aware of developments post-dating the end of 1821. The Greek uprising continued, with some Greek success in guerilla warfare against cumber-

& that all the world was at peace   We found Hadje Ahmet the Ghadamis
Merchant [had] told them that the English made them all keep the peace
– that we had cleared the Sea of all robbers

Amongst other questions was the never failing one of what have you
come for we told them to see the country and the Inhabitants and every
thing that was worth seeing that all the men & women in England could
read and write[5] that we knew most all the world already and that we
wanted to know the rest – and that if any of their people went to our
country on his return would not every one be asking him what are the
people like how do they dress are they rich or poor good or bad or
have they fine houses &c very true they said we are just the same but
they were much surprised that all the english people could read & write

The D[r] Made the Sultan a present of one of the swords sent out to us
from england which was very much admired for the gilt work on the
handle & scabbard – the blue on the blade was also highly praised but
they said they would have like it better had it been sharp on both sides[6]

The Sultan or Sheikh of Ghaat is between 50 & 60 years of age about 5
feet 8½ inches high no difference in his dress between him & the better
class of the towns people   His name is Belgashem – and to give a slight
idea of his grandieur the room nex[t] to the one we sat in was occupied
by his horse and one of the young princesses came in during our visit
with nothing but a ragged breachcloth on and ran into her fathers arms

---

some Turkish armies, through 1822-23 until the intervention of the land and sea forces of
Mohammad Ali, Pasha of Egypt, the following year. Clapperton probably represented the view of the
conservatives among the post-Napoleonic European Great Powers who saw the Greek rebellion as
merely a part of a general revolutionary wave in the south and a minor, disruptive disturbance which
the Sultan would quickly bring to an end.

[5]The literacy rate in Britain at this period – a problematical figure, traditionally estimated by reference to signatures in parish records, especially marriage certificates – was probably around 20%,
and relatively somewhat higher in Scotland than in England. [C.R.M. Jones, Institute of Comparative
Education, London, personal communication.]

[6]Oudney subsequently recommended to Lord Bathurst that a gift of a sword, especially one made
to Tuareg design, would obtain more credit with Tuareg leaders than other, more expensive, gifts
[letter to Lord Bathurst of 16 August, 1822, quoted by Bovill in *Missions*, Vol. II, p. 289].

who embraced her very tenderly   I could not help smiling at this slight mistake of the young and thoughtless princess   neither could the Tuaricks who were present   on the Sultans perceiving the cause of our mirth he sent her to the Sultana   at the same time giving her a slap on the bare breach for disturbing the gravity of the Levee –

After taking leave of the Sultan we were taken to the house of the Cadi who is at present in Ghadamis   we were received by his son   one of the finest young men I ever saw   he has travled a good deal in Marocca and would very gladly go with us to Bornou and England   his name is Lamim   he offred us his house to stop in in the heat of the day – we thanked him but said we preferred the tents – after some time staying with him   during which we were very much at our ease   we returned to our tents where we found some boiled Mutton Fatat a basket of ripe dates and another of Grapes[7] sent us by the Sultan

Sunday 28[th]

Our tent at an early hour was crowded by the Tuaricks beg[g]ing tobaco of which both men and women are very fond – the men consistantly carry on their left Arm a large leather pouch of Soudan workmanship that contains their tobaco, pipes, flint, steel, & Match   we had brought some of the Morzuk tobaco with us for the purpose of giving them and we accordingly distributed it amongst them-

We had a mess of Kuscassou and mutton sent us by our worthy friend Hadje Ahmet the Ghadamsa Merchant and on the Tuaricks taking leave of us we had our breakfast – it came on to blow after 8 A.M- a Strong gale from the EN.E accompanied with Sand the same as yesterday – we had again to wrap ouselves up and lay under the lee of our baggage untill near sunset when the gale ceased and we got a little respite   When the

---

[7]Al-Barkat [Ar., lake or lagoon], one of the outlying oasis-villages of the Ghat complex, noted for its abundant water and date palms. [Details in Scarin, *L'insediamento umano*, pp. 46-55; plan on p. 51.]

Tuaricks came I was cleaning my sextant from the sand which had penetrated into the inside through my trunk ["through" deleted] the leather
case and the wooden case which though well bound with brass is considerably warped and shrunk from the dryness of the climate so that the
sand can get [in] though [we] take ever so much care we had to explain
the uses of all our instruments and we allways called in the assistance of
the Hadjes to explain appealing to them if they had not seen such things
on their voyage to Mecca – this maneauvre allways took the trouble from
us and the Hadjes would never fail to say as we said after wards – after
the men went away we were visited by the women who we found could
ask for what they wanted as well as the men – we wanted them very
much to sing but they were too much afraid of Hatita but they said that
if we could get him away they would sing to us –

Made the Latitude by Mn. Alt^{de} of Formalhaut 24°-47-[ ] N^8

Monday 29th
– our tent as usual surrounded by our friends showing their empty tobaco pouches & knocking the ashes out of their pipes & begging for tobaco but it was now too late we had given all away so they had to smoke
their own –

Morning and evening the D^r was beset with patients wanting medecine
for present use and he has had never had an application for medecine to
make the women bear male children or has he had any for Madam to
help an impotent husband – we advised with Hatita about what we
should give as presents to the heads of the people and it was accordingly settled that we should give to young Lamim the Cadi's eldest son a
white bournouse a clasp knife razor pair of scissors and three dollars
to Hadje Mohamed^9 a white turban knife razor a pair of scissors and

---

[8]Log, and later journal entry [Wednesday 31st July] has 24°-57' – which is correct.
[9]Not further identified; a merchant of Ghat or perhaps another of the visiting Ghadamis traders.

three dollars – We had no other presents with us & the white bornouse was mine that I had given to the D^r I gave the Sister of Hatita a fine barrican

we were sorry that we had no other presents to give as there were a number of others equally deserving   particularly Hadje Ahmet – the Ghadamis Merchant – we begged him to excuse us not sending him a present as we realy had nothing to Send – this evening our camels were [to] have been brought in as we intended starting in the morning – but they as usul did not make their appearance

Tuesday 30th
Clear & fine – to day as usul we were surrounded by paitents – and no camels made their appearance – We had a visit from another Sultan who Hatita says is greater than them all[10]   he offered to conduct us to Soudan or any part of Timbuctoo or Tuat[11]   we were at some loss to Make up a present for him   at last we agreed with Hatita that it would be better to give him a red bornouse that we fortunately had left   a Knife   a pair of scissors and [ ] to buy tobaco

In the evening Hatita wished us very much to Stay for 2 days longer as Also the Cadi's son Lemim who said he wished to accompany us to Morzuk but that he would be unable to get ready in less time

Wednesday 31st
Clear & fine   we had a visit from the principal ladies of Barcat   both men & women belonging to that town had expressed a great desire for

---

[10]By "great man", Hatita was possibly here seeking to translate (into Arabic) for Clapperton the Tamasheq word 'imohaghan', a term used to refer to the aristocracy and ambiguously combining the qualities of personal excellence, old age and superior status.

[11]Interesting as a reflection of the territory where the Tuaregs felt at home. Timbuktu was used as a general term for the region of the western Sudan known as the Niger Bend.

us to go there & see them but as Hatita would not go he and Jobar the
Sultan having quareled 4 years ago Since which time he had never set
foot within its walls – and as we had come to the country under Hatita's
protection we would not pay him such a bad compliment Jobar wrote
to Hatita in the affair making him an apology but Hatita was in flexable[12]
– we had another and the most powerful reason want of means to make
them the presents they would expect & Jobar was one of the principal
persons in opposing our comming to the country

Hatita and the rest of the Tuaricks were in the tent when the Ladies
arrived they were very free & talkative & we had to show them all our
inventions such as the kalediscope &c we made them a present of a pair
of scissors a small looking glass each with which they were very much
pleased –

they were dressed in long blue tobes the same as the men over which
they wear the light howli or Baraccan at the corner that hangs down
they had a number of large beads hanging by way of ornament – Round
their necks hung a belt of finely plaited leather on which were strung a
great number of charms – and each had their little looking glass which
appear to be the glass of a watch silvered on the concave side & put into
a small wooden box to prevent it breaking both men and women are
very fond of admiring them selves looking at their teeth & their eyes &c
& not a hair must be out of its place they were not a little scented with
civet which they get from Soudan[13] two of the women were painted
with red ochere as far up the face as the eyes

---

[12]Richardson remarked on Hatita's quarrelsome nature some 23 years later: "They [Hatita and
one Hadje Busheer] had made it up... [Hatita] could be cantankerous" [*Travels*, Vol . I, p. 213].

[13]Ar., *zabad*, a civet cat – a striped carniverous quadruped from the central African forests (*vinerra
civetta*) and also parts of Asia. A yellowish or brownish unctuous substance, with a strong musky smell,
is obtained from glands in the animal's anal pouch and is much prized for perfume-making.
According to the British traveller Simon Lucas, the cats were trapped and kept in cages and period-
ically irritated untill "a copious perspiration is produced" and civet-musk is secreted under the tail.
This was scraped off and preserved in bladders, or small boxes made of hide. "After a short interval"
Lucas reported, " the operation is renewed, and repeated from time to time, till at the end of twelve
or fourteen days the anmial dies of fatigue and continual torment. The quantity [of musk] obtained

They were good looking women & wore the hair dressed over the forehead – & falling in two long tresses on each side of the neck which is plaited & put up in a loop when they are not in dress

at Sunset all the principal people of the town came out to visit us & to beg us to prolong our stay for 10 days more – but we had to refuse their kind offer as we expected the Kaffle to be getting ready for Bornou and answers to the Drs Letters – We might by complying with the wishes of these kind people lose an opportunity of proceeding to our destination – Hatita & young Lemeem begged hard for the Dr to stay till Miday tomorrow but he was not to be moved but we promised to wait 10 Miles from Ghaat till they came

[GHAT COMMENTARY][14]

The Tuaricks have very little commerce   they being principally employed in carrying the Merchandise of the Fezzaners Ghadamsies & Tripolines & in protecting it & the Merchants from being plunderd –

They call themselves Tuaricks – or in the singular Targie[15] they inhabit the greatest part of the great desert – and are spread from Fezzan on the East to the Atlantic Ocean on the West bound on the North by the Barbary states – and the Negro countries on the South – they occupy

---

from one cat is generally about half an ounce." [*Proceedings of the African Association*, Vol. I, p. 159-60]. Civet cats and their musk were so valuable, according to George Lyon, that even in Sudan "a savage old cat will produce ten or twelve dollar's worth in three heats. Their price is enormous, some being sold for three or four slaves." [*A Narrative*, p. 154]. So important was the civet cat in perfumery that it was a common sign for perfume shops in 18th-century London. [See A. Heal, *Sign Boards of Old London Shops* (London, 1957) pp. 45 and 147.]

[14]It is evident in this passage of commentary that Clapperton generally approved of Tuareg society, in particular in a positive comparison with that of the Arabs. Some allowance has also to be made for Clapperton's rather sweeping generalizations, obscured perhaps, like many that have followed, by a tendency to see Tuareg society as a closed and timeless entity – whereas, particularly at this period, its structures were almost certainly in a transitional stage as they adapted to external influences. [M Ole-Nielsen, SOAS, personal communication.]

[15]See Chapter Three, n. 27.

several towns in the northern part of Soudan – of which Aghadez is the principal[16] – They speak the Berber tongue and say that the Berbers speak the same as the Sultan of Morocca sent one of that nation as his ambassador on a late occasion when the son and nephew were at war but the Tuaricks would take part with neither[17] – They have written characters amongst them which most of their men and women can understand and use for putting their names upon their things and they are very fond of cutting their names on the rocks – & hills both in their own country & in Fezzan –

They said they did not know where they came from but that they thought they came from the countries north of the desert[18] – Ganat is the oldest Town they know of and is 2 long days journey South of Ghaat and five days with loaded camels as they have to go round the hills – it consists of only a few houses and some date trees

The Tuaricks who live in the country do not cultivate the ground but live principally upon the Milk and flesh of their goats sheep & Camels and the Wadan Ghazale & wild ox which they procure by hunting – the Wadan I have seen it is like a large red goat with long shaggy hair hanging down the neck & breast[19] the White ox I have never seen they say it inhabits the sandy part of the desert has a black nose & horns & is very fine its traces I have seen the feet is of the size of our smallest

---

[16]For a general account of the Tuaregs of Air, see Rodd, *People of the Veil*.

[17]An obscure reference which might relate to a centuries-old folk memory of connections with the Kunta Sheikhs of the western Sahara. (Until the 11th century, before the advent of the Arabs in the west, there was no distinction between Tuaregs and Moors. In the 12th century the Almoravids moved both west and east, and the Kunta moors reached Timbuktu). Alternatively, this could be a reference to an actual visit by a Sheikh of the Kunta tribe. Leading Kunta Sheikhs went into the Hoggar as mediators, and could speak Zenaga. In either case, Clapperton's interlocutors evidently regarded the Moors of Mauritania as relations in a sense. [H. T. Norris, personal communication.]

[18]Not incorrect. There have been many claims that the Tuaregs are descended from the Lamta of northern Libya [H. T. Norris, personal communication].

[19]Some confusion on Clapperton's part here. The goat-like animal he describes, and known in Fezzan as the 'wadan', is the moufflon, *Ammotragus lervia*, rare but still to be found in the massifs of the central Sahara. Clapperton's "white ox" might refer to the oryx, *Oryx gazella ssp. leucoryx*. Received accounts, however, were easily confused by the Arabs' use of the general term *'bakar al-wahshi'* for both wild cattle and antelopes which look like cattle [Nachtigal, *Sahara and Sudan*, Vol. I, p. 261n].

horned cattle – they annually import a quantity of Wheat and dates from
Fezan which the[y] receive in exchange for their Senna leaf which the[y]
bring from Soudan   and a load of Senna at Aghadez is given for a load
of dates[20] –

The Tuaricks of this country[21] never eat fowels or their eggs or any thing
that has been cooked with them   the[y] could give us no reason for so
doing but Hadje Mohamed a Ghaatian said it was for the best of all reasons they could not get them as it would be next to impossible to rear
them in the country   the Ghaatians and other Tuaricks who live in
towns are by no means so nice and live the same as the rest of the
Moslims – they never eat in their own houses between sun rise & sunset
and like all wandering people they are able to eat a great deal at a meal
without injury and to fast for a long time-

at the time of the ripening of the dates they come in from the country and
live round Ghaat and Baracat living upon the new dates the[y] beg from
the Ghaatians & Barcattians   they do not cultivate much ground only a
little round the towns which is done by their slaves – The country what
parts of it that we have seen would produce more than Fezzan particularly Wady Sirdilis – which could all be made into Gumah fields – and
watred with very little labour – but the Tuaricks of the country hold as
mean to cultivate the ground & call the Ghaatians & Baracatians their
servants – When the[y] told me they thought the Bashaw would try to
take their country from them I told them the Bashaw had more reason
to be afraid of them taking his country from him & I told them if they
were not too lazy they need not be indebted to Fezzan for dates & Wheat
very true they replied the Fezzaners are slaves – There are also very fine

---

[20]Senna became an increasingly important commodity in "legitimate" Saharan trade in the 19th
century. When he was in Ghat in 1845-6, Richardson recorded that 130 camel-loads, valued at 15 dollars each, were offered for sale at the great winter fair.

[21]Clapperton's sources for this passage of commentary are not stated, but we may perhaps take it
that he is refering to the Tuaregs of Ghat and the related semi-nomadic and sedentary clans in
Fezzan, rather than to the nomadic Ajjer clans.

grapes & peaches grown here   the grapes they sometimes dry – or eat them when ripe but they never make any wine

The people of the country live in tents made of the Skins of the Goat the Wadan & the Ghazale – the houses of the town are in every respect like those in Fezzan

They have been a long time at war with the Tibbos – but are at present at peace –

Their arms[22] consist of a sword & dagger three spears and a Musquet or pistol if they can get them – which has but been of later years – they pro-cure them from the Ghadams Merchants & Tuat – they are the same as the Moorish guns and very bad – their powder they procure from Ghadamis & Fezzan and it is a very indiffrent sort & they have no Idea of loading a gun & serious accidents happen some times from their bursting which is not seldom – the sword blades are of European man-ufacture and are procured from the same place some of them are very ancient & the date [on] one of these was 1577 – it had a head with a ducal crown stamped upon it very well executed[23]   after they purchase them from the Ghadamis or Tuat merchants they take or send them to Aghadis to get hilts & sheaths fitted they are long straight & sharp on both sides and they are not unfrequently peirced near the hilt to make them longer – They wear them different from any nation I have ever seen having them slung over the right shoulder the hilt hanging down-wards over the ["right" deleted] left arm   they are by no means good swords men as they do not know how to guard give a good cut or do

---

[22]The Tuareg distinguished between their traditional "white" arms and firearms. Men were armed (and presumably encumbered) with a broad two-edged sword; an arm-dagger; a throwing-spear or two; some javelins; and a large but light antelope-hide shield. Flint-lock hand-guns were rare in the early 19th century and were unwieldy, primitive and ineffective. [Duveyrier, *Les Touaregs du Nord*, pp. 444-6.] See also Rodd's account of Tuareg arms [*People of the Veil*, pp. 233-7 and Illustration facing p. 236].

[23]Tuareg, *takuba*; a straight, double-edge bladed sword, the hilt a plain straight cross guard, gen-erally known today as a Kaskara. Manufactured in various European cities, these blades were traded from the fifteenth to the late nineteenth century. [T. Del Mar, Sotheby's, personal communication.]

they ever make use of the point though the swords are well formed for that – they say they are good marksmen with the gun but I have only their sworn words for that never having seen them tried but we have seen two or three with miserably cut faces & hands from the bursting of their guns[24] – they fire them in the same way as all the negrose which [is] the gun being loaded they the[n] hold it in the left hand place the right on the end of the but[t] as if they were going to dart it at somthing – they then look along the sight at the object put the but[t] about the middle of the collar bone & fire throwing the gun forward at the same time as if that would add to the force and saying damn your father at the same time – the Stocks of their guns are much shorter than ours and [if] they were to put the but[t] against the shoulder joint their eye would be over the lock –

Their Spears are from 8 to 4 feet long and are of three diffrent kinds one is all of Iron & ornamented with cross wire – and is mostly worn by young men another is about 4 feet long and is used by both the princi-pal people when they walk or ride on their Mahareys   they use it then to scratch the animal on the neck or flank to make it quicken its pace it has not got a head like the others but may more properly be called a staff with a long iron point at the lower end   the other is about 8 feet long having a head shaped like the halberts of our sergents and – of the same size but without the cross bar   at the lower end there is a socket with a flat end fixed on by two clumsey rings this serves for sticking it in the groun[d] when the[y] halt – they use the spears more as an ornament than any thing else   they confess they do not know well how to use it the Tibbos excell them much with the spear but they allways beat them with the sword – they never excercise throwing it –

The daggers are worn by a broad leather strop attached to the upper part of the Sheath & through this strop they thrust the left hand the hilt lying as it were in the hollow of the hand & the sheath going along the Arm –

---

[24]Log: "which are very bad and the same as the guns used in Tripoli".

the hilt is in the form of a St. George's cross ornamented with pieces of brass – as is also the sheath – the daggers are all made at ["Soudan" deleted] in Aghadez   the dagger is their constant arm they never taking [it] of[f] but to pray & then they lay it down in reach of their eye –

The Shield is of Ox hide dressed like a pallet – it is also made in Soudan – about 3½ feet in height and 2½ in breadth with highly ornamented St. Georges cross as if hanging down from the upper part it has a thin iron plate on the inside to which the handle is fixed   as it is very light it is held in the left hand   it is not fit to keep of[f] a good blow with a sword or the thrust of a spear unless comming slant ways – and this is the way they pary the blows – they take great care of the shield covering it with a cloth – when ever they halt & sit it carefully up against their spear – so that nothing may spoil or dirty it of their sword and daggers they are greatly careful and when ever we killed Hatita allways received the Marrow and he would sit for an hour in the sun rubing it & leting it melt into the blade – When they lay down to sleep at night the spear is stuck in the ground at their head & the shield laid against it their sword is laid under their head the dagger remains on the wrist – if they have a musquet or pistol it is laid down along side of them –

The dress of the common people consists of a coarse woolen Shirt or frock with short very wide sleves [which] comes down within 2 or three inches of the knee a pair of loose trowsers that come down a little lower than the calf of the leg   they wear a narrow belt of leather or woolen around the waist and a pair of sandals on the feet – of camels hide those from Aghadez & other parts of Soudan are very well made – the turban is of blue cotton cloth made also in Soudan and the web is only about 4 inches wide one Twist of the turban is opened and passed over the fore head – & forms a shade to the eyes an other is brought round about the Middle of the nose and falls down over the face mouth chin and neck this part is generaly a separate piece of cloth – from the turban

Those of the richer inhabitants consist of one or two blue or blue & white

Tobes of Soudan Manufacture they are large loose blue shirts with long sleeves about one half the length of the body or better a pair of blue trowsers also of Soudan manufacture their turban is worn in the same excepting the part that covers the face which with the rich is generally of a piece of blue cotton cloth highly glazed and tied behind the back of the head with two long loops hanging down the back – under the turban is worn a red cap – the manufacture of ["Soudan" deleted] Tunis to it is added a piece of blue cloth all round the rim which makes the cap appear higher and serves for the shade over the – eyes they have all-ways a belt of finely plaited thongs hanging over the shoulder strung *nearly* full of charms sewed up in leather – also to another belt hangs the Mohametan prayer book in a case of leather or some times of silver it is in Arabic though few of them can read a word or know a letter they never fail to have one – it looks like a we[e] touch box[25] at first sight –

they can give no proper account why they cover the faces up – in the manner they do one saying that Mohamet did so another that their attention may not be taken up looking at the young women – when I said was it not to preserve the Mouth & eyes from the sun & wind they said it was for that also – it certainly requires some[thg] of that kind in traveling – to preserve the lips & eyes – it would be an excellent disguise for a thief round the blue Turban they wear a white cotton cloth[26]

The diseases amongst them are few if we except the eyes – and the ague and liver some times[27]

---

[25]A box for 'touch-powder' or 'priming-powder', formerly forming part of a musketeer's equipment [ShOED].

[26]The origins of the legendary tagilmus have been much debated [Rodd, *People of the Veil*, pp. 288-90] but one cannot generalize; the reasons given for wearing it vary from tribe to tribe [Prof. H.T. Norris, personal communication].

[27]On the basis of research done in the 1950s, L. C. Briggs concluded that in spite of the generally healthy Saharan climate, "the life of an individual native is often eventful medically" [*Tribes of the Sahara*, p. 248; see also Chapter Nine: "health and diseases"]. Under-nourishment and protein deficiencies led to broncho-pulmonary infections. Rheumatism, diseases of the respiratory system, tuberculosis, digestive troubles, malaria, trachoma and venereal diseases were all common.

They are about the Middle size though there are amongst them some very tall men – well formed slight rather than muscular – and have an upright walk and the most unbounded independence in their looks and actions – the colour of their skin is the same as the inhabitants of the south of Spain with fine fore head arched eye brows dark hazle eye rather high cheek bones – a common nose inclining slightly to a bend upwards in the middle – a small formed mouth and teeth a good chin Unlike the Arabs – (Chin which is very short) & they have a good supply of hair on the beard

[faint line drawing of a profile]

They [are] strict Mohametans in their religion[28] very superstitious and will believe any story however extravagant of the Devil and his agents – and many extrodinary ones are they told by the diffrent Merchants traveling through their country in all of which the[y] firmly believe

They believed that all christians were children of the devil before we went there and many a wonderful story was told about us before we came – but now all that prejudice is happily removed and the D[r] has got a high reputation for courage for his visit to Jinoon and every new commer is sure to ask him about it if he did not see the horses or camels the date trees or the people – &[c]

Their Standard of Morality comes nearer the christian than any other Mohamedans I have seen – they never get drunk having the greatest abhorence of all intoxicating drinks Marry only one wife at a time – they are very friendly to one another though murders happen at times the pirpitrator flies to Fezzan where he wait[s] until he or his friends can buy him off – the men & Women eat in company and they the females have as much liberty of speech as in any other country in the world and

---

[28]Not entirely true, as many other travellers attest; and in conflict with some of Clapperton's own evidence elsewhere.

are as virtuous but not more so – the younger branches of the family are kept in very great order particularly by those who live in the country they not being allowed to marry before their elder brother not allowed to smoke if he does not & should he be sitting down they must take a seat behind him – not eat in his company without [being] expressly permitted[29] –

They have got a very neat Mosque at Ghaat – much better than any one in Fezzan they make no use of water before prayers but go through the motions – and do not take the trouble of going to the Mosque at all times but clear away a little place in the sand and if there is a number of them they stand in a row & pray together one of them acting as Mouaddin and calls the people to prayers – along their tracks you frequently meet with small places cleared away for praying and I used hardly to be able to avoid laughing at one of our camel men who used regularly to call to prayers as if there had been a multitude of people – so much are these people bound to forms the[y] have a great number of charms hung around different parts of their bodies – and in their turbans They also wear the *tagtega*[30] or Mohametans lock different from any others – for instead of wearing a round lock they wear it in the form of a crest from the forehead to the back of the crown & when they have no tagia or cap[31] this flowing crest of long shaggy black hair gives them a wild and savage appearance

[note of tifinagh letters in margin]

They are under the Government of a Sheikh or Sultan as they call them in this country and that situation is hereditary ["in the male line" insert-

---

[29]These practices, characteristic of Saharan people generally, surprised, even shocked, travellers of different periods.

[30]Possibly a local word linguistically related to the Arabic root-word *taj*, crown (as in Taj Mahal). Today young Tuareg boys have their hair shaved off but as teenagers grow it into plaits. The practice of some ancient Libyan tribes of trimming the hair into a crest was noted by Herodotus [*The Histories*, Vol. IV, p. 175]. Gustav Nachtgal in 1869 found Tebu boys' hair so treated and thought it gave them "a very droll appearance" [*Sahara and Sudan*, Vol. I, p. 211].

[31]Berber, *tarqia*, a skull cap.

ed] but they have no authority whatever and every one acts as free as the winds of heaven[32] – & then there cannot be a more convincing proof of the goodness of these people's dispositions than their good & moral conduct which is superior to that of all the Mohametans I have ever seen and were the fear of Hell fire and the laws removed us in Britian there would be few able to live in it and I look upon England as the Most blessed place on the face of this earth – it may be said that their gross superstition may make them so but this cannot be the case as they are surrounded by people on all sides of the same religion equally supersti-tous who are guilty of every vice and where it is not held to be so where rapine injustice & Murders are comitted with impunity and [the] guilty not looked upon as the worse for it – with such examples before their eyes – shows their dispositions to be realy good as nothing has such an affect it will be allowed as example

The Cadi is chosen by the Majority of the people but his situation [is] for life of course –

Their letters or characters[33] are as follows and are written either from the right or left and sometimes up & down

[3 page vocabulary – see Appendix 1.]

the people of Sockna Ghadamis Augela Speak the Berber tounge[34] Ghaat is in – Lat^{de} 24°-57-[ ] N by Mn Alt^{de} of For^{ht} and Long^{de} [ ] East by an Eclipse of the Moon and lunar obervations it is built on the point

---

[32]As Tuaregs are normally matrilineal, this shows the influence of Islamic practice. Where there was a Sultan – in Agadez, Ghat and elsewhere – social tensions surrounded this type of succcession. [H.T. Norris, personal communication.]

[33]Tifinagh, a system of writing the Tamasheq (or Tamahag) language of the Tuaregs.

[34]Berber languages or dialects of the Hamito-Semitic group are spoken all over North Africa, from Siwa oasis in the Western desert to Senegal, and notably by the Tuareg of the Sahara, in northern Algeria, in the Rif, Atlas highlands and south of Morocco, and in modern Mauritania. There is little or no intelligibility between dialects which have become much influenced by Arabic, Punic, Latin and sub-Saharan languages. Berber speech has been retreating for centuries in the face of the advance of Arabic.

of a rocky ridge of hills – that come from the Jinoon range – the town is built of mud & stone and walled around   the houses kept in good repair and the streets clean – it is about ¾ of a mile in circumference surrounded with high walls having 2 gates   one on the south side being walled up – the gate is large and high and in the walls are loop holes for musquetry – The town is well supplied with good water & outside the gates is a very copious spring of sweet water which serves to water a great number of gardens and fields without more trouble than making a channel to convey it to them – the Town was once on the top of the hill under or on the point of which the new one is built but from the giving way of the rock on which it was built   a number of the houses came down with it – and some of the inhabitants in them this made them build their nests where they now are some of which are now in danger should the rocks which over hang them give way

Their marriges   they buy their wives from the fathers giving as many as 8 or 10 camels for a wife if she is very handsome and so on   paying according to their beauty – but they court them first and Hatita told us that the young men & women made evening parties[35] – any young woman who wishes to give a party send[s] round to her friends and acquaintances that she will meet them at night in the desert where she will have mats spread   the[y] come on their Maheries every young woman attended by her lover or brother if she has one – they each bring a cushion and the women sitting in a circle on the mats sing and play on the Erbab[36] untill near morning & then return to their homes – Hatita said that the greatest propriety prevailed that any breach of indecency would be punished with death – They have nothing to eat or drink at these evening parties but the ladies & gentlemen take a drink of sour milk when they go home & go to sleep – he told me also that the young women sometimes are with child before marrige   when this happens her

---

[35]Tuareg social gatherings of men and women, with music, singing and flirting, take place either in the afternoon [*tendi*] or at night [*ahal*], as described by Clapperton. Both types characterize the relatively free but mutually respectful relationship between the sexes in Tuareg society.
[36]Guitar-like instrument, common throughout North Africa and the Sahara.

parents and relations give her a good drubbing and the father has to take care of the child – I suspected that Hatita had one child if not 2 in that way as he told me this himself and asked me what we did with them in our country[37] though he denied the charges   I could see he was a great wag amongst them   and as he has never been married – his brother Sidi Mohamed is not allowed to take a wife untill he does which is the case with all those who do not live in the towns the younger brothers can not take [a] wife smoke or eat unless his elder brother does the same   those living in the towns are not so particular

in their burials they do not bury the children in the same church yard [sic] as the growen up people but in a small one close by

They have only 4 horses at Ghaat & Barcat.[38]

---

[37]Clapperton's own situation – see Introduction, p. 39.

[38]Much traded across the Sahara from North Africa to the Sudan, horses became rare in the desert after the introduction and diffusion of the Arabian camel in the first Christian centuries. Although expensive to feed and maintain in the Sahara, horses were faster and more agile over short distances than even the best riding camels, and were thus valued and prestigious mounts. [Bovill, *The Golden Trade*, pp. 15-16].

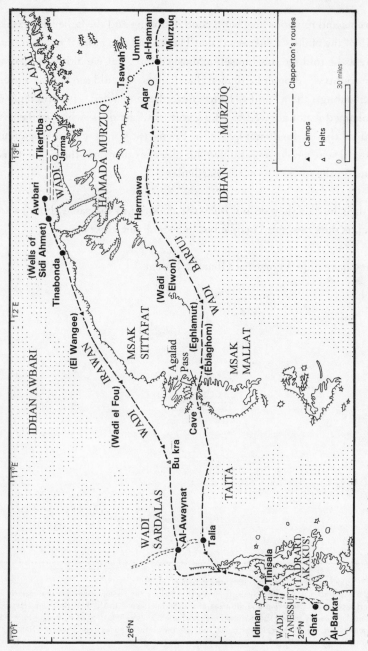

Map 8. Western Fezzan and the roads to Ghat II

CHAPTER

7

Return to Murzuq

Thursday August 1ˢᵗ 1822

Struck our tent at day light but could not get away untill 7-30. AM– the whole of our friends came out to take leave   amongst the rest was the Sultan himself – they said they were sorry they could not prevail upon us to stay but should we ever be so kind as [to] come back to them we should never want for friends & protection

at 11-15 after traveling over the same ground we had done when we went to Ghaat – we halted and took up our quarters under the wide spreading branches of our favourite Atilla that had proved such an excellent shade to us before and was now as willing and in as good condition as ever to do it again

we had just lain down to rest when we were joined by a Dervise[1]   his man Servant boy a camel & jackass   we had seen him at Ghaat & he told us there that he would accompany us to Fezzan where he was going to claim some property that was left to him – His name is Hadje Ahmet

---

[1]Use of the word 'Dervish' indicates the Ottoman connections of Clapperton's interlocutor(s); and 'black' normally indicates slave status. The traveller was probably a pilgrim attached to some sufi order (probably Karaziya, but the Sahara was rich in various Sufi orders from the sixteenth century onwards), and a native of Tuat who happpened to be born of mixed parentage. [H.T Norris, personal communication.]

a native of Tuat – and of black parents – he took up his quarters under
a neighbouring tree – and at three o'Clock in the afternoon we were
roused by the little boy of Hadje Ahmet calling the people to prayers as
if he had been calling from a Minaret or mouadan   the whole of our
mohametans attended except my servant who is by no means given to
praying but is as honest a man never the less as ever I have met with –
the rest of the people look upon this holy man comming as a great blessing and are sure we will prosper   after Sunset we were joined by Hatita
Sidi Mohamed his brother and young Lamem who we learnt with much
regret was not able to accompany us to Morzouk – as the whole of the
people of the town had come and begged him not [to] leave them fearing that he would go altogether   he is a most aimiable young man and
had gaind our friendship by his kindness mildness and the great desire
he had to learn every thing and particularly english of which he had
learnt a few words from us   he had read most of the Arab books they
have in the country which are but few[2] & traveled to Marocca and
Soudan & he expressed a great desire to accompany us in our travels
and return with us to England of which he has formed a high opinion
he is about 5 feet 9 inches high with particularly mild and intelligent
countenance [more so] than most of his countrymen but that may be
from his keeping himself cleaner – a great deal [more] than the rest

Friday 2nd

our friend Lemem left us at Day light   he had made us a present of a
very fine Soudan sheep that followed the Kaffle like a dog[3] and would
eat out of our hand

The D[r] young Ben Hadje & I set of[f] ahead of the Camels and arrived

---

[2]At that time books in Arabic were in manuscript (and therefore extremely rare and expensive),
the first printing presses arriving in the Arab World only in the 19th century, particularly through the
influence of Christian missions in the levant. [A. Hourani, *Arabic Thought in the Liberal Age, 1798-1939*,
(Cambridge, 1983) p, 63.]

[3]Sheep were capable of going 6 days without water [Richardson, *Travels*, Vol. II, pp 250-1]. See also
Bovill [*Golden Trade*, pp. 17-18 & n.] on the relative endurance of pack animals in the desert.

at the well of Tinasala at 11 A.M- very thirsty and not a little tired   we found [him][4] lying under an Atilla tree – we here drank very heartily of cold water which made me throw up a great deal which I thought was helped by some unripe peaches I had eaten at Ghaat a few days before and which had given me a pain in the Stomach

at 1 PM the Camels arrived and we having bought a sheep at Ghaat for 3$ we had it killed & gave our people & ourselves a feast – we found the Kuscassou & dates we had buried quite safe and untouched –

Made the Lat^de of the Well of Tinisala 25°-15'- [ ]" N by a Mn- Alt^de of Antares – & the Long^de by Eclipse of the Moon 10°-57' [ ] East of Greenwich[5] – we told the people there was going to be an eclipse that they might not be alarmed – Hatita says that the Tuaricks are not alarmed at an eclipse of the Sun or Moon being eclipsed but that they think they are sick when that takes place[6]

Saturday 3rd

at 5 A.M Sidi Mohamed Hatita's brother left us to join their people who are enc^d 4 days journey to the north^d of this place[7] he would have liked very much to have accompanied us to Mor[zuk] but Hatita would not allow he even durst not ask such is the respect they pay to the elder brother   Mohamed is a much stronger man than Hatita and taller with a bold resolute look and figure   he complained much that his brother would not Marry as he wanted to take [a] wife but could not – untill his brother did – he has been out on several of there [sic] war partys where he has got a great reputation for courage and ablities – he was allways

[4]Log: "Mohamed the Tuarick whom we had left in charge of our dates & Kuscassou".

[5]An estimate of longitude made by comparing the local time of the end of an eclipse (calculated here by an altitude of Antares) with the time for the end of the eclipse at Greenwich published in the Nautical Almanac. The result was a good one; the correct position being 25° 10' N, 10° 15' E.

[6]The diary of Abu Bakar b. al-Tahi Tashi, born 1657, in the "Agadez Chronicles" includes an account of the effects on the population of a solar eclipse and phenomena attributed to it [quoted by Norris in *Tuaregs and Islam* pp. 85-6].

[7]Log has "N.W.", i.e. at the northern end of Wadi Tanessuft.

kind and obliging while he was with us & he wished me much to stay with them – he is less orthadox than his brother Hatita whom he generally calls the Maraboot to us when he is away

at 5.20 AM. left Tinisala and traveled up the same road we came down by untill 3 PM when we turned into the hills   at first we could not perceive in what direction the pass lay as we saw nothing but steep rocky precipices on every side – at last we came to the foot of the mountains when there we could discover no pass for the camels there being only a narrow rugged & rocky & steep zigzag foot path made by nature and assisted by *art* as far as the rolling of a [number] of the lightest stones could assist or better it   we thought that camels never could look at such a path as this and were looking around to see what all this meant

we were soon made to understand that this was the pass by the camels braying and commencing their ascent – we walked behind to pick up any thing that might fall off and be ready to give any assistance   we found them *secured* much beyond our most sanguine expectations – but the least false step or jolting would have sent any of them to the bottom head long but the animals from instinct or some other cause know their situation and though a hand was placed at the head of each   camel it would only move at its own pace & when a place of steepness or crossed by a rock occured it would rest upon its fore knees keepin[g] the load on its back as even as possible [&] crawl over in that way –

about half way up Hatita's Mahery being the hindmost of the Kaffle I perceived a large number of ticks sticking on the off hind leg thin[kin]g this must give the animal a great deal of pain and weaken it I with a very simple and foolish heart stoop'd down and was *draging* them off when the offended beast gave a kick on the breast that sent me reeling against the rocks as much as to say take that for your humanity   had it been the near foot with which I had been kicked I would have been sent to glory before my time and lain at the foot of the rocks untill the day of judgement if the Kites and Ravens had not carried me away piece meal –

at 6- we got to the top from whence we had an extensive view to the Westward – observed that the hill of Jinoon formed part of a high range running N.W. by compass   at 7 P.M – halted – in what may be also called the pass – it being surrounded by Steep rocky hills which produce a beautiful echo – the pass is called El Lughlaghan – Course   N.NE 18   NE 3   E. [by] N. 2

Sunday 4th

at 5 AM – a beautiful morning we started our road still lying through the wady and the hills on each side gradually getting lower & opening more out into vallies – on which a few mimosas mixed with bushes of the agool grow   the dry beds of the mount[ain] torrents bear evidence of its raining heavily at times and the Tuaricks tell us that at times the whole of these wadys are covered with water – at 8.40 AM we arrived at the wady Talia & pitched our tent near a spring of good water – we here intend halting for the day to let the camels feed before we take [to] the desert again – this is a beautiful spot appearing just like a garden & the spring is covered over with trees that makes it look like a little bower which it is for if you chuse to sit round the spring you may enjoy the cool spring water in the shade but with all the joys of this world it has its dangers which here are snakes of a venomous kind called Liffa which here lay wait for the feathered tribe who may come to quench their thirst besides numbers of mosquitoes which fill this delightful bower with their song and I suppose *accomp*[y] the snakes in quality of nightingales as they like that vile reptile delight to live near Woody bowers and springs and prey upon the weary and luckless traveler – who may chance to prefer a bed of grass to a bed of sand –

it came on to blow very hard and it laid our tent level with the dust   we did not attempt to pitch it again but took shelter under some attilla trees at some distance from the well   our people employ[ed] filling the Gerbas

The low flat plains composing the desert from this part look like low hills rising above one another this is only a continuation of Wady Sirdiles in passing down the wady we passed some fine stratum [of] red and yellow ochre

E by N ½ N 2   SE 2 ½   E by S 3 ½

Monday 5ᵗʰ

owing to the usual delay of our camel men we did not get away untill 6 A.M– our road was over gravel & sand hills composed of a coarse slate at 12 – we had high Sand hills to the South at the distance of about a mile their marches appeared to be the low slate hills at 7 PM – we halted in the Taita or desert Course E ½ N 30 Miles

Tuesday 6ᵗʰ

at 3.30 A.M- Started – without breakfast our road lay over a gravelly plain untill 1 P.M- when we arrived amongst some [of] the detatched mounᵗˢ of the Fezzan range – in which there are a number of natural caves in the lower Stratum of Firestone[8] which lies above the slate & in one of these we took up our quarters & had some tea we were here joined by a – *Douro* – or begging Tuarick[9] we asked him where he was going he said he was just looking round – fellows of the kind frequent the roads leading to Soudan & Tumbuctoo and attach them selves to travelers as guests for 2 or 3 hundred miles – living upon them and begging for presents – this worthy appeared to be very well off having a good she camel loaded with provisions which he had got from a Kaffle going to Soudan & his wife attends his flocks in the mountains – his name is Hadad or Iron[10] – & he now travels with us –

---

[8] A soft calcareous sandstone [ShOED].

[9] Ar., *dawra*, to circulate. The *Ineden*, travelling tinkers or blacksmiths, or both, were a special class, rather despised – and feared, being supposed to indulge in suspect magical practices – but credited as story-tellers [H. T. Norris, personal communication].

[10] Ar., *haddad*, blacksmith.

at 3 PM we left the cave and entred the pass of the mountains by the dry bed of a Mountain torrent which they call the *Shakir* or street[11] as it is worn out of the solid firestone rock – about 50 feet wide in some places in others not above 12   the blocks being overhead sometimes to the height of some hundred feet formed a fine shade and beautiful echo   we were 2 hours winding up this place and at 5 PM we by a gentle ascent got amongst the highest of the hills which now form a wady opening to the East[d] called El Ughamoot[12]   we traveled on untill 8 P.M- when we halted for the night – our Course to the cave E by S. 18 – & from there to El Ughamoot 8 miles E by S ½ S

Wednesday 7th
(Started at 5.20 AM)   Morning fine and Clear   we found our selves in a fine wady with plenty of food for the camels – consisting of large tufts of grass and Tallah trees – they call this and Some of the road a head by way of conveniance the Mirrour[13]   however there are a number of Liffai amongst the grass   one of which our new companion the Duro killed with his spear   we examined his mouth & found the fangs which were of a good len[g]th   it is the same as described by Jackson[14] who I think has given a very correct drawing of it –

at noon we fell in with a Kaffle of Tuaricks going to Fezzan   they had left Ghaat 4 days before us but had delayed on the road for the purpose of enjoying our good company and partaking of our spare dates & Kuskassou   we found here 2 wells or holes of rain water   which the Tuaricks dig in the winter & the water continues in them through the year – at 5-40 PM. halted at the head of a mountain Wady called still El Ughamoot   our Course E by S ½ S 26 Miles   this Wady convey[s] the

---

[11]From the root word, Ar., *shaqq*, to cut across or traverse; cf. shaqirqa – a wady bed.

[12]"Elghom-ude, or the Valley of the Camel" – with its subsidiary, Wadi Telisaghe, the site of notable pre-historic rock engravings first described by Barth in 1850 [*Travels*, Vol. I. pp. 173 et seq.].

[13]Ar., *al-miraya*, a long stretch of open, flat desert.

[14]J. G. Jackson, *An Account of the Empire of Morocco* (London, 1820) – with an elegant drawing of the horned asp [Plate 3, facing p. 110].

winter rains from the East[a] side of the Mts & supplies the wells as far as Zuela[15] -

Thursday 8th

Morning Cool & Clear   at 5-40- Started   our road was over broken pieces of sand stone and some times in the wady when it lay in our way at 1 – P.M- we halted at a place called Elwon where there were two holes of water[16] – we did not pitch the tent but took our quarters up under a Tallah tree   great Nos of which with bushes of the agool grow in this wady and we pass a great no- of camels feeding on them – we could now barely see the Fezzan hills stretching to the Southd – and those on the north side had sunk in the horizon but descend gradually to this wady in a Stony plain   Course E ¾ S 16 Miles   this part of the wady is called Elwon

Friday 9th

Started at 5-30 A.M- we here were left by our Duro – which if he could mind [=mend] pots and pans or use the soldering iron at all – I should have called him a Tinker their mode of life being much alike the D[r] gave him a dollar & a few dates with which he was well pleased & he went to visit his wife who was feeding his flocks in the Mountains   our road the Same as yesterday we have high Sand hills about 5 Miles to the South on the north the stony deserts – at 6.30 PM. we halted on the plain   Course E ½ S. 28 Miles

Saturday 10th

at 5 A.M- Started our road the same as yesterday   at 5-30 P.M halted

---

[15]Incorrect. The end of this wady lies in the Harmawa district, some 30 miles west of Murzuq and 600 feet below the level of Murzuq, at the wells of Sharaba.

[16]Elawen, at the head of "the eternal Wadi Aberjush [Barjuj], with all its little side branches" [Barth, *Travels*, Vol. I, p. 170].

for the night in the wady   Course E by S   24 miles – this part of the Wady is called Harmawa

Sunday 11th   at 4-30 A.M- Started   at 7 AM we arrived among some low alluvial hills – after crossing which we had stragling date trees   at 4 P.M- we saw the Town of Agar bearing North 8 Miles   at 6-30 we arrived at Humum – we instantly despatched a man to Morzuk to send our horses out at day light and to acquaint them of our safe arrival as they had had many curious reports about us

We were soon surrounded by a no- of people   we bought some grapes & had some bazeen made but we could not get to sleep for all our long days march – at day light we sent for the camels which had been found at that time but they were not going to part with us on such easy terms The[y] accordingly kept them untill 7 oClock when we started – and at 9 am we had the pleasure of meeting Mr Hillman who had brought all the horses we arrived in town at 1 P.M –

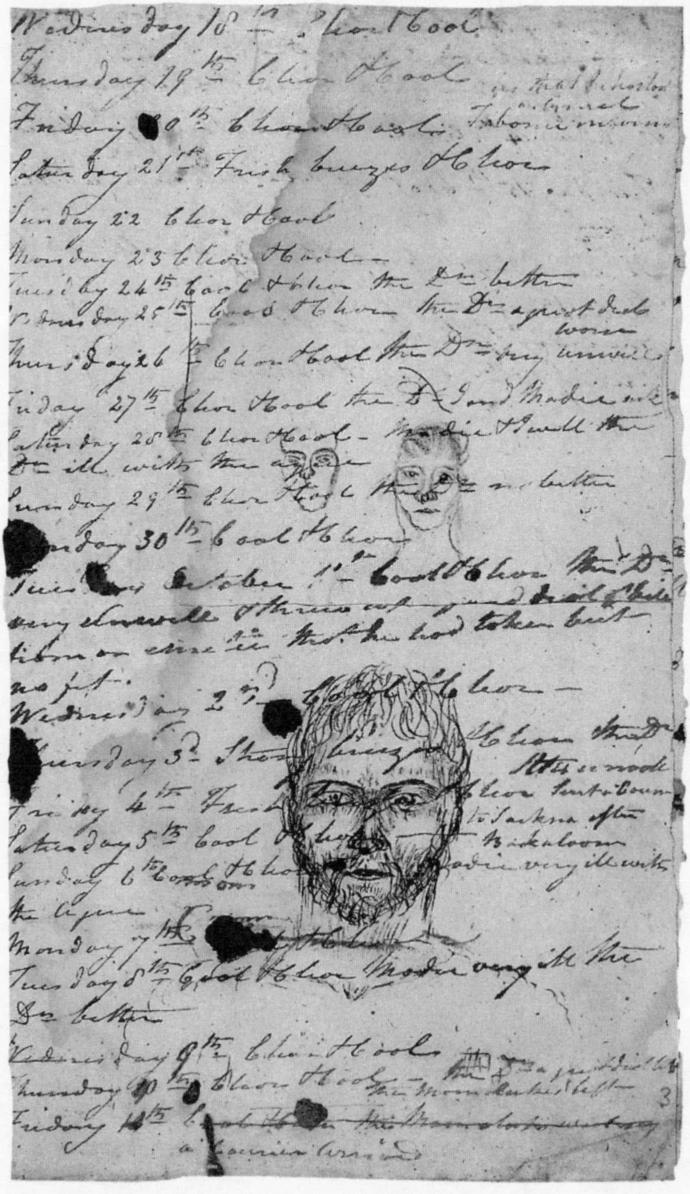
Wednesday 18th — Clear Cool
Thursday 19th — Clear & Cool
Friday 20th — Clear & Cool
Saturday 21st — Fresh breezes & Clear
Sunday 22 Clear & Cool
Monday 23 Clear & Cool —
Tuesday 24th Cool & Clear the Dr better
Wednesday 25th Cool & Clear the Dr a great deal worse
Thursday 26th — Clear & Cool the Dr very unwell
Friday 27th Clear & Cool the Dr and Madie [illegible]
Saturday 28th Clear & Cool — Madie & [illegible] the Dr ill with the ague
Sunday 29th Clear & Cool the Dr no better
Monday 30th — Cool & Clear
Tuesday October 1st — Cool & Clear the Dr very unwell [illegible]
[illegible]
Wednesday 2nd Cool & Clear —
Thursday 3rd [illegible] & Clear [illegible]
Friday 4th [illegible] Clear [illegible]
Saturday 5th Cool & Clear [illegible]
Sunday 6th Cool & Clear [illegible] Madie very ill with the ague
Monday 7th [illegible]
Tuesday 8th Cool & Clear Madie very ill the Dr better
Wednesday 9th Clear & Cool [illegible]
Thursday 10th Clear & Cool [illegible]
Friday 11th [illegible]

Figure 9. Remark book

CHAPTER
8

A summer in Murzuq

[Sunday 11ᵗʰ August continued]
we found that a courier had arrived bringing us the intelligence that the Bashaw was not yet preparing to send an escort or army into the interior we however found that a Kaffle was going to Bornou 14 days after the feast el Asser[1] to comemorate the meeting of the pilgrims at Mecca – and they would be glad of our company – they were the people of the Sheikh of Kanem who had arrived here with goods & Slaves on his account during our absence   My Lord Bathurst not approving of Mʳ Tirwhit's remaining here as our Consul   he is in consequence going down in 5 days – the Dʳ & I have offerd to make up the amount of his salary out of ours if he will remain as it will be of the greatest consequence to us   particularly if we go with the Kaffle as we intend   and in that case we will have to leave part of our goods behind which it will be necessary to foreward up to us –

During the time we have been away at the Wadys Shati Gharbi & Ghaat – the wind has from 8 AM– untill Sunset blown from the E.N.E. increasing grandually [sic] to Strong breeze & sometimes a gale about 2 PM – then gradually lul[l]ing to a calm after sunset and in the night veer

---

[1]The *Id al-Assura*, which celebrates the death of Hassan and Hussain, the sons of Ali, son-in-law of the Prophet, at the battle of Karbala in 680 A.D.. The *Id* fell on 27th August.

167

with light airs & Calms round to the South, West, & North The Thermometer in the heat of the day in the shade was very regular being 102° & 103° of Farnheit in the hottest time before sunrise 82° of Farnheit

in the Wadys where we halted in the heat of the day we used to Start as early as possible taking a cup of coffe breakfasted upon tea in the heat of the day and went to Sleep we were a great part of the time without sugar and at [the] last we were out of all but we found not the want of it on the road to Ghaat & back as there was no halting in the heat of the day we had generally Bazeen before day light 3 draughts of water between that time & sunset and then bazeen or Zurmeta – we felt no great inconvenience from this mode of Traveling & living and as we made greater progress & were more regular I would prefer it to the Arab way which is to halt in the heat of the day – we allways followed the example of the Tuaricks & had our bornouses wrapt round our heads to keep out the heat – had we not done this [we] would hardly have stood out 2 days

Monday 12th
Clear & Warm

Tuesday 13th
D"-

Wednesday 14th
Clear & Warm

Thursday 15th
D"-

Friday 16th
D"-

Saturday 17th
D"-

Sunday 18th
D"-

Monday 19th
Clear & Warm   Mr Tirwhit left at day light to return to Tripoli   we
accompanied him as far as Deliam a village 13 Miles to the E of Morzuk
where we parted   the D^r and I had offered to make up his salary from
our own if he would stay   as   in the event of our having to go to Bornou
and leave part of the baggage behind   he would be of the greatest service in forwarding our things up – and for keeping up a comunication
with Tripoli and us – but he said he would not think of it without Lord
Bathursts approval   he was very popular with all the inhabitants who
regreted his departure as much as we did

Tuesday 20th
Cloudy & cool   wind North

Wednesday 21st
Cool & Clear

Thursday 22nd
Cool & Clear   this Morning the whole of Morzuk was thrown into the

greatest alarm by a letter which Mohamed el Lizhari[2] received from the Son of the Sultan who was Murdered by Mohamed el Mukni the late Bey of Fezzan the letter was summoning Lizhari to come down instantly to Oubari where this person said he was with the whole of the people of *Ghaour*[3] with the people of Wady Shiati & Gharbi   and that he was comming to take possession of his late fathers kingdom and if Lizhari delayed an instant he would take his head of[f] –

I waited on Lizhari to offer my ass[tce]   I found him in his house surrounded by all the principal people of the Town and the letter in his hand   they all appeared in the greatest consternation and not knowing what to do – after sitting a little while during which time not a word was spoke I returned to the house where we thought it would be our most advisable plan to guard our own house in the event of an attack as we would have as much to fear from the maj[ority] of the towns people as we would have from the new Sultan & his men as we were well satisfied by the fickelness of the people and their dislike of the Bashaw's government   we accordingly got all our arms in order and loaded them determining to sell our lives dearly should we be attacked – in the meantime they began to collect the warriors of the town[4] – and as we had got all ready I went out to see their forces

at the Bab Sherer[5] or outer gate of the castle I found about 30 people with musquets sitting round the outside of the gate round a large wooden bowl with skin over it – to serve as a drum   this was struck with a

---

[2]Received in his capacity as acting Governor in Al-Ahmar's absence in Tripoli. Lizari was a principal Mamluk of Fezzan and close henchman of Al-Mukni and Yusuf Pasha Karamanli. Lyon records [*A Narrative*, pp. 250-2 & 268] that he had been one of the commanders of the expedition to Bagirmi in 1819; and that around this time Al-Mukni became jealous of him and Lizari feared for his life.

[3]It would not be surprising if rebellion was imputed by the Murzuq leadership to the Gharian Berbers who were the first of the tribes of the interior to rise up against Yusuf Pasha in 1803-5, declaring themselves free of the customary annual tribute and cutting off the road to Fezzan. As a result, the district was garrisoned by troops loyal to Yusuf Pasha. It was with these troops that Al-Mukni captured Murzuq and overthrew the Awlad Muhamad dynasty in 1811 [Folayan, *Tripoli*, pp. 47-52].

[4]The official guards (*bindags*) and others, such as the Mamluks, armed with muskets.

[5]Ar., *shara*, street.

stick like one of our big drum sticks every half minute – then came Lizhari from his house on horseback with [a] pocket handkerchief tied round his mouth & hanging over his chin   he waited a few minutes without dismounting while 6 horsemen (all they were able to muster in the town) made their appearance heading to the castle   he Gallaped out holding his musquet over his head with the but[t] to the approaching horsemen who were gallaping up to meet him holding the[ir] musquets in the same manner as he did calling ya walied ya walied which sounds in their quick manner of repeating it exactly like you lad you lad in english – which it Clearly is not or possibly oh boy or ah lad   when that group joined they rode round the town with a sort of drum beating before them the women particularly the elderly and ragged came out to encourage them with their cries of joy which [is] done by calling lo lo lo in a rapid and shril manner – at the same time waving their rags over their heads the Bindags or warriors ans⁣ᵍ in their cry of ya walied   If a man or englishman or any other european christian encounter them if he was frightened he would imagine that the infernal regions had sent forth a troop of furies and their male companions to seize upon him – to us who knew what was going on it afforded much amusement to see the old withered beldames waiving their rags over their heads and yelling as loud as they could to encourage the seven horse men the Flower of Fezzan who with their inefficient arms and doubtful courage would fly from an english dragoon for they would never stand his attack

-when they returned to the Bab-Sherer a brass 3-pᵣ was brought mounted on a carrige with *wood* and iron enough to make a carrige for a 4 ½ pᵣ – for this queer thing has neither spunge ram[m]er or scourer[6] and only pieces of old iron for shot – being willing to assist them Mᵣ Hillman our naval carpenter turned to and made them a spunge and rope scour but

---

[6]A term for the tool, fitted to one end of the rammer or sponge and often consisting of a coil of metal shaped like a spring with a sharpened point, which was used to dig out of the chamber of a gun any unburnt material which otherwise accumulated to form an increasing bulk, eventually preventing the flame from reaching the cartridge. [Brig. K.A. Timbers, Royal Artillery Historical Trust, Woolwich, personal communication.]

they having no iron for the ramer this could not be supplied – the Neapolitan Renegado was amongst the people at the Bab Sherer as drunk and insolent as drunken men generally are   he was abusing every one and calling them fools and cowards   when the vagabond had got drunk himself from fear

we got Lizhari up to our house to take a cup of tea – to be out of the way of the drunken Renegado who is his brother in law – he told us there were only 40 men in the town whom he could depend upon   I asked him if he had any provisions in the castle   he said no   I told him the best thing he could [do] would be to get all the provisions he could into the castle instantly   that as there were only 40 men upon whom he could depend upon   it would be no us[e] to attempt diffending the Walls of the town which were 3 Miles in circumference and in many places broken down – that he ought to have the 3 pounder at the inner gate of the castle and not to fire it untill they were close too [sic] – to repair all the breaches in the walls   send a man out to reconiter with orders to be back before sunset and as they had a well in the castle they could easily hold out untill the Bashaw sent a force to relieve them – as they could not possibly have any great guns to batter the walls down – all this he promised to do – and he sent off a man immediately to reconiter – in the evening the man sent to reconiter returned having been 15 Miles to the westd wihout seeing an enemy

as soon as it was dark – we sent our servants out and we dug a hole in the floor and buried all our valuables   this plan we adopted from the advice of Hatita who also said that when the enemy came we should sit down and take no notice of anything but be scratching holes in the sand with our hand   this last advice we were not determined to follow but as soon as they began with us we should turn upon them and if they forced our house   to sell our lives as dearly as possible   Mr Hillman having compleated their gun carriage repairs and made them a rammer and spunge with a bit of coir they fired it off at sunset – and two or three times during the night –

[Friday 23rd]

we slept very little and at daylight when we went to the Bab Sherer we found the Bindags had been up all night and looking very very tired for want of sleep we had heard them beating the large bowel [sic] or Noba as they call it[7] all night – they sent 2 horsemen out at 8 AM to reconitre – who returned in the evening without having seen an enemy they went a few miles beyond Humum which is 15 Miles West of this place on the road to wady Gharbi where the letter said the lawful Sultan and his army were encamped –

we had a great many applications for powder and ball none of which we complied with to some [of] them I put flint into their pistols as we had plenty of them and to spare – the same noise and dust was carried on in the town to day as yesterday but the [gates] were all kept shut and visited by the Bindags hourly – in the heat of the day the town might have been taken by boys – as all hands went to sleep except in our house to which we kept very close only going out one at a time to hear the news and see how they were getting on

Saturday the 24th

the Morning presented the same scene as the two former days only the Bindags were talking very big at the enemy not making their appearance and two horse men were sent out at day light with orders to go as far as Tesawa if possible and inquire of the Maraboot who commands the town[8] the number of the enemy and where they were that if they had not left the wady Gharbi to send a Tuarick as a spy to see what they were about and if they were gone any other road –

later in the afternoon they returned as fast as their horses could carry them bringing intelligence that they had been at Tessawa where the

---

[7] Ar., *nawba* – a ceremonial drum.
[8] See Sunday 9th June above

Maraboot took them out to view the camp of the enemy at [a] short distance from the town   they found their immense force to consist of the Son of the former Sultan and an old man who was driving his camel they were encamped under a date tree with a large pot of Lackbi between them   a beverage his [=he] is very fond of   and it being very strong and supplied in great quantities to him at Oubari – in his cups he had thought himself commanding a large army and so sent the formidable and threatening letter to Lizhari – which had caused the inhabitants of Morzuk and us so much trouble and Alarm and money – he was comming here to se[e] his mother[9] who lives here with two or three daughters who are very profuse in their favours to any one that will give them a dollar – but now he had to decamp with his army and go to Ghaat to be out of the Bashaw's power   who could instantly take his head off if ever he is caught after this maneauvre – the night was rejoicing and feasting – and we were not the least happy people in the town   and though I should have liked very well to see a little fighting after so much trouble yet I am of [the] opinion that we have been more fortunate as we could have been plundered by friends & foes

Sunday 25th

This was a day spent in rejoicing by all the inhabitants of Morzuk except the mother of the drunken scamp who was the cause of all our fears & tribulations

Monday 26th

bought 3 Camels

---

[9]That is to say, a wife of the late Sultan Muntasar, still residing in Murzuq after the coup against the Awlad Muhammad dynasty.

Tuesday 27th

gave the carcases of 2 Sheep & a portion of wheat to the poor on account of the feast of El Asser   in the evening they fired the four [sic] pounder and a great many musquets

Wednesday 28th

Early in the morning the people were dressed in their best – paying and receiving visits   the boys of the town dressed in their fathers cloaths gallaping about the town on asses & horses &^c   the principal inhabitants visited us & we gave them coffee   the four pounder was fired several times during the day – & in the evening we set off 5 rockets[10] to the great amasement of the whole town   Hatita & the nephew of the Sheikh El Kanemi[11] were with us when we set them off

Thursday 29th

Clear & Warm

Friday 30th

D"-

---

[10]The Mission had a supply of Congreve rockets. Primitive rocket technology had reached Britain from India at the end of the 18th century. Sir William Congreve improved on this, developing rockets with explosive or incendiary warheads, explosions being timed by trimming the fuse to the appropriate length before launching. Congreve made eight different sizes of rocket, weighing up to 60 lbs. and with a range of up to two miles. They were used in many engagements in the Napoleonic Wars and in the American war of 1812. There were further post-war improvements.

[11]No further detail emerges in the Mission papers, but probably a maternal relation. Murzuq was a regular home of members of Al-Kanami's family. Al-Kanami, whose mother was the daughter of an Arab merchant of Murzuq, was born in Fezzan [L.Brenner, *The Shehus of Kukawa* (Oxford, 1973), p. 49]; he owned property – houses and date plantations – there, and, as we know from the Mission's susbsequent affairs, one of his wives and at least two children were certainly in Murzuk in 1823. [Folayan, *Tripoli*, pp. 80 & 94-5].

Saturday 31ˢᵗ
Clear & Warm

Sunday Septʳ 1ˢᵗ 1822
Warm & Clear

Monday 2ⁿᵈ
Clear & Warm

Tuesday 3ʳᵈ
Clear & Warm

Wednesday 4ᵗʰ
Clear & Warm   news arrived of a Kaffle having arrived at Gatrone from Waday[12] and of their having had a battle with the Tibboos of Borgoo wherein 15 of the Unfortunate Mamelukes who had fled from upper Eygipt[13] had been killed & severall Trabolizes[14] & Fezzaners

Thursday 5ᵗʰ
clear & warm

---

[12]Before the slaving Sultanate of Wadai opened a direct trans-Saharan link to the Mediterranean at Benghazi via Kufra and Awjila, its links with North Africa were either through Darfur and the Nile valley, or by the roundabout road through Borku and Tibesti to Fezzan. As this second road was particularly long and dangerous, slave caravans rarely used it once the direct Benghazi link had been firmly established in the 1840s.

[13]The cause of the trouble in Borku was a quarrel about a servant of the Mamluks having cut down date trees [Log]. See Chapter Two, n. 6.

[14]The people of Tripoli.

Friday 6th

clear & warm   a courrier arrived from Tripoli with – letters from the Colonial Dep^{t} & Consul Genl Warrington – & to our astonishment we learnt that Major D– Denham had left Tripoli for England – without writing me a scrap or leaving me any instructions that Bk^{m} was app^{d} to conduct us to Bornow^{15} – we had all packd up ready for starting after the Aid Kerbeer^{16}

Saturday 7th

Clear & Warm

Sunday 8th

D"-

Monday 9th

D"-

Tuesday 10th

Fresh breezes & Clear   Lizhari being a little merry this afternoon – he told us by the way of adding to his mirth that he had put to death the Sheikh of Sockna some 6 years ago by the Bashaws orders – & also 7 of the Walid Sulimans by Muknis [orders]   so much for the customs of the countries – in one the office of executioner is held as infamous in others as honourable   I inquired of others the truth of what our worthy friend had said & had it confirmed from others   indeed I never had reason to impeach his veracity much

---

[15]See Introduction, p. 26 and letters in Appendix I; also Friday 11th October.

[16]The Islamic year was 1238 A.H, and the next major festival would have been the *Id al-Mawlid*, celebrating the birthday of the Prophet, falling on 12th of *Rabi al-Awal* (i.e. 26th November); but the reference here might have been to a local festival falling in the intervening period.

Wednesday 11th
Clear & fine

Thursday 12th
D"-

Friday 13th
Clear & Cool

Saturday 14th
D"– Lizhari borrowed our horses to go out & meet the Mamelukes

Sunday 15th
Clear & Cool

Monday 16th
Clear & Cool   we visited the Mamelukes in company with Lizhari &
Boubuker – they were seated in the window and a No– of the Morzukies
were there some as spies & others – as idlers   their No– is now reduced
to 5 – and 2 Beys are of the N^o Ali Bey – & Mohamed Bey   the other
3 are common Mamalukes they are all Circassians – & fine looking men
Mohamed bey in particular

Tuesday 17th
Clear & Cool   we were visited by the Beys to day – the other 3
Mamelukes as also some of their slaves were armed and carefully
guarded all the doors – allowing no one to pass in unless we ordred it –
we treated them with coffe to which they said they had long been

strangers – Ali Bey whispered in my ear to give him a little Argula which we call rum *of Tripoli*   I told him we had none but that we would send them a little wine & rum in the evening – they are much afraid of going to Tripoli & say they want much to go to England as firmans are out against them through all the Grand Senyors dominions   they begged our advice as to what they should do

Wednesday 18th
Clear & Cool

Thursday 19th
clear & Cool

Friday 20th
Clear & Cool   in the Afternoon the Man whom we had hired to take care of the camels Abdullah Taboun an Arab – came & told us that he was a camel short   that he was short of one camel & that our servants had not brought the proper N°. out – the servants swore that [they had] taken him out 13   we sent for Lizhari who sent for Mr T. to the [ ] where he said he would soon find out the truth   they applied the Bastinado which had the desired effect when he confessed he had sold one of our best camels to [a] Tibbo who had gone to Bornou   he is to be kept in prison untill he pays the ammount

Saturday 21st
Fresh breezes & Clear

Sunday 22nd
the Dr taken ill with the head aches & pain in the bones & Chest & loss of appetite

Monday 23rd
Clear & Cool

Tuesday 24th
Cool & Clear   the Dr Better

Wednesday 25th
Cool & Clear   the Dr a great deal worse

Thursday 26th
Clear & Cool   Dr no better

Friday 27th
Clear & cool   the Dr ['s] complaint turned into an ague   Madie my servant & Myself taken ill

Saturday 28th
Clear & cool   Dr still very unwell   Madie & I a little better

Sunday 29th
Clear & Cool   the Dr no better

Monday 30th
Cool & Clear

Tuesday October 1ˢᵗ 1822 –
Cool & Clear   the Dʳ very unwell & threw up a good deal of bile from an Emetic[17] that he had taken but had no fit

Wednesday 2ⁿᵈ
Cool & Clear

Thursday 3ʳᵈ
Strong breezes & clear   we are all very unwell

Friday 4ᵗʰ
Fresh breezes & Clear   sent a courrier to Sockna to see if B-km had arrived there & if he was not there to wait 4 days & then return with all speed & we would set off to Bornou without him – he was to have left Tripoli on the 15ᵗʰ Sepᵗʳ according to the Consul's letters

Saturday 5ᵗʰ
Cool & Clear

Sunday 6ᵗʰ
Cool & Clear   The Dʳ very ill with the Ague as also madie my servant

Monday 7ᵗʰ
Cool & Clear

---

[17]Oudney used a treatment of epsom salts with 3 grams of emetic tartar in tamarind water to relieve the symptoms of his consumption [*Missions*, Vol. II, p. 395].

Tuesday 8ᵗʰ
Cool & Clear   Madie very ill   the Dʳ better

Wednesday 9ᵗʰ
Clear & Cool

Thursday 10ᵗʰ
Clear & Cool   the Dʳ a great deal better

Friday 11ᵗʰ
Cool & Clear   a courrier arrived from B-k.m & Major D– the latter having been overtaken at Marsallies by a courrier that informed him an escort had been appointed & he has returned in time to join it

Saturday 12ᵗʰ
Cool & Clear

Sunday 13ᵗʰ
Cool & Clear   Mʳ Hillman the Naval Carpenter taken ill

Monday 14ᵗʰ
Cloudy   Hillman much worse

Tueday 15ᵗʰ
Cool & Clear   Hillman better

Wednesday 16th

we are all a little better to day

Thursday 17th

Cool & Clear

Friday 18th

Cool & Clear   From this day to the

2nd of November

I was unable to write from the severe Ague that I had

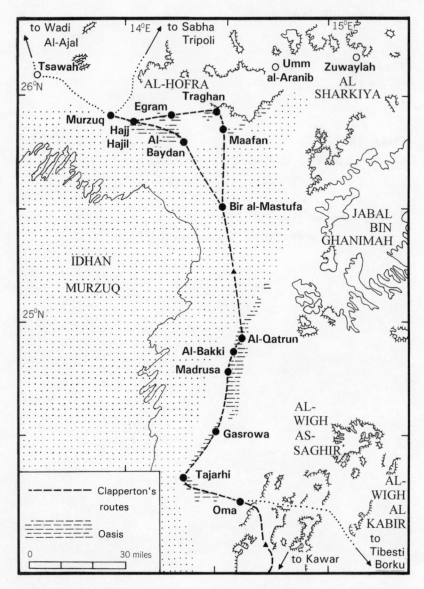

Map 9. Southern Fezzan

184

CHAPTER
9

Southern Fezzan

[Sunday 17ᵗʰ November][1]

We left with 29 Camels[2] leaving one behind by mistake besides that for M[ajor] D– baggage

Monday 18ᵗʰ

having been all ready for some weeks before and the camels arriving late last night we commenced loading at day light our Howdas or saddles[3] for the camels which have come up from Tripoli being at Bookalooms they denied them when we sent for them wishing to put off our departure for some days more – though we had waited 3 days since the appointed time – for our final departeur from Morzuk – and though the Bashaw since Bookalooms arrival had sent up orders for him to start on the 15ᵗʰ and if unable to send his brother – if he did not comply he was to lose his head

---

[1]Clapperton made no diary entries from 3rd to 17th November. He may have suffered a relapse (see 2nd November, above) or been preoccupied with preparations for departure or both; in any event, the first page of this journal is left blank - and any notes on loose paper have become lost.

[2]As well as for baggage, camels were needed to carry water (six 50lb gerbas each) to support the horses on passages between wells - on average one camel per horse [Lyon, A *Narrative*, p. 93]. See Chapter Five, n. 21.

[3]Ar., *hawdaj*, a palanquin (for a lady) or litter; a widespread term, taken, for example, into Urdu as *howdah*, and by extension or local usage here, a pack-saddle.

after some squabeling between our servants and the brothers of Bookaloom we got their saddles and – at 3 P.M– we left Morzuk – I rode out of the town alone before the camels after having taken leave of all our friends and in a little time I was joined by the D^r & Mr Hillman – Major D– prefering to stay behind and to come with B–k–m – Karaka & the sheikh of the Bahr al Ghazale & a native of Borno – to both of whom we had been as kind as our circumstances would admit particularly to the latter who stood much in want of it – the D^r said that B.k.m. had visited him before he left the house and said that his brother Hadje Ali should join us at Hadje Hajel with the camels and that he would leave Morzuk on Friday – after the afternoon prayers which I had suspected & told Major D– would be the case when I saw we did not start last Friday wither he keeps his word this time or not time will only show – but I doubt him much – at 5 P.M. we halted about ½ a mile south of Haje Hagel – Hadje *Ibrahim Ali Golliah* the greatest miser in Morzuk sent us a basket of cakes

Tuesday 19th

at 6 A.M Started and at 2 P.M– we arrived at Egran – as we passed the Maraboot of Sidi Busheer at Hadje Hajel our servants begged us to give them some thing as an offering at the shrine of this saint to ensure a safe journey as it is customary for all travelers on going or returning to do so the D^r gave a dollar which was taken by the servants & presented at the place to b[u]y fowels & wheat to be given to the poor– it is a shabby looking place close to Haji Hajel on the south side of the road – at Egran we were waited on by part of our escort who were encamped there – they are Arabs of the tribe Magerha[4] (they made no secret that they were sent to take slaves and that they had brought Irons for securing the prisoners [)] they wished to saddle them selves upon us but we referd them to B-k-m

---

[4]The Magarha is an important Arab tribe based on the Wadi ash-Shati and the adjacent Zallaf palm groves, but nomadizing as far north as the heads of the great Wadis Zam Zam and Bey al-Kabir, between the Hamada al-Hamra and the Sirtica. This pugnacious tribe's usual hostility to the Awlad Sulayman and its allies was exploited by both the Turkish and Italian conquerors of Fezzan.

Wednesday 20th

at 8 A.M started for Tragh[an]   we were accompanied by our Arab
friends who do not like to part with us – and as I forgot to Mention
before – the Wife of Major D– serv[ts] and ["another Male & Female"
deleted] and 2 other freed blacks – a male & female who are going to
their country – the wife of Barca and the other woman are going to
Wady – the Man to Gobir[6] in Soudan – we have also 2 Orfilly Arabs
["who accompany us to" deleted] &   3 Fezzaners to take care of the
camels besides Jacob the Jew the late servant of Major D– who has
brought up a new servant from Tripoli – so the D[r] has taken the jew
more out of compassion than the use he will be of – at 12–50 we arrived
at Traghan – we got well supplied with provisions from our old friend
the Marabo[ot]   M[r] Hillman is again taken ill and complains much of
his head too – also Madie my servant has got another attack of the ague –

Thursday 21st

Morning Cold & Clear – after break fast we were waited on by our old
Friend the Maraboot Hassun[7] – who had supplied us & our cattle with
a good store of provisions – for us bazeen for our servants Fatat & for
the horses & Camels Gussub & dates we also purchased a bag of the
round and good dates called mug mugs[8] to eat on the road after making
a bad breakfast – and when we could not halt to make a dinner – ["11.3[0]"
deleted] we made the old man a present of about a pound of coffe he Asked
for some sugar but we excused ourselves giving as we had very little   Major
D– having brought up but 2 loaves – we gave him 4$ for the prov[isions]
he had sent us – and treated him and his attendants to a cup of coffe each –

---

[5]Barca returned to Fezzan in 1824 with a new wife, Zalegi, and 8 slaves. [See List of Merchants,
Appendix IV and Tuesday 28th September 1824].

[6]An ancient Sudanic Kingdom, on the western fringe of Hausaland, which from 1818 had been in
rebellion against the Caliphate of Sokoto. [See D. M. Last, *The Sokoto Caliphate*, (London 1971); H.
Clapperton, *Journal of a Second Expedition*, (London, 1829) pp. 186-8, 207].

[7]See Thursday 2nd May 1822.

[8]Perhaps a local name; many varieties are grown in Fezzan, "an irreplaceable form of food there,
serving equally the needs of men and animals" [Nachtigal, *Sahara and Sudan*, Vol. I, p.116]. The dates
were compressed into large, dense blocks for transport.

at 11–30 A.M the Dr & the camels set off and I remained behind with one of the men to take a Mn Alt^{de} of the Sun – which made the Lat^{de} of Traghan 25°–54'–52" N – at 1 P.M– I came up with the camels I found Mr. Hillman very ill so much so that he was obliged to be supported on the mule to prevent his falling off – he complains of great pain in the head & weakness   poor Madie was also very ill at starting but Barca's wife who is a bold looking queen laid hold of him & forced him   and I made him ride my horse

after traveling over the salty plain   which in some places looked like a ploughed field and in other places like mud or ice   at 2 P.M– we arrived at Maafen which consists of a ruinous village made of – mud houses and some of the branches of the date tree –   the Sheikh told us that it was once a flourishing place but that the Bashaw had taken the herds of the greatest number and all those who possessed any money lost their hous-es   he made the attack on the Ougla⁹ Arabs for cheating him of the date tax   these unfortunate people were of that tribe and carried on a great trade to Soudan and other parts –   now there is no trader amongst them and all they possess are the date trees which they say are no good–   we bought a Sheep for 2$ and got dates & Gussub for our horses & camels – in the evening Hillman and Madie much better –   there is a stripe of date trees to the south of the Salt plain – about ½ a mile in breadth   the water at Maafen very good

Course from Treghan to Mafan by C^{a} [=compass] South 5 Miles – Lat^{de} by Mn Altde of Formalhaut 25°–51 –10" N

Friday 22nd

at 9 A.M– left Maafen and after passing through the date trees which run about ¼ of a Mile to the South of the town – we came amongst sand hills and sand plains – over which we had not unpleasant traveling par-ticuly as Hillman & Madie were a great deal better –   I gave Madie my horse to ride and walked –   near sunset it got very cold with a north^{ly}

---

⁹Walid Awjila, whose homeland is the oasis of Jalu in Cyrenaica. Bu Khallum was of this tribe.

wind and as there was not a blade of grass or particle of wood or drop of water we had to travel untill 8 PM – we ["arrived at Mesitootar" inserted] only pitche[d] one tent and all went under it – Man & beast in our Kaffle were both tired & hungry – I was threatened with an attack of the ague – Course S.SW – 29 miles

Saturday 23rd

Cold & Clear Hillman very ill and delirious – about a mile due South of our encampment stands the ruin of a large Moorish castle having been built of sun dried bricks & has been surrounded by a ditch with square flanking towers at the corners – near it there is a well of very excellent water – the castle stands a[t] the S.W end of a fine Oasis – of about 6 miles in length and 4 in breadth plenty of grass & bushes of the agool growing over it –

we rested today on account of Hillman who is very ill sent the camels out to feed on the Oasis had the sheep killed & gave our men a feast as they have all behaved very well

Noon Mn Alt^{de} Suns Lower limb gave the Lat^{de} 25°–30–56" N in the night our dogs kept up a continued barking which we could not account for our people said that it was Foxes that smelt the blood of the sheep we had killd but we thought it was Tibbo people come to steal our camels– I got up and followed the dog[s] who led me to the fresh tracecs of a camel at about a Mile from the tents this put our men on the alert and a guard on the camels all night

Sunday 24th

Cold & Clear at 8–20 AM Started crossing the Oasis near the centre we entred upon a plain of sand having low ridges of quartz rock running in an East & West direction lightly covered with sand – which scored the feet of both horses & Camels – we saw the fresh traces of a Kaffle going to Morzuk that had passed us in the night – after noon we came on to a beautiful level plain of sand – outside the Oasis there is not the slightest blade of grass or shrub

at 4.20 P.M– Mr Hillman not being able to go any further we halted for the night   Amp^{de} not well defined over the horizon being cloudy 258° *Kator*[10]   Lat. Mn Alt. Form^t [=Formalhaut] 25°–13– 44" N   Course South 18 miles

Monday 25th
Morning cold & Clear   Mr Hillman very unwell Madie better   there being neither food for the camels or water for us we could not stay for Hillman – & at 7–50 A.M– we started 2 of the camel men walking on each side of the mule & supporting him to prevent his falling off Madie not being so unwell rode my horse   our road was over the same level Sandy plain which in the after noon changed to long ridges like the swell of a long rolling sea on the south side of the ridges the sand was light and soft the camels sinking in some places mid leg deep   it is owing to the finest sand blown there by the last gale – and a strong breeze from the Southd would blow it on the north side where it will ly [=lie] untill shifted by another gale –

the camels at first were affraid to cross – but after they had got over the first they did not stop at any of the others   one of our camel men of the name of Ali who has been 4 times at Waday once at Bornow, and twice at Soudan says that near Waday there are places in the sand that neither man or beast can travel over – that if the[y] attempt they sink and are

---

[10]Amplitude describes the difference between 90° east or west and the azimuth of the sun at the theoretical rising or setting above the horizon; used in calculations, with appropriate tables and corrections, to calibrate a magnetic compass, here before setting out on the long desert journey [*Admiralty Manual of Navigation* (London, 1955), Vol. III, pp. 239-243]. Clapperton was using an hygrometer, designed by Lieut. Henry Kater, an engineer and inventor serving with the British Army in India, to measure the effects of humidity on terrestrial refraction [W.E. Knowles Middleton, *Invention of the Meteorological Instruments* (Baltimore, 1969), pp. 100-01].

lost for ever – that he has been on the edge of some where he has sunk in with one leg to the thigh while the other leg has been on firm ground – on asking him if there was water underneath he said yes but I suppose he thought we wished such an answer

at 4 we came in Sight of the date trees surrounding Gatrone[11] and descended into a level plain composed of clay sand & gravel in traveling over which one of our heavy loaded camels broke into a hole with its near fore leg the off one falling out before its body – it was quickly unloaded and the people dug away to bend the other leg under the body & then hauled the other out of the hole fortunately the poor animal had received no injury and it was loaded & proceeded on as if nothing had hapnd had the same incident happened to a horse or mule he would have either had his near leg broke or the off shoulder out of joint – but the camel though to appearance is a very stiff looking animal it has the most flexible joints of any large animal I have ever seen at [ ] Tufra Soft sand at 5–40 P.M– we halted on the south side of Gatrone poor Hillman was so ill that I had to carry him into the tent in my arms like a child –

we sent into the town to the Maraboot who is the greatest man here for food for our selves & Cattle – and were soon supplied with bazeen & Kuscassou one of our camels having had a premature birth in the morning when loading the life was in the young animal and that was all– when its throat was cut in the name of god & brought away by our Mohametan servants & camel men & at night they have made a feast only giving the neck & entrails to the dogs the feet were just put in the fire for a few minutes then taken out the ashes & dirt slightly rubed off and then eaten with great relish – if properly dressed I dare say they

---

[11]Al-Qatrun, the foremost of four small, impoverished settlements along the Wadi Ekema and Fezzan's most southerly outposts on the Central Saharan road to Lake Chad. A floating Tubu population lived in palm huts outside the walled village. George Lyon was at Al-Qatrun in December 1819 and again in January 1820, finding that "the language of Bornu" was more widely spoken than Arabic [*A Narrative*, p. 224]. Gustav Nachtigal visited in 1869 and again in 1870 – see in particular *Sahara and Sudan*, Vol. I, pp. 200-08, with plate on p. 202.

would have made a very rich dish for people who like such things – I certainly should have tried the taste of it but my mind revolted at the Idea of eating an animal just reeking from its mother's womb –

Course S. by W. 22 Miles

Tuesday 26ᵗʰ

Morning Cold & Clear – Mr Hillman no better – sent the camels out under the charge of the 2 Orfillas to feed on the Agool – which is in this neighbourhood in great plenty   we had bazeen sent us for breakfast by the Sheikh but so bad we could not eat it – Noon took a Mn Alt^{de} which makes Gatrone in 24°–53′–15″ N –

we had a visit from the Maraboot whose name ["& style" inserted] is Sidi Hadje Mohamed Rashid   he is a black man of the middle size   about 50 years of age with a short white beard & a pleasing countenance   he possesses all the trees & granaries in and near the town & [is] therefore looked upon as a very great man –   he by his own account has been a great traveler and visited Soudan Waday & Bornou sev^l times   he asked kindly after C^a L^{12}– & if he was well and where he was –   he said he thought the world was near an end as Mislem fought against Mislim   & spoke much against the present Sultan whose squeezing gripe he had felt & made to launch out 300 $ and feed his army in their stay here on their going and returning from the late expedition   he is troubled with the rehumatism & sore eyes – for which the D^r is going to give him some medecine – we treated him to a cup of coffe – he was very free and affable in his manners –   it being the feast of Milood the people of the town kept dancing & singing all night & beating on the drums & Gangahs^{13}

in the evening Hillman little better

---

[12]Captain George Lyon – see Introduction pp. 15-17 & n. 67.
[13]Gungaa: for a description see Saturday 7th December.

Wednesday 27th

Cold & clear Hillman very unwell people empld repairing the *Hawdahs* or Camel saddles and restuff[ing] them with straw evening Cold & Clear Hillman no better evening Amp^{de} 265° – 30'

Thursday 28th

Cold & Clear[14] Hillman still very unwell – at 4–30 PM– Haje Ali the Brother of Bookaloom & his slaves arrived on horse back they had been dispatched by Bookaloom & Major D– to our defences they fearing as they had broken faith with us that we would set of[f] without them which from our former movements having allways taken place when we appointed a time – they feared that it would be so now but the illness of poor Hillman has put a stop to it this time and Bookaloom and the Majors staying is rather a fortunate event than otherwise

Friday 29th

Cold & clear Hillman little better – this evening our servant[s] made a complaint that the Maraboot M. had threatened to beat the D^m Servt & that for demanding the wood he had brought from a woman who refused to give it to him that a poor lad who had accompanied us from Traghan had been refused admittance into the Mosque because he had been working for us on the day of the feast – he said that they told him to go with the infidels –

– in the evening they complained to us in a body and said they could not think of being mocked for serving the Shaitan[15] we thought it was a trick of B–k–ms Cⁿ [= Captain] to make himself of consequence with respect to the beggar from Traghan I told them that must be a falsehood for on walking through the town on the same day on which he said he was insulted – the Mouaddan or person who calls the people to prayers

---

[14]The entries for 28th, 29th and 30th November were probably made all at one time, as Clappperton's entries here are made over and around, evenly-spaced, pre-written dates.

[15]Ar., *shaitan*, Satan, the devil.

was very pressing for me to go into the Mosque but I excused myself as I would have to pull my boots off – and as to the Mar^{bt} threatening to Bastinado the D^{rs} serv we said that he must have been doing some thing very bad or he would never have done such a thing but we would enquire in the morning –

Hillman a little better

Saturday 30th
Cold & Clear   after breakfast we went & waited on the Maraboot taking with us the D^{rs} servant and one of the camel men – when we told him what we were come about [he] said he had the power to bastinado the man for he had talked to him with more impertinence than even Mukni or the Sultan Mustapha had done and with an air of greater authority with respect to their being insulted by the people of the town for serving the christians we must be conscious that must be a false hood as no one in the town that he knew & he knew them all but what were our friends – and told the people to bring forward the people who had used the insulting language to them – this neither the Traghanite or the s[erv]^t could do – so we convinced them that we knew it to be a falsehood – for the people had ever behaved to us with the greatest kindness and attention   Mohamed the D^{rs} servt– got a severe reprimand from his Master – and the Traghanite was sent about his business after begging as many dates & as much wheat as would last him to Traghan – I   had I had my will would have given him a beating & sent him back – but the D^{rs} christian virtue would not follow my advice – we today bought dates for our camels – to feed on in the desert

about 8 P.M– a dispute between Hadje Ali[16] and the Major's late Servant the Jew Jacob arose about an Iron oven for boiling the kettle the Jew

---

[16]Hadje Ali Bu Khallum, brother of Abu Bakr, who accompanied Clapperton and Oudney to Wadi Gharbi [Saturday 8th June 1822 *et seq.*].

having bought it the day before for us – Hadje Ali being half drunk said
that he had bought it this afternoon   I called the Jew to be silent but he
either did not hear me or was too much engaged in dispute to atend – at
last they got from little begin[ning]s to very high words when Hadje Ali
insulted the Jew by calling him infidel and the other replied by damn-
ing the prophet   this was quite enough for the whole of the Mislems
were up in arms in a mom' & the drunken Whelp Hadje Ali flew to me
to interfere & punish jacob for insulting his religion – I paid no attention to him but went out & ordered my servant out of the ["sun" delet-
ed] way into my tent and told him in the hearing of the whole to get my
pistol ready – The D' Came out also & we got the peace made up for the
night by Hadje Ali & the Jew making friends – this little drunken
wretch I firmly believe has caused these disturbances on purpose – –
however the Jew had he been in Tripoli would if not put to death on the
spot would have had to turn Misslem or have his throat cut –

Sunday December 1ˢᵗ 1822

Cold & clear   Hillman a great deal better this Morning   the D' is sending Jacob back to Tripoli as it would not be safe to take a person with us
who had offered such an insult to the faith of our – servants & those
whose friendship we were bound to cultivate however bad they were[17]

Monday 2ⁿᵈ

Cold & clear   we found that some of our camels had got the itch ["or
Jerab"[18] inserted] which our servants had been too lazy to inform us of
before – at 4 P.M– part of [the] escort arrived[19] consisting of one horse-
man & 6 footmen Arabs – They do not deny their intention of going a
slave hunting – when they arrive at Bornou

---

[17]In the event, Oudney kept Jacob Deloyice on – no doubt, as before [Wednesday 20th November],
on grounds of compassion – but he continued to be disruptive.

[18]Ar., *jerab*: mange

[19]Denham arrived in Al-Qatrun, with Bu Khallum and his party, on Tuesday 3rd December.

[no entry Tuesday 3ʳᵈ]

Wednesday 4ᵗʰ

Cold & Clear *emply*ʲ²⁰– at 4 P.M about 30 Mounted Arabs arrived amongst which was Abdullahi Tabonie the man who stole our camel

Thursday 5ᵗʰ

Strong breezes & very cold – emplyᵈ on²¹ in the evening we saw a dance by – a dance of Tibbo women before B.k–ms Tent – Strong b[reezes]

Friday 6ᵗʰ

cold & clear – we did not travel to day as Book–m had not got his papers²² ready –

Gatrone is in Latᵈᵉ [　] situated at the Westʳⁿ point of one of those places where the Atill – agool & Gigi²³ grows and where the water is not above 10 or 12 feet below the surface and often not above three or four – these places in Sp[ring] appear ["like" deleted] to run in streams like rivers – and are commonly called wady such and generally having a stony plain or hills on one side & sand hills on the other²⁴ – This of

---

²⁰Incomplete.

²¹Incomplete.

²²Presumably letters for Al-Kanami, the Sultan of Kawar and Tubu Shaikhs on the caravan road to Borno. [See Appendix I. iv, p.185].

²³Nachtigal [*Sahara and Sudan*, Vol. I, pp. 109 & 198-9] lists some of the camel fodder plants and grasses common in southern Fezzan and the mid-Sahara.

²⁴Fezzan and the Sahara received a much higher rainfall during the Pleistocene and especially the Holocene up to about 5,000 years before present. Much of the shallow ground water encountered by Clapperton, and known to the inhabitants for generations, is derived from rainfall from these former times and finds its surface expression as discharge areas at topographic lows in favourable geological strata. These discharge areas may give rise to discrete springs but also occur as *sebkhats* (see Chapter One, n. 22]. When the latter are dug through, water may rise via wells over wide areas. Much of this palaeowater remains fresh since the rocks (sands and sandstones) are quite clean, and any salinity is likely to be the result of evaporation of rainfall and accumulation over long times. [Prof. M. Edmunds, British Hydrological Survey, personal communication].

Gatrone runs to the N.E– and South – The town is small and the houses in a very ruinous state having three gates none of which can admit a
man on horseback the suburbs are large and the houses built of the
branches of the date tree some of which are plastred over with lime they
are all inhabited by Tibbos[25] owing to the conection of the present Mar[bt]
whose mother was one of that nation those inside the Walls are mostly
Fezzaners who are from jet black to red – or half to three quarters breed
– owing to the mixture of the Arab blood with the Negro and Tibbo

– the Maraboot Hadje Mohamed Rashid is Lord of all the land and dis-
tributes justice to the Inhabitants and he keeps them in very good order
tho a Gaide or Governor is appointed by the Sultan over this place and
Tegerhy with all the land between – his duty only consists in collecting
the taxes on the Date trees & Gummah fields – and sending a correct
account of all Kaffles comming from the interior their n[os] of slaves and
other Merchandise[26] – so that they may not cheat the government by
sending part of the Kaffle by another route than Morzuk where the
duties are paid – The present Gaide is Mohamed ben Abdullah – the
Neapolitan Renegado who – looks miserably ill from the effects of
indulging too freely in lackbi – indeed this place appears very sickly
from its situation and the no– of stagnant wells about the town – ["and
the town" deleted] it also stands in a hollow surrounded by sand hills
which cover what a few years ago were gardens and gummah fields this
sand was brought by a strong Eastly gale which collected the sand about
the Atill & date trees – and they are now about 40 feet high[27]

---

[25]The sedentary Tubu of southern Fezzan also had their own gardens, with vested title, on which
they employed *haratin* sharecroppers [Briggs, *Living Races of the Sahara*, p. 106].

[26]See Saturday 13th November, 1824.

[27]*Neulinge* (German) – hillocks formed of sand or debris accumulated around vegetation in the
hatiyas. "The *etel* bushes mostly grow on more or less substantial sandhills to the formation of which
they have themselves contributed;" [Nachtigal, *Sahara and Sudan*, Vol. I, p. 196].

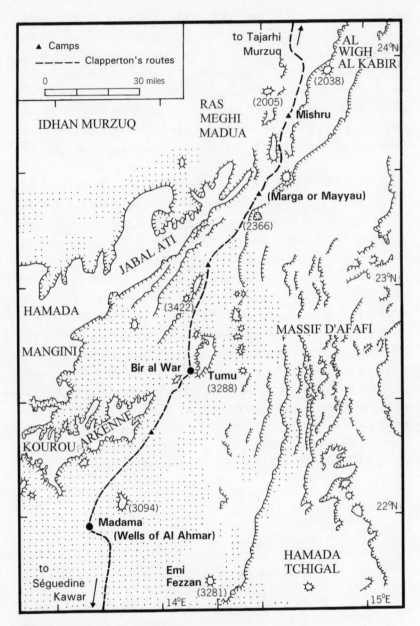

Map 10. Fezzan-Tubu borders

CHAPTER

10

Fezzan-Tubu borders

Saturday 7ᵗʰ

Morning clear & Cold   at 10.40. AM– Started   our road lay for the most part through date trees & Mounds formed by the Sand blown round the Atill trees   out of the town we passed the remains of a large Moorish Castle called Burghi and another to the Eastᵈ called Kamba or the Castle of Small appear–   at 3 P.M– we halted at Medroosa a small village consisting of about a dozen small houses – surround[ed] neally [sic] with stagnant pools of brackish water – we encamped to the South of the town amongst the sand hills   the road was pleasant today but the illness of poor Hillman & Columbus Major D.'s servant – took away the pleasure we would otherwise [have] enjoyed – from The freshness of the Day the pleasantness of the road & nature and the various Nº of people who compose our Kaffle who consist of Arabs[1] – Fezzaners and liberated slaves returning to their country who when all together form as curious a group as can well be imagined and when loading or halting – the confusion of Tongues is like Babel –

at this place like Gatrone young Tibbo Girlls came out accompd– by three of their Men beating on the Gunga – which is the half of a gourd

---

[1]Denham lists the Arab parties, and their chiefs, numbering some 210 in all, principally of the Magarha tribe, at that time "in great favour with the Bashaw", and of small tribes from Wadi ash-Shati. [Denham, *Missions*, Vol. II, pp. 162-8].

with a sheep skin over it like a small kettle drum and beat either with the hand or a small stick – they were headed by the Sheikh of the place who exerted himself in an extra^{dy} manner to make the Girls exert themselves in the dance –

Course S. by W ½ W 8 Miles

Sunday 8th
Cold & Clear – at 8–40 A.M. Started   we were the last that left the ground owing to our loads being always to be made up & the small number of our hands – our road was as yesterday through Mounds of sand crownd with the Atill or rather mounds of sand formed round the atilla trees leaving the tops uncovered and thereby making it appear like a bush on the top of the sand hills – on the West side of the road we had nothing but a Sandy desert and to the East^d stony plains   at 10 saw the hills of el Weaght Saghir[2] or the little weaght hills running from S.W to N.E.   our people said that – there they procured plenty of Alum[3] which is taken to Morzuk for sale   the hills are in the form of Broken cones and running higher as they go to the N. Eas^{td}   the Great Weaght is crossed in going to Waday and appears to be the same range they describe running through the country of Tibesty & the Tibbos of Borgoo which is further to the S. E^d

– at 4 PM halted at Gassur Owa[4] amongst the date trees   our sick people had stood it out very indiferen^{tly} but the day was milder than what we had experienced for some time before –

Course S by W ½ W 14 Miles   at the halting place there are 2 wells of

---

[2] Al Wigh as-saghir (little) is the northwestern spur of a chain of hills which at its southern end swells into the Jabal al Wigh al-kabir (great). [Nachtigal, *Sahara and Sudan*, Vol. I, p . 212].

[3] A whiteish, transparent, astringent mineral salt (Ar., *shabb*); used principally in tanning and in medicine and widely traded over the centuries throughout the Sahara.

[4] From the Arabic, *gasr*, castle, and *rauwa*, well-watered [Nachtigal, *Sahara and Sudan*, Vol. I, p. 212, n. 1].

very good water about 6 feet deep   it smells a little at first – but in taste it is very good

Monday 9th

Clear & Cold   at 8–10 A.M St^d leaving the date trees which turn to the east^d – about a mile & a half to the South – we came to the ruins of the castle[5] which gives the name to this place   it is a large square building having square towers at each angle and one in the centre of each side with loop holes for archery – it is built of Sun dried bricks and has been built by the same people and at the same time as the Great Mosque at Zuela and all the castles to the East of Morzuk are built in the same stile – with sun dried bricks on the out and inside the middle being filled up with clay and gravel – square flanking towrs & surrounded by a ditch and bridge built with a work outside the ditch & bridge   the castles to the westard of Morzuk are built with clay or mud dried in rough lumps – with round towers at the Angles and no ditch –

at 2 we passed the S.W. end of the hills called the little Weaght   our course has been over a gravelly ["road" deleted] plain having patches here & there of date trees to the West^d & beyond that the Sandy desert our sick stood it out much better than usual and at 3–30 P.M– we arrived at Tegerhey [arabic script added] and encamped to the southd of the Town on a sandy spot elevated considerably above the level of the town –

Bookaloom told the D^r that it was customary for all Kaffles going to the interiour to give a Boozafer[6] or present to the persons who had been there before or what in England is called paying a footing – and that he

---

[5]This was the castle 'Gusser Hallam' that George Lyon passed but did not visit on his way to Tajarhi in January 1829 [*A Narrative*, p. 237]. The various castles of the Wadi Ekema (effectively frontier country between Fezzan and Tubu domains) were well built, mainly with fired bricks, and on a regular, usually rectangular plan. [E. Scarin, *Le oasi del Fezzan* (Bologna, 1934) Vol. I, p. 165.]

[6]Ar., *Bu safar* – the father of the journey; a festive meal marking the inauguration of a journey [Nachtigal, *Sahara and Sudan*, Vol. I, p. 215]; and, more generally, a traditional feast on important occasions in a journey, such as the crossing of a border.

was going to give 2 Camels & we had better give one & some Kuscassou – the D^r said he would give the latter but the Kuscassou we could not spare – after the Sunset the Arabs surround the camp hooting & Crowing like cocks others calling Wauk Wauk – as at the death of a person – untill they were told they were to have next day a Boozafer Course S. by W. ½ W 12 miles

Tuesday 10th
Morning Clear & Mild   our sick a great deal better –

Bookaloom brought the camels for the Boozafer which were soon killed and divided   a good portion to each person in the camp for 2 days – noon Made the Lat^{de} of Tegerhy by Mn Alt^{de} of the Suns lower limb 24°19'12" N

in the afternoon our camp was all mirth and joy firing guns feasting and 3 marriges took place with the Arabs and – liberated slave women who marry for the voyage to Bornou only – stipulating that they are to have a camel to ride all the way – and that on her part she will cook and keep the husband warm at night – –

the young Tibbo girls came out here & danced before the Tent of B–k–m as at the other places

our sick much better but the poor D^r is worse than all – this afternoon when he & I were taking a walk he was so much exausted that he had to lay down to recover himself though we had walked but a short distance

Wednesday 11th
Mild & Cloudy – our sick much better – we hired three Maherry to carry dates & Water across the desert for which we are to pay – 3$ each evening amplitude 14° -1' West –

we heard today that the Sultan Mustapha had ["hired" deleted] taken the government of Fezzan for 3 years more[7] & that he was shortly com-ming to Morzuk – also that Hadje Mohamed and several others were comming to join us and would join us on the morrow – a Maraboot who had accompanied the people of Omlaranib – kept beating on a tam-bourine the whole of the night Shaking his head backwards & forwards as if he would have thrown it off and calling allah, allah, allah or god, god, god or it appeared more like a song – than said the whole of the people made him a present of something & they consider it as necessary that he gives them some little thing in return to pres[erve] them from harm – one of these fellows accompany all Kaffles as far as this place & then return & I dare say the rogues make a good thing of it – for they receive a present from every one in the party rich or poor in return he gives some trifle such as a pinch of gum or a scrap of paper & prays for them when absent I could not help thinking it was something like what used to take place in – other countries not many years since when the most villainous actions were all done in the name of god and the church

Thursday 12th

Morning amplde 14°- 9' W   Tegerhy [arabic script added] is in Latde 24°-19'-12" N at long^de [ ]   it is situated at the S.W. end of the Little Weaght hills which from the accounts I was able to gain from those who had travled often to Waday & Tibesty appear to be a branch of the range that runs past that place and which form The Tadarart Mountains at Ghaat – & the Mountains on the South Side of Wady Gharby the main range – I expect to pass on our road between this & Dirkie – the Soil is composed of a greenish clay under which there is water at the depth of from 3 to 8 feet all the way from Gatrone – the[n] like that place also it is bounded by a Sandy desert on the west and the date trees & grass

---

[7]Mohammad al-Mukni's apppointment as Bey of Fezzan had been renewed for a further three years in January 1820, on condition of paying $80,000 to Yusuf Pasha Karamanli during that period. But this contract became worthless because Al-Mukni was almost immediately replaced by the Georgian renegade, Mustafa al-Ahmar, on the same terms.

run about one day's journey to the S.E at the foot of the Little Weaght hills

It appears from the ruins of several moorish castles & Garden walls built of sun dried bricks to have been once of greater import^{ce} than it is at present – as also of g^{tr} extent – in one of the old gardens we saw 4 trees of the dome date a spec[i]es of palm[8] – also a large mimosa where the skin or cover of whose fruit or the hull of the bean for it is just like the small French bean serves for diying their wool & leather black[9] –

The town is not walled but built round an old castle whose walls are [sic] only standing – and inside the Mamaluke[10] has a house it is about 200 feet by 150 & built of mud and appears to be of the same date as the castle of Morzuk[11] –

the inhabitants are mostly Tibbos who un–like there [sic] country men at Gatrone live in the mud houses of the town some of which are very neat and clean with inscriptions from the Koran over the door – there is a small lake of brackish water here formed I think from the clay being taken away for building on the North & East is a salt Marsh or plain reaching from the foot of the Weaght hills to the town and surrounding it for the breadth of 2 or 3 Miles on the North & East Sides – on the South and close by the town is the little Lake of brackish water in which there is a n^{o} of rushes which are frequented by wild ducks of which I saw upwards of thirty – on the West for about a Mile there is a few gardens in which they grow barley Gussub & Gaffoly – but very little wheat – and beyond that are the Sand hills of the desert – There are no houses of date tree branches here The Tibbo who compose the greatest population of the town inhabit the clay houses

---

[8]Ar., *dhom* – *Hyphaene thebaica*, an equatorial palm of many uses, which this far north would be cultivated not wild.

[9]The tannin-rich fruit of the *Acacia nilotica* [Nachtigal, *Sahara and Sudan*, Vol. I, p. 135].

[10]Presumably the Neapolitan renegade Mohamed ben Abdullah, "the drunken Mamaluke", now the kaid of the district [Friday 6th December].

[11]i.e. late 16th century; cf. Lyon's description [*A Narrative*, p. 239].

Friday 13th

Morning cloudy   at day light there was no appearance of starting – but at 8 A.M. B.k–m sent to say we would go as far as the wells of Oma or Matan[12] which is a name for the gathering place of all Kaffles whither it have any other name or not   this Hadje Hagel is called a Matan – and so with all other places whe[re] Kaffles assemble before they proceed on their j–y – before starting observing a hubub near the tent of B-k-m I went to see the cause   when I found it to be one of the liberated slaves getting a bastinadoing for beating his wife who was with child and had been straying in the night either to warmer quarters or where the food was more plentiful – there certainly was a great disparity of ages – But I should think intrigue was in great measure driven out of their minds by fatigue and hunger – except for the purposes of filling their bellies

at 10–30 Left Tegerhy   our road lay over the desert which is here com-posed of sand & Gravel – & having the stripes of date trees & atill on our left and the hills of the little weaght on the other side of them – to our right was the sandy desert – –

at 2– P.M– the date trees crossing our course & go about a mile to the west – we turned East amongst them untill 3.30 PM when we halted at the wells of Oma or the Matan   they are situated amongst sand hills date trees & Atill trees and from the great N^o of human skeletons[13] ["of human beings" deleted] one would take it to have been the only remains of an anc^{nt} city whose only remains were the bones of its inhabitants – the great N^o of the Sk^{ns} may be usually accounted for – as at this place all

---

[12]Ar., *mawtan*, the halting place at Bir Omah.

[13]For northbound slave-caravans, the passage over the Tummo saddle was the last and hardest sec-tion of the journey across the Sahara to Fezzan. Many wells on the main Saharan slaving routes were surrounded by the skeletons and scattered bones of humans and animals. It has been suggested that this was due to slave children, in particular, falling by the way side and dragging themselves to the next well, only to find the caravan had gone. Sick animals would also be abandoned at wells. [H. Vischer, *Across the Sahara from Tripoli to Bornu* (London, 1910) p. 226.] But Fisher and Fisher suggest that many slaves died when wells were found to be clogged and took long to clear [A. G. B. Fisher and H. J. Fisher, *Slavery and Muslim Society in Africa* (London, 1970) p. 79]. For an account of the destruc-tion of an entire caravan on the Lake Chad-Tripoli road in August 1849 when a clogged well failed, see FO 160/12, Gagliuffi to Reade, 14th September 1849.

Kaffles wait untill joined by their friends who usually travel two or three days apart for the purpose [of] leaving water in the wells[14] – The wells are about 8 in No– lying under a S^{tm} of ["Clay" deleted] sand the Water good & plenty about 4 feet to the water

Saturday 14th

Clear & Mild at 11– AM– Hadje Ali left with the half of the party to proceed before us – 2 days March Made the Lat^{de} by Mn Alt^{de} O. 24°–14′–37″ N we had a visit from the Gayde of Tegerhy who was drunk – a supply of wood – & grass sent an man on with H.A. to fill skins the D^r paid him 10 dollars for this – an old Woman Came & asked me if I would give her water on the road – which I agreed to

Sunday 15th

Dark & Cloudy W^r at 8–30 A.M– we left the wells of Oma and traveling W by S– to clear the oasis saw a ridge of Sand hills which runs from the little Weaght hills at 9–50– we rounded the Sand hills whose bases appear to be composed of ridges of quartz rock running in a East & West direction – –

at 11–30 AM we traveled S ½ E the hollows between the ridges being filled with sand made the traveling easy for man & beast – we saw a great no– of Locust which the blacks caught & eat when roasted[15] – at

---

[14]As Clapperton explains, large caravans broke up into separate sections, travelling at a few days' interval from each other, to ease the enormous pressure on the limited capacity of wells. A slave caravan of hundreds of people and animals needed thousands of litres of water to quench immediate thirst and to fill containers for the journey's next stage. For a record of how separate sections of the same caravans would arrive in Tripoli over several days, see FO 101/20 Dickson to Bidwell, 17th November 1848, enclosed *Return of Caravans Arrived at the Town of Tripoli from 1st January to 31st August 1848*.

[15]A traditional and favoured food throughout the Sahara; see, for example, Ibn Battuta's observations in Tuat in December 1353: "The food of its inhabitants consists of dates and locusts, for there are quantities of locusts in the country; they store them just like dates and use them as food. They go to catch the locusts before sunrise, for at that time they cannot fly on account of the cold." [Ibn Battuta, *Travels*, p. 338].

3– PM. halted   Course W by S 2 – S.S.W– 3   S ½ E 7

Monday 16th

at 7–40 AM– Started Course S ½ E – over stony ridges the hollows of
which were covered with sand – at noon Saw the Mountains of Mishru
to the Southd bearing from W by S. to East   at 3– PM we entred
amongst the hills and at 3–30 we descended into a valley   the hills are
composed of sand[ste] clay iron stone & blue & white slate the same as
those of Taradart & Wady Gharbi & from 5– to 600 feet – high –

the valey is of clay and to the East[d] of the road are several Mounds of
clay of about 12 or 14 feet high which had appt[y] the height of the Wady
but washed away by the water[16] they having that ap[ce]

5–45 P.M– halt[d] at the wells of Mishru[17] – we had passed the skeletons
of what they said were slaves – one poor Mabrook[18] – took the trouble
to cover some – but the people laughed at her – all around the Wells for
a dist[ce] of ¼ Mile each way was covered with skelitons of human beings
and other Animals the former the greater N[o]   our tents were pitched
over these[19] – the cause of so many deaths is they say owing to the slaves
– drinking too much water after a long fast from food & water the Lat[de]
by Mn Alt[de] Sirius 23°-44'-23 N   C[ourse] S ½ E – the Gerbas filled

---

[16]Nachtigal [*Sahara and Sudan*, Vol. I, pp. 216-220] gives a detailed account of this section of the
caravan road. Clapperton describes here a common feature of the landscape: a small erosion valley
with outcrops or tablelands, known as a "witness" or, by the German term, "Zeuge", which have
survived weathering and "witness" the former level of the terrain. This valley was known ironically
as the Dendal, or promenade of the Ghaladima, since it resembled a town when large slave caravans
halted at the wells of Mishru [H. Vischer, *Across the Sahara* (London, 1910), pp. 222-3].

[17]An important well between Fezzan and Tubu country – a border which was never clear. Denham
[*Missions*, Vol. II, pp. 196 & 8] refers, for example, to celebrations held "on entering Tebu country" at
Tajarhi. For Barth, on the other hand, writing in 1855 [*Travels*, Vol. III, p. 620], the border lay 16 miles
south of Mafaras, "the southernmost well of Fezzan". Nachtigal in 1869 [*Sahara and Sudan*, Vol. I,
p. 216] held the border to lie north of Mishru. J-C. Zeltner ["Islam et sociétés au sud du Sahara:
Tripolitaine et pays toubou au XIXe siècle" in *Cahiers annuels pluridisciplinaires*, No. 3 (Paris, 1989),
p. 92] sensibly concludes: "La véritable frontière était le désert, qui n'appartenait à personne, et
qu'aucun Etat ne songeait à revendiquer."

[18]Clapperton means *mabruka* (f.). By the time a black trade slave reached the market in North

but the man we had sent with them gone on – found some stone trees
the heart knots – & rents [are] chalk – & the layers of diff^t stone   others
like wood opal & some flint[20]

Africa, he or she was already a nominal Muslim, with an Arabic name. As Professor John Hunwick
points out,

These names were often peculiar to slaves and tended to have meanings which were redolent of
happiness, good fortune and favour from God; for males Khayr Allah (goodness of God), Jar Allah
('neighbour' of God), Kafar (camphor), Anbar (ambergris), Murjan (gem); for females Umm al-
khayr (mother of goodness), Bakhita (fortunate), Mabruka (blessed), Mahbuba (beloved), Sa'ida
(happy), Za'faran (saffron) etc., ...

[J. O. Hunwick, "Black Slaves in the Mediterranean World: Introduction to a Neglected Aspect of
the African Diaspora" in E. Savage (ed.), *The Human Commodity* (London, 1988) p.13.]

[19]The camels enjoyed chewing the dried bones [Oudney, *Missions*, Vol. II, p. 202].

[20]See Chapter Three, n .5.

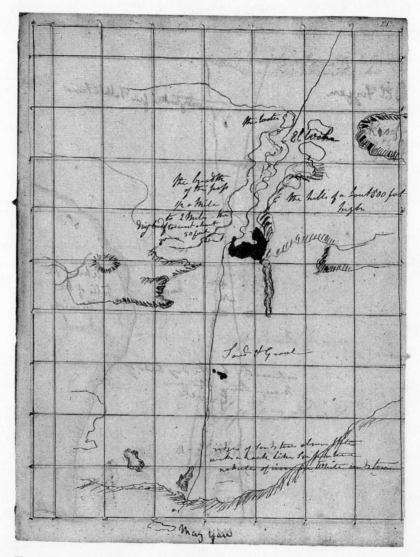

Figure 10. Course map, the road to El Waur

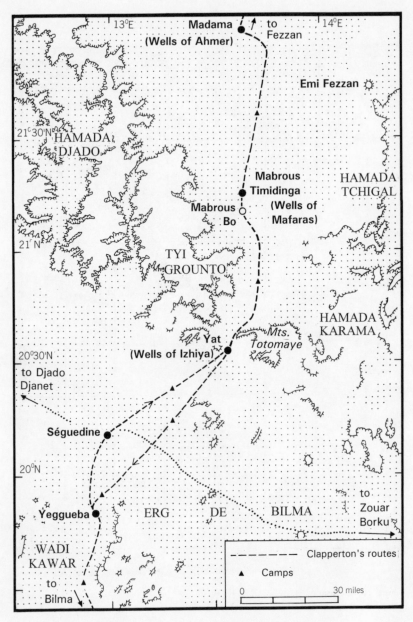

Map 11. Central Sahara

CHAPTER

11

Central Sahara

Tuesday 17ᵗʰ
Clear & Cold – at 7–40 – Started   we left the Wells of Mishru which
are 3 in Nᵒ and about 20 feet deep the Water sweet & Good – we found
our gerbas filled but the Man whom we had sent the[re] had gone on
with Hadje Ali   being offred to stop with them untill we came up –
though when they are in a body the dead bodies appear to give them no
concern – in the day light the place had something like a ressurection
from *inter*mixture of the dead & living black & white & speaking a number of languages –

we ascended by a rocky pass directly from the wells – there is another
pass about 2 Miles to the Westᵈ but as the sand had filled the hollows in
this we ascended without difficulty   our Course South untill 9 A.M–
when we descended into another valley of great breadth Studed with
black rocky hills   our Course S by W. ½ W – we crossed a nᵒ of vallies
which run in a direction E by N & W by S – the road to day was strewn
with the skeletons of the dead   amongst some of which by the plaited
lock of hair on the crown and the face turned to Meca that the Master &
Slave lies unb[urie]d where they fall here – the road good being sand
& gravel composed of flints agates & coarse cornelians – the hills of red
& white sand stone – Clay iron stone & blue & white slate the bottom of
the valley covred with gravel over clay and some times ridges of a stone

appng to Serpentine – & the hills allways appear black – ["the outside of" inserted] from the weather – there is also a great quantity of iron stone & nodules of iron stone[1]

at Sunset we came to a very black hill – called by the people in going to Bornou May–Yau when returning from Bornou to Fezzan Marga or soup[2] – after rounding this hill we halted at another place covred with dead bodies – at 6–35 P.M– Course S by W ¾ W

Wednesday 18th
at 7–20 AM Start   at 8 A.M – we descended by a winding pass called by the Tibbos Le Gubbu & by the Arabs Tinea and Hormut Tinea[3] – the bottom & sides of the pass had a very curious app^ce from the long train of camels winding down the groups [of] camels sitting on the black bar-ren rock & the skeletons of Men & animals lying on the path and on each side some of them had fallen in groups or had been thrown together out of the way – & 2 Conical black high & rugged hills on each side – on the side of the pass we got sp^les [=samples] from a yellow vein in the s^te [= sandstone] rock – when we got down our course was SSW ½ W over a Wide valley – the hills composed of sandstone Slate white & black with a yellow vein running thro the sandstone – in the valley are Obs^d great quantities of a rock like serpentine & alum slate & the gravel of the valley flints agates – nodules of iron ore – & a fine white sandstone in which the nodules [are] like small shot studded in the stone like pepper

at 1 PM– we ascended another ["valley" deleted] hill – we have found

---

[1]The stones observed here – agates and cornelians – are varieties of chalcedonies, a semi-trans-parent or translucent sub-species of quartz with a waxy lustre. These, and silicates such as flints and serpentines (a hydrous magnesium silicate, of a dull green colour), are all typical mineralogical fea-tures of the gravels of the mid-Saharan pleistocene [Prof. M. Edmunds, personal communication].

[2]Ar., *maraqa*, soup. The term '*may-gau*' is perhaps a local dialect word, but may stem from the root-word *maraq* which has the sense of traverse.

[3]Nachtigal refers to the precipitous descent into the "Lagoba Buia, the great valley". Clapperton appears to have confused the terms he heard: *khuma*, [Ar.,] is a narrow passage or pass; *teniya*, Tubu for a road. [Nachtigal, *Sahara and Sudan*, Vol. I p. 218].

the descents allways steeper on the North side than the south – the approach being to the latter More gradual caused by the sand being blown against the side

after ascending this hill our road for 2 Miles was over coarse slags of sandstone & then we come on to the gravel & coarse sand which covered the slags to the depth of a foot or two in most places

a She camel ["of Bkms" inserted] brought forth she was assisted by the Arabs – and 5 Minutes afterwards was reloaded & went on after her young one which was carried on a mule before her a piper & dancer before B–km at 5– halted & pitched on the desert after^a Cloudy

Lat^{de} by Mn Alt^{de} Sirius 23°–6′–16″ N   Course S.S.W ½ W

Thursday 19th
at 7 AM– Started our road over a gravelly plain S.S.W ½ W to the pass [&] hills of El Waur or the difficult – at 10 we passed hills ["to the East – a range" inserted] the day was cool & pleasant we found a Small bird that had been blown by some gale from some other country – also the head of a wood pecker – they were both quite dry

at 4–20 PM we entered between the hills that form the pass – these are of the Same Structure of those of Wady Gharbi & Tinderart [&] of the same app^{ce} – and about 800 f^t high[4] we passed few dead bodies but at near the entrance of the pass we passed the bodies of 2 Much mangled the[y] had not an arm lying one way &^{c}

at 5–20 P.M– we ent^d the pass which is the dry bed of a torrent – between the Mountains – we had great trouble & diff^y from the rugged-

---

[4] The valley floors of the deeply-fissured central Saharan plateau lie generally at some 1,800 feet above sea-level, with the surrounding mountain tops and tableland at around 2,800 feet; Mount Tummo itself rises to 3353 feet.

ness of the road – the exausted state of the camels – & we would have gladly staid any where but Bkm was ahead – and we had to proceed on though our poor camels lay down from fatigue several times – and at 3 or four places only one camel could get down the passes at a time & the hurry of those behind – the roaring of the camels & impatience to get on ad^d no small confusion & the illness of poor Hillman who today was much worse – added not a little to our miseries – –

at 9–30 halted near the water and the Wind blowing strong & the loose gravel of the bed of the torrent wh^r we encampd would not hold the tent pegs so we secured them with – bags or boxes   had Kuscassou for dinner   Course S.S.W ½ W 20 – SW. 8 –

Friday 20th
Strong breezes & Cloudy   at day light B.k.m came and kicked up a dust with our men for not being at the wells filling the gerbas – & the poor camels had not drunk for 7 days & now they have to go for 2 more without water – after 8 A.M– B–k–m sent to the D^r that we would halt for the day as the Arabs complained much of fatigue – we therefore sent our camels of[f] to drink & all our empty skins to be filled

the Water is found in the bottom of a hill bearing E.S.E– from the halting place and is found in great quantity   there are 5 holes cut into the place – and the water is sweet & good

noon Made the Lat^de by Mn Alt^de of the Suns lower limb 22°–40'–27"N– we had one of our camels that was lame on the near fore shoulder   burnt with a red hot iron   the manner is to secure its legs & turn it over and taking a red hot iron burn near the place in lines of about a foot or 6 inches – acc^dg to the damage the number is less or more – this burning is a general remedy for all diseases in Man & beast[5] – afternoon Clear & fine

---

[5]see Chapter Three, n. 31.

214

Saturday 21st

Clear & fine   we commenced loading an hour before day light and left the halting place of El Waur or the difficult (so called from the stony pass) – at 6–40 A.M– our road was over stony ridges for 4 Miles when we came on a fine gravelly plain bounded to the North by the black hills that form the pass of El–Waur which stretch to the East & West for as far as the eye can reach – and to the West^d there runs a range of hills of the same appearance – nearly North & South – and appears to be a branch of the same range we have been passing through for these some days past   at 4–20 P.M– we passed between two Isolated hills – and at 6–P.M– halted

We passed today the half decayed bodies of a great No– of the unfortunate slaves who had been taken at Bagirmi by Mustapha the present Sultan of Fezzan   the bodies were only in part decayed and their skins looked like parchment & their bodies & skeletons remained as the life had left them   some had their hands at their eyes others were lying with the hand under the head & some with their arms & legs stretched out & lying on their backs – the body of one poor child had the Hands stretched out as if in supl^{ct} [=supplication] not to be left to die in such a place

from giving our camels too many dates after their drinking they were all drunk   Course SW by S –

Sunday 22nd

Morning fine & Clear   at 6–40 AM– Started   before starting Bkm gave the D^{rs} servant a beating without asking the D^{rs} permission –

our road was over a fine gravelly plain S.W. by S. & as we felt a little tired the D^r & I we rode on a head of the Kafle to take a nap before the camels came up – we let the camels pass for about a mile and then started on our way to join them   we fell in with ["some others" deleted] Bk^m the Major & the rest of the Escort as usual – but on our comming we

were not a little surprised at his flying into a rage at our staying behind
– saying that he was ans^ble with his head to the Bashaw for our safety and
that we were in a very dangerous place and surrounded with enemies –
the whole appeared to me as a plan to put us out of humour or to quarrel for some reason of his own that I cannot at present Scrie into – for
before he went to Tripoli all was safe & clear & he would forfeit his head
if he did not take us in safety without an Escort – now he has got an
Escort all is danger and we must not go out side of this Escort and of
course the ruin of the Mission and an end to our journ[ey]ing further
than Bornou – Noon we passed a few Tallah Trees the first grown thing
we had seen since we left Oma seven days [ago]

at – 4–20 we came ab^st [=abreast] of the hill that forms a land mark for
the well – we also saw a hill with 2 peaks bearing S. by E called Fizzen
bearing S. by E Dist^d about 30 miles   it is one of the halting places for
Kaffles & 2 day[s] from El–Waur   it is on the road to Wady [=Wadai]
Bhr El Ghazale & Kanem   at 5–30 halted at the wells of El–Ahmer or
the red so called from the colour of the sand & Clay which is of a dark
[red colour]   all round the well are the strewed the bodies of human
beings and animals in all states of decay – & lying those that withstand
kicking about preserving the form in which they had died   by the side
of one of the wells is a Mother & child from the app^ce of the bodies   the
water is about four feet from the surface & in great plenty   we found
Hadje Ali and the Kaffle here & were not a little surprised to find that
our man was not with him as they say they had left him at the Well &
given him Wr [= water]   Lat^de 21°–59′–11″ N by the Mn Alt^de of Sirius

Monday 23rd
Clear & fine amp^de 128° 30′ – at 7 A.M– we left the wells of El Ahmer
– the water is good & in great plenty – and for the first time since we
left the wells of Oma have we seen the traces of any living creature save
those of passing Kaffles – but here we had the pleasure of seeing some
traces of the Ghazale – though every where you turned we saw the bod-

ies or skeletons of human beings though we now think not much or feel
little concern on passing these – except the thought of their capture is
present in our minds and I suppose we will be as bones too in time –

our road was over an extensive plain broken into ridges running E. & W
– which in some places rose to little hills – the rock of these hills & ridges
are composed of a Slaty stone & a very fine sand stone which appears as
if it had undergone a great heat but it is from exposure to the W [=
weather] for all the exposed stratum are generaly the same way

at noon we came to a gravelly surface underneath was a fine Soft sand
like brown ochere – in this place there were a no– of air holes & app^ng
as if the water was not far distant – it caused very heavy treading for
man & beast at sunset Fizzan bore E. by S– Evening amp^de 259° we
have not passed so many dead bodies to day as in days past – and all of
those here appear to have not been long dead – I suppose owing to the
trouble it takes to make a hole here we had a strong gale and the fine
sand blown along with it particularly from that raised from *hot [a]ir*
caused both man & horses to sneeze and was painful to the eyes & the
poor D^r suffered much from breathin[g] it & coughed a great deal at
6–P.M– halted Course S.S.W – 23 miles

Tuesday 24th

Morning Clear & Cold At 6–40 AM– Started S.W by S – over the
same gravelly plain as yesterday – at 10 we crossed a range of low gravelly hills composed of fine sand stone & clay iron stone &^s saw a range
of hills running from W.N.W. to S.E. not very high & [two words illeg.]–
from this place we crossed several gravelly ridges untill 3 PM we came
on to a sandy & Gravelly plain over which there was strewed several
crusts of gypsum – and a very beautiful white gypsum was on the banks
of the dry beds of stre[ams] and on some of the ridges looking like white
Stratum of rocks but when examined proved to be only a crust from 8
inches to 1 inch in thickness –

the plain we had passed over part of yesterday and the fore part of this day appears at times to be over flowed – & I must also observe that at some seasons & times that there must be a considerable quantity of rain fall from the hills to the northrd of the Wells of Mishru into this place[6] – from the dry beds of streams crossing the desert in different directions and when joined must be of considerable size and also amongst the hills

one of our she camels foald or calved – to day – a fine young she calf – but unfortunately about an hour afterwards she lost the use of her hind legs – and we had unfortunately to take her life   she was the best in our Kafle   so strong gentle & walked so well – we were congratulating our selves on the fine supply of milk we had got when the accident took place –   she was soon cut up by the Arabs and borne away to the last morsel –   the whole of the blame of her illness was placed to a poor old black woman – who from humanity I had fed from Tegerhy and now and then given her a ride on the camels –   every one that came near cried out the evil eye had kil[led] the poor beast & we could not convince them to the contrary   the poor Niger agreed with us and said it was the will of god –

at 7 P.M– we halted at the well of Mafrass[7] – we had to clear the well[s] of mud & sand – & to get Bkm to send a Showse to let our people have a Well   Course S.W by S

Latde of Mafrass by Mn Alt^de of Sirius 21°–13'– 51" N

Wednesday 25th
Cool & Clear   at 7.30 left the wells of Mafrass   they are three in no– –

---

[6]The Buddema depression [Nachtigal, *Sahara and Sudan*, Vol. I, p. 44] lying between Mangeni and Tchigai plateaus.

[7]Ar., *mafaras*, the mare's spring; an important staging post in this barren region mid-way between Fezzan and Kawar. According to Saharan tradition, water was divined here by the early Arab conqueror of North Africa, Oqba ibn Nafi [Norris, *The Tuaregs*, p. 17].

& the water lying under a Stratum of blue clay about 4 feet thick   the
water is abundant and good   they are situated in a hollow formed by
ridges of fine sandstone which to the West about ¼ of a Mile Dist.ce form
low hills   the lower Stratum is a fine Soft slaty sand stone containing
stalaktites lying horizontaly – like the rusty barrel of a musquet filled
with ice[8] – there is a small valley running to the West.d in which are a N.º
of Atill trees – round the wells are a few young date trees – 2 Miles to
the South of the Wells – we came amongst a considerable quantity of
strong grass where we let the camels & our horses feed untill we sent to
B–k–m – (who stays behind with the horse generaly for an hour or more
after the Kaffle starts) – to see if we should stop & let the camels feed for
a day but ["they were" deleted] he sent orders for us to proceed we had
stoped for about 1 ½ an hour and then proceeded over a plain to the
S.E. end of the range of hills mentioned yesterday – at 11 we came upon
a bed of shells of which we collected a n.º but the[y] broke in pieces in
our hands – mostly – they had the appearance of Oyster shells & what
they call the scalop shells – the latter the greatest no   they have many
worm holes through them and it had every appearance of a bed of shells
when left by the tide[9]   on each side there were ridges of lime stone not
high running East & West   we crossed several ridges of lime stone the
hollows between which were filled with sand   we therefore could not
see what was below

at 4–20 P.M– we came abreast the hills spoken of before over which we
traveled the ridges that were mountains   at 7– P.M. halted – in the dry
bed of a Mountain stream   Course S by W ¾ W 22

---

[8]These interesting structures, likely to be casts of roots or vegetation that have formed a nucleus
for mineral growth as the sediment was buried, occur in the sandstones and especially the ironstones
of other, similar, regions of the Sahara [Prof. M. Edmunds, personal communication]. There are two
wells named Mafaras, some 19 miles apart [Barth, *Travels*, Vol. III, p. 622]. From Clapperton's course
notes, the site described here would appear to be near the southern well.

[9]Fossils of both sea-water and fresh-water molluscs are to be found in the Sahara. The former date
to the Cretaceous period; the latter arose (carried by water-birds of passage) in the swamps and lakes
of the Holocene (10th to 2nd millennium BC). These shells (notwithstanding Clapperton's description of them as 'sea-shells') are more likely to relate to the former presence of freshwater lakes and
may well be Cardium species [Prof. M. Edmunds, personal communication].

Thursday 26ᵗʰ

Cold & Clear   the wind blowing from the North   at 7–30 A.M– Started
our road – as tha[t] in the afternoon of yestʳ – was within the ["points
&" inserted] ranges of hills which here stretch further to the S.E – and
open into narrow vallies & ravines to the Westᵈ and to the Eastᵈ form
loose ranges & isolated hills – they are composed of iron stone clay iron
stone but the Val[eys] had sand stone thin white soft Slaty sand and a
green sand stone   at 8– PM halted ["at the wells of Izhiah¹⁰" inserted]
we had been stoped sever[al] times by the giving up of Bkms camels –
and Hadje Ali had to remain with four all day – when we arrived every
one was as tired as could be & for myself I have walked these 2 last days
owing to the shoe of my horse having lamed his near fore foot – but I
have walked thru parts of every day since we came out   Course S by
W ½ W 9   SW ½ S 14

we had for our Christ dinner Kuscassou and a case of the english *meat*¹¹

Friday 27ᵗʰ

Clear & pleasant   we gave one of our camels to be Slaughtered & B.km–
another which was served out to all hands   we had a visit from Tibbos
who come from a town called [   ]¹² 2 days journey to the Westd

Latᵈᵉ Mn Altᵈᵉ Suns lower limb 20°–32'–36" N

in the evening it came on to blow from the N.E. bring[ing] with it showers of sand

---

¹⁰Jehaya or Yat, the largest hatiya between Fezzan and Kawar, some 12½ miles long and 2 miles
wide.

¹¹Illegible; possibly 'meat' – that is to say, dried meat, at that period commonly pressed and dried
in lozenge form; or perhaps 'spirit', that is to say, port, with which the Mission had supplied themselves, partly, to be taken with 'bark' [*chinchona*, quinine].

¹²Djado [see Sunday 29th December below].

Saturday 28th

Strong breezes with clouds of sand – we were unable to stir out of our tents all day   in the evening at Sunset it Moderated a little but came on to blow a strong gale with clouds of sand from the N.E.

Sunday 29th

Strong gales & cloudy with Clouds of sand – & very cold   Izhiah is an Oasis of about 3 miles from West to East & 1 ½ from N– to S– Surrounded on the North, East & west Sides by hills of Sandstone clay Iron stone &c & hills & ridges of the Same having a very rugged and barren app[ce]   the Water is plentiful & good lying every where in the Oasis within a few feet of the Surface – the face of the Oasis is covered with tufts of a coarse grass on which the camels feed   there are also a No– [of] dome date trees & the Tallah[13] tree that serves for fire wood – here the Kaffles supply them selves with grass for crossing the desert – the soil is Sand over clay – there are 2 towns   one called Jebado & Segaden[14] 2 days journey to the West[d]

Monday 30th

Cold & Clear   at 8 AM we left Izhiah & travelling over a gravelly plain broken in many places with ridges of Slatey sand stone – which rose in to little hills in some places – the tops of which were covered with the same red sand stone as the ones we had passed some day[s] before & also the clay iron stone with the black vitrified app[ce] –

at Sunset one of our camels that had been sick from the time of leaving El Waur we had to leave behind & the poor old negress was also blamed for – this looking with the evil eye –

to day we heard from the people that the cause of all this cold wind was

---

[13]Ar., *Talh, Acacia seyal* [Bovill, *Missions*, Vol. II, p. 205].

[14]Djado and Siggadim, the latter being the northern outpost of Wady Kawar and a principal cross roads and staging post on today's trans-Saharan routes.

owing to a Tibbo's having lost a charm that he had paid a dollar for at Tegerhy to a person who was able by his wr[= writ, or writing] to still the winds

at 7 P–M halted   Course – S.W. ½ S –

Tuesday 31st
Cold & clear with very little wind   at 7 A.M– Started our road over a gravelly plain broken in to ridges of sand stone and in some places the ridges rise into little hills   at 3. P.M– we entred a wide sandy valley

at 4 PM halted having lost our way   the poor camel that had given up had followed us in the Morning but he gave out about noon & we left him again to his fate   Course SW ½ W

Wednesday Jan[y] **1**[st] **1823**
at 7 A.M. Std   at day light – we discovered our selves to be near the Wady and Wells   at 9– we halted & pitched our tents – at the Hatias & Wells of Irguba

at 10 A.M. Came on to blow a gale from the N.E– which brought clouds of Sand along with it & filled & covered every thing   the fine sand penetrating through the canvas of the tents caused a disagreeable sneezing & Coughing

Thursday 2nd
Stong breezes & Cold cloudy AM   this Morning a Heayena[15] was brought into the camp nearly dead with hunger   it did not attempt to touch any thing not even our dogs   who barked at it a little and then look'd at it at a respectfull distance

---

[15]Rare in the central Sahara today.

the Oasis of Irguba is situated on the South side of a small range of sandstone hills   the water is within a few feet of the surface   very good &
sweet ["and about 3 feet below' inserted]   the face of the Oasis is covred
with trees of dome date   the Tallah and bushes of the gush[16] a coarse
grass on which the camels feed   it runs allong the foot of the Mountains
for the distance of 4 or 5 Miles about ½ a Mile in breadth   to the South
is a sandy plain & to the East the low sand stone hills & rocks – in the
centre of the plain are some sand stone rocks that have once been much
higher   Underneath is a Stratum of blue & white pipe clay – the wells
are within a 100 y^{ds} of the above rocks and on the north side

noon Moderate breezes   Lat^{de} by Mn Alt^{de} of the Suns lower limb [ ]
3 of Bkms camels had been left behind from fatigue – and we wait for
them to day

Friday 3rd
Morning Cold & Clear & blew a fresh breeze from the N.N.E   at 8
A.M– we Started   our road was over a plain composed of Sand & gravel & here & there appeared the Stratum of pipe clay rock the same as
forms the lower part of the hills for ⅔ of their height   on the top is the
red sandstone & Clay iron stone   at 10 we crossed a point of the range
that runs a few mile[s] to the westd– we then descended into a gravelly plain having the hills to the East   to the west the gravelly plain
extended like a sea as far as the eye could reach –

at 6 PM we halted at the foot of a branch of the above range that runs to
the West^d and over which we cross[ed]   the *Aalam*[17] or guide on one of
the hills is just like a Martello tower[19]

Course S by W – 18

---

[16]Possibly, Ar., *'ushb*, spring herbage [Bovill, *Missions*, Vol. II, p. 205 n. 3].

[17]Ar., *alam*, a direction or marker point; some landmarks were made more conspicuous by the
addition of a cairn to which passing travellers would add stones.

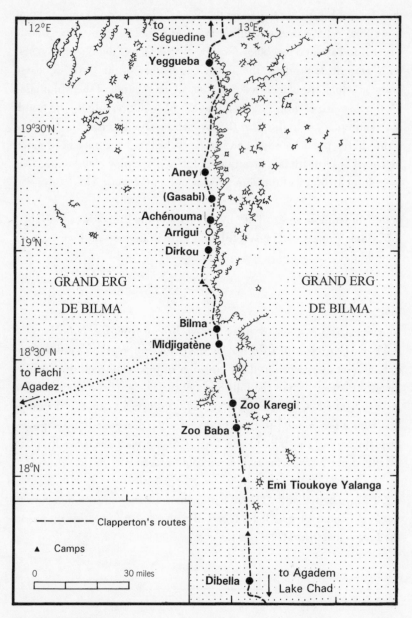

Map 12. Wadi Kawar

224

CHAPTER
12

Wadi Kawar

Saturday 4th

Cold & clear   at 8 AM– we left our encampment at the foot of the hill –
and crossing near to the point of the range we entered into what they call
the Wady Kawar[1] which we traveled through untill 1–30 P.M– when we
halted at Ani the first Town on the road belonging to the Tibbo's – the
houses are built of Stone & Mud – in the same form as those in Fezzan
some indeed are plastered outside with lime – and others are made of the
date branches in the form of a bee hive have a door some thing in the
same proportion & a large court built of a fence arround it –

The town is built on top of 2 hills or rocks – and have a very singular
appearance – the first or East[d] is att[d] [=attached] to the range and can
only be app[d] [=approached] in 2 places – by horses or camels the rock
being steep or forming a precipice every where else except whereas –
the other is built on the top of [a] hill or large rock –

the Water is excellent and about 18 inches below the surface

---

[1]The Wadi Kawar, a long, narrow north-south chain of wells and oases, has always been a vital link
on the main central Saharan road between Tripoli and Lake Chad and an important centre of salt
production for the largely saltless Sudan. The Wadi marks the main ethnic and linguistic divide
between the east Sahara (the black Tubu and associated peoples) and the white Tuareg confederations of the west. It has long been disputed by rival peoples and powers.

The date trees & Grass extend for ab[t] 2 Miles to the West[d] & is then bounded by the Sandy desert which rises a little above the level of the Wady – to the East or the rocky hills – small gardens & a great No of recent[ly] planted date trees we saw few men but a great N[o] of women the old ones are great beggars

A Maraboot which is held sacred by the Tuaricks[2]

Course S by W 8 Lat[de] by Mn Alt[de] of Sirius 19°–22'–10" N

Sunday 5th

Cold & Clear – at 9– A–M.. left Anni and after 2 ½ hours traveling through a coarse grass & date trees we arrived at Gazabi[3] – we saw a great no of date trees that had been planted last year & those that had been planted in appeared to be kept in good order and taken great care of – it also appears that the date has not been long an inhabitant here so it is a sign that the people are improving and that they are able to live in peace and enjoy the fruits of their industry which the poor people (what with the Arabs on one side and the Tuaricks on the other who hunted them through the desert like wild beasts) were never able to do before the Bashaw took Fezzan into his own hands[4]

The Town of Gazabi is in Lat[de] 19°–19' [ ] by Mer Alt[de] of the O – it is built on a rising ground having a No– of date trees & Grass between it & the Mountains to the East & to the West[d] the desert the town is not walled around & the houses are built – in a strageling manner of Stone & Mud instead of Mortar – the inhabitants are civil the D[r] had a great

---

[2]Incomplete entry.

[3]The ancient capital of the first settlers of Wadi Kawar, the Gezebida, a people of mixed Tubu-Kanuri origins. See note 26 below.

[4]The implication is that Arab tribes who for centuries had wandered and raided into this region ceased doing so when Fezzan fell to direct Tripoli control. Nevertheless, any such interval of peace was short-lived. For an historical account of the ups and downs of economic life in Kawar see M. Le Coeur, *Les Oasis du Kawar – une route, un pays, Vol. I: le passé pré-colonial* (Paris, 1950).

No– of patients and from the manners of the women great No– of w^m [=whom] came to the Camp I should think they sell their favours[5] – we were offered a fine sheep for sale – but as we had bought a goat at Anni we did not buy it – though we bought a pot of honey for – [$]7– which they bring from Bornou & Soudan –

A Tibbo who has often travled from this place to Aghadez & Ire[6] says that it is due west or they travel in the direction the sun sets to Aghadez 5 days to travel well which may be about 24 or 26 geographical miles a day when traveling easily 6 days & part of a seventh and says that Ire is 3 days further West than Aghadez[7] –

a No– of the Tibbo's came & danced before B.k.m –

they were examining the Escort in firing at the scul of a camel at about 30 yds distance or pistol shot few of them hit though they had a rest made of saddles

Monday 6th
Morning Clear & fine at 8–30 A.M– we left Guzabie or Gusabee Bkm had a breakfast sent us of sev^l dishes carried by young Tibbo Girls our road lay along the foot of the Mountains some times traveling among the Stripe of Grass & some times on the sandy or gravelly plain according to the winding of the stream of grass & trees –

Bkm was very gaily dressed having on a Bornouse of cloth of Gold & all

---

[5]Murzuq was a notorious centre of prostitution: "the women of Murzuk are . . . of bold aspect and depraved manners. All the lower classes of females . . . will commit acts of immodesty anywhere." [Richardson, *Travels*, Vol. II, p. 348]. Other centres of the Saharan caravan trade, and particularly the trade in young females slaves, apparently offered similar facilities.

[6]Correctly *Ayar*; today usually written Aïr.

[7]Clapperton's account is confused: the track from Kawar runs directly west across the Ténéré desert – the road of the annual Tuareg salt caravans [see note 25 below]- to Agadez, the capital of Aïr. Agadez is situated in southernmost Aïr, from which point a journey of a further two or more days would indeed be required to reach central Aïr.

his accoutrements shining with it or silver   the Standards were borne before him – & the Noba or drum was carried by 2 young slave boys while a third kept striking it about every half minute with a piece of a rope for want of [a] stick – the Arabs on foot were in the center before Bkm as also the Standards which were borne by men on horse back – the Arab horse were on the wings & Skirmished across the front – only the camels bring up the rear

during the March a dust arose and seeing a squable – the Dr Mr H. & I rode up to see what was the Matter   we found B.k.m & his slaves beating one of the Arab horse men – who they said had fired with ball which cut the shirt of one of the Magerhas which he had meant to Kill – after this worthy had got a beating – a no– of the foot on being called to proceed on refused to join the cavalcade – which on Bk^m seeing he drew his sword & rode arr^d laying it about the shoulders of all he could   they ran instantly to their posts like well bred spanials and began to go through their play as they call running across holooing & hooting with their guns at arms length above their heads with the butt ends presented to each other –

at 1.30 P.M. we arrived at the town of Ashinuma or Asinuma – which is built close under the foot of the Mtn and contains a good n^o of houses there is also here a town on the top of the hill in which they keep all their goods &^{c} & to which they fly in time of war or danger – the hill is about 250 feet high forming – in 2 precipices near the top each about 30 feet high the houses are both built on the top and excavated out of the sides the ascent is by a narrow winding foot path which will only admit one man at a time –

the rock at [the] top is comp^d of Strata of white sand stone the lower Strata a pipe clay or fine sand & pipe clay and most of the houses are built & plastred with this clay – The inhabitants are very civil and said to be rich the D^r had a no– of p^{ts} but none seriously ill – When I went through the town on my way to shoot at some birds the women &

228

Children were very much frightened but when I told them not to be
afraid that I was only [*"with some serv^{ts}"* inserted] going to shoot some
birds they came around me all begging to look at my double b^d gun^8 and
I believe every woman in the town came to see & we were as informal
as if [we] had [been] acquaint[ed] for years – I shot a kind of small egal
or large falcon with a bald head^9

Lat^{de} by Mn Alt^{de} – Sirius 19' 8' [ ] N   Course SS.W

Tuesday 7th

Morning fine   Arose at day light and went to visit a lake which I had
seen yesterday from – the top of the hills   on my way down and about
200 y^{ds} to the West^d of our camp I obs^d some crows & Kites surrounding
and eating at some thing black which I took for the carcase of a young
camel – I fired amongst them and when I went to pick up my prize I
found that instead of the carcase of a young camel it was the body of a
slave that had been laid there last night that the place on which I stood
was the Churchyard which only for some of the heads & feet sticking
out through the sand I would not have knowen from any other place as
the bodies are laid on the ground and a little sand scratched over them
and the wind bringin[g] more makes the place appear like many others
here as if a few small mounds of sand gathered round a tree or dry bushes of grass – on enquiry after wards if I was right in think[ing] it to be
a burial place they told me it was and as we had seen nothing of the kind
before at any of the other towns^{10} nor would I have known this only for
the above cir^{ces} these birds had eat part of the shoulder & hip – &
though these birds live on such food yet the Arabs Tibbos & blacks eat
them & whenever I shoot any there is generally a squable for the body
by our people – I turned from the scene with horror for though I have

---

^{8}Probably a "fowling piece" – a double-barrelled flintlock sporting gun, most likely a 6-bore, used
principally for wild-fowling. [G. Gardiner, Sotheby's, personal communication].

^{9}From the description, not a falcon; but possibly a juvenile Egyptian vulture.

^{10}Clapperton had presumably seen burial grounds in Fezzan, but not birds scavenging on them.

seen dead bodies in hundreds at a time many k^d [=killed] in all ways yet I never saw beast or bird making a meal from the dead body of my fellow creatures before –

I proceeded on to the lake through groves of date trees & tallah trees – when I arrived I shot 3 plovers with a grey back black wings white belly w[h]ite ring round the neck & black tail & long legs it has a small claw on the outer bend of each wing[11] the cry very like to the green plover of Britain

The lake is about 2 miles in length & a ¼ of a mile in breadth having a no– [of] small isl^ds– in the Middle which look like whitish rugged rocks and on a nearer approach like small islds– of dirty drift ice – on ex^m I found it to be Salt & Mud & Sand which is thrown up by some means I do not know or it may be by the fine sand blowing on shallow places & the high Winds blowing the spray from the lake over this sand form their app^ce some of them are about 12 feet above the level of the lake the lake is shallow in most places with a black muddy bottom over which is a redish scum which makes the lake appear like the colour of small beer – the Banks are Mostly covered with grass – and on the sides and in the lake are a No of long reeds – the Salt oozes Under the grass like moss of a yellowish & wihte [sic] colour and untill I put my hand down to procure some for the D^r I thought it was – moss – on the East^n side the water boils up in several places with great force – and within about 20 yards from the same place on the bank is a fine spring of Fresh sweet water and a bay of about 20 y^ds in breadth which shook under me when I went to the spring to wash the Mud & brine of[f] my limbs that I had got in wading in the *slime*

The taste of the lake water is salted & bitterest I ever tasted in my life – it is situated from Ashinuma S.W– about 2 Miles

---

[11]The Spur-winged plover (*Vanellus spinosus*), common in open country and near fresh and salt water.

the[y] have a No of Cows here as various in colour as in Britian and about the size & make of what in Scotland are called the Galloway breed – they have horns slightly bent upwards & about 2 feet long[12] – their sheep are what are called the Soudan sheep – & a N<u>o</u> of goats & some poultry – they have a few fields in the Neighbourhood in which nothing is growing at present but from what I could learn Gussub is the principal grain there of which they have a N<u>o</u> they buy in Fezzan from the Arabs

This evening a little before sunset an afray of rather a serious nature took place in the town between an Arab sheikh and a Tibbo about a dollars worth of dates which the Arab had bought – however no sooner was the hue & cry set up that there was a dust then every man flew with his gun to shoot the tibbo right or wrong our servants to a man went in spite of orders or advice – This Tibbo who had offended was brought by [ ] to the camp before B.k.m who during the fray appeared to be in a rage at some thing or else was fitting himself for appearing to be in one – when the Tibbo was brought before him – who with little or no ceremony the poor Tibbo (who appeared to be a lad of 16 or 17 years of age) was thrown on his belly and every one who could get near with a stick kept beating him on the back and legs for about 10 m<u>ts</u> when B–km ordered them to desist and he was bound hand & foot and 2 of the principal persons came from the town to beg him off but first a slave of B.k.ms was sent with a Tibbo to the lads house to bring 4$ as a fine for his offence –

The truth was the Arab was the offender – this Sheikh Abdullah had sold the Tibbo a camel part was paid in dollars & part in dates – and the S<u>k</u> not liking the dates took them back to be exchanged or else to have money In maneauvering over the dates an altercation took place

---

[12]Apparently humpless longhorn; common in iconographic representations in the Sahara, ancient North Africa and Ethopia, yet today confined to a very small region of western Africa. The cattle Clapperton observed may have been genuine 'living fossils', brought across the desert in pre-historic times, or, perhaps more likely, brought into Kawar by kanuriized pastoralists from the Lake Chad region. [See R. Blench, "Ethnographic and linguistic evidence for the prehistory of African ruminant livestock, horses and ponies" in T. Shaw et al. (eds.) *The Archaeology of Africa* (London, 1993) pp. 71-87 for a discussion of the origins of sub-Saharan cattle.]

between his man & the Tibbo and   from words the servant proceded to
beating him with a stick   when the Tibbo drew his sword and made a
thrust at the servant which went through the folds of his barecan but
without further injury   Abdullah then knockd him down – and the servant set up the alarm – which being heard at the camp caused all the
Arabs and every man who could raise a weapon to proceed to the place
– to take part against the Tibbo right or wrong – B.k.m also sets his own
price upon every thing that they have to sell to the camp so that power
with the Arabs & Fezzaners is both law and justice – Slaves of the most
abject kind to their superiors & the most unjust & cruel tyrants to those
they have it in their power to oppress

Wednesday 8th

Morning Cold & Clear   it blew very hard during the night & from the
loosing of the sand on which we were encamped the whole of our tents
were blown down   we succeeded in pitching them again – but mine had
not been up half an hour before it was blowen down again – and I would
not take the trouble of pitching it again but slept in the open air the rest
of the night – my servant whom I have allowed to sleep in the tent during the cold weather   caught a severe cold – acc[d] with violent vomiting

at 7–20 AM we left Asinuma or Ashinuma and traveling along the foot
of the hills came to Aligi a long stragg[ling] town built partly on a shelf
at the foot of the hill & partly at the foot of the hill the houses built in
straggeling clusters extending for about ½ a mile to the south

the D[r] M[r] Hillman & I riding ahead of the camels we met a n[o] of women
& girls accompanied by three men beating on their sort of drums to the
sound of which the women danced waving a brush or fly flapper made
of the date tree over their heads Some times striking their backs with it
and other times as if sweeping the dust from before us – we alighted &
sat down – the women continued to dance & call lo, lo lo – after a little while perceiving that we were not the persons that they had come out

232

from Aligi to honour they enquired for B.k.m and we told them he was
by this time on his way from Asinuma   they left us to meet him – one
of the drummers was rather fantastically dressed about the head having
a cap of jackall skin with the hair on made with 2 large flaps that come
down by the ears   a wicked crown – with the scalp of the animal in
front[13]– the grinning face of the fellow added not a little to the grotesque
appearance – he appeared to be master of the band –

From Aligi I saw another lake bearing W ½ S distant about 4 Miles   the
people of Aligi told me that the name of it was Fatima & that it was Salt
like the one West of Ashinuma whose name they said was Egelan – on
riding through the town I saw the principal people assembled before the
Mosque ready to go and meet B.k.m when he appeared before the town
– our road was through bushes of grass date & Tallah trees & at 1 P.M–
we arrived at Dirkee or Dirgou as it is called by the Tibboos but Dirkie
by the Arabs & Fezzaners &[c] we pitched our tent to the South[d] of the
town – one of the horse men in skirmishing before B.k.m near to the
town where the in[hts] had planted some young date trees his horse fell
with him at full gallop & he was fortunate enough to get off with little
damage either to his horse or himself this is the first accident of the kind
– though they do not wait for a proper place but gallop through thick &
thin rough or sm[th][14]

the D[r] had a N[o] [of] patients with the usual comp[ts] [=complaints] & the
camp was soon filled with women old & young   they had heard from
some of their country men who had seen the pictures of the Tibbo
women in Cap[tn] Lyon's book and all were anxi[ous] to have a look at
them – it was accord[ly] shown them and they were quite in raptures –
with it   we saw none here with the silver rings represent[ed] in that

---

[13]Rock engravings (dating between the third and first millenium B.C.E.) of hunters wearing jack-
al-headed masks featured in the finds at In Habeter III near Tel Isaghen in Fezzan. [C. McBurney,
The Stone Age of Northern Africa (Harmondsworth, 1960) p. 264 & Plate 21.]

[14]See H. J. Fisher, "The Horse in the Sudan" in *Journal of African History*, Vol. XIV, 3 (1973) pp. 369-
371] for an account of deployment of horses in celebrations in Sudan.

work though from the great no– who have come into the camp I should suppose every woman in the town to have had a look at the camp not at us for we are not noticed more than the rest of the people & the D^r will be the only man remembred amongst us – they had heard the Month before the last Rhamadan[15] that he was comming through their co^{try} to Bornou & that he was a very good man I saw 2 girls at Gatrone dressed quite in the style of Capt^a Lyon's portraits but none of the men like his

Thursday 9th

Morning clear & Mild   at an early hour the camp was filled with Tibbos principally women who were busy buying and selling dates & camels meat – & the small wares of Soudan such as small plaited leather strings for tying charms round the neck or arms leather bags Tobes & Sheep – it appears here that the women here are are the Mistress of their own house for every one carries a bunch of keys[16]

Dirkee or Dirgoo is in Lat^{de} 18°–59'–53"" N by a Mn Alt^{de} of the Suns lower limb   it is situated on a rising ground & the houses are built of mud unlike the other tibbo towns we have seen[17]   it has a salt Marsh extending for about ½ a Mile on the North side & part of the East   to the South is a small salt lake about 200 yds to 300 in breadth from which they procure a considerable quantity of salt[18]   on the west at about a ¼ of a mile commences the sandy desert – and the range of hills are about 4 miles to the East having a stripe of date trees between them & the town

---

[15]That is to say in April/May 1822, when the Mission had only just arrived in Murzuq.

[16]Briggs [*Living Races of the Sahara Desert*, pp.104-5] comments on the customary privileges and dominant role in the household of women in Tubu society.

[17]Dirki, the political capital of Kawar and residence of the Sultan. Nachtigal [*Sahara and Sudan*, Vol. III, pp. 61-2] remarks on the Kanuri character of the layout, building and traditions of the town – which in 1869 was a larger town than Al-Qatrun.

[18]A centre of Kawar's natron industry of continuing importance, its salt a pinkish colour distinguishing it from the white natron of Bilma [K.S. Vikor, "The Desert-side salt trade of Kawar" in *African Economic History*, 1982, No. 11, pp. 115-144].

– They say that the Tuaricks come here for salt that some times they pay and some times they do not that last year they come in greater N^{o} than usual & took every thing they could lay their hands on & that a Kaffle of Tuaricks had left this place only a few days ago but they had behaved well this time[19] – they say here that it is 7 long days j^{ny} to Ire and give the bearings the same as at the other place viz where the sun sets –

the people here are well dressed & app[ear] not to be very ill off for all they say of the Tuaricks – the Dr– asked them what made them exact tribute from travelers   they said they only did so untill they know them after that they were as well of[f] and as free as a Tibboo

on the D^r asking them if it ever rained here & at what times   they said that it some times rained for a day but at no particular season   that when that occurred they come out & prayed to God & the prophet that he would cause it to cease and not to wash their houses down[20]

the water in the wells is very good & sweet but hard – & within a few feet of the salt lake – like all the other places here & in Fezzan good fresh water is found within a few feet of salt wells & marshes & some times as at Traghan in the midst of a soil containing a great quantity of salt

we bought 2 Sheep for 2 ½ $ each as our stock of preserved meat was getting low   A party of Arabs who had been sent to Steal or take the Tibbo camels as B.k.ms were done up   returned with 10   that not being sufficient a^r [=another] party go off in the Morning in search of more

---

[19]Barth [*Travels*, Vol. III, pp. 613-5] remarks that the Tubu here were protected to some extent by the Tuareg because they fulfilled a useful function as salt brokers. Clapperton's accounts indicate a steady if small volume of Tubu activity in the salt trade. In mid-century the Tuareg had come to dominate it wholly and Kawar suffered depressed times – the "dilapidated town of Bilma" and the "miserable hamlet"[Barth, *Ibid.*]; but the Tubu peoples' situation had apparently improved again by the time of the Nachtigal's visit to Wadi Kawar in 1869.

[20]Norris [*The Tuaregs*, pp. 200-201] writes of the legendary control of rain by Tuareg priests, the Ineslemen, supposedly able to prevent total drought or assure regular and seasonal rainfall by prayers and other acts of intercession.

Friday 10th
Morning Clear & Warm   we had quite a fair in the camp to day again
but the Tibbos are very much displeased at the Manner in which their
Camels are taken from them   B.k.m told them it is the Sultan of Tripoli's
orders and that he will take them where he can find them[21] –

the party returned in the evening with 6 more camels   before sunset
Old Hadje Mohammed his 2 Sons the brother of the Cadi of Morzuk
& another Mercht arrived   they left Morzuk 6 days after us witht any
escort or guards   so much for B.k.ms account of the roads and the danger to be dreaded when an Old man of 65 and his 2 son's dare to travel
without guards even when they had this offered and scorn to ly up inside
the Camp – fearing the Arabs

Saturday 11th
Morning Cloudy & Warm   at 8 AM– Started   our road was in a line
with the hills amongst tallah trees & Grass Bushes & agool occ[ly] broken
through by low ridges of pipe clay and sand stone   at 1.30 halted &
pitched our tents at what the[y] call half way between Dirkoo & Bilma
the wady stretches for about 5 miles W[t] from the foot of the hills & then
the des[ert]   Course S by W ½ W *8*

Sunday 12th
Clear & Warm   at 7–40 S[t] our road the same as yesterday   saw a N[o] of
Ghazales one of which an Arab shot[22] –   I have rode a camel today &
Yesterday having cut my leg in wading in the Salt lake at Ashinuma after
birds   at 2– halted on the Southern Side of Bilma   Course S. by W ½
W 12

---

[21]"An excursion that was sanctioned by the Sultan, who gave them instructions as to the route
they were to take." [Denham, *Missions*, Vol. I, p. 212].

[22]Probably the *Antilope arabica*, called *Al-ariyal* by the Arabs [Barth, *Travels*, Vol. II, p. 65], common
in the southern Saharan desert and the steppes of the Sudan.

Monday 13th

Cloudy with a fresh breeze   the D[r] at this place as well as those we have
passed has had his tent burst from morning to night with patients principally women – but he has only one application for medecine to make
a woman fruitfull

Today the D[r] and I went to visit the salt pits – they are situated to the
west of the town & look like [a] cluster of little Volcanic hills or rocks
taking that appearance partly from the earth that is dug out of the hole
at first & partly from the sand that occ[ly] blows in & the salt forming
round it assumes the Shape of a piece of dirty ice or rough stone and is
thrown out or built up round the top in the form of a wall   the place is
something like a tanners pits the hole being of an irregular size with little salt banks bet[wn] for the gatherer to walk on – at this Season of the
year the pits are full of salt water to the depth of a foot to 18 inches or 2
feet with a scum of salt on the top some thicker than others according
as the salt has been taken off – on the sides of the pits are some beautiful Stalictites – in the summer they say there is little or no water and
that the salt is procured in great quantities – they put it up in the form
of large sugar loaves for the purpose of carrige – the salt is clean pure
from sand and free from any bitter taste   the loave salt is white as our
basket salt in Britain – some salt is procured from the lake at Dirkie and
the other places but not so good as here

Boolma or Bilma is in Lat[de] 18°–40'–44" N [Lat[de]] by Mn Alt[de] O   situated on a rising ground in the centre of a salt plain which looks like as
if ploughd over without any of these large blocks of salt & mud   as in the
other plains of the same kind in this country & the Kingdom of Fezzan
in this plain are a No. of springs of fine fresh water which look like little plots or islds– left unploughd as they are generaly covered by green
grass & reeds and above the level of the plain some feet they have a very
beautifull appearance   besides there is a feeling of pleasure in looking at
a spring of fresh water that none who have not travled in such a country can feel   the Salt plain to the East is bounded by the same range that

comes unbroken from Iguba but ["at this place turns to the east^d " inserted] 2 or thr[ee] Miles south of this place turns to the East^d on the South & West sides there are high sand hills & to the north the Wady Cawar or Kawar –

the houses are built of Mud but in a very ruinous state it has since been s^d [=surrounded] by a wall which the greatest enemy it ever had could not wish to be in a worse condition there is another town about a mile to West^d amongst the salt pits – but distinguished by no other name both are called Boolma and considered as one town[23]

COMMENTARY

The commerce carried on here is in salt which they carry to Bornou & soudan & receive in exchange slaves, tobes, &^{c} & what is not made use of in this country is taken and sold at Morzuk – They say that to the ammount of 30.000 camel loads is taken or bought by the Tuaricks ["every year into Soudan" deleted] who carry it into Soudan where each loaf is sold for a dollar or its value last year they say that the Tuaricks came to the amount of 13.000 and carried of[f] besides all the salt from this place & Dirkie every thing else that they could lay there hands on[24]

Their name is Tibbos or Tibowi – they are the same people as those of Tibesty which they say is 7 days Journey to the East^d and Borgoo which is 15 days Journey to the East^d they have a language of their own approaching very near to the Bornou language if I may judge from the sound of the words but those Arabs and Fez[aners]– who understand

---

[23]The western settlement beside the salt pits is today called Kalala.

[24]The annual Azalai (Tg.,*Taghalam*) of the Tuareg. These values correspond to an annual export of some 1,000 to 3,000 tons (based on loads of 95kgs per camel) – figures which Lovejoy [*Salt of the Desert Sun – Salt Production and Trade in the Central Sudan* (Cambridge, 1986) p. 97] posits as a more likely annual average than Nachtigal's estimate, later in the century, of 6,300 tons.

the Bornou language say that it differs greatly[25] — with respect to their N[os] I am very uncertain [if] I were to say 3.000 in Kawar I dare say that I may be near the tenth on one side or the other[26]

They sow very little grain owing I suppose to the honesty of the Tuaricks & Arab Merch[ts] I suppose who would save them the trouble of reaping it their date trees are few in No— compared to those in Fezzan in an equal extent of country fit for the growth of the date tree besides the dates are much smaller than those of that country —

Their Weapons consist of a sword of a very peculiar ["construction" deleted] shape — and is either used to strike with or thrust in a horizontal manner at the enemy and what ever part strikes is sure to wound it is called — Mizari[27] The dagger is about 2 feet long in the blade roughly made straight & very sharp with a piece of leather moulded round the handle to make the iron firm enough & large enough for the hand — the sheath has a leather grummet or ring for putting over the left wrist but they generally carry it in the left hand it is called Lowi[28]

They also carry 5 or 6 spears one longer than the rest called Adibory the others light and made for throwing to a distance they are not feathered at the ends to make them go true & further but the heads are dread-

---

[25]There are two dialect clusters of 'Tubu' [lit., the people, *bu*, of *tu/i*] (the same root word as ti in Tibesti): Teda and Daza. The term 'Teda-Daza' is generally used today to denote the whole language. This remark by Clapperton is the first record by a European of the relationship between Teda-Daza and Kanuri, which was later confirmed by Barth and subsequently Nachtigal, who added Zaghawa to the group. Teda-Daza is part of the 'Saharan language family' within the Nilo-Saharan phylum. [Professor N. Cyffer, University of Vienna, personal communication].

[26]The French administration's census of 1906 gave a population of 2,280, of whom about 800 were Kanuri [Vikor, "The Desert-side Salt Trade", p. 140 n.4]. Peter Fuchs [*Das Brot der Wüste, etc.*, (Wiesbaden, 1983)] estimated the population at 2,800, comprising 1,300 mixed Tubu-Kanuri (the sedentary Gezebida), 1,000 in Kanuri communities, and some 700 immigrant Tubu (the Tubu Brawia, the original settlers from the north,) in Kawar and its outlying oases.

[27]The word 'misari' for sword does not appear in J. Lukas [*Die Sprache der Tubu in der Zentralen Sahara* (Berlin, 1953)] or Ch. Le Coeur [*Dictionnaire ethnographique Téda*, IFAN, No.9, (Paris, 1950)].

[28]Tubu, *loii*, *épée* [Le Coeur, *Dictionnaire*]. Denham refers to the term "hunga-munga" for a sword, presumably from the Arabic root word *anjar*, a slit or cleft.

fully jagged – for making the wound more dread they have also bows
& arrows some of their arrows are poisoned short & without feathers
the head is of iron barbed & if shot inside the barb would leave the iron
in both the bow and shaft of the arrow is *cane* they call them
Adikoonoo the small throw spears the Bow Kaffee arrows Kifee[29]

Their diffensive Armour is a shield & steel cap with a chain net that
hangs over the neck the links of which will not admit the point of a spear
– a long piece of iron runs down before the nose like a handle – or take
away the chain from behind and it would make a large ladle[30]

Their food consist[s] of boiled rice gussub a grain that eats something
like wheat, dates & Milk & camels flesh – the Atir & Gussub [they] procure in Bornou they have also a Nº of Cows & sheep the latter are of
the Soudan breed –

Their dress consists of a Turban over a bl[ue] cotton cap the turban is
generaly narrow blue cotton cloth highly glazed & made in soudan – one
turn is always taken over the mouth & Chin – a Tobe or large shirt with
wide sleeves the size of the body the colour generaly blue or light blue
& white stripes some are altogether white & a pair of blue or white
trowsers that come down to the ancles if they can afford it the[y] wear
2 or 3 tobes at the same time some times carrying one over each shoulder

The women dress in a tobe of blue cotton cloth the sleeves not so large
as the Mens with a square piece of blue cloth or striped blue & White
thrown over the head – a no– of them also dress with a square piece of

---

[29]*Adiboory* and *adikoono* are evidently compound nouns, from the root-word *edi*, javelot, lance [Le
Coeur, *Dictionnaire*]. Lukas [*Die Sprache*] notes *kapi* for 'bow', related to the Kanuri *kafi*, or *kife* .
Clapperton's *kife* for 'arrow' is probably an error. Lukas has *fere* for 'arrow', and Le Coeur notes *here*.

[30]The kulakhudd – a semi-spherical, domed, bowl-shaped helmet (of Indo-Persian origin) with a
sliding nasal bar and chain-mail neck defence, common in the 17th to 19th centuries. More elaborate
versions included quilted lining, a spike and plume holders and intricate damascene decoration. [G.
Gardiner, Sotheby's, personal communication.]

cloth tyed over the left Shoulder of blue or white & a piece thrown over the head the same as above they have the long flaps over each ear the same as at Gatrone – but I have seen none here with [ ]

Their diseases appear to be few from what we saw being mostly sore eyes & complaints of the breast though all want medecine They are of a light spare form with rather short faces large eyes – generaly a large mouth & good teeth small flat nose in general but their countenances are very diversified their foreheads are in general high with a prominence over the eye brows & not falling back the chin small & beard thin of their dispositions we have had little opportunity to judge – but I should think from their countenance that they were a lively good natured set what ever the Arabs & Fezzaners say who treat them very ill call them infidels & rob them when ever they dare – so if they retaliate at times it cannot be [a] matter of surprise

Their Religion is Mohometan and a No of them can read & write Arabic They are governd by a Sheikh who is called Sultan he is a middle aged man & called Dinomoo[31] he has very little authority and in his dress & ap^{ce} is not to be distinguished from any o^r [= other] well dressed Tibboo

Tuesday 14$\underline{^{th}}$
Clear & mild on enquiring at the Tibbos today what the Tuaricks called Bilma or Boolmo they said Doolmoo or Doolomba – & that there was another town called Aghram[32] 3 days West of Bilma with a lake and a

---

[31]In the published Narrative [*Missions*, Vol. II, p. 208], he is merely referred to as "Sultan Tibboo". According to Cline [The Teda, p. 19] a medieval tradition has the name 'Diulumana'. The Arabic origins of this, Dhu'l Amana, imply a person having possession of something (in this case, salt mines) under licence (here, Kanuri authority) and responsibility for its security [H. T. Norris, personal communication].

[32]Agram [Berber, 'town'] is more widely known today as Fachi. It is a salt-producing village with a principally Kanuri population, some 160 miles west of Kawar and usually considered part of it [Vikor, "The desert side salt trade", p. 118].

great no. of date trees — they say that they call salt Doolmoo in Soudan[33]

The Tibbos of the Whole of the towns we have pass[ed] pay tribute to the Tuaricks as also the inhab[s] of Aghram who are Arabs[34] very poor the tibboo say

---

[33]Etymology uncertain. Salt is *gishiri* in the Hausa language; the Kanuri word is *manda*; and the usual word in Teda-Daza is *gereni* – also *ere* in dialect – and the related *galin* or *gilin* [N.Cyffer, personal communication].

[34]More likely Arab tribes from the region of Chad than from the north. [Prof. H. T. Norris, personal communication].

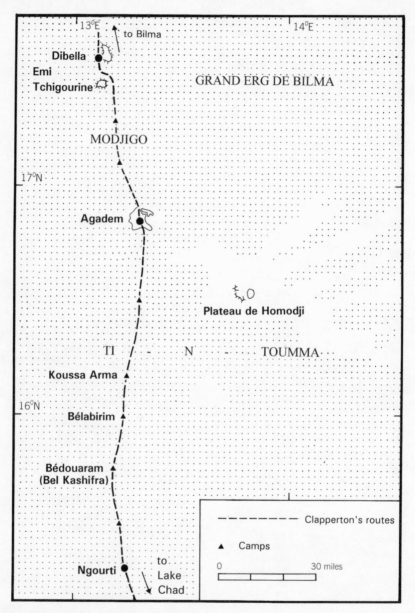

Map 13. Southern Desert

244

CHAPTER

13

Southern Desert

Wednesday 15th
at 8-40 A.M– we left Bilma and after winding round ascend^g and descending amongst the sand hills we halted at 1– P.M– at a small Oasis and wells   on the South was a point of the range of hills we have passed along from Ieguba to this place where they Turn to the S.E   the Wells & Oasis is called Mis, ka, ti, noo   Course   South 8

Thursday 16th
at 7- A.M – Started   after crossing some of the sand hills to the south of where we had halted we Ob^{sd} that instead of the range which we had come along from Yeguba being broken & turning to the East^d it proved only to be a valley and that we are now traveling in a vally covered with sand as are a No– of hills to the East & West   our road is intersected by large dykes of sand which have accumulated in the place the[y] now are since the last gale from the marks of the old road at the foot of some of the dykes   the Mountains or hills are comp^d of the same Substances as the other but are Much broken into valleys to the East & West & the hills more of cone shape than before

our camels to day were in a very Weak state & one we had to kill as we could not bring it along after unloading it – at 7 halted– between 2 hills

Lat[de] Mn Alt[de] Sirius 18°–21'–11"N the halting place called ["Kaffleron" deleted] Zow Dubhe[1] Course S ½ W 14

Friday 17th

morning Clear & fine   at 6–40 A.M. Started   our road for a Mile & [a] half was over the ridges of rock ["formed by" deleted] running from the hills to the East[d]   saw a small Oasis on the West side of the hill under which we had halted all night   after crossing the rocky ridges which are composed of the same Substance we obs[d] the hills running to the W.SW as far as the eye could reach   to the south[d] of these was a large valley filled with Sand hills & from the top of which I could discern another range of rocky hills to the south[d] – the range still continues to the south – at Noon we halted at the Oasis of Zow[2] – where we found good feeding for the camels & plenty of wood & water Agool & green grass & tallah – took distances between the) – O[3] the Oasis runs from a point of the hills to those that branch out to the West   there water & grass &[s] growing round the point – for the distance of 2 miles and about a mile in breadth

Sent our camels out to feed filled our Water Skins and did every thing but say we must stay to B.k.m over the next day – but he is getting short of provisions for his men & horses   he having only 13 days for a Journey of 22 days

Long[de] by Dist O – C – 12°–48'–30" E[d]   Lat[de] Mn Alt[de] Sirius 18°–13'–11" N[4] Course South 8

---

[1]Clapperton's Zow Dubhe would appear to be beside the Tenga-tenga hills at the northern end of the Zoo oasis complex.

[2]Zoo Baba.

[3]Symbols for a calculation of longitude by the lunar distance method – using the distance between the sun and the moon.

[4]A fair sighting; actual position is 18° 14'N, 13° 3' E.

Saturday 18th

at 8 A.M – we left Zow   a no– waited behind some time so that others
might go ahead & indeed B.k.m kept the greatest part of his own camels
behind – & we were sent on after the Shiblean[5] as usual –

when on the top of one of the high sand hills – which are here about 400
feet obs^d that the range still continued to the south but at the distance of
about 8 or 9 Miles – but a hill ["to the West^d bearing N.W ½ N" insert-
ed] where there was an Oasis & Well – it is Called Kaffleron[6] and the
place we halted at on the 16th is called Zow Dubhe or the mother of
Zow – the hills to the East^d are nearly covered to the top with sand and
the sand hills we travled over to day are formed of sand over Small hills
– from their shape as in some places I perceived the stratum where the
sand had blown off – at 7 P.M – halted after a very fatiguing days journey but just before we halted we had nearly all our baggage upset by a
rush a party of Arabs made ["with their camels" inserted] to get on to the
the halting place after keeping behind all day they descended a sand hill
like a torrent right into the Midst of our camels and only for the exertions of our men we would not only [have] had our things smashed to
pieces but our camels killed I galloped to B.k.m who sent the Showse
to keep them in order and prevent their attempting the same thing over
again

B.k.m had to kill 2 of his camels as they were unable to proceed –
Course S ¾ W 13   Lat^{de} 18°–1'–51" N Mn Alt^{de} Sirius

Sunday 19th

Morning clear & fine   at 7.40 AM – started the sand hills decreasing in
size and our road much easier –   at 9 we came up with a part of the
Kaffle which had taken another road and got a head of us – B–k.m gave

---

[5]Lyon [*A Narrative*, p. 59] gives Ar., *Shiblia*, a cloth-covered, wooden-framed litter carried on a
camel; here, by extension, the baggage train.

[6]*Kaflorum* means simply a halting place. The hill bearing N.W. is Yoo Kareri (1778 feet).

them a good blowing up – for not stoping for us – we were here Abreast of the end of a Black hill ["bearing East" inserted] called Ama, che, qoi, ma[7] and it is cons[d] the halting place for Kaffles – here we found tufts of grass on which our poor camels fed   at 6 P.M– halted   just before halting when we were going to water our horses we found out of 14 skins we had filled at Zow that we had only 5 and as our horses had not drank since yes[dy] morning we could only allow them about 2 gallons – we had all left the Kaffle to the charge of our servants & they said our skins were bad – I suppose they had given away or sold the greater part but they stoutly denied the charge   sent our camels out to feed on the tufts of grass that are to be found in the hollows of the sand hills – before halting we came to a mound of pipe clay & blue clay   it looked like a Stratum of rock

Course S. by W 14   Lat[de] by Mer Alt[de] Sirius 17°–48'–38" N

Monday 20th
at 7 A.M – Started   we left the camels to be brought on by our servants – and as none of the horses in the Kaffle had drunk for 2 days we proceeded on ahead   our road was over low sand hills between which there was plenty of grass –   saw the traces of Ghazales which were very numerous –   at Noon we arrived at Some Mountains nearly covred to the top with sand – the part exp[d] was composed of Quartz & sandstone in the hollows – between some of the sand hills the pipe clay stratum was exposed – which confirms the opinion I had formed of the sand hills having for their nucleus low hills composed of the same range as Kawar hills

at 1 we arrived at the wells of Dublea [arabic script added] which are situated at the foot & to the southd of a small range of rocky hills in an Oasis having sand hills to the North & East

---

[7]Emi [Mount] Tioukoye, the mountain 'half way' [Tubu] between the Zoo oases and Dibella.

248

at 6 P.M– the camels arrived   we filled our gerbas as soon as the tents
were pitched   the water has rather a bad taste & smell but not so bad as
we had been led to expt   the water is in great plenty about 18 inches
below the surface in the lowest part of the Wady[8]

Course S ¾ E – Lat^{de} by Mer Alt^{de} Sirius 17°–32'–5" N

Tueday 21st

We had a fresh breeze all night which sent our most of our tents flying
& made the surounding Sand hills look as if it [was] snowing round
them – at 8.40 A.M we left Dubleh – and ascended the sand hills to the
south of the Wady   before we got to the top 2 of our camels gave up so
that we have 4 now that are unable to bear any thing whatever not even
their own saddles –   the Camel gives up at once from c[ar]rying the
heaviest load to being hardly able to move along and some times they are
left to perish & some times they are killed – if they will not be at the
trouble to bring them on

– at 4– P.M– halt^d as the place afforded grass for the camels which we
sent out to feed   our road after as^{cdg} the sand hills was over a series of
ranges of sand hills having gentle ascents & declivities running E & West
– at 1 P.M we came to grass growing amongst the sandhills – after halting took distances between the O & C   we passed 3 black rocky hills
about 2 Miles bearing to the West^d of the road called *Chegrum*[9]
Course S. ¼ E 11 Miles   Lat^{de} by Mer Alt^{de} Sirius 17°–21'–43" [N]

---

[8]These wells lie at the southernmost end of the 200 miles long Wadi Kawar water course.
Nachtigal comments on their reputation for poor quality water which caused intestinal troubles; and
it was here that Henry Warrington, a son of Consul Hanmer Warrington and a member of the
Central Africa Mission led by Barth, died in 1854 [Nachtigal, *Sahara and Sudan*, Vol. II, p. 83 & n.].
[9]Tchigoubine (1710 feet).

Wednesday 22nd

Morning cold & Clear   at 7.30 A.M— Started   after leaving the vally
in which we had halted all night we ascended on the Sand hills which
wave in an East & West direction and were they covered with grass
would be called Lease [= leas] or gentle hill & dale – our camels travled
very well we having given each a quart of dates & the weak 2 [quarts]
that and the little grass they had last night – quite revived them but had
to give up 2 to be killed as they were not able to come on a little before
sunset we came to plenty of grass – the Arabs wanted much to stop but
Bkm went on and at 6 halted – in a vally where the grass was in
Abundance and after unloading we sent the camels out to feed just after
we had had our dinner an alarm was given that the camels were attacked
by an enemy which turned all the horse & foot out

Course S by W ½ W 18 miles – Lat^{de} by M Alt^{de} Sirius 17°–4'–38" N

Thursday 23rd

Clear & fine   at 7.30 AM— Started our road was over the sand hills as
before – waving from E.S.E to W.S.W. so that we had the hills in a slant-
ing direction   after leaving the place we halted at all night we had not
[had] a blade of grass or shrub and only for its having raind for some
time lately we would have had none at the former place as those who
had travled the road before said that they had never met with grass there
untill this time[10] – at 4 P.M – we rounded the West end of the hills of
Agadim[11] and halt^d near the – Well – & sent the camels out to feed this
range is like the former & the people agr^d – say that they are the last we
will see – they run in a direction [ ] and as I said before the nucleus of
all the sand hills appear to be of the same –

---

[10]Depending on the season of travel, most desert shrubs and grasses being ephemeral.
[11]An extensive wadi and the largest settlement between Kawar and Chad; "a great rendezvous,
and the dread of all small kafilas and travellers.... frequented by freebooters of all descriptions"
[Denham, *Missions*, Vol. II, p. 219].

There is plenty of grass in the Wady also a no of trees called [ ] bearing a red or purple fruit bigger than a ["straw b" deleted] current berry[12] – in several places there is a Crust of Trona – appearing like the salt marshes in Fezzan –

In crossing the sand hills we found several pipe formations of sand resembling coral outside but hollow in the inside – they are rough on the outside like coral and form small branches from the stem & knobs – in the inside they are quite smooth some of one colour & some of another the most common colour is grey – formed of the particles of sand and some natural cement which is like transparent paste or izing glass[13] – we found them in great quantity sticking up through the sand like as if they served for funnels for evaporation & I am of [the opinion that] they are as the Tibbos say they find More after the rains and say that the remdr [=remainder] of the water comes through they pound them to a fine powder and put it in their ears when troubled with the ear ache[14] – Course S by W ¾ W 15 – Lat^de Mer Alt^de of Sirius 16°–49'–22" N –

Friday 24th

Clear & Warm sent our camels out to feed at day light – our people emp^d filling our Water skins &^c The people acquainted with the road say we will have grass all the way to Bornou from this place the Arabs brought in 2 Ghazales which they had shot – I was unable to go out all day from the pain in my legs[15] & have had cold poultices of henna[16] all day applied to it – when the rains are plentiful at Bornou it rains here

---

[12]Ar., *siwak*, *Capparis sodata*: "a tetrandrous plant, called suag, with a heavy narcotic smell; its fruit a small dropa" [Oudney, *Missions*, Vol. II, p. 219 n.].

[13]isinglass; mica, translucent gelatine [ShOED].

[14]Calcified reeds; well described from several parts of the central Sahara, for example, around Kufra, where they mark out the former extent of quite large lakes [M. Edmunds, personal communication]. Barth [*Travels*, Vol. III, p. 610], mentions some traditional explanations, such as the effects of lightning, or the runs of white ants in the guinea corn, for these "remarkable crystallized tubes called 'bergom chidibe' by the Kanuri and 'Kauchin Koassa' by the Hausa people...".

[15]See Chapter Four, n. 16 on the cause of these uncomfortable leg swellings.

[16]Henna, Ar. *hinna*, *Lawsonia inermis*, used in Fezzan and the Sahara for a variety of medicinal as well as cosmetic purposes [Nachtigal, *Sahara and Sudan*, Vol. I, pp. 118, 136-9].

Saturday 25th

Morning cool & Clear   at 8 A.M – Started   our road was the same as on ["the 2 days before we came to Agadim" inserted] days past over low sandy ridges   we had little or no grass and one of our camels got drunk with eating the [   ][17] and drinking soon after – though he was a stout camel & walked well on other occasions   he fell so often that we had to unload him – the Arabs opened one of the veins of the Nose & took abt ½ a gallon of blood from him – when after falling they could not get him to rise he was thrown on his broadside & turned round in that way   after which he always got up

2 courriers of the Sheikh of Kanem[18] arrived bringing letters to B.k.m & several others   he had heard we were on the way and sent to wish us welcome – he had only arrived at Bornou 16 days ago – from an expedition he had ["been" deleted] made to Bagermie where the people had all fled on his approach except the old and infirm   he brought of[f] all the camels & Cattle he could lay hands on – at 6–30 P.M. halted   course S by W ½ W.   17   Latde Mn Sirius 16°–32'–32" N

Sunday 26th

Morning cool & Clear   at 7 AM – Started   our road the same as before at Noon we came to plent[y] of grass on which the camels & horses fed greedily   notwithstanding 2 of our camels that had given up some days before were unable to proceed – we therefore had to kill them   and all we got for our share was one of the hearts and the kidneys   the Arabs began before the life was out of them to cut them up   every man where he could lay his hands on without stoping to skin it – when ever they see a camel droop they hover arround like so many wolves & When the word is given to kill every man cuts or tears off as much as he can without regarding the owner who oftener than otherwise goes wt [= with-

---

[17]Suag; see note 12 p.201.
[18]Muhammad Al-Kanami of Borno.

out] a morsel   we saw numerous tracks of the wild ox which they say is all white[19]   as also of several Ghazales

one of our camel men killed a Leffa in the afternoon   which was about 18 inches long and had the poiseonus fangs –

at 7 halted & sent the camels out to feed – from the haziness of the hori- zon we could not see the eclipse when she arose   took the time at the ending and the appt time by an Alt^{de} of Sirius – [1]7°–50'–3"   the end of the Eclipse Green^h time   6–58

$$-52–3 \quad 13o–[0']–45" \text{ East}$$

Course S by W ¾ W– 18   Lat^{de} by Mn Alt^{de} Sirius – 16°–13'–52" N[20]

Monday 27th

Cool & Clear   at 7 A.M. Std–   our road was down a narrow vally in which in some places there were a few Mimosas growing   both the low hills & the vallies are covered with tufts of fine grass on which the camels fed as they went along – at 10 we met a Kaffle consisting [of] about 20 slaves ["and about" deleted] – belongs to some of the Bornou people they were acc^d by about 10 Tibbos –   they had left the Well of Bel Kashifra yesterday M^{ng} & Kuka the capital of Bornou 16 days ago – as I was some miles ahead of the Kaffle they made a n^o of inquiries and I could plainly see that the people of Bornou did not like the Idea of the Arab escort at all –

the whole of the vally we are traveling through is marked with the feet of Ghazales & the wild cow – some of the former we saw but none of the latter – they must have been here in myriads but a few days ago   as the soil is a light sand & both hills & vally are like sheep fold[s] with the marks of their feet – we killed another Leffa today   the fangs very long

---

[19]The Mendes antelope or addax, *Addax nasomaculatus*, a large antelope distinguished, when fully grown, by its whitish colour and one metre long corkscrew horns.

[20]Koussa Arma (16°12'N, 13°13'E).

for the body about 18 inches or 2 feet at 7– PM halted – Lat^{de} by Mn Alt^{de} Sirius – 15°–55'–49" N   Course SW by S ¾ S– 19

Tuesday 28th

at 6.20 A.M– Started the horse going ahead as some of them had not drank for three days – yet never the less the Arabs gallaped before B.k.m. in their usual manner without any regard for the condition of their poor horses – at 10 A.M– we [halted] at the Well of Bel Kashifra so called in the Bornou and by the Tibbos Be, doo, woree – we had to send the people down to clear the well of the sand with which it was nearly filled up – it is 5 feet in depth – and when clear of sand the water plenty and good – it is frequented by a tribe of Arabs called Goonda[21] – ["Sheikh's name" inserted] Taher[22] – who come here to sell their fat, sheep & milk to the passing Kaffles but hearing of the approach of the army or escort – they had all fled –

The well is situated in [a] circular valley about 2 miles to the Westd of the one we have been traveling in for the last 2 days – and from the appearance of the place I do not think the tropical rains constant[l]y extend this far north though there is plenty of grass yet as the bottom of the valleys are clay there is no tracks or marks or any traces of water which would be the case were the rains to take place here as in other tropical climates

at Noon the camels arrived when we pitched the tents & sent them out to feed – Course S.W. by S ½ S   Lat^{de} by Mn Alt^{de} Sirius 15°–40'–53" N

---

[21]The Gunda Tubu, a sub-tribe of the Teda of Tibesti formerly from Tchigai, with a population of some 800, occupied the desert oases from the southern fringe of Kawar to Agadem and were principally engaged in camel-herding. In the 19th century they became mixed with the cattle-herding Daza Kecherda of Manga. [Chapelle, *Nomades noirs*, pp.116-117.]

[22]According to Denham [*Missions*, Vol. I, p. 224] Sheikh Mina Tahr ('the black bird'), aged 25, was a hereditary chief of the Nafra Gunda Tubu tribe.

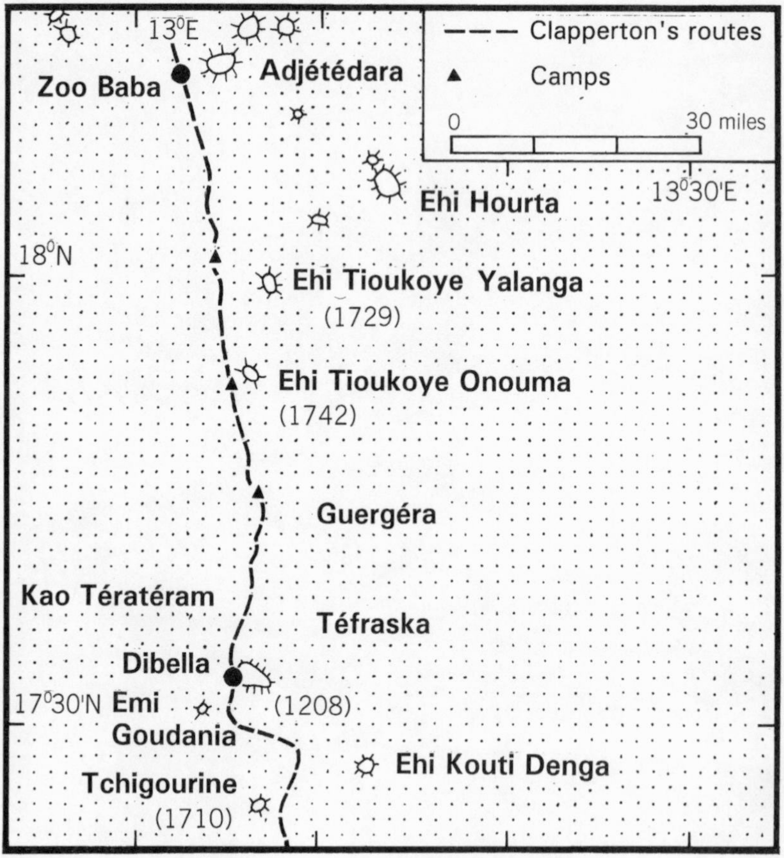

Map 14. Return to the Desert

CHAPTER

14

Return to the Desert

Thursday 23ʳᵈ [September 1824]
at Day light Sᵗᵈ & at 11 AM arrived at the well of – Belkashefra or the
upper well – a large encampment of Arabs or Tibboos who would only
allow us to water our horses – they watering their own which ammount-
ed to thousands Camels sheep & bullocks In the afᵗⁿ visited by Mina
Taher who said we would have the well all night – & that he wished us
to go on our journey next day – we filled our water skins but were not
able to water our cˡˢ night squals of Wind & lightning with slight
Showers of rain

Friday 24ᵗʰ
Clear & Warm – no water but great promises from Mina Taher in ques-
tioning him to day whither they were Tibboos or Arabs he said Tibboos
of Wady Kawar that their lighter colour was from god that they were
the same people though lighter in colour than the Tibboos of Fezzan and
Kawar – diffrent in features having higher noses more like arabs –
speaking in general both the Shouack Arabic & the Tibboo languages

The Tibboos of Kawar & Fezzan have flat broad nostrils in general wide
mouths & Short faces – the women cleaner dressing their hair diffrently
– the women of Kawar wearing the large flaps of plaited hair over each

ear – the Tibboos of this place wearing it like the Kanumboe women in ["plaited" inserted] bobbins having the fore head shaved a considerable way up and a plaited ornamented row of hair in front – They are thieves to a man – rob Gaffles when they Dare – & Steal from all –

we have had sad work about water Mina Taher wanting his fees – or as much as he can get from the Arabs before he will let them have water or even us though Major D has given him a good Tobe a Turkadee & a red cap yet he wants me to give him another – says he "are you a boy or a poor Man Rais Abdullah that you cannot give me a present like Rais Haleel" – I said you are a very knowing fellow Mina Taher & do you think I am going to put a blush on the face of Rais Halel who has given you a very handsome present – and you have not even let him have water for his camels – he burst out a laughing & struck my hand as much as to say you are not to be done

the Major had to go down & see his camels watered himself as his people were not only prevented [from] watering his camels & filling their skins but if they attempted to put their bucket in the well – my people had filled their skins during the night & got the camels watd– with a little patience by sunset – I exchanged my horse for 4 good camels one of which I let Major D. have – at 30$

Saturday 25th

Clear & cool Mina Taher brought a Tiger skin to me which he said was a present to Sultan George – I gave him a Turkadee & some tobaco as I realy could not withstand this appeal & returned him his old Tiger skin which I suppose was the best article he had to give telling him at the same time that Sultan George had more Tiger skins than there were Tigers in the land of Slaves.

The Ague has been very prevalent in our little party – from what cause I know not except from the heat of the sun. Major D. has 2 serv'ts ill

& Hillman   I have one

at 2.30 P.M. left Bellkasheefra   I had recovered considerably from the pain in my left side by drinking warm camels milk with which we had been supplied by the natives in a abundance at a very cheap rate for gussub, Tobaco, Khol or antimony and Gubja[1] at 7 P.M. halted as Major D. was behind with his Gaffle[2] & Hadje Boo Zaid's Gaffle had halted when old Hadje Boo Zaid having remained behind had lost his way & we heard him hallooing & firing to the East of My camp – I sent my people & brought him quenched his thirst with some tikery[3] and sent him to his own Gaffle which was not far distant – Course N. by E

Sunday 26th
at Daylight S[td] – Major D– joined   the Morning hazy with a Slight wind from the East[d] which caused the haze by bringing showers of light sand which powdred the faces of all the blacks & dim[m]ed the Suns light & rendred surrounding objects nearly invisable – at Noon halted –

Calm at 3 P.M. St[d] at 8–30 halted   Course N by E ¾ E –

Monday 27th
at 4–30 no Stars to be seen the guides differing greatly about the roads I could not see the compass – but by the light of the fire – & found our old guide to be right – at day light we saw Hadje Boo Zaid a long way to the East & turning back to find the place they had left but when they saw us they followed on to join us –

at 10 A.M. we met a gaffle from Fezzan 70 days who had letters for us

---

[1] Common trade goods from Borno brought to pay the costs of the desert crossing.

[2] See Chapter Ten, n. 14.

[3] "Guinea corn pounded and seasoned with pepper dried in the sun and mixed with milk or water – a sour taste." [*Clapperton in Borno*, p.193].

they had left Agadim yesterday

at 3. P.M. Started – and at 8 P.M. halted – Course N.N.E –

Tuesday 28th

at 4–A.M. St^d after day light they bothered our guide so much that they led him out of his [ ] at 10 they thought they had lost the road and Major D– & the Maraboot Moh^d Sia went to the top of the sand to look for the hills of Agadim which on not seeing them when the Maraboot abused our guide in a shamefull manner telling him he had killed him and all the people with thirst – saying there we are all dead men by your villany – the old guide now gave up – & they were traveling on to the East or E by N. I left the Gaffle with camels knowing the old guide was right and went on our old course N.N.E & N by E ¾ E and at the top of the first sandhills saw the Black rocky hills of Agadim a head – My people called out to the Gaffle & the greatest joy was testified by the whole party who following the old foolish Maraboot were giving them selves up to despair –

at 11 AM arrived & halted at Agadim at the Eastern well we found that part of the Gaffle which had left us the night of the 26th had not arrived and already great fears were entertained for their safety by the whole Gaffle – about an hour after our arrival 2 men on foot came from them who were perishing with thirst who said they had left them the night before and that they were lying in the most deplorable condition with-out a drop of water unable to move either back wards or for wards The poor men were in a very bad state but they were only allowed to have a little water at a time and people washed their heads & necks Major D^s servant who had his wife & 8 slaves[4] went of[f] to them with 2 camels & Water at 3 P.M. 6 camels came in from the poor people – who said they were still alive I sent one of my camels & [*"bag"* deleted] water off by

---

[4]Now counted, at least by Clapperton, as a merchant – see Appendix 4.

the wish of Major D⁵ serv' who had arrived I offred the whole of my camels but could not get a man to go –

Wednesday 29ᵗʰ
Clear – at 11– the Kaffle consisting of Ebn Taleb[5] & the Mesurata people[6] arrived they fortunatly fell in with the lost Gaffle supplied them with water & brought the most of them in with the rest remaining to collect their goods & come in slowly –

Tintuma is a journey of 3 days across from Agadim to bel Kasheefra the course from the East ͩ – Well ["of Agadim by compass" inserted] SS.W. for the first day – & half of the second[7] if you leave Agadim you come to the trees in the hollows where you can hardly mistake the road – this part above consists of shifting sand hills which leaves no trace an hour or two after the travler has passed being effaced by the wind – the greater part of the ["hills' deleted] sand it being now the rainy season is covred with tufts of grass – but on our going to Bornou not a blade was to be seen – the night was hazy & not a star to be seen which was the cause of these people loosing their way –

this desert is inhabited by what they call the white bullock – I have seen numerous traces of them the print of their feet is like a young bullock – they by the descriptions of the Arabs & tibboos have long thin horns [and are] of the size of a Calf or larger & quite white[8]

---

[5]A merchant from Sockna, who became well known to Denham and Clapperton during their stay in Borno and had been helpful over negotiations concerning Hadje Ali Bu Khallum's debt to the Mission [*Clapperton in Borno*, p. 173].

[6]Misurata, 150 miles East of Tripoli, had been an important trading centre and Mediterranean port since the Middle Ages. Although smaller than Tripoli, it had certain geographical and tax advantages, and in the early 19th century was sending trade caravans to Fezzan, Wadai and the countries of the Niger Bend. Black slaves were sold there for local agricultural and domestic use and for export. Misurata merchants, like those of Tripoli, were to be met throughout the central Sahara.

[7]The correct course is broadly South by East, i.e. half a point to a point ($5.75° – 11.5°$) more easterly than Clapperton's estimate.

[8]The addax; see Chapter Thirteen, n. 18.

Thursday 30th

Clear & Cool – in the evening the whole of the party of the people that were lost on the sands arrived without any deaths

Friday Octr 1st 1823

at Sunrise Moved on to the upper well where the rest of the Gaffle had halted – ready for starting –

Saturday 2nd

Clear & Cool   filled our water skins & waterd the camels as we intend starting at 2 P.M. –

– at 2 P.M. left Agadim   the Mesurata people remained behind to hire camels from some Tibboos of Belkasheefra who had followed the Gaffle with camels to sell & hire –   On our ascending from Agadim obs^d Hadje Boo Zaid   Ebn Taleb & the rest of this Gaffle taking a long streatch to the West^d   Our Guide and all the people wanted me to follow but I convinced them they were wrong that they were now on the direct road & to follow it   I had taken the courses out of my book from Agadim to Billma so that we may not loose the road again or have the poor guide abused any more by the Maraboot & Others –   Course N. by E ¾ E   the sand hills steep & difficult   saw the tracks of No^s of the white bullock –   At 9 P.M. Strong gale with thr & lightning   halted –   midnight rain –   after starting saw a poor slave boy dying by the road side of Flux[9] from bad food

Sunday 3rd

Slight rain   Sunrise Std   Saw the hills of Agadim bearing from S by W ¾ W to S.S.E ½ E –   the sand hills as usual – steep difficult & numer-

---

[9] An early term for dysentery, or other internal illness involving abnormal discharges (of blood, excrement, etc.), as opposed to ague, an acute fever, with shivering and shaking, especially malaria [ShOED].

ous   from the rain last night the loom[10] on the sands was very great   the bones of a camel looked like a large pile of ["white" inserted] rocks – Noon halted for the heat of the day – N by E ¾ E

At 3 P.M. S^t & at 7 P.M. halted on account of a little grass being near for the camels   the other Gaffles came & halted near   they had no less than 14 camels knock'd up – sent the people out to cut grass for the camels to eat during the night

Monday 4th

at 4– A.M. St^d and at 11 AM halted at Duble
Course N. by E ½ E or N by E ¾ E –
this Afternoon one of the merchants of Jerba[11]   a town to the Westd of Tripoli   died   he had 2 towns men in the Gaffle but they let the Mesurata Merchants bury him – as they would not take the trouble –   he died of a Flux caught at the Town of Burwa in Bornou – from the No of camels dead & knockd up 65 & 70$ is now the price of a decent camel   Ebn Taleb sold 3 at 70$ each to be paid at Morzuk

Tuesday 5th

Clear & Cool – filled our water skins & watered the camels – at 3 P.M. left Dublee – the road very difficult and fatiguing for the camels from the height & Steepness of the sand hills which run in a general direction from East to West   the Nueclus of which I take to be the remains of old hills or rocks from the broken rocks I found some times on the tops of the sand hills & by the *broken* slate in the vallies between – at 8 P.M. halted   at midnight a large Gaffle ["left" deleted] of Tibboos with Salt passed us for Bornou

---

[10]The indistinct or exaggerated appearance of an object on the horizon, in darkness, haze, etc. [ShOED].

[11]An offshore island of small settlements in the Gulf of Gabes, subject to Tunis but close to Tripoline territory. It was a centre of coastal trade in local produce and in goods and slaves brought across the Sahara.

[sketch map with note: "Zow 8 days by a courier to Tibesty No Water".]

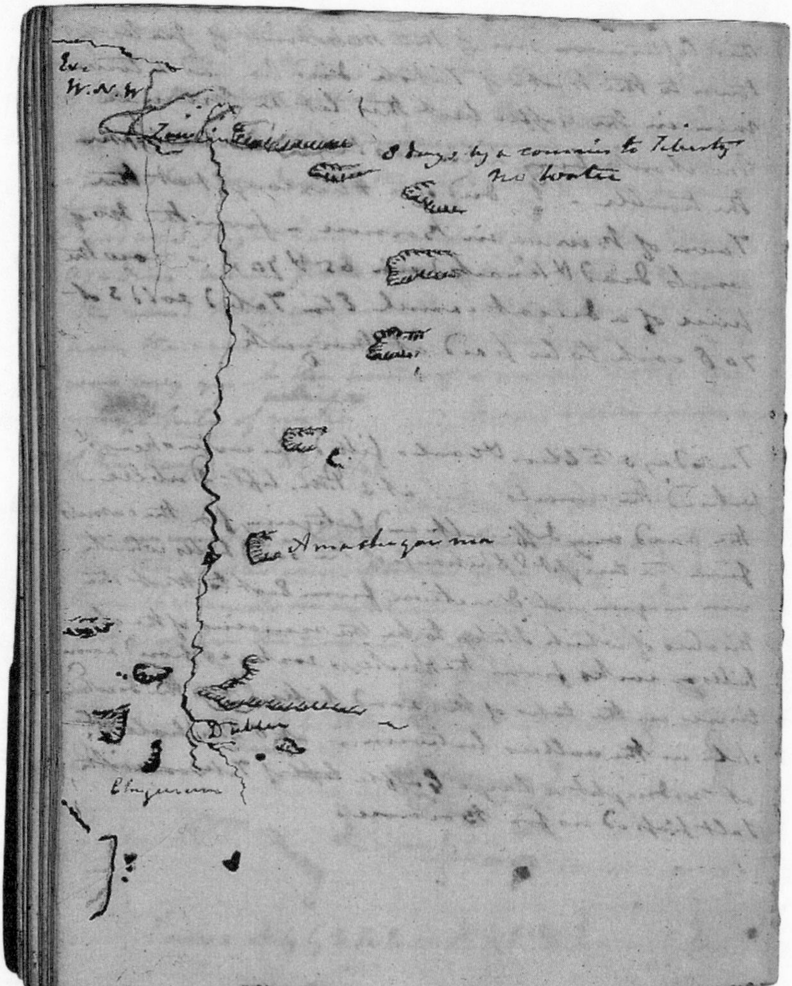

Figure 11. Sketch map of Dibella to Zow

Wednesday 6th

at 4– A.M. the Wind cool & Sharp – road very difficult – Noon halted abreast of some Rocks called Ama che qo ima   Met another Gafffle of Tibboos with salt for Bornou about 100 camels   At 3 P.M. road like a ship beating to windward – from the height of the sand hills many of which we had to cross   the camels of the Arabs giving up ["very fast" deleted] in great No– – *one* Mesurata Mercht has lost 8 his whole stock the Slaves in this case have to carry the loads on their heads[12] – Sunset Zow hills N. by E. the West Ex^t [= extremity] at 8 P.M– halted for the night   the greater part of the Gaffle passed on a head –

Thursday 7th

at 4–30 AM. St^d road as usull [sic] a no– of camels of the Arabs without loads – Noon Arrived at the Oassis of Zow – waterd the camels & sent them out to feed   a gaffle of Tibboos with salt

Friday 8

Cold & Clear – in the aftern– I was very ill with fever[13]

Saturday 9th

Cold & Clear   very ill with fever & billous [sic] vomiting   sent my people out to cut grass for the camels as we would halt at night where there was none   At 3 P.M. St^d road difficult from the steepness of the sand hills   saw from the camels back that the chain of rocky hills are all joined

---

[12] All but the most valuable slaves crossed the Sahara on foot, but their general treatment and chances of survival depended largely on who drove them. The Tuareg were relatively humane, clothing slaves decently, allowing one camel load of provisions for every four people, limiting marches to five hours daily and not making slaves carry loads. The Tubu, by contrast, hardly clothed their trade slaves, allowed only one camel of provisions for every ten slaves, drove them by forced marches, manacled most of them, and expected all but small children to carry up to 20lbs. on their heads. [Wright, *"Nothing else but slaves"*, pp. 228-32.] In this instance cited by Clapperton, slaves may have had to share out a total burden of up to three quarters of a ton if the camels had been fully loaded.

[13] Reflected in Clapperton's shaky, thin handwriting in this journal entry.

between Zow – & Billma breaking into small low wadys or ravines which run but a short distance – I had to kill a favourite white camel this after noon from a putrid sore on its near fore shoulder which prevented it walking so it was better to kill it than leave it to perish for want in the desert – it had been from Kuka to Sockatoo with me was fleet & docile and I was often solicited by the Tuaricks when in Haussa to sell it at 8 P.M– halted a very cold wind from the N.W. Course N ½ W

Sunday 10th

day light Cold & Clear loaded the camels & St^d at noon halted at the Oassis of Mis ka ti noo I was very ill all the way and threw up a great quantity of Bile

Monday 11th

Sunrise St^d Very sick at 11 AM halted at Billma on the south side no improvement has taken place in the town on the contrary I think that in the course of a few years more it will be no more if they do not take the trouble to repair & Build a new – they are in hourly expectation of the yearly visit from the Tuaricks & who they have heard are halted in the neighbourhood the most of the Males and all the young women in consequence have fled – they come some times to the amount of 4000 camels[14]

Dates are the only thing sold here I was asked 4$ for a quart & Major D. was asked 7$

---

[14]Nachtigal [*Sahara and Sudan*, Vol. II, pp. 68-9] observes that, "Larger caravans such as are equipped by the Tuareg to carry salt to the Hausa states – and each might on leaving Ahir, include perhaps 3,000 camels – set out perhaps only three times a year; but there is an immense number of smaller parties of Tuareg and Tubu which export the salt to their homes, or to Kanem, Bornu and Hausa."

Tuesday 12th

Morning Cold & Clear   a little better to day

Wednesday 13th

Morning cold & Clear – a no of people belonging to the gaffle taken ill
of flux and ague   At 3 P.M. left Billma & at 7 P.M. halted at the road
side   Night cold & windy

Thursday 14th

Cold & Windy   sunrise St^d – at Noon halted for the heat of the day   saw
great no^s of Bullocks sheep & goats – at 3 P.M– St^d & at Sunset halted
on the North side of Dirkee

Friday 15th

Cold & Clear   after Sunrise the Tibboos to the ammount of about 30
came in a hostile manner to the camp – amongst them was the nearest
relation of a man that had been shot by one of the Mesurata Merchants
on his way to Bornou for – attempting to throw a spear at him – they
were brandishing their spears & uttering cries of deffiance – the tuble[15]
was beat & we flew to arms – when the *gents* after a little noisy talk took
themselves off

The Tibboos demand the price of blood   the Arabs say they owe them
blood that they are seve[rely] in their debt

Laid in a stock of dates 5$ worth for men & Camels and 1$ gussub which
was ground into meal for the men

---

[15]Ar., *tubal*, drum.

Saturday 16ᵗʰ

Cold & Clear with the wind from the North   Columbus the Servᵗ of Major D. very ill as also three of his men with flux & ague

The Sultan has given orders that the Gaffle shall not depart as he says that he has not had his dues which are – as much as he can get no fixed price being given   ["formerly in the time of Mukni's Sultanship at Agadim & Izhiah they paid a white tobe or ¾ $ for each camel" inserted][16] if he is stronger than the gaffle he takes what he pleases if the Gaffle is stronger than him he takes what they give[17]   the Mesurata people and Ebn Taleb have paid but the Sheerefs the Mamelukes of Fezzan & those descended from Maaraboots or holy men refuse to pay as they say it is not their custom – though they trust to the strength of the Gaffle not a musquet or pistol or sword being worn or in the possession of the whole of them

Sunday 17ᵗʰ

The Mesurata people & the Sultan could not Settle about the blood of the Tibboo & he forbids them to start   which Order they care not to disobey – the new Sultan of Fezzan[18] has sent him a letter declaring his sorrow for the crime and telling him to kill the authour

2–30 P.M. Started – at 7 P.M– halted in the Hatia having taken the Western road being the nearest – halted abreast of Ashinuma – Major D. had a loaded camel left behind on the road in [the] charge of 2 men

---

[16]Customs dues of variable amounts were levied on slaves and other goods in transit at such Saharan entrepôts as Bilma, Murzuq and Ghadamis, and again at the Mediterranean ports of Tripoli and Benghazi, and at such final destinations as Constantinople and Smyrna. Total dues on a trade slave (male or female) taken from Hausaland to Constantinople via Murzuq and Tripoli might amount to as much as $23 out of total estimated travel expenses of $39 [Wright, "*Nothing else but slaves*", Table 7. 6: "Expenses of moving slaves Hausa-Constantinople, $/Head."].

[17]"The, more or less orderly, system of 'salams', payments and exemptions" [Nachtigal, *Sahara and Sudan*, Vol. II, p. 62].

[18]Mustafa Al-Ahmar died in late 1823. The exact date of the appointment of his successor, Sidi Hassain, is not evident from the Mission's papers, but he only arrived to take up his post in Murzuq in November 1824 [Monday 22nd and Tuesday 23rd December 1824].

5 Tibboos came & plundered the load threatening to kill the men who were in charge of it & taking 5 Tobes belonging to a poor idiot in Major Ds service

Monday 18th
at Sunrise St^d and Noon halted under the shade of some Mimosa for the heat of the day – Major D. sent a man one of those who had been in charge of this camel that was robbed & who said he knew the robbers to our guide who had gone to Ashinuma – and at which town they said the robbers lived

at 3 P.M– Started and at 5–30 PM. halted at Gusabee or by the Arabs Kisbee encamp'd on the North side of the Town

Tuesday 19th
Cold & Clear the Guide & Major D^s Servt brought one of the men that was acused of robbing the camel – he offerd to swear that he did not rob the camel & was not near it Major D^s 3 *men* offerd to swear he was one of the principal the poor man who lost the tobes would not allow them to swear said that if they all swore some body must swear falsely & that he would not make them come into a sin that god would give him more he hoped

Sultan Dinuma arrived intending to try and get more duty from the Arabs –

bought a very lean sheep for 2$ for which they asked me 6

Wednesday 20th
dull & cloudy very ill with flux gave ¼ $ for about ½ pint of sour milk

Thursday 21ˢᵗ
dull cloudy Wʳ

Friday 22ⁿᵈ
at 7 AM [left] Kisbee and at 10 halted at the Springs of Anai for the
Arabs to arrᵍᵉ the hiring of their camels – the Town S.S.W. 2 Miles
under a rock like a castle

Saturday 23ʳᵈ
Strong Wind & Cold at 3 PM Stᵈ at – 8 P.M halted cold Windy night

Sunday 24ᵗʰ
Cold Morning at Sunrise Std & noon halted at Noon halted at the
Oassis of Iegaboo the Rocky hills connected to the Easᵗᵈ all the way

Monday 25ᵗʰ
Cold & windy at 7 A.M. left Iegaboo along the ["Eastⁿ" deleted] Westᵈ
Side of low rocky hills N ½ W we at Sunset arrived at the Oassis of
Sigadim at sunset on the S.E. side of which there is the ruins of a
Tibboo Town & Castle which were destroyed by the [ ] inhbᵗˢ killed by
the Tuaricks of Ghaat 21 Years ago[19] the Oassis is about 6 or 8 miles in
circumference a Nᵒ of date and Mimosa Trees and springs of fine water
– & a salt Marsh from which in the Summer produces fine Salt – there
is a rocky conical hill on the S.E side opposite the town the rocky hills
to the East & to W.S.W. these rocky hills they say extend to Ghat from
which it is distᶜᵉ 70 days Gaffle traveling – its name of Sigadim is Arabic

---

[19]The original inhabitants of Segguedine were Tubu of Djado [cf. Nachtigal, *Sahara and Sudan* Vol.
II, p. 49], but in the last decades of the 18th century, with both Borno and Fezzan weak states and
unable to impose their influence on the central Sahara and its caravan road, the Tuaregs had become
all-powerful in Kawar and the central Sahara. Segguedine and northern Kawar came to be dominated by the Tuaregs of Djanet; and central and southern Kawar and Fachi by the Tuaregs of Aïr.

& Bornou meaning a place where there is no law or government or where the place is governed by Women[20]

Tuesday 26th
at 8.30 AM. left Sigadim and on asending between the hills by a sandy road we continued to ascend gradualy untill after miday the Ranges of the hills to the north & West running from N.E. to SW. ["E.N.E. & W.S.W." inserted] 3 or 4 to the N.W. of considerable height above the others   At Sunset halted under the lee of some rocky hills[21]

Wednesday 27th
we had a mild night & calm morning not with standing our elevated situation   at Sunrise St^d and descending gradually to the Oassis of Izhiah where we arrived at 1 P.M–. halted on the north side of the Oassis   the Water Salt & bitter

Thursday 28th
cold & Windy all night bringing with it showers of sand so that the people could not go out to cut grass   every thing was filled with a fine sand[22] – the Arab Merchants applied to one [of] the Tibboos to still the wind by writing for which he demanded 2 $ & we were to have no wind for 7 days B.k.m when we were here before gave a pair of red cloth breaches to a Tibboo for the same purpose – The arabs when they want Wind to clean their grain in harvest after it is trod out have certain characters

---

[20]The Berber root-word *gedem*, common in Saharan place names, e.g. Agadem, Sogdem, refers to a place where a track biforks in an area clear of desert – having the sense of both staging post and crossroads [H. T. Norris, personal communication]. There is no obvious Kanuri derivation; but perhaps a Tubu dimension in the ironic reference to the dominant role of women in society [cf. Chapter Twelve, n. 16].

[21]The rate of travel through this *hatiya* was slower than normal, presumably to allow the animals to browse before, as here, or after the demanding caravan passage over the Tummo saddle.

[22]The *ghibli*, see Chapter Five, n. 29. For accounts of the trials of Saharan travel during a *ghibli*, see *Nachtigal, Sahara and Sudan* Vol. I, pp. 47-8 and R. Caillé, *Travels*, Vol. II, pp. 108 et seq..

written on the blade of a knife which [is] stuck in a wall & When they want a wind they pull it out & stick in again when they want the wind to cease so that the practice is Wid[e]ly extended – – one of My best camels died today

Friday 29th
Moderate & Cool the Tibboo will get a great deal of credit for his writing for we have every prospect of a Moderate day of wind! we have been enabled to cut grass & gather wood for the journey to Tegerhay – The Water in the well was Salt & bitter when we arrived but after use got a great deal better – one of my best camels died today – hired anothr for 7$ to Tegerhay

Saturday 30th
Cold & Windy at 8.30– AM left Izhiah at 4–30 P.M. saw high sand hills to the East^d – road rocky & dreary – passed a young male slave lying dead on the road side that had belonged to Gadum a Blacksmith of Morzuk a cruel hard–hearted wretch who drives his slaves along like beasts more than like human beings

at 8 PM halted for the night Course N.E ¾ N Cold & Windy all night

Sunday 31st
Cold & Clear at 7 A.M. S^t cold wind all day – at 4 P.M– halted at the wells of Mafrus – obs^d the connection of the rocky range of hills – to the west^d– which at Mafrus go to form a deep laing [=lying] to the Westd in the dry bed of a river with trees here & there running to the S.E we had crossed a No– of others all running in the same direction

found on our arrival ["that" deleted] those of the gaffle who had preceded us busy clearing the Wells & making others – the night before the

272

people went to rest filled our gerbas & watred the camels   N.E by N –

Monday 1ˢᵗ Novʳ 1824
Cold & Clear   at 7 AM– Stᵈ   left the greater part of the Gaffle behind
as they remained for the next day to hire fresh camells from the Tibboos
who are accompang the Gaffle from Izhiah & to refresh their slaves   at
4.30 P.M. halted   Met a Gaffle of Tibboos with dates from Fezzan[23]   the
road sand & Gravel and several rocky ridges   great quantities of
Gypsum &ᶜ

Tuesday 2ⁿᵈ
Cold & Clear   El Fizzan E by N–   at 7 AM. Stᵈ   Met a Gaffle laden
with dates   Tibboos   at 7–30 P.M. halted at the Wells of El Ahmer –
filled our water skins   Course N.E ¾ N.

Wednesday 3ʳᵈ
Cold & Clear   El Fizzan from the Wells S.E ½ E –   at 7–30 A.M– Std
Gypsum   at 8– P.M. halted under the lee of some rocks the hills to the
Westᵈ dist about 6 or 7 miles   night cold & windy   Course N.E by N –
passed a no of dead bodies on our road – very ill all day

Thursday 4ᵗʰ
Cold & Clear   at 7.30 Stᵈ   at Sunset halted at El–Waur in the dry bed
of a torrent ["amongst" deleted] the bones of Animals and human beings
no place here being clear of them on which we could pitch our tents – I
was here very ill every one said with juandice [sic] or as they call it the
yellows of the road   the body or skeletons of an Arab his camel & 3

---

[23]For the complexities of Tubu Saharan commerce, and the willingness of these people to travel
great distances for apparently modest gain, see Chapelle, *Nomades noirs*, pp. 210-21 and Le Rouvreur,
Saheliens et Sahariens, Carte 30: "Principaux courants commerciaux".

females lye together just before comming into El.Waur who died of thirst El.Waur is the most dreary place in the desert – Surrounded by high black dreary rocky hills the sides of which are covered from top to bottom with small *pinacles* the valley between of ridges of the same black broken stone clays and gravel intersected by the dry bed of a torrent covred nearly by the bones of human beings and camels with here and there the ashes of the fires of passing Gaffles – a cold N.E wind added to the ddrearyness of scenery arround us – sent our camels to drink and filled our water skins the hills to the West continue and here called *Akroof*[24] – Dist – 7 or 8 Miles

Friday 5th

The morning cold & Chilly remained untill 10 A.M. to rest our people who had been up the greater part of the night filling water [skins] & watering the camels at 7 P.M. halted – not being able to make our distance we have met som[e] Arabs with 7 camels & dates wheat &[c] comming to meet Ebn Taleb – from them we got a supply and Major D. sent me a bowel of camels milk which he got from them he having hired some of their camels – the Milk was a real blessing as we have had no tea or coffee for this some weeks past & I am undable [sic] to eat any thing we have I can still discern the connection of the hills to the West[d] during the day from *my* elevated situation on the top of the camel a branch runs to the East[d]

Saturday 6th

Cold & Clear road dreary & Stony – met 4 Camels with dates going to meet the gaffle or us or if we did not hire them they proceed to Kawar Sunset ["halted" deleted] – Met a Gaffle with dates

at 7 P.M. halted night very cold N.E by N –

---

[24]*Akruf*; etymology uncertain, probably a local word for a mountain; here the Jabal Ati.

Sunday 7th

at 7 A.M. St^[d] close to May yau one of my camels died that had travled with me from Bornou to Sackatoo to this place carrying still the heaviest load – I felt a little at loosing this old friend as I had intended to have given him to the consul at Tripoli which would have been like giving him his liberty – but poor fellow he could not come up the hill even without his load – That Monster Gadum left a poor female slave to perish on the road today   her head was terribly swelled & unable to walk & insensible   when I fell in with her one of his male serv'ts was waiting by her untill she died   not to bury her but to bring away the few rags she had on – I stoped intending to have carried her on my camels but she could not hold on being quite insensible and we would likely have shared the same fates had [I] waited to bring her to   which was apparently hopeless – a Cold Wind from N.N.E all day

at 7– P.M halted   Course N. E by N & N.N.E ½ E

Tuesday 9th [= Monday 8th]

Cold & Windy   Met another Gaffle   at 7 A.M. Std and at 10 halted at the wells of Mishru where we watred our camels with the loads on & proceded on our journey   at Sunset halted – we here met a gaffle of Tibboos with dates for Kawar

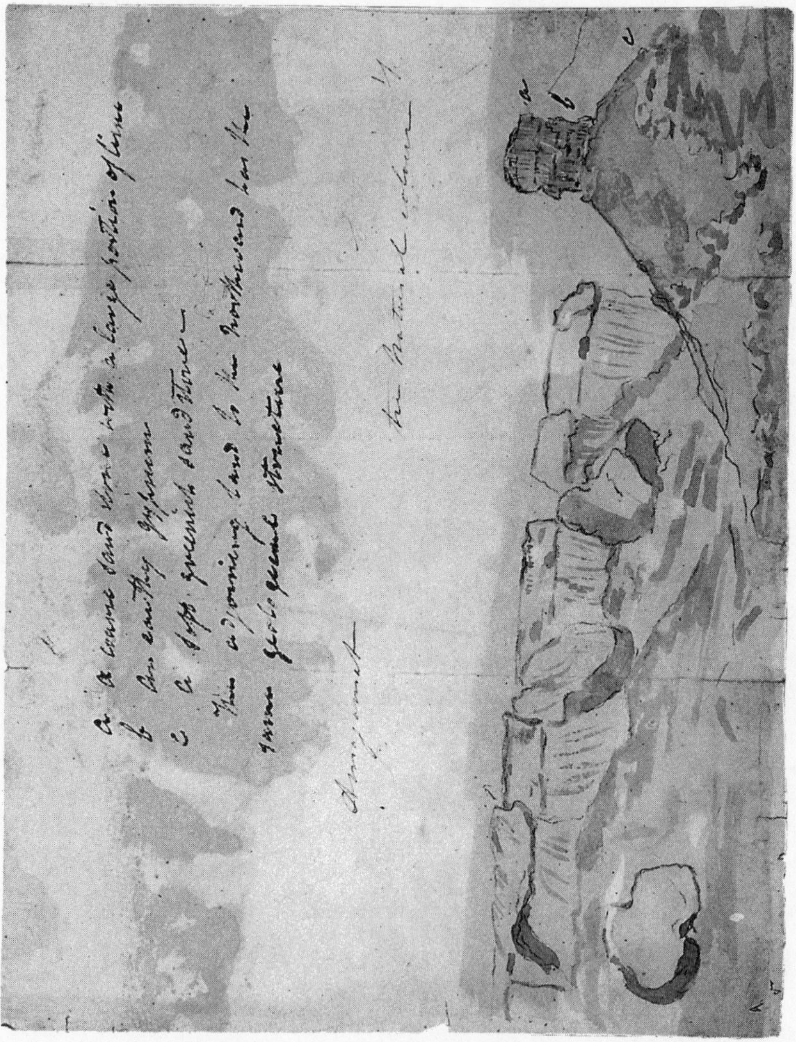

Figure 12. Amyamat, a hill near Omm Al-Abid

CHAPTER

15

Return to Fezzan

Tuesday 9ᵗʰ

Cold & windy – at 7 AM. Stᵈ   after Starting Met a Gaffle of Tibboos
with dates going to Kawar or to sell them to the Gaffles comming from
Bornou – at 1 P.M. saw the date trees of Oma to the N.E.   every ones
heart rose within them   the poor slaves sick lame & the weary all joined
in the cry of joy – at comming again so near the country of living men –
at 7 P.M. halted at Tegerhey   one of my camels gave up just as we entred
the date trees – & though the night was excessively cold & windy I had
to send my people to bring in the load on their backs & leaving a little
grass with the camel   they left it for the night as it was unable to come
on the place of our encampment

Wednesday 10ᵗʰ

Cold & Windy   the guide waited on us in the Morning full of promises
and compᵗˢ [= compliments] &ᶜ & made us a present of a Sheep & some
bread   for the sheep he told us he had paid 8$ one half above the price
but he expected the larger present from us – I gave him 4$ I believe the
Major did the same   he then begged hard for a tan[n]ed hide of Soudan
saying he had just bought a new garden & had no draw bucket – then
could I not give him a Turkadee for his Wife or stirrup leathers for his
saddle or a Soudan bridle   to all [of] which I leant a deaf ear – we got

plenty of water Melons in exchange for tobaco or wheat which is the small money of Fezzan – always nothing else but dates or wheat – we bought flower & dates as we were entirely out – in [the] evening the Mesurata Merchts arrived

Thursday 11th

Fresh breezes from the N.N.E & Cold   all the Gaffle came in the evening old Hadje Boo Zaid had to leave 6 camel loads of goods at El. Waur for want of camels – which he hired here & sent off for them on the instant of his arrival

Friday 12th

Cold & Windy   at 8 A.M. left Tegerhey   Ebn Taleb in company – and at 3.30 halted at Kassirowan – the camel that gave up died to day – there are the ruins of 2 old castles to the West^d of the road I did not see on our journey to Bornou –

Saturday 13th

Cold & Clear   at 8 A.M. [started]   & at 2 PM halted at the village of Medroossa   we were here met by the Sheikh El–Saug or Clerk of the Market at Morzuk & 4 horse men come to take an account of the slaves & goods of the Gaffle[1]

Tuesday [= Sunday] 14th

Cold & Clear   at 8 A.M. left Medroossa and at 11 AM halted on the North side of Gatrone   in the evening the Maraboot[2] sent us soup bread

---

[1]Evidently Madrusa, on the southern approaches to Al-Qatrun, served as the clearing port for desert arrivals; but on this occasion there was also a second head count after leaving Al Qatrun – see Wednesday 17th November. As Clapperton points out [Friday 6th December, 1822], this was a control mechanism only, and the dues were not paid until the caravan reached Murzuq.

& some water melons excusing himself from waiting on us by ill health

Monday 15th
Cold & windy   very ill all day

Tuesday 16th
Cold   all the Gaffle that remained at Tegerhey behind us arrived to day
sent the Maraboot Sidi Mohamed Rashid a present of a Dollar and a
Turkadee as he had sent us meat every day with water Melons & Dates &^c

Wednesday 17th
Cold & windy   at 8.30 AM left Gatrone – after we got clear of the date
trees the Sheikh el Saug came & counted the slaves in the Gaffle & the
no– of camels with goods –

at noon halted at the Well of *Narij* to the East^d of our former route   here
are the ruins of a larger town than Gatrone built in the same stile as the
castles & ruins of Tegerhey   that is broad sun dried bricks outside & in
& filled up with clay and gravel in the Mid[d]le –

Thursday 18th
Cold & Windy   at 7–30 AM left Narij   Very cold   at Sunset halted being
unable to reach Meastoota

Friday 19th
Cold & Windy   at 8.30 A.M. St^d and at 11 A.M. arrived & halted at the
oassis of Mestuta

---

²Hadje Mohamed Rashid – see Tuesday 16th November.

Saturday 20th

at 8–A.M. St^d & traveling N.N.W at Sunset Major D. & I halted the rest of the Gaffle proceded on to Bethan[3] ["they" deleted] which was at a considerable distance they not having provided themselves with wood & Water –

Sunday 21st

Cold & Clear at 7 A.M. Started at 8.20 passed the Village of Bedthan I here exchanged one of my camels that had given up for a sheep – worth 3$ – at 2 P.M. halted at the village of Hadje Hajel – killed our sheep & gave our servants a feast[4] Ebn Taleb & the rest of the Gaffle that went to Bedthan last night – had gone on to Morzuk

Monday 22nd

at 9 A.M. left Hadje Hajel & traveled on to Morzuk – at which place we arrived at 1 P.M– we were waited on by Lizhari Hameda Bookhaloom & all our old friends – we found our house in a very dirty state though the Major had written to *request* Lizhari to have the house put in order –

The Sultan arrived yesterday from Tripoli and the Mamelukes were all bedizened with sliks [=silks] & lace – and nothing was talked of but the new Sultan we here found a courrier from Tripoli with letters & Tea Coffee Sugar &^c

Tuesday 23rd

Cold & clear – in the afternoon waited on the Sultan – Bey Hassan[5] an elderly man very kind and communicative and is a clearly decent fellow

---

[3] Al-Baydan, on the southern rim of the Hofra oasis complex.

[4] To celebrate journey's end at the marabit of Sidi Bushir where, two years earlier almost to the day, they had made their votive offerings on departure for Borno [Tuesday 19th November 1822].

[5] Al-Ahmar's successor, Sidi Hussein [*Missions*, Vol. III, p. 498].

– about 40 or 45 years of age a Circass[n] by birth – and is getting the castle in very good order we were present[d] with Tea & Sherbert – but on his asking if we had all come home but one he let his under jaw fall and asked why Mr T remained behind – in the evening he sent us a present of 2 sheep some corn & oil he told us he was going to send courrier to Tripoli if we wished to send letters a thing we never have been informed of by any other since we left Tripoli

very ill with ague Hillman has also had a severe attack

Saturday 27th

– we waited on the Sultan today to inform him of our intention of leaving for Tripoli on monday next – he said we had hardly time to draw breath yet and as I was in a weak state he thought we had better stay a few days longer particularly as there was a Gaffle comming from Wady now at Gatrone in which there were 4 Merch[ts] of Darfor – we might hear some news[6] – we agreed – to his wish he was very chaty talked of an action the Bashaw's vessels had had with the Greeks in which the turks had taken 2 – & lost 16 we were sorry to hear this news but did not believe it as the Turks never lose a battle by their own account[7] – he is a good natured fellow this Sultan & apparently the best and most liked of the whole of the Bashaw's people I have seen he has quite won Hillman's heart by his *likeaby* [= likeability]

---

[6]Presumably, news of the Niger and the Nile and other geographical information relevant to the Mission's researches.

[7]Clapperton was no doubt aware of the strength of the Greek fleet, their greatest military asset, but would not yet have heard of the Ottoman campaign, spearheaded by the Egyptian fleet, to reconquer the Peloponnese by sea. Tripoli's naval contribution to the Sultan's war against the Greeks in 1823 had been so small that a special envoy was sent from Constantinople to reprimand the Pasha – who as a consequence began to buy new vessels between 1823 and 1824 [Folayan, *Tripoli*, p. 107].

Tuesday 7ᵗʰ [December][8]
part of the Gaffle came in from Wady   they were in miserable condition
they lost better than half the Nᵒ of slaves they left Wady with from
hunger & cold[9]

the Arabs of Boo *Shall*[10] – Marabootans or descendants of holy men –
wait on the Sultan of Fezzan and present him with a bridle   he has in
return to give them a female slave in return   they do the same to every
new Bashaw – the first of the *tribe* who gets there gets the prize   he that
waited on this Sultan came to me the first by and by   begging greatly
Saying that every Sultan gave him [something]   why we english would
give him nothing – I told him we gave to people who were poor and in
want not to rich people like him – he then sham[m]ed Mad   threw of[f]
his cap in deffiance but I sent for the servts and turned his holiness out
of doors

Wednesday 8ᵗʰ
rode out with the Sultan in the afternoon

Sunday 12ᵗʰ
Fresh Gales   we intended to have left Morzuk today but the owner of
my camels having a she camel killed by a male he begged that I wᵈ stay
another day that he might be enabled to sell the meat and bring away the
skin   aftⁿ showery

---

[8]There are no diary entries from 27th November to 6th December inclusive, nor from 9th to 11th
December.

[9]Most Saharan slave caravans avoided travel in winter, otherwise too many slaves died of cold in
the frigid Saharan nights. As Richardson observed [*Travels*, Vol. II, p. 224]: "These nigritian people
cannot bear the cold. Our northern cold affects them more than their southern heat does us. Heat
can be borne better than cold in Saharan travelling."

[10]Possibly a reference to the marabutic Walid Bu Saif.

Monday 13ᵗʰ

Clear   at 11 A.M. sent the camels forward with orders to halt at Delaim
– waited on the Sultan who wished us to remain to see the principal
Man of the Tuaricks who was expected to come in to town to day – but
we had seen enough of their great men and kindly thanked him & took
our leave   at 3 left Morzuk   we were accompanied out of the town by
Hadje ben Hamid & his cousin Hadje zy abe deen –   at Sunset not having found the place where my camels had halted – I Scouted untill midnight & not being able to find them I returned to where Major D. had
pitched & remained in his tents all night – slight rain during the night
E by N. 9 Miles

Tuesday 14ᵗʰ

before day break I left Major Dˢ encampment – & found my people
encamped at the Wells where after filling water & getting breakfast we
left & joined Major Dˢ Gaffle on the road – to Wady Nishuwa[11] – the
road full of broken Stones & the day cold & windy   at Sunset halted in
Wady Nishua – which breaks off from the wady above Tessowa to the
West running to the East of Ghudwa 5 or 6 miles bends to the North &
enters Omlabeid   in it there is plenty of Atill Trees & Tullach with agool
– & grass & wells of good water about a fathom in depth – Antilopes –
& hares are to be found here the latter rather numerous –

Course N.N.E 24 – N by W. 12   night Windy & Cold

Wednesday ¹⁵ᵗʰ

Cold & windy   at 7 AM. Stᵈ & traveling E by N down the Wady – at
4–30 halted at Ghudwa[12] – we could get neither eggs or lackbee   the

---

[11]Wadi an-Nashu, (Ar., sand).

[12]Ghudduwa. Sacked in Yusuf Pasha Karamanli's campaigns against Fezzan in 1810-12 but the
"many remains of former well being" were still evident 40 years later [Barth, *Travels*, Vol. III, p. 627].

283

Sultan[13] they said had eat all the former & his attendants drank all the latter it appeared they had also run away with all the young women for we could se[e] none this time though crowded with them before – all that we saw were two or three old women apparently half starved – occl showers during the night – Course E. by N. 18 Miles

Thursday 16th
Cloudy & Cold at 7 AM. St[d] at 4–30 PM [halted]

Friday 17th
dark cloudy W[r] at 7 St[d] day cold at 4 – halted on the North side of Sebha[14] – we were waited on by one of our old friends Sheikh Abdullah[15] who has got as fat and round as a But[t] and his beard quite grey – he was as kind as ever Course N. by E ¾ E –

some of the Arabs of the Magraha tribe who had been on the Ghazie with the late B.k.m– were here as they winter in the Wady and in Shiati

Saturday 18th
Clear halted to day gave Sheikh Ab[h] a Tobe & pair of Stirrup leathers – Sebha is the only town I have seen in Fezzan that is improving the late Sult[n] Mustapha had built a house here for the purpose of residing in during the sickly season at Morzuk the walls are in good repair & the gardens of wheat & indian corn surround the town – No[s] of Magerha arabs passed to their winter quarters in Shiati today

---

[13]Ambiguous – but probably a reference to Sultan Al-Ahmar.

[14]A thriving town, fully described by other travellers. The Italians made it the capital of Fezzan in the 1930s as a more healthy site than Murzuq.

[15]Abdullah ben Shibel [*Missions*, Vol. III, p. 500].

Sunday 19th

Clear & Cold   at 7 A.M. left Sebha – at 3.30 P.M– halted at Timenhint
Course N.N.E ½ E   2   N.E by E ¾ E 14 Miles

we were supplied with grass and provisions by the Sheikh of the Town
who took care to ask what was to be given him before he sent any thing

Monday 20th

a raw cold morning   at 8 AM left Tim^t– we had to halt twice to make
fires to warm ourselves & the poor slaves   at Sunset halted at Zeghan[16]
Course N.E by E ½ E –

Tuesday 21st

Cold – I was very ill all day   Nos– of the Magerha Arabs here – who
are proceeding to Shiati – the water of Zeghan is now quite brackish
the well from which they procured the good water from before having
fallen in   they have been too indolent to rebuild it or clear it out   heard
from an arab to day an account of an ["ancient" inserted] castle & town
["in ruins" inserted] built of stone & lime in Om la beid which we had
not seen on our way up   I doubt it is an Arab story

Wednesday 22nd

Clear & cold   at 7 AM left Zeghan – at noon arrived & halted at the
Wells of Om la beid[17] – on the road we fell in with a No of the girlls [sic]

---

[16]Northen Fezzan, comprising Sabha and its surrounding villages, Tamanhint, Samnu and
Zaghan, is agriculturally productive (particularly dates) and economically important because of its
position on the junction of trade routes.   The northernmost village of Fezzan proper is Umm al-Abid.
In the early 19th century the northern boundary of Fezzan was Abu Njaym [Lyon, *A Narrative*, p. 66].
North of the Jabal as Sawda lies the geographically and ethnically very different region of Jofra.

[17]Umm al-Abid, (mother of slaves), where slave caravans stopped to take in a good supply of water
for the four days' travel ahead without wells on the road towards Tripoli [Richardson, *Travels*, Vol. II,
pp. 393-4].

of the town going to gather wood   they gave a loose to their tounges in fine style on our men attacking them and soon put them to silence – I went to se[e] the old ruins of the town & castle – but found all an exageration – the remains of an old clay Castle certainly were standing part of the lower wall was faced with stones – & Clay – and the Appearance of clay foundations – saw some fine hares & the tracks of the Antilope

the Well of Om la beed is old – and there is a continuation of wells all conected by a drain below to the spring head – at distances of about 10 or 14 yards from one another – such like I have seen in other parts of Fezzan near the site of old castles[18] – the Arabs or Fezzaners of the present day know not who – made them!

Om ya mat[19] above Omlabeed bore N.E. ½ N.   filled our Water Skins & collected wood for crossing the desert –   Course N.E ¾ N

Thursday 23ʳᵈ
Cold & Clear – at 7.30 AM. Started – at sunset halted on the desert – Course N by E ¾ E–   met a gaffle from Sockna

Friday 24ᵗʰ
Calm   at 7 Stᵈ   Met a Gaffle from Tripoli who told us they had beeen expecting us at Tripoli for some time past – One of Abbas' she camels brought forth – about a quarter of an hour was taken up in arranging the young camel <u>on</u> the back of the Mother when we marched on   Sunset halted – saw El Goff or the heads[20] bearing the Westⁿ [extremity] N.N. E ½ E   Eastn N. E by E –   Course N.N.E ½ E –

---

[18]See Chapter One, n. 13 on *foggaras*.
[19]Garim bu Guffa; identified on Lyon's map as 'a turret-like hill'.
[20]Ar., *al-Qaf*, head, top or summit.

Saturday 25th

Christmas day   cold & clear   at 7 AM St^d   the day excessive cold
Sunset halted – at Wady Timishee about 6 miles inside the Assoda or
Black hills[21]   we had warm brandy and water in the Tent of Major D–
in the evening

Sunday 26th

Cold & hazy, with rain at times   after traveling about an hour we halted
in Wady Shirkha libben   the cold wind & rain increased to Such a
degree that we were glad to come too [sic] – in the Aftⁿ it cleared a little – collected a n^o of plants   this is a fine Wady   No^s of trees plenty of
grass and it is frequented by arabs from Zeghan and Sockna in the
Winter with their camels   Old Abbas[22] brought a plant called libben or
gutaba – which is dried & pounded and given three fingers full as a dose
for the *bell[y]*   a purge – another khala for the kidnese when injured
another for rheumatism[23] –

Showers during the night   a party of Arabs from Zeghan halted near
they had camels which they had brought to fatten – when arabs who
come out & live in this manner   dates and Milk is their only food   except
on religious feasts – when bazeen or a little fat is added to their zumeta
and boiled and is then called – *muta bugh or cooked*[24]   if they can possibly
have meat they have it

Course   like Tacking   to the North^d

---

[21]The Jabal as-Sawda.

[22]not identified further – the old guide or perhaps a merchant travelling with them.

[23]Ar. *luban*, gum, or, more widely, an exuded milky substance (including frankincense); but perhaps some confusion on Clapperton's part over 'khala' (Ar. *khulya*) which means kidneys.

[24]Ar., *bukh*, cooked.

Monday 27th

Cold & hazy with rain at times – at 7 St^d roads difficult – filled water
at the Well of Gutfa   at 4 PM– halted in Wady *Ill malagi* –
[Course] E by N

As we have now arrived on the West^a side of the black hills as they are
called – I shall attempt to give an account of their extent and formation

– To the E.N.E they extend to a town called Zilla near Bengazi[25] a distance of 4 days journey ["or 90 miles" inserted] to the West from where
we crossed 3 days from North to south [ ] Miles

the upper surface is covered with basalt – broken in pieces as if by the
hand of man – they are so smal[l] and the bases of the basaltic pillars
which can be seen on the sides of the Mountain are also broken in the
same manner but remain in their original situation cemented together by
a petrified lime stone – some of the basalt is very porous – and like the
cinders from a black smiths forge   some of the porous basalt – is full of
small christals – the bases of the hills are composed of limestone containing petrified sea shells – some of the hills on the West side are all
together of limestone lying in a very irregular Manner shook & broken
like the basalt   other places the strata is perpendicular some horizontal
in most places the ["limestone" deleted] is broken like the basalt and at
a distance looks like clay – the basalt rests on the limestone – & a dread-
ful convulsion it must have been to have shook those hills into so many
small pieces –

in most of the narrow vallies there is wood & plenty of grass – on which
the camels of the Arabs feed during the winter – and the Wadan, the
Antilope, and the Ostrich feed all the year through – there are no Wells

---

[25]Zilla, some 110 miles east of Sockna on the edge of the Sirtica desert, was a moderately impor-
tant staging post on the main pilgrimage and slaving road from Fezzan to Awjila, Benghazi and the
Nile Valley. Benghazi lies 250 miles east of Zilla. Clapperton was probably told "Zilla, on the road to
Benghazi".

on the south side   they have dug to the depth of 40 fm^s without finding
water – on the south side the ascent is gradual almost imperceptible on
the north – the hills end in Steep or precipatous sides

Wednesday 29th

at 8 left Ill Malagi ["or the meeting of the Wadys' inserted[26]] and at 4
arrived at Sockna[27] – I now riding alone and a head of the Gaffle – near
the town I met a young girl who – paid me a n$^{\circ}$ of compl^{ts} taking me for
a servt of the Bashaw's I suppose on seeing my red small cloths – "god
be praised you have returned from the wars – at which you have been
on account of us every one is glad in the town to hear that you are comming – may your friends in your own town be the same no doubt your
wife and sisters [are] waiting with open arms to receive you – may god
bless you and preserve thank god you have returnd from the wars" I
could not get in a word edge ways – so had to leave her –

Major D. had sent the Maraboot in to procure a house for each – the one
he had appropriated to me uninhabitable – I by the assistance of Old
Abbas hired a good one for a dollar – the Sheikh of the town was in a
sad fright about the house he said we had all lived in the same house at
Morzuk the Major was in a large house able to hold us all why could
we not go there – I begged he would not be the least uneasy he had
done his best – he sent me provisions for myself servt & horse

Thursday 30th

Clear – I waited on the friends of Ebn Taleb and Hadje Mohamed Hair
Treag[28] the brother was very ill with enlarged spleen for which he had
all his side open with burnt scars not yet healed up he gave me coffe

---

[26]Ar., *maltaqa*, crossroads.
[27]See Chapter One, n. 28.
[28]Haj Mohammed Hair Trigge, one of the richest inhabitants of Sockna, who had lived in Cairo
[*Missions*, Vol. I, p. 155 & Vol. II, p. 503].

and his ["house" deleted] room was decked out like a kitchen the walls covred with plates dishes bottles and jugs arranged on shelves on the walls from the floor to the rooff – the wife of Ebn Taleb's brother Misa I thought very beautiful – she is young and has been married 3 years 2 of which her husband has been in Soudan – she said why did I not bring him with me why did he stay and a no– of complaints of his absence – it is too bad of these fellows   they marry a young handsome ["wife" inserted] leave her at home for years – if she goes astray they cut her throat while they live openly with concubines & have children who are entitled to same right as those born in wedlock –

The language is a dialect of the Berber that people having once inhabited this place[29] there are the ruins of 2 Walls extending from the ["SE" inserted] gate to the gardens – which are walled round – to prevent the arab horse taking & killing their wives & servt as they were going to & from the fields

Friday 31st

Clear & Cold – it is held as bad and offensive to talk of women or any thing connected that way or sing before a relation

Saturday Jan[y] 1st 1825

Cloudy & Cold

Monday 3[rd][30]

No camels   this is an unlucky day and so was yesterday lord help us for all that we know of these people they just do as they like with us and it is no use getting in a passion with them – when ever they say god willing

---

[29]See Chapter Six, n. 35.
[30]No entry for Sunday 2nd January.

to any question asking what is to be done   be sure they will not do it

I breakfasted with Old Mohamed Hair Treag   his wife has been a great beauty once   her fine eyes are still the same   and her kindness and attention make up for the loss of the rest – she has been [on] the pillgramage to Mecca but ["the" inserted] her journey has given her more behaviour of a christian dame than a sour bigoted Mohamadan   after I left there [sic] house I went to take leave of Ben Taleb's Wife and his brother Misa – I was taken through every room in the house

Tuesday 4th
[no entry]

Wednesday 5th
after a good deal of trouble set off from Sockna at 10 A.M.   the weather cold & Cloudy   we have got most of the male and female slaves who accompanied us from Morzuk   the poor creatures were so glad when they met us as if they had met their fathers & mothers

Sunset cold & windy with Showers of sand   Course N. by W.

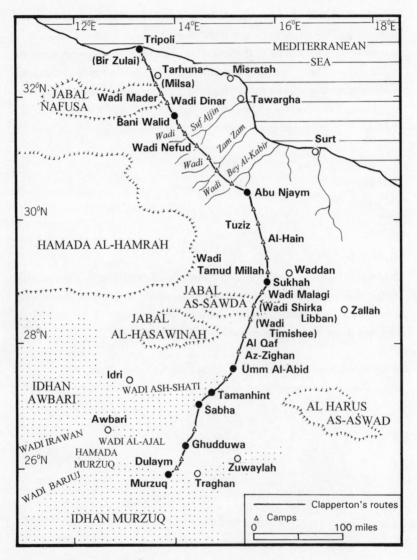

Map 15. Murzuq to Tripoli

292

CHAPTER
16

Return to Tripoli

Thursday 6ᵗʰ

Cold & windy at 9 started at 1 PM halted at the well of Tamud Millah
– cold & windy all night filled 2 days water & very ill with ague all
day

Tamud or the water found under the earth

Friday 7ᵗʰ

Cold & Calm – at 7 A.M Sᵗᵈ N. ½ W. at 9. AM Major D. parted compʸ
taking the road to Grizah[1] – Noon strong cold wind from the N.W.
passed several patches of barley belonging to the Arabs of Hoon in
which our friends allowed the camels to have a good *nip*–

at 4 halted in the dry bed of a stream that rises at the foot of the hills and
takes its course to the north and East and is joined by another comming
from the Hormut Tuziz to the N.E. of which it forms a lake the night

---

[1]While Clapperton remained on "the old road by Bonjem", Denham made a detour to visit the
remains at Ghirza, a late Roman site and its surroundings which include a large settlement, cemeteries and a series of spectacular monumental tombs [see *Missions*, Vol. III, pp. 503-510]. Nearby in
the Wadi Ghirza is a Roman agricultural flood system [D. Brogan and D. J. Smith, Ghirza: A *Libyan
Settlement of the Roman Period* (Department of Antiquities, Tripolitania, and Society for Libyan Studies,
London, 1984)]. Clapperton and Denham met up again at Bani Walid on Thursday 20th January.

cold & windy   there is much rain in this part of the desert – 2 days journey to the N.E of the hills of Hormut Tuziz – where the water halts

Saturday 8ᵗʰ

at 7 AM– Sᵗᵈ   Cold with a strong gale from the N.W.   saw plenty of
antelopes   none of which I could get within gunshot – saw also the
traces of an ostrich – at 3 P.M. halted in the wady which is here called
El haad   found water about 4 feet below the surface – the water in several parts of the wady had but sunk under the earth a short time before
– on our route to Fezzan in 1822² we saw nothing of this water course
and the Sockna people come here and in its neighbourhood to feed their
camels in the winter season and say that when the rains are plentiful in
the winter season the bed of the river is full and carries every thing
before it – which present appearance confirms – filled our water skins
cold & windy all night – Course N ½ W

the plain and on the banks of this River is covered with foliated gypsum
and *opal*   Sunset Halted to the Northᵈ of *El. Haim* or the tent³   night
cold & Windy

Sunday 9ᵗʰ

Cold & clear   the Whole ground covered with hoar frost – at 7 AM–
leaving the bed of the river to the Eastd we travled slowly over the ridges
that form between the river and the hills of Tuziz   allowing the camels to
browze on the budding scanty bushes as they passed through the vallies
which now look green and fresh   far different to what they appeared
when we passed over this place in 1822 – then their roots were only to
be seen but dry parched roots as no rain had fallen that winter – the
roots of this bush serve the Arab for fire and its budding tops a good food
for their camels –   when we passed the Hormut Tuziz and at the

---

²In the month of March.
³Ar., al-Khaima, tent, and, by extension, home.

Northern intrance Mukni had opened a well and at the depth of 30 fms had found a little brackish water the late Mustapha el Ahmer had it dug 10 *fms* deeper and lost what little they had found at 30 –

Monday 10ᵗʰ
Cold N. ½ E. our road difficult and rocky skirted to the Eastᵈ by barren rocky hills & to the Westᵈ by high sand hills or low Rocky hills covred with sand the rocks covered with brown *bushs* – to the Westᵈ of the Sand hills & to the East of the range of hills running from Wady Orfilly called the Gerzah hills is a lake of water of considerable depth ["considerable for this country that is it will take a man to the *waist*' in the deepest parts of it" inserted] which continues some times through the summer[4] –

Sunset halted on the Side of the hills of Tuziz under a point running out to the Westᵈ called the father of the goats or Bu Naga[5] – Course N. by W–

["Monday 10ᵗʰ Cold" deleted]

Tuesday 11ᵗʰ
Cold – at 7 A.M. Started   cold & Windy at Noon – at 3.30 P.M. halted at the Wells of Bonjem – during the night heavy rain

Tuesday 11th the Orfilly Arabs had once a settlement ["to North" deleted] at Bonjem but owing to the guinea worms they gave it up[6] – to the

---

[4]The large wadis, Wadi Bey al-Kabir and Wadi Zam Zam (see Thursday 13th January), as well as the Wadi Sofeggin further north, run roughly parallel, from south-west to north-east, draining the country between the Hamada al-Hamra uplands and the Gulf of Sirte. As occasional water-courses, they offer some opportunity for cultivation of barley and other crops by local and more distant tribespeople.

[5]Clapperton made a slip here; Ar., *naqa*, she-camel, not goat.

[6]See Chapter Two, n. 20.

eastd of the Castle there still remains a considerable No– of date trees but they only go up there at the time of impregnating the female trees and in the harvest to gather the fruit   Course N.[7]

Wednesday 12th

Cold Windy & Cloudy   at 8 AM– left Bonjem having waterd our camels and filled our water Skins

at 4 P.M. halted in Wady Bey – the day was so very cold that I went a head frequently to light a fire for the poor slaves to warm themselves – as they suffered greatly by the cold – Course N.

Wady bey comes from Gerzah and enters the Sea at Taurgha – there is water in different places in its whole course which is like a river of trees and grass for the whole way   on each side is barren gravelly and rocky desert – at Taurgh[a] near Misurata it is a running stream   in this Wady several tribes of Arabs feed their flocks in the spring and sow their grain each tribe having their separate parts – principally the Magerhas and Wallid Boo Seafs

Thursday 13th

Cloudy   at 8 AM– left Wady Bey – the day cold & Windy – at Sunset halted in Wady Zem zem   this is another river of trees and grass and joins Wady Bey 3 days j[ny] to the East[d] of this road   Course N. by W

the night being very cold with a little rain one of the female slaves named Lafia who had been the life and joy of the whole of the others[8] by her wit and mimickry   particularly of the owner of the house she stoped   at in

---

[7]A second entry for the day, made on the opposite, otherwise blank, page.

[8]George Lyon remarked that the female trade slaves in a caravan were much less exhausted by travelling than the males: the women and girls walked together and sang in chorus nearly the whole day – "which enlivened them and beguiled the way" [A Narrative, p. 326].

Sockna a blind man who used to keep rather too strict a guard over his dates and female slaves in Lafia['s] opinion – I have not escaped myself some times from her – but this night she gave up she was cold wet and hungry and began singing in a mournful tone what had she done in her lifetime to cause her to be taken from father mother and husband to be made a slave I called her into my tent gave her some Kuscasou and when she had filled her belly she was as merry as ever I enquired of her how she had been sold she said that she was going to a neighbouring town to see her father and Mother and her brothers sold her to Tibbo Slave dealers –

Friday 14th

at 8.30. AM– weather warm & Clear the slaves all merry as possible – as they had suffered by the cold since we left the Wady Kawar my Friend Lafia who is from Mandra and another female slave from Wodie in Borno[9] had a battle about the superiority of their towns a great cause [of] quarrel amongst both males and females of the interiour they fought and tore the cloths of[f] one another when the Master of the wodie girl comming up was going to beat Lafia this I prevented by telling him if he laid hands on her I should certainly beat him – saw great flocks of Antilopes which were very shy Sunset halted – course N.N.W

this evening the people who were with [us] being short of water the Male slaves all lads kept calling out to their masters you like money dont you – if you dont give us water we will die and you will lose it – they were going to be beat for their impertinence but I interfered and made them give each an allowance for the night

---

[9]Mandara, a pagan country in mountainous region south of Borno raided by Borno for slaves; the town of Wudi lies on Borno's northern border on the western shore of Lake Chad.

Saturday 15th

Morning clear & fine   at 7. AM St^d   a little after Starting Hadje Ali the owner of the camels which carried my baggage Had been severely wounded by a Magerha Arab – as he was plowing up the Harvest the Arab had put 2 balls through him   one through his breast which was nearly healed and the other through his Arm below the shoulder and Splintered the bone – this also was nearly healed   and he was going down to Tripoli to complain to the Bashaw – in mounting his ass which was a very obstinate one he fell and broke the bone   the lower part of which appeared through the old wound in the Arm   I was a head and they came hollowing after me to come and give my advice and assistance they were leading the poor man Supported by 2 of my servants who when he met me I was glad to see he was so quiet and resigned saying only that god had written it and he must bear it – when we got up to the camels I made them halt and had a fire made and one of the camel men a native of Sockna being a doctor he made [a] splint from one of our soudan canes anointed the arm with warm grasses after placing the bones in their proper position and then bound the splinter [sic] round the arm and placed him on a camel

at 4 P.M. we halted in Wady Nefud – which with the adjoining wadys are beautiful beyond description after comming off an arid desert – greater part of the wady is now sowen with barley by the Orfillies – we had some trouble in getting fire wood and all the trees were green & woods [sic] not burn

Sunday 16th

Morning clear with a heavy dew   at 8. A.M. left Wady Nefud   I crossed the Mountains in a direct line – the camels following the road through the ravine – after getting to the Northd of the hills I met a Sheikh of the Boo Tuble arabs¹⁰   he was very anxious I should go with him to his tents

---

¹⁰Not further identified; perhaps a minor clan?

and he would kill a sheep and make a feast – he told me that consul Warrington had been waiting for ["me" deleted] us for – this month past in Beneolied –

at 4 PM Cold with sleet and rain   halted near Gerla Mountain   Hadje Ali very ill   poor Lafia sat up with him all night –   Course N.N.W and – N.W

Monday 17ᵗʰ
at 8 AM– Started   at 4 P.M. Fresh breezes & Cloudy with rain   Halted in Wady Gharbain   this wady is now planted with barley which is about 4 inches high   N.N.W ½ W

Tuesday 18ᵗʰ
Clear & frosty   at 9 left Wady Gharbain – at Noon arrived at Beneolied – and halted near to the castle – N.N.W. ½ W – waited on the Govr who is here getting the tribute

Wednesday 19ᵗʰ
Cold with rain at times   went up to Where the consul had halted when he was here   found a good supply of every thing to eat & drink[11]   I was much pestered with beggars to day   that is every Arab is a beggar   they stole My bornouse leaving me an old one in rags in its place   the Govr begged the tobe off my back   another a pair of breaches –   the Maraboot's brother begged my shirt

---

[11]Barth was similarly met at Bani Walid by a messenger from the Consulate "who, besides a few letters, brought me what was most gratifying to me in my exhausted state, a bottle of wine, a luxury of which I had been deprived for so many years." [*Travels*, Vol. III, p. 629].

Thursday 10ᵗʰ [= 20ᵗʰ]
Cold & frosty

Friday 21ˢᵗ
Cold at 10 AM – left Beneolied at 4 halted at Wady *Dinah* in the bed
of it

Saturday 22ⁿᵈ
at 7 AM left Wady *Dinar* Cold & Windy – at 4 P.M– halted at Wady
Mader received a messenger from the Consul – Course ["N. by W."
deleted] N.W by W Cold & Windy all night

Sunday 23ʳᵈ
Cold & Clear at 8 AM– left Wady Madir which is now full of Water and
there is a Nᵒ of ["ancient" inserted] Ruins here – with the Walls of a
prety large town at 4-30 P.M– halted at *Milsa* where we had little or no
fire wood a dead camel with a circle drawn round it and the Orfilly
Star[12] –

Monday 24ᵗʰ
Clear at 10 Warm at 4 halted on the South side of the Mountains

Tuesday 25ᵗʰ
at 8 AM– Started and at 4 PM halted at the Beer *Zulai* the Consuls bro-
ker met us on the road they had been out 2 days with the Consul who
had rode home last night and left orders for a messenger to be dispatched

---

[12]Ambiguous. The Orfilly star was probably branded on the camel, but might perhaps have been
drawn in the sand.

when we arrived   When we arrived at the Well we found a carpet spread
toast Sandwiches and Coffee[13]   it proved to us a princely feast

[Notes on fauna[14]:]

Spoon Bill   white iris   red legs – red & greenish bill[15]

Habara   grey iris   pupil black[16]

Duck   black & White   a beautifull black eye[17]

Mohur Arab –   Garchiga   Bornow   – beautifull ["black" deleted] red &
White Antilope   beautifull black eye   long legs   leaps & bounds[18]

Corigum   black on the thigh outside   the female a dusky red approaching to brown – light hazle iris[19]

---

[13]And "huge draughts of Marsala wine" [Denham, *Missions*, Vol. III, p. 510].

[14]Jottings on the last used page of the journal, relating to observations made or specimens collected, mostly in Borno; see *Narrative* (1st. edition 1826), Appendix XXI: Zoology, pp. 183-207.

[15]The African spoonbill, *Platalea alba*.

[16]Ar., *hubara*, a generic word for a bustard. Here possibly the Nubian bustard *Neotis Nuba*
(*Kretzschmar*), eye stone grey; a bird of the desert edge confined to the Sudanese arid belt [C.W.
Mackworth-Praed and C.H.B. Grant, *Birds of West Central and Western Africa*, 2 Vols., (London, 1970)].

[17]Possibly the Knob-billed duck, *Sarkidiornis melanotos melanotos*. The female has no knob; but
Clapperton had earlier remarked on the beautiful black eye of a male he had shot in Borno [*Clapperton
in Borno*, p. 212 & n.].

[18]*Gazella dama mhorr*, [Ar., mhor], a dark form sub-species of the Dama gazelle [T. H. Haltenorth
and H. Diller, *Säugetiere Afrikas und Madagaskars* (Munich, 1977) p. 93].

[19]*Damaliscus lunatus korrigum* [Kanuri, *kargum*], also known as the Western hartebeest [Haltenorth
and Diller, *Ibid.*, p. 81].

APPENDIX I

CORRESPONDENCE FROM FEZZAN

Borno Mission – five unpublished letters from Fezzan (May and November 1822)

Two issues were on Clapperton's mind in the seven months spent in Fezzan in 1822: first, how to obtain the official escort Yusuf Pasha had promised to provide, or how otherwise to cross the Sahara to Borno; and, in the latter months, Denham's dereliction of duty in his attempted return to England [see Introduction, p.26]. Bovill provides a summary of these affairs in his Introduction to *Missions to the Niger* [Vol.II, pp. 32-59], documented by a selection of the Mission's correspondence, official and private. Clapperton's journal, however, adds further to our understanding of events and the reactions of the travellers to them; as do two letters he wrote from Murzuq to John Barrow at the Admiralty in June and September 1822. These form the substance of this appendix (Items I.i and I.ii)[1]. Accounts in letters written at the same period by Denham and Oudney also widen the perspective:

• Denham's private remarks to his brother Charles in mid-May 1822 on the eve of his departure on his return journey to Tripoli (I.iii)[2] ;
• Oudney's account to John Barrow of the state of affairs in November 1822 immediately before final departure for Borno (I.iv)[3];
• Denham comments to his brother on the low state of morale in the Mission when he rejoined his colleagues in Murzuq, also written at the beginning of November 1822 (I.v)[4].

---

[1]Royal Geographical Society (R.G.S.), London, Library Ms. File, Mus. No. 403/3: two letters of Hugh Clapperton.
[2]R.G.S., The papers of Major, later Lieutenant Colonel, Dixon Denham (D.D.) Library Ms. File, AR 64, D.D. 17/21: three letters from Denham to brother Charles 1822-24.
[3]R.G.S., Mus. No. 408/7: four letters of Walter Oudney.
[4]R.G.S., D.D.1 7/20: thirteen letters from Denham to his brother Charles 1821-24.

Note on chronology

The Mission arrived in Murzuq on 7 April 1822. On 30th April Oudney and Clapperton made a short excursion eastwards to Zawila, with the aim, among others, of finding a supposed mountain of saltpetre which did not exist[5], while Denham remained in Murzuq to continue putting pressure on the Sultan, Mustafa al-Ahmar, to mount the promised escort to Borno.

By the time Clapperton and Oudney returned to Murzuq on 9th May, it had become clear that there was no prospect of immediate travel to Borno. In discussions on 15-16 May Denham volunteered to go to Tripoli to report the state of their affairs to the Consul-General and to remonstrate with Yusuf Pasha Karamanli. He agreed with his companions (17th May 1822) that he would return in 3 months, i.e. August, if nothing had been achieved. When Denham left for England, however, to complain in London after the fruitless audiences wth Yusuf Pasha, he implied to Warrington that Clapperton and Oudney had agreed to his being free to do so. This was untrue. Furthermore, Denham's letters reveal that he was in fact content to remain in England and not return to Malta and Tripoli again until November[6] – in other words, he did not intend to rejoin his colleagues in Murzuk until, at the earliest, January 1823.

When Clapperton and Oudney returned to Murzuq on 11th August after their journey to Ghat, they found a letter from Warrington written in early July confirming a lack of progress with Yusuf Pasha at that date – but with no reference to Denham's departure for Marseilles and England. Clapperton and Oudney, now even more confident that they could travel safely in the Sahara without any escort, set about making plans to travel with a caravan of merchants due to depart for Borno in mid–September. On 6th September, however, they received Warrington's letter of 21st July saying that the Pasha had agreed to provide an escort commanded by Bu Khallum; that Denham was now on his way back; and that the expedition was ready to start out from Tripoli in mid–September. Their replies to Warrington, with frank accounts of their frustrations and anger, were intercepted and read by Denham at Sokna on the road from Tripoli to Murzuq[7] – an inauspicious start to the reconvening of the Mission.

---

[5]R.G.S., D.D. 17/21.

[6]Denham letter to Charles, 5 August, 1822 [R.G.S., D.D. 20].

[7]It would have been an acceptable, and indeed sensible, practice in terms of the Mission's arrangements to intercept official communications from other members of the Mission in the field to their prime support base, the Consulate General. Bovill quotes in full [*Missions*, Vol. II, pp. 54-55] Denham's reactions in a letter to Warrington written in Sokna on 11th October 1822.

I.i Letter from Hugh Clapperton to:
John Barrow Esq
Admiralty Office
London

Mourzuk 4th June 1822

Dear Sir

As yet we have only acquired knowledge of the disposition of the people and got a little acquainted with the language – however trivial these may appear they are still necessary for the Grand end of the expedition

The D^r and I have been at Zuela and set off to morrow to the Tuarick country for the purpose of extending our [knowledge] and inquiring among a people who are widely distributed and command all the tracts from here to Timbuctoo and Soudan   some think the step imprudent because it is pericleous and no doubt the over cautious will believe so but it is necessary to do something that may tend to further success for be assured if we go with the army neither of the ends of the Mission can be accomplished – the D^r is so convinced of that that I would not be astonished if he departs for his destination when we return from Ghraat should no change take place in the Bashaw's views   it would be well were there any danger but we find on the contrary from those who come in every week the road is perfectly safe & the people well disposed

His Highness is overcareful partly from friendship and partly from the reward promised – We would have been better pleased had he sanctioned our proceeding foreward – though we do not regret coming here on the contrary [we] feel glad from the opportunity afforded us of constantly gaining information respecting the interiour   I could tell you a great deal as we converse every day with those who have been many times in Bornou & Soudan but that we do from mere curiosity never expecting any information useful to science from people who have [no] inducement to observe any thing except what relates to their convenience

we cannot form the least conjecture respecting the Niger you know as much about it as we do the general opinion is that it ends in the Nile to the South^d of Darfur there are certainly a number of streams in Bornou and the countries adjacent and one flows from Soudan the Waou which people say passes by Yaourie if that were authenticated the identity of the river near Timbuctoo and the Waou in Bornou would be certain – but I give very little cred^et to the accounts of the Merchants in determining the courses of a river navigable only in some parts and winding in various directions

– The Moors travel far certainly but it is generally in a beaten track and if you ask them their reasons for believing that such a river runs into another or joins it they can give you no other than [that] they think so or that they have been told so – Allow the identity of the Waou and the Niger How does it get to the Nile [?] one has *heard* and yet almost all agree that it ends there the uncertainty in which the matter is involved in place of [one word illeg.] ought to increase our energy and urge us on without an army if we go with one we must all return with one and farewell to the discovery of the course of the Niger or the Dr's forming an establishment and of the the English nation and character being known [in] those quarters – If we are so unfortunate to go as intended we can only be associated with the conquerors

– We find Mourzuk a tolerable town to live in and far from being unhealthy it is now dull from the Bey having gone to Tripoli and the greater number of those belonging to his government – I have determined the Longitude of the place by means of several Lunars on both sides of the Moon to be 14° 49' 30" W^8 – & the Latde by Mn Altde of Spica in the south and Dubhe in the North to be 25° 54' ["] N

– Both the D^r and myself regret not having brought two good pocket chronometers and a telescope for Jupiters Satelites^9 for we are anxious to settle as many points as possible and do all the good for science we can

---

[8]Clapperton meant to write 'East'. The actual position of Murzuq is 25°55' N, 13°55' E.
[9]A calculation of longitude gauged by the motions of Jupiter's planetary moons.

We all enjoy good healths and my worthy friend the Doctor requests me to give the best regards to you and hopes he will be able to write you a long letter on his return from Ghaat for he has really a great deal to do his fame is widely extended as a physician and people come from all quarters for his advice which will perhaps form as good a protection to us by and by as the Tescaras of the Bashaw – I hope that in five months after this you will hear from us at Bornou on the banks of the Niger and believe

me Sir your Most

Obedient Servant

Hugh Clapperton

I.ii Letter from Hugh Clapperton to:
John Barrow, Esq. LLD FRSi, &c &c
Admiralty, London   **Mourzuk 19th September 1822**

Sir,

I have the pleasure of informing you that we will certainly leave this place in the course of nine or ten days – We would now have been seven days on the road there – had not a courrier arrived from Tripoli on the 6th informing us that the Bashaw had sent an escort

– Dr O and I have been at Wadys Gharbi Shiati and Ghaat we travled in the hottest months of the year viz. May June July and August the Thermometer in the shade being from 102° to 106° of Farnheit in the heat of the day and though obliged the greatest part of that time to travel from before sunrise to sunset without halting having only two meals a day one before we started and the other after we halted at night we experienced not the slightest inconvenience save slight colds owing to the great change of temperature between the night and day and our sleeping in the open on our mats every night –

We have everywhere met with a kind reception and on no occasion have we met with a disposition to obstruct us in any observations which have all been done in the most public manner on the contrary the people have been anxious that we should see every thing and if they thought there was any thing we had omitted they would kindly point it out – We have settled the geography of all the principal points in Fezzan and 18 Miles NNE. of Ghaat we had the good fortune to get the longitude by the Moon's eclipse on the 2nd August last

It is much to be regretted that we did not bring a good Chronometer or Telescope as the M[essrs]. Beechey[10] took the latter instrument belonging to the late M[r] Ritchie – and I can assure you that with [a] common case instruments and chronometers are as easy to be preserved here as in any other country – as a proof our sextants are as good as the day they were brought from M[r] Jones' shop[11] though they have been more used than if we had been on board a ship for the same period

I must refer you to D[r] Oudney's itinerary for a particular account of our proceedings it will be accompanied by a chart of our route which is on a plane scale and I hope you will excuse its not being done better when I tell you that it was done upon an old twisted rickety table that we brought from Tripoli – but I shall do a better when I return to England though this is correctly laid down from sketches taken on the spot and the table of courses will enable any person to construct another[12] should I not return again which is not in my power to foretell our lives being in the hand of him who made all things –

---

[10]Capt F. W. Beechey and his brother H. W. Beechey were carrying out a survey of the north African coastline. See their *Proceedings of the Expedition to Explore the Northern Coast of Africa* (London, 1828). Clapperton and Oudney had expected to be able to collect articles from the Ritchie – Lyon expedition which had been left with the Consul General in Tripoli, but Oudney blamed Capt. W. H. Smyth. "The Beecheys behaved very kindly in giving us a few but the ones we principally stood in need of had been carried away by Capt. Smyth in the Adventure." [R.G.S. Mus. No. 408/7; Oudney to John Barrow (Admiralty), 25 October 1821.].

[11]Probably Thomas Jones of 62, Charing Cross, fl. 1806-1861, maker of navigational instruments [C.Southon, Sotheby's, personal communication].

[12]A fair boast; see Appendix II for the detail of Clapperton's itineraries.

With respect to Major Denham he has left us on the 20ᵗʰ of May for Tripoli for the purpose of laying before the Consul the true situation of affairs here with respect to the Army going to Bornou and to procure if possible letters of recommendation from the Bashaw to his friends in the interior and we would proceed with the first Kaffle – You may judge of our surprise on the arrival of the last courrier when the Consul's letters informed us of his having gone to England as if a matter that we had been previously acqauinted with   It has left me without instructions of any description   Neither has he written to the Dᴿ however his absence will be no loss to the Mission and a saving to his country for Major Denham could not read his sextant, knew not a star in the heavens and could not take the Altitude of the sun –

The naval carpenter William Hillman[13] we have found a most excellent man trusty and zealous for the good of the service – I hope he will not be forgot at the navy board when an opportunity offers

With the most sanguine hopes of success in our future Journey
I remain Sir
your most Obᵈ Serᵛᵗ
Hugh Clapperton

I.iii Extract from letter from Dixon Denham to his brother Charles Denham dated 15–17 May 1822

… Our departure from this, [(]to you I may say altho' I do not use such strong expressions to my employees) miserable depot of mal–aria & disease, appears to be less likely than ever to take place. The difficulties and dangers of travelling, after passing the frontiers of Fezzan, render the attempt impracticable with a smaller escort than 200 ["Horse" inserted] Men. Their force from many reasons cannot be furnished as double the

---

[13]See Introduction p. 24 & n. 77.

number of camels would be necessary to accompany such a Force in passing deserts 7 days without any supplies – but the Sultan assures us that we may wait and go with the ["Army" deleted] Expedition which ["army is not more" deleted] the Bashaw is about to send altho' no preparations are yet making for such an undertaking. –

something or other must be attempted, as every thing is to be dreaded from a delay during the hot months in Mourzuk. This capital has already formed the grave of one of our predecessors & of the Mission to which he was attached – and a constant exhaustion of money, health & strength must be the consequence of it[14]. The Sultan has this morning refused an offer I took upon myself the responsibility of making of 3000 dollars if he would forward us in any way to Bornou so that we might there await his arrival with the Expedition – 10000 he said would not induce him so to sacrifice our lives, recent events had rendered the journey more difficult. The Natives of Waday, a very warlike people to the Eastward of Bornou had broken with Kanem thro' which country our road to Bornou lies and had murdered the Chiefs & carried off many people. I then declared we should either go on alone, or that I should return to Tripoli & state to the Bashaw how wretchedly he had kept his faith with the British Government, demanding redress. The Sultans reply was just as you please & we left the Castle – I cannot express to you the feelings of disappointment with which we entered our dwelling after this audience.

17th May

We had last night a long debate on the state of our affairs. In council is strength, says somebody, but that must depend on the ability of the Chamber. Every thing looks like an attempt to neglect & delay us here, to meet a similar fate to that of poor Ritchies – which there appears to me but two ways to avoid ["it the one" deleted] meeting as bad a one[:]

---

[14]From these remarks Bovill imputed cowardice in Denham's "anxiety to escape what he believed was the lethal climate of Murzuk" [*Missions*, Vol. II, p. 44]. One should perhaps not, however, make too much of them. Denham had many faults but physical cowardice was not among them.

by going unadvisedly on, ["the other" deleted] or returning to Tripoli personally remonstrating with the Bashaw & the Consul & insisting on a performance of his promise to me – a promise [for] which he was but too ready to demand a Sum of Money in advance – I should now say too willingly granted him. The difficulties of this alternative troubled us – no Escort, the expense, the advanced state of the Season & 1200 Miles in such a country preparatory to as many on returning to be performed in advance of Mourzuk – all these I however overcame by offering myself to go with one Arab & two Camels. my companions remonstrated and wished that we should draw lots I however was peremptory, and two days more will not find me here.

I shall see the Sultan off which will put an end to all possibility of more favourable prospects until his returning & I shall then move & pass him on the road. My Arab assures me that such a proceeding will not be allowed for altho' he will be 50 days on the road no one must go before. I shall however ask no permission and I dare say no one will attempt to stop me. If I can at all judge of the wishes of HM Government they will approve of the steps I am about to take. Their ["object in' deleted] negotiating with the Bashaw for his protection as far as Bornou must have been under the idea that so far little risk should be incurred and that the Mission should thus arrive in a state to prosecute its enquiries and ultimate objects with more strength and vigour than could be the case were it to move in an unprotected state & subject to attendant deprivations & anxieties previous to being established at Bornou supposing this suppostion to be true how could we arrive in such a manner, if at all, were we desperately to move on in the worst season from Mourzuk throwing off by ourselves the protection of the Bashaw in acting in opposition to our Instructions & by that means rendering useless the arrangements which HM Government have made for purchasing our safety of that Prince –

You will say that remaining in Mourzuk is equally destructive to our Mission. So it is, but then it must be remembered that we are here by

placing too great confidence in the representative of those to whose protection we were consigned & not by or on our own responsibility.
remonstrance is now in our power, and I am not inclined tamely to suf-
fer these Moorish authorities to insult the Nation by making representa-
tion to its agents in direct opposition to truth – ...

I.iv Letter from Oudney to
John Barrow Esq
Secretary Admiralty &c &c
London   Mourzuk 4th November 1822

Sir,

I do not know how to apologize for omitting writing for so long but I
really have been much harrassed since I left England – our prospect at
times gloomy, at times smiling, alternating so that a sensible impression
was made on our spirits   Matters you must I know were very unsettled
in Tripoli, and all for the responsibility the Bashaw took upon himself
for the handsome sum promised. I was consequently not left a free agent
but secretly opposed in any undertaking that had the slightest danger so
as to try to deter me from it. You perhaps have heard of the protest sent
to Consul Warrington on my going into the Tuarick country. From the
difficulties experienced in our setting out on that journey, I anticipated
greater on signifying my intention of proceeding to Bornou with the first
Kaffle, but in that I was mistaken, for from Sidi Mohammed Lizari acting Sultan I received every assistance & the promised letters to Sheikh
Canmie Hadji Lameen ruler of Bornou, and to all the Tibboo Sheikhs
on the route. Thus while matters were in a doubtful state in Tripoli, we
would quietly have been on our journey to our destination had the courrier not arrived when we were all ready, and put a stop to proceedings.
It was the greatest chance in the world my worthy friend Clapperton
was not at Gatrone for a few days before we had agreed that he should
go forward and I was to meet him there with the lighter baggage   had
that been put in force it would have decided at once the course we were

to pursue and enabled us to get to Bornou four months before we stand a chance of arriving there.

The Consul's exertions have been most praiseworthy — in every thing respecting the Mission he has acted a most energetic and laudable part — the Bashaw is a curious man to deal with and like most of his kind his great policy consists in deception   It may do once or twice but is very soon detected. He perhaps took the only step that made His Highness take an active part and sanction our going. The road is perfectly safe, and our personal safety is doubly assured by Escort of 60 or 70 Arabs I should think but of the exact number I am not as yet perfectly certain. For my part I would most gladly have dispensed with them, as I dread they may be a thorn in our side, but let us hope for the best. We have a good man in Boo Khullum — he knows the people well, and is highly respected by all. I am sanguine of success ...

My valuable friend Lieu^t Clapperton desires to be remembered to you. He is just what I told you he was, and I think you ought to do something for him   he deserves it   he possesses spirit & enterprise — he has good sense and has several acquirements useful for a traveller   he has not the faculty of making trifles appear as matters of great moment & clothing in fine words what ought to be plain language   caution is very well but it is unbecoming a traveller to have too much of it   he foresees dangers that have no existence

I have not experienced any opposition on account of being a christian and Briton   There is not that [one word illeg.] for the christian name nor the prejudice which one might suppose — it is much easier for us to suppport our own characters than one that must set but awkward even after several years experience. I am sparing of paper it is scarce here and we have a long journey before us   I will write you from Bornou. I am Sir
Your most ob^d serv^t
William Oudney

I.v. Extract from letter by
Major Dixon Denham to his brother
Charles Denham   **Mourzuk 4th November 1822**

. . . .

I found Dr. O extremely ill & weak being a few days risen from a bed of
sickness and Clapperton on his Bed which he had not left for 15 days.
The Carpenter who was the only person that could come out to meet me
was so weakened that for a moment I did not know him   they had all
been afflicted with the fever & ague, had been delirious and only relieved
by strong Emetics – my appearance with Boo Khouloum has enlivened
them a little altho not as much as it might because they do not feel as they
ought. We all were up at dinner yesterday but they are dreadfully pulled
down and do not venture out until the Sun has nearly reached the meridian
with such prospects before me it is with the greatest difficulty I keep my
spirits . . .

These letters or characters are as follows and are written either from the right or left and some times up & down

Tuarick —

+ or X	yet	Miamooee — what is that
∴ or ⋮	yuk	Takaoba a Sword — Takeobawie Swords written ☉ ∴+
☉ or ▣	yes	Teluttela Dagger Telighe Daggers ‖+
♡ or ◻	yeb	
⨅ or ⊏	yum	el Baraoka gun el Barota guns
⨆ or E	yind	⨆☉‖
‖	yil	azel a Sheep Ezella Sheep
#	yuz	Darga a Shield
⤚	iz	aise a horse eisan horses
⊢	yint	Tibdjout a moon
		Rijan a Makera or light Camel Rijana Dhe
⋮	yuk	Alis Man Mid a man tie of Men
⋮	Eguh	Tamut woman Tedeghtton woman
⋀	yed	aok a Tree iskken Tree Takia a piece of bread Tellaou bd
◻ or ○	yun	aman water
⅛ or W	yi	asiem South Aisa Meat awit bring
⌐	ish	Kala no
∙∙	yu	Iwo come Sera here
∙∙∙ A	A	Ragi ain Go away Baraka road
/	yin	Manistaket how far or how much
∨ or ε	yesk	yo gik afar distant
U	yuf	yo hag near
⋈	yig	ahal a day chelan days
∪	yid	Talat a month Talat Months ikhel a year

Figure 13. Tuareg Word List

APPENDIX 2

A TUAREG WORD-LIST

In the chapter of the published account of the Mission's proceedings entitled *Excursion to Westward of Mourzouk*, written by Dr. Oudney, there appears a list of nineteen 'Tuarick characters' over the brief comment:

> These characters will be sufficient to enable the learned to trace the connexion of the language with others that are now extinct. Here we have no opportunity of making inquiries into this important subject[1]

Clapperton at least made an attempt to enquire further; the results being the word-list below. Since he had no knowledge of Tamasheq, beyond perhaps a few customary forms of greetings and essential everyday words, we may assume that the vocabulary was taken down with the help of an Arabic-speaking intermediary, such as Hatita, or the son of the Qadi, Al Amin, who so impressed Clapperton, or one of the visiting Arab merchants of Ghadamis[2].

---

[1]Oudney, *Missions*, Vol. II, p. 193.
[2]See 27th July, first and last paragraphs.

Clapperton's Tuareg word-list
A three-page note written in Ghat, 31st July, 1822

[1]

Their letters or characters are as follows and written either from the right or left and sometimes up & down

[left hand column³]

+ or x	yit
.. or :	yik
⊙ ⊡	yis
◑ ⊡	yel
⊐ or ⊏	yum
Ǝ or E	yud
Ⅱ	yil
⊞	yuz
≻—≺	iz
H	yint
⋮	yuk
⋮	Egugh
∧	yid
⊓ O	yur
⪯ or W	yi
ⱦ	ighs
..	yu
.	A
/	yin
ʕ S or C	ish
U or ⊓	yuf
⋉	yiz
U'	yid

---

³On the first two pages, Clapperton's notes were compressed into two, approximate, columns of script. For ease of reading these have been presented separately.

[right hand column]

Tuarick[4] –

Miamoon	what is that		
Takuba)	a Sword	Takoobawi	Swords
written ⊙ ∴ +)			
Teluk)	Dagger	Telighi	Daggers
∶ll +)			
el Baroot)	a gun	el Barota	guns
Ǝ O ʘ II)			
Uzel	a Spear	Uzela	Spears
Darza	a Shield		
aise	a horse	eisan	horses
Tibadjnet	a mare		
Rijan	a Mahery or Light Camel		
Rijana Plur.			
Alis	a Man	*Ali∂*	a number of Men
Tamutt	woman	Tedighthan	Women
Ask	a Tree	iskhan	Trees
Takima	a piece of bread	Takawa	bread
Aman	Water		
Asiem	Soup	Aisa	Meat
Awit	bring		
Kala	no		
Iwo	come	Sera	here
Ragi ain	Go away		
Baraka	road		
Mamitafutt	how far or how much		
yagesheafa	distant		
yo haz	near		
ahal	a day	ehelan	days
Taluta	a month	Taleel	Months
dahel	a year		

---

[4]Problems of transcription of Clapperton's handwriting described in Appendix 6, pp.347-50, apply *a fortiore* to a word-list such as this, with many single words or short phrases out of context and composed of a run of ambiguous letters. A measure of guesswork is nevitable. The Tamacheq words are therefore all best treated as "looks like".

[Page 2]
[left hand column]

Amaki	a [illeg.] vessel for carrying water		
Matalid	How do you do		
Hair Ras	very well		
Okigara hurit	I hope you are quite well		
Matigum	what are your news		
Ki	thou	nick	I were he
Afinak	the head		
Airef	Fore head		
Amar	eye brows		
Teat	eye	Teatawin	eyes
Tainhan	nose		
aisne	Mouth		
esina	Teeth		
ilis	tounge		
Tineart	chin		
evia	throat		
ukfat	give me		
ukfa	I will give you		
Zing	to buy		
Sing	to sell		
atoo	gun powder		
libal	a musquet ball	libale	balls
Fuda	thirsty		
Ruk	to wish		
isoo	to drink		
Tafo	Sun		
Eywa	Moon		
Ehare	Stars		
Amila	White	Emilen	Whites
Enotafa	black	Enitafan	blacks
yakugra	red	yakughan	reds
yugharan	Green		

[right hand column]

Tine	Dates
Anoo	a well

320

Ehegun	deep or long		
yezit	sweet		
yahoosir		beautiful	
aisen	Salt		
Yishot	Bitter		
yurza	sour		
agh	Milk		
Amis	a Camel male		
Agintalim	Camels Milk		
tis	a Cow		
Eghier	an Ass		
aburat	a boy		
Tibirat	a girl		
Aliba	a water skin		
Abis	a Water Skin		
Sanuk	I know		
win sina	I do not know		
Alak	take care		
didagh	this place		
tarakaf	a Kaffle		
Minas laket	where are you going		
aghmim	city or town		
Manitafalid	where are you come from		
Artoofat	God be with you		
Eymora	a camp		

[Page 3]

Taminas	a cup		
Tadawad	a battle		
Tabu	Tobaco		
Takooinan Tabu	fill the pipe		
Tebooa gemsek	shoes		
Ablatin	a Stone	Eblatin	Stones
Egidi	Sand		
Amadthak	a Clay soil		
Tearei	a Goat	Auli	Goats
idi	a dog	thoor	dogs
Ekia	sheep	Akasu	Sheep

321

Egitat	a bird
Amarhi	my love
amadeke	my friends
ahaibus	a Caftan or loose gown
Kirhaba	Trowsers
Tiboohayan	boots
get	[illeg.]
loza	hungry
Timse	fire

Eyon	1
Sin	2
Karat	3
Akoze	4
Simenze	5
Sithies	6
Isa	7
Etam	8
Tisa	9
Murow	10

Agharcir	to ride a horse
insa	to sleep
yaka Kwak	to lye on one side or lounge
Takoomloot	the red cap or Tagia
Takumisi	a long shirt – or tobe

It is evident that Clapperton's list of words was taken down – in his own particular orthography, complete with some french spellings (e.g. 'ou' for 'u', as in Mourzuk) – just as he heard them. It is made with no reference to root consonants, and using his own approximations at vowel sounds. The list is in every sense a practical, work-a-day affair with particular emphasis on matters of personal interest, such as animal husbandry, provisions and arms. Despite these limitations, Clapperton's notes represent a rare, if short, glimpse of the Tamasheq language and Tifinagh script as used by the Tuaregs of the Ajjer region in the period before contact with Europeans.

It is interesting therefore to compare[5] Clapperton's notes with A. Hanoteau's *Essai de Grammaire de la langue Tamachek*, a study completed in 1859-60[6]. One might for example compare the Tuareg (Lybico-Berber) alphabet [Hanoteau:, 2-3] and the names of numbers [ibid:, pp. 127-8]. Like Hanoteau, unlike others, Clapperton reproduces some examples of the Tifanagh script now largely defunct. Hanoteau also records stray inscription-like texts and an extensive transliteration of these [ibid. pp. 204-6]. Clapperton introduces random and incomplete Tamasheq phrases, whereas Barth[7] and Hanoteau [ibid:, pp. 227-80], in appendices in particular, offer extensive dialogues and a narrative, with commentary.

Examples in Clapperton such as, on p. 2,

> *Mamitaffut* – 'how far/ how much?'
>
> *Matulid* – 'how do you do'

are sufficiently correct to indicate their occurence, elsewhere, amongst the Tuareg, and are recognisable; others are very loosely rendered. For example, [p. 2] *'artoofat'* – 'God be with you', would be closer rendered by expressions such as 'until tomorrow', *'à demain'*, *'hasta mañana'*. Arabic is worked into many Tuareg phrases and, indeed, on p. 1 'al-Baroot' (gun) is without doubt the Arabic *al-barud*, 'gunpowder'. On p. 2 Clapperton renders the well-known Tuareg phrase 'nought but good' as Hair ras, whereas Hanoteau [pp. 227-8 and 251] transcribes this as *el-Khir-ras – Hair/Khir* being in fact the Arabic loan word, *al-khair*, 'the good', which, as E. Lane indicates in his *Lexicon*[8] , has many shades of meaning and numerous Qu'ranic associations. Another example where Clapperton and Hanoteau may be compared is on p. 2 where Clapperton translates 'where are you come from' [sic] as *Manitafalid*. In Hanoteau [pp. 241 & 251] this expression is rendered by *d es tefeled?*

---

[5]The editors are grateful to Professor H. T. Norris, formerly of S.O.A.S., London, for the comparisons elaborated and commentary contributed below.

[6]Second edition, (Algiers, 1896) – with the Preface dated Dra el Mizan, February 1859.

[7]*Travels*, Vol.3, pp.724-63.

[8]E. W. Lane, *An Arabic-English Lexicon*, etc., (2 Vols., London, 1863, repr. Islamic Texts Society, Cambridge, 1984)

The following examples from Clapperton are compared with the words to be found in Ghoubeid Alojaly's Lexique Touareg-Francais[9]:

Clapperton [with page ref.]		Ghoubeid [giving sing. & plural forms; [with page ref.]
Takuba [p.1]	a Sword	takoba/tikobawen [87], épée[s]
Teluk [1]	Dagger	teleq/telghen [11], petit[s] couteau[x]
aise [1]	a horse	ays/aggosan [206], cheval[aux]
Alis [1] plur. Inid	a Man	alas/meddan, [118], homme[s]
Aske [1] plur. ishkon	a tree	ashek/pleshkan [183], arbre[s]
Baraka [1]	road	abaraqqa/ibbaraqqan [10], chemin[s]
Sera [1]	here	ser [177], au moyen de
shal [1] plur. shelan	day	ahal/ihallan [78], galante[s] des jeunes (Gh) elan [108], année[s]
ilis [2]	tongue	iles/ilesawan [118], langue[s]
ukfat [2]	give me	akfu [89], donner
Fuda [2]	thirsty	fad [36], soif
Tafo [2]	sun	tefuk/ tofuken [37], soleil
Amila [2] plur. Emalin [2]	White	imlal/mollul [128], blanc
Enotafa plur. Enitafan [2]	black	izdaf/sattaf [219], noir foncé, (terne)
Tine [2]	Dates	tayne/taynawen [206] ,datte[s]
Anoo [2]	a well	anu/enwan [137], puits
tis [2]	a Cow	tast/shitan [169], vache[s]
aburat [2]	a boy	barar/bararan [11], enfant[s]
aghmim [2]	city or town	aghrem/ighoram [72], ville[s]
Ablatin plur. Eblatin [3]	a Stone	ablal/iblalan [7], pierre[s] dure[s]
idi plur. thoor [3]	a dog	idi/idan [16], chien[s]
Egitat [3]	a bird	agodid [50], oiseau[x]
loza [3]	hungry	laz [50], faim
insa [3]	to sleep	ansu [149], passer le nuit
Takoomloot [3]	the red cap or tagia	tagolmust/tigolmast [52], voile[s] de visage de l'homme Tg.

---

[9]Ghubayd agg-Alawjali, *Lexique (Awgalel) Touareg-Français*, (Copenhagen 1980).

Clapperton's Tifanagh alphabet list concurs almost fully with those provided by both Hanoteau [pp. 4-5] and F. Rodd[10], although the latter identify further minor variations in symbols and in direction of writing (up/down, left/right). Clapperton's list of numbers one to ten is similarly fully recognisable:

Clapperton	**Hanoteau**[11]	
	(masc. form)	symbols
Eyon	iien	IΣ
Sin	sin	I⊙
Karat	keradh	∃O∴
Akoze	okkoz	ⵣ ∴
Simenza	semmons	⊙ⵎ⊙
Sithies	sedis	⊙Π⊙
Isa	essaa	. ⊙
Etam	ettam	ⵎ+
Tisa	tezzan	. ⵣ +
Murow	meraou	: Oⵎ

[10]Rodd, *The People of the Veil*, Plate 33, p. 266 and p. 269.
[11]*Grammaire Tamachek*, pp. 127- 8.

APPENDIX 3

CLAPPERTON'S ITINERARIES

Clapperton's log of itineraries, reproduced here in full, represents the first scientifically assembled record of the caravan roads through central and western Fezzan and across the Sahara from Murzuq in Fezzan to Kukawa in Borno. Alongside these course notes, Clapperton also kept up a set of charts sketched during travel. The record is comprehensive and accurate[1]; and its significance in terms of additions to geographical knowledge at the time is evident in the maps drawn by, for example, the London cartographer J. Arrowsmith before and after the Borno Mission.

We have a second, fair copy, version of the Itineraries for one period, from Thursday 21 December 1822 (Maafan) to Wednesday 29 January 1823 (The Wells of Dugasheemee). In this tidied version Clapperton recorded intermediary compass points in degrees rather than in half and quarter points, for instance, S 20 E for SSE¼S. In this version, he was systematic in entering a daily running estimate of longitude – corrected when opportunity arose – and also created a column to record observations of Amplitude[2], in which, however, in the event he only made one entry.

While the text of the journals presented in this volume ends at Bel Kashifra (*Bedouaram,*) on 28th January 1823, the data for the itineraries through the remainder of the journey to Kukawa in Borno is shown, for the sake of completeness, in this Appendix.

---

[1]See Appendix 5: Cartography.
[2]See Chapter Nine, n.10.

327

From Mourzuk & Zouela [April-May 1823][3]

Date[4]	Course	Distce.	Latitude[5]	Place where halted[6]
Apr				
30	EbyS¾S	15		to Zaizou
				Latde 25.52.38N
May				
1	EbyS¾S	18		to Treghain
2	ESE	8		to Towela
	ENE	8		to Mughwa
3	ENE	8		to Taleb
	EbyN¾N	8		to Hamera
				Latde 26.6'N
4	E½N	9		Missaguin
	E½S	8		to Zuela
6	NW½N	5		to Omleranib
	SWbyW½W	12		to Mughwa
7	[illeg.]			
8	[illeg.]			Haje Hajill

Fom Mourzouk to Wady Gharbi, Shiati & Ghat [June-July 1823]

June				
8	WNW	12		Humum
	NW	13		Tezawa
9	NbyW	18		To a Well & Tullah
				trees in the Desert
10	North	8		to the South side of
				the range forming the

---

[3]The record of itineraries in this remark book starts on Friday 29th March 1822, being the continuation of a record, now lost, covering the journey from Tripoli to Murzuq where the travellers arrived on 7th April. The text presented here starts with Clapperton's departure on 30th April on his and Oudney's short excursion eastwards from Murzuq to Zuwaylah on 30th April .

[4]In Clapperton's log, this column has the title 'Month, Week & Days. Days of the week have been omitted for reasons of space.

[5]Clapperton records the astral data. $\underline{O}$ = the Meridian Altitude of the sun's lower limb.

[6]And other notes; at times including a running estimate of longitude. Modern place names, where applicable, are shown in the maps accompanying the text of the journals.

	NWbyN	2		South side of Wady Sherge & Gharbi
	North	6	Mn Altde Spica	
			26.33.55N	in the pass of the hills to Tikertiba
12	W¾N	4	Mn Altde Spica	
			26.33.30N	Kharfa
16	WbyN½N	8	Spica Mn Altde	
			26.32.45N	Germa
19	WbyN	10	Antares	
			26.34.35N	Oubari
24	WbyN	5		in the wady
25	WbyN	10	Antares	
			26.32.35N	Well & Maraboot of Sidi Ahmet
26	ENE	6		at the side of the Sand hills near to Oubari
29	NNE	4		
	EbyN	6		
	NEbyE	8		amongst the Sand hills
30	NE	5		Tigadefa
	NEbyN	5		
	North	2		amongst the Sand hills
July				
1	NE	6		Wady Jamar
	NWbyN	1		a wady no name
	ENE	3		Wady Tawel or the long wady
	NNE	2		
2	NEbyN	6		
	ENE	1		
	NEbyN½N	5		at a well & date trees brackish
	NNW	2		
	NWbyW	1		
3	NW	10	Antares	
			27.26.3N	to Idri
5	SEbyS½S		Mer. Antares	

				27.19.12N	13.22
	SE½S	15			Bingebara
6	SbyE	17			The Well of Dakoon
	SWbyS½S	3			Wady Bilawagi
7	South	6			The Well of Inshea ["in Wadi *Taer*" deleted]
	S by W	5			Well & Wady of Lakersha
8	SbyW½W	8		Mer. Antares 26.54.43N	Wady Trona
9	SbyW¾W	8			
	SbyW¾W	6		Mer. Antares 26.40.40N	Mandra Salt Lake & village
10	SbyW½W	8			To Tikirtiba
16[7]	West	14			to the Well of Tinebonda
18	W½S	24			in a part of the Wady called el Winga amongst Tallah trees
19	WbyS½S	29			at 4PM passed the end of the Mounts of Fezan which here take a bend to the South in a direction SSW El Fow or the Wady of Cool breezes
20	WbyS	27			in the desert
21	W½N	30			at 8.30 A.M passed Bookra or the limping father a
				Antares 25.47'N	Small hill Wady Sirdilis
24	WbyS	2			
	WNW	3			the entrance of the pass in the hills
	WSW	2			Cleard the hills and Entred the Wady Ghat
	SSW	17			

---

[7]Clapperton made no record of the subsequent return journey to Ubari by the route previously travelled through Wadi al Ajal on 12-16 June

25	SSW	14	Antares	
			25.15'	Wady Tinisala
26	SW	10		Tallah tree in the Wady
	SSW	10	Formht.	
			24.57'N	Ghaat
August				
3	NNE	18		to the entrance to the pass in the Mountains
	NE	3		the pass called El Luglughlan
	ENE	2		in a wady in the mts called El. Lughlughan from the pass
4	EbyN½N	2		
	SE	2½		through a mountain pass to Wady Talia & a spring 3° 30'
	EbyS	3½		
5	E½N	30		passed sand hills on each side from noon to 4 PM in the Taita or desert 3° 30'
6	EbyS	18		to a natural cave in the Fezan Mountains
	EbyS½S	8		up the bed of Mountn torrent whose Sides were like the a wall of freestone rock
7	EbyS½S	26		at 4 on a plain – sand hills to the south Elghamoot
8	E¾S	16		wady elwan well
9	E½S	28		on the desert plain
10	EbyS	26		Harmawa
11	ESE	29		at 4 AM amongst some low hills saw Agar at 4 PM about 8 Miles to the North at 6.30 arrived at Humam

[From Traghan in Fezzan to Kukawa in Borno, November 1822 – February 1823]

November

21	Treghan		Mn Altde O	
			25.44.50.N	Treghan
21	South	5	Formht.	
			25.51.10.N.	Maafen 15.23.36. S15E-
22	SSW	21	Mn Altde O	
			25.30.56.N	Meastoota 15.21. -. S7W
24	South	18	Mn. Altde O	
			25.13.44N	desert 15.25.42 S15E
26	S½W	20	Mn Altde O	
			24.53.15N	Gatrone
				Evening Amplitude
				260-30′ 15.29.30

December

7	SbyW½W	3	24.45.15	Madroosa 15.24.12 S2°W
8	SbyW½W	14	24.31.15	Gasserawa – the Castle
				above
				[illeg. 15.35.32. S2W]
9	SbyW½W[8]	12	Mn Altde O	
			24-19-12	Tegerhe S 2W
				15.20.18 Long^de E
				variation morn. 14°1′
				& eve. 14°9′W
13	S½E	6	Mn Altde O	
			24.14.47	The Wells of Oma
				15.30.24 S20E
15	WbyS	2		
	SSW	3		
	S½E	7	24.4.7	on the desert 15.30.36
				South
16	S½E	22	Mn Altde Sirius	
			23.44.23	Wells of Mishree
				15.39.24 S22E

[8]Fair copy has S20E.

17	South	2		
	SbyW½W	20	23.24.23	Marqa or Mayyau
				15.38.6 S4W
18	SSW½W	20	Mn Alt Sirius	
			23.6.16	on the Desert 15.32.54
				S13W
19	SSW½W	20		
	SW	8	Mn Altde O̱	
			22.48.27	El Waur S18°W 2S –
				15.24.24
21	SWbyS	24	22.17.35	on the Desert S19W
				15.16.56
22	SWbyS	22	Mn Altde Sirius	
			21.59.11	The Wells of El Ahmer
				S19W 15.9.44
23	SSW	22	21.37.23	on the desert 15.6.36
24	SWbyS	26	Mn Altde Sirius	
			21.13.51	The Wells of Mafrous
				14.50.8 S19W
25	SW¾W	22	20.51.57	in the dry bed of
				Mountain Torrent S5W
				14.56.14 Amplde Ed
				260°30'[9]
26	SbyW½W	9		
	SW½S	14	Mn Altde O̱	
			20.32.36N	Izhiah
				Water trees & grass
				S20°W10 14.50.14
30	SW½S	22	20.12.26	on the Gravelly plain
				S24 W22 14.41.20
31	SW½W	26	19.51.8	between 2 hills
				S35.W26 – 14.26.26
January				
1	SW½W	2		
			Mn Altde O̱	
			19.49.24	the Wells of Uggeba
				Hatiya – on the South

---

[9]From fair copy version.

				Side of a range of hills running ESE & WSW
				Long^de S35 W2
3	SbyW[10]	18	[19.31.24]	at the foot of a detached hill [Long^de 13.51.26][11]
4	SbyW	8	Mn Altde Sirius	
			19.22.10N	Town of Ani
5	SW½W	5	Mn Altde O	
			19.19.12	Town of Guzabee or Gusabie
6	SSW	11	Mn Altde Sirius	
			19.8.11	Ashinuma or Asinoma
8	SSW	9	Mn Altde O	passed a town called Aligi 3 Miles from Ashinooma – a lake abreast of it
			18.59.13	Dirkie or by the Tibboos Dirgoo in the Wady
10	SbyW½W	8	[18.50.13][12]	
12	SbyW½W	12	Mn Altde O	
			18.40.44	Bilma or Boolma
15	South	5	[18.34.56]	Mi ska,tinoo an Oasis
16	S½W[13]	14	Mn Altde Sirius	
			18.21.11	["Kaffle oasis" deleted] Zow Dubeh Oasis
17	South	8	Mn Altde Sirius	
			18.14.11	Oasis of Zow Dis. O – C Westn Long^de 12.48.30 E
18	S¾W	14	Mn Altde Sirius	
			18. 1.51	Ama che quoima
19	SbyW	14	Mn Altde Sirius	
			17.48.38	on the desert
20	S¾E	18	Mn Altde Sirius	
			17.32.5	The Wells of Dubelah

[10]For this, and the next entry, the fair copy version has S4E.
[11]From fair copy version.
[12]Left blank. Data for this, and for log entry 15th January below, taken from the fair copy version.
[13]The courses for this and the following three days' march are recorded as being East, rather than West, of South in the fair copy version.

				Oasis at the foot of rock hills south side
21	S¾E	12		Mn Altde Sirius
			17.21.43	Desert O – C[14] [Long^{de}] 12.37
22	SbyW½W	17		Mn Altde Sirius
			17.4.38	Desert
23	SbyW½W	15		Mn Altde Sirius
			16.49.22	Agadim to the Southd of a range of Hills running from [ ] distant a Mile & a half
25	SbyW½W	17		Mn Altde Sirius
			16.32.32	Tintuma desert
26	SbyW¾W	18		[illeg]
			16.13.52	Eclipse 13.45 East[15]
27	SWbyS¾S	17		Mn Altde Sirius
			15.55.49N	Tintuma Desert
28	SWbyS½S	8		Mn Altde Spica
			15.48.53	Belkashifra
29	SWbyS	14		Mn Altde O
	ENE	2	15.36.13	Well of Dugasheemee
31	S¾W	18		Mn Altde Sirius
			15.19.28	on the Bornou road
				February
1	S½E	15		Mn Altde Sirius
			15. 4.58	Bornou Road
2	S by E	18		Mn Altde Sirius
			14.40.28	Wells of Kaffee [o]r Koofee
3	SSW	20		Mn Altde Sirius
			14.29.46	The wells of Hummam or Maetema
4	SSW½W	13		Sirius
			14.19.6	The town of Lari N.W end of Chat Lake 5th AM. O – C 13.44

---

[14]See Chapter Thirteen, n. 3.
[15]See Chapter Seven, n. 5.

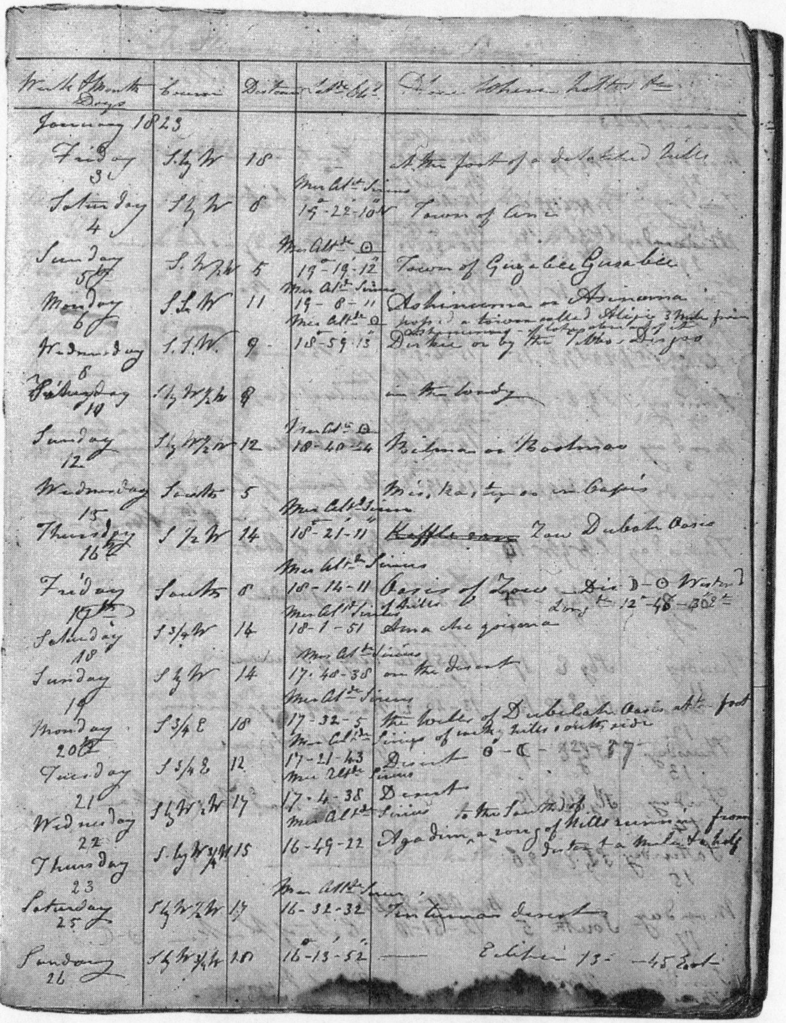

Figure 14. Log of itineraries: December 1822 to January 1823

6	SWbyW	10		Banks of Chat
7	SWbyS	8	Sirius	
			14.5.22	Town of Woodee
11	S by E	17	Sirius	
			13.51.26	City of Burwa
12	SbyE½E	12	Sirius	
			13.40.21	Banks of Sugalarum
13	S by E	9		Yow City & river
14	SbyE½E	19		on the road to Kooka *13.47*
15	S by E	20		
17	South	5	Mn Altde Dubhe	
			12.51.18N	City of Kooka O – C
			13.47.36 E	

Figure 15. Watercolour of Idni

APPENDIX 4

A LIST OF MERCHANTS

A list of merchants, with their camels and slaves, travelling to Fezzan from Borno on 12th September 1824[1].

[Page 1]

Merchant	Camels	Slaves	M. & F
From Mourzuk[2]			
Hadje Boo Zaid			m80 f12
["Mohamed Ebn Taleb" deleted]			
Hadje Mohamed Zy Abeden		23	
Hadje ben Hamed		37	
Mohamed Gadiran	6	26	
Mohamed ben Hadje Mohd			
& Mohd Mameluke W.R.		40	
Abdelaziz ben Hadje Abd		30	
Mohamed en Gorgadee		12	
Sultan ben Dumbarina			
from Sockna			
Mohamed ben Ebn Taleb		70	
& Bozherera			m8 f12
Mohamed ben zedoa		5	
& Boobuker		6	

---

[1]Sunday 12th September, 1824 [*Clapperton in Borno* pp. 215- 216, amended].

[2]Listed on page 1 by town of origin, the latter being written sideways across the margin.

Merchant	Camels	Slaves	M. & F
from Misurata			
Mohamed Bughula	5		15
Salem ben Abdullah	3		19
La mem boo fooness	5		16
Boobuker boo fooness	7		13
Mifta el Ghaowel	6		32
Hamed el Muturdi	2		9
& Touzela. abd. Sumat	7		22
& Yussef, Abed Abrachman el Furzanee			
from Jerba			
Hadje Abraham			
& Massoud	9		45
Abderabu	2		12
Fughaboo	5		
Mohamed. Sia	2		5
Barca	3		7

[page 2]

Merchant	Camels	Slaves	M. & F
Sheeref Raschid	3		8
" Ottman	6		22
" Brahim	2		15
Bookhaloom	20		45
Boobuker BukooBoum			8
Mabrook ben Shinor	2		9
Massoud be drachman	2		12
Ougela	2		6

There is no other list of the merchants in the caravan with which Clapperton and Denham travelled from Borno back to Fezzan. The caravan was formed of merchants who had been engaged on business, some for over twelve months, in both Borno and the Hausaland. Its departure had originally been planned for August but had had to be put back when heavy rains delayed the arrival of the contingent from Kano.

Clapperton and Denham's arrangements to travel with this caravan were made with the assistance of Shaikh al-Kanami, who had an interest in assuring that proper assistance was available to them – guides, couriers and other helpers. Al-Kanami would have felt some responsibility for the safety of British travellers returning to Fezzan, especially since arrangements had just been made for John Tyrrwhit to remain in Kukawa as the official British vice consul to Al-Kanami's court and state. Similar responsibilities were probably impressed on the leader(s) of the caravan (Hadje Ben Hamid, Hadje Mohamad zy Abdun of Murzuq and Mohamad Ebn Taleb of Suknah) who were all trusted connections of al-Kanami's and already well known to Clapperton and Denham[3].

Clapperton evidently had time as the caravan assembled in Wudi, two days before its departure for the Sahara, to establish who his travelling companions would be on the return journey to Fezzan. It is impossible, however, to say how systematically he approached the collection of his information. On one previous occasion he had noted a departing slave caravan comprised of merchants who had travelled to Borno with Bu Khallum and the Mission in 1822-23 [*Clapperton in Borno*, Wednesday 16th July, 1823, p.160]:

> there were 5 of them with about 120 female and Male slaves – viz Hadje Ahmet 57 Showa Bendou 13 Mohamed Fitif 10 Abdul Whaid [ ] & a man from Mesurata"

Here we see an average of 24 slaves to each merchant but Clapperton offers no information on the number of camels in the caravan.

By any standards, the numbers returning to Fezzan in September 1824 represent a considerable slave caravan: 35 merchants, 637 slaves and 94 camels. Presumably there were also servants (or personal slaves), guides, slave-drivers and camel-drivers who might have raised the number of travellers to at least 700. What is striking about Clappperton's list is the fewness of the camels: he counts only 94 in all. Even if all of them were carrying food and water for the caravan, and nothing else, and if not one of the merchants rode, there would have been a ratio of seven humans to every camel. This in turn suggests that the slaves, in particular, would have been on very short rations: the Tuareg normally allowed one camel load of provisions for every four slaves in transit across the desert, while the Tebu provided a starvation diet of one camel-load for every ten slaves[4]. No doubt the merchants of Clapperton's caravan expected to meet on the road Tebu traders willing to sell dates to augment the dangerously meagre supplies the caravan itself carried.

---

[3]See, for example, *Clapperton in Borno*, Chapter 5, pp. 170-174.

[4]FO 84/919, Vice Consul Gagliuffi to Consul General Herman, 31st December 1852, enclosed in Herman to Foreign Secretary Lord Clarendon, 14th March 1853.

It may well be, of course, that Clapperton failed to list all the caravan's camels, or counted only camels carrying trade goods. The figures as they stand, however, are notable. One merchant (Hadje Mohamed Zy Abeden) had 23 slaves, another (Mohamed ben Hadje Mohd) 40; but apparently neither had any camels. It is difficult to understand how they fed and watered their slaves, unless several fellow-merchants carried supplies for them, which seems an odd arrangement.

The large number of male slaves owned by three merchants (Hadje Boo Zaid – 80 slaves; Abdelaziz ben Hadje Abd – 30 slaves; and Mohammed ben Ebn Taleb – 70 slaves) raises serious questions about security. For, on the face of it[5], it is not clear how these three men managed to drive a total of 180 sullen, malevolent boys, youths and even full-grown men (outnumbering the merchants by 5:1) across the Sahara without the help of a considerable body of armed and whip-wielding guards that Clapperton does not mention at all.

---

[5]Some individuals counted as 'slaves', for example, may have already been in the employment of the longer-term visiting merchants.

APPENDIX 5

CLAPPERTON'S CARTOGRAPHY

In general, I can not praise too highly the zeal and accuracy (allowance being made for his positions of longitude) with which this eminent and successful traveller, who crossed the whole breadth of the African continent between the Mediterranean and the Bight of Benin, has laid down his various journeys.

[Barth, *Travels*, Vol. III, p. 125]

An official 'General Map' of the Borno Mission was published in the *Narrative*, but information in the present journals allows us to construct a more complete and accurate account of the routes the travellers followed.

The maps accompanying the present text are based on the itineraries, course descriptions and other observations contained in Clapperton's journals, together with, in the case of the trans-Saharan journeys, reference to his own sketch-maps which have not been published. Locations and routes have been plotted against the following:

Michelin: Afrique, Nord et Ouest, Map No 953 [1:6,000,000],
Paris, 1990; general outline and trans-Saharan journeys.

National Atlas of the Socialist People's Libyan Arab Jamahiriya,
Libya [1:3,500,000]: Secretariat of Planning, Surveying
Department, Tripoli, 1977; Fezzan general.

Russian General Staff, North Africa [1:1,000,000 and 1:500,000],
Ministry of Defence, Moscow, 1987; central and western Fezzan,
[Djanet (NG32), Sebha (NG33)], and Central Sahara, [Shorfa (NF33)].

Carte Internationale du Monde [1:1,000,000]; Institut Géographique National, Paris, 1974; central Sahara and Niger [Djado, NF33, Bilma, NE33 and ND33, Ndjamena, ND33].

U.S.A.F. Tactical Pilotage Charts, Algeria, Libya [1:500,000], Defense Mapping Agency, Missouri, 1981, H-3C andH-3D; Fezzan, and Ghat.

Cross reference has been made to the published maps of later missions of the nineteenth century, and detailed modern maps published in works by, for example, by Daniels, Mattingly (for Wadi al-Ajal and Jarma), and M. Le Coeur (for Wady Kawar)[1].

The regions of Fezzan east of Murzuk and south as far as Al-Qatrun were accurately documented by Lyon. Here Clapperton's work added little that was new. West of Murzuk however the published official map of the Mission does not do justice to the material available in Clapperton's records, and is in parts inaccurate[2]. Clapperton provides a detailed account of Wady Gharbi, and a record of two routes across the Ubari Sand Sea. We also have here the first full account of two caravan roads between central Fezzan and Ghat. For the journeys across the Sahara and back the journals add more details than were published at the time. The routes between Tripoli and Fezzan had already been mapped by Lyon and have not been studied in detail here.

Clapperton's calculations of latitudes are notably accurate[3]. He also attempted, with reasonable success, occasional calculations of longitude by the lunar distance method. A comparison of his estimates [see Appendix 3] with the true positions of principal towns, settlements and wells visited often demonstrates the accuracy of his calculations.

In addition, Clapperton kept a running estimate of his position by dead reckoning –

---

[1]The editors wish to record their particular thanks to Simon Pressey, cartographer, for his expert presentation of the present maps.

[2]See Clapperton's letter of 19th September 1822 to John Barrow [Appendix I. ii]. Clapperton was of course not present in London to oversee preparation of the maps to accompany *The Narrative*. The result was that a number of errors emerged in the published work, as Bovill, for one, remarks: "his [Clapperton's] map showing the route he and Oudney followed on their visit to Edri and Ghat does not make sense..." [*Missions*, Vol. II, pp. 122-4].

[3]Clapperton had been well trained in the Royal Navy. On the Great Lakes of Canada in 1815-16 he served under, and for a short period alongside, one of the great naval hydrographers of the day, Capt. W. F. W. Owen R.N., whose three-year study of the complete coastline of Africa was one of the masterpieces of post-Napoleonic War naval survey. See P. A. Penfold (ed.) *Maps and Plans in the Public Record Office, Part 3. Africa*, (H.M.S.O., London, 1982) Items 200, 254-5, 459, 716, 862-4.

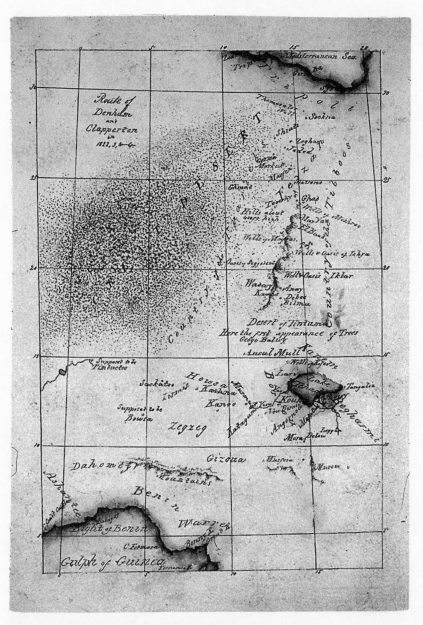

Map 16. Early 19th century map of the Sahara

a method of only moderate reliablity, despite accurate estimates of distance marched thanks to the regular pace of a caravan[4]. Considerable difficulties attach to the necessary multiple calculations when bearings from a hand-held compass are taken while travelling a constantly winding route through a featureless terrain, and in a loom created by the hot desert air that exaggerates distances – and errors in the recording of course notes or slips of arithmetic have of course a cumulative effect. Thus, the record of routes Clapperton travelled in an east-west direction is more liable to inaccuracies whereas in a broadly north-south direction, i.e. crossing the Sahara, it is sound – as he proved to his own satisfaction when guides became lost on a starless night on the return journey. Some of the records of courses marched in a southerly direction indicate that readings by Clapperton's hand-held compass were perhaps one point ($11\frac{1}{4}°$) or more West of true[5].

From his combined notes we can establish fully Clapperton's routes. The journeys were, of course, for the greatest part on established camel tracks between places of habitation or wells identifiable today. The editor finds some lack of clarity in the navigational record only in the middle section of his journey across the empty quarter between central Fezzan and Al Awaynat in Wadi Sardalas. Also praiseworthy – given the fallibility of oral information – are Clapperton's not unsuccessful efforts throughout his travels to obtain and assess information on adjacent lands and route[6].

Transscription into English of Arabic place-names is hazardous, and in the case of Fezzan in the early 19th century, with a multitude of languages and dialects, it would be impossible to adopt an academic system of transliteration. There are also some problems with Tubu and Tifanagh, not least on account of transliteration into different European languages, notably French, German and Italian. In the maps accompanying the text, names of identifiable places in Fezzan have been written following offical Libyan practice today, and in central and southern Sahara following the French-based spellings adopted in the Republic of Niger. Clapperton's spellings have been retained where place-names no longer apply (shown in brackets on the maps); and locations or halts which can only be roughly estimated, are marked ' Δ '.

---

[4]"By repeated measuring with our chain, we found that, on tolerably even ground, our ordinary rate as the Tawarek travel was half an English geographical mile in thirteen minutes." [Barth, *Travels*, Vol . I, p. 168]. Note: 10 nautical miles = 11.5 statute miles = 18 kilometers.

[5]Despite occasional attempts to calibrate his compass (see Chapter nine n.10). Clapperton makes, for example, the course for the route from Agadim to Dibella to be North, whereas in fact it lies North by East.

[5]See for example accounts garnered from Hatita, and perhaps others, on the road to Ghat about the lie of the land to the south [Wednesday 24th and Thursday 25th July 1822].

APPENDIX 6

EDITORIAL PROBLEMS AND PRACTICES

The present diaries have been transscribed and reproduced in a form as close as possible to the original raw material. The approach and practices adopted for handling some of the editorial difficulties encountered are summarised below.

i) Illegible words and passages. Damaged paper or ink smears sometimes obscure single words or groups of words. Some text is squeezed in at the end of the lines or around deletions. Insertions meander between paragraphs. Poor materials – scratchy, thin writing, where tails of letters have faded, or large blobs of ink – take their toll. Where such words could not be made out clearly, italics have been used, as in other cases of doubt, signifying "looks like". Some have had to be marked as irrecoverable or illegible.

ii) Poor grammar, confusion in word order, missing words or gaps in the text. The vagaries of phraseology and poor grammatical control in Clapperton's journal arose mostly from loss of train of thought – for example, when sentences were left hanging in mid-air, or were repeated or begun again half way through. No editorial alteration or guesswork has been attempted. Gaps, including a number left intentionally by Clapperton for later completion, as in the case of proper names, are indicated by a space surrounded by square brackets.

iii) Punctuation. Clapperton's approach to punctuation is perhaps best described as an irregular system of dots and dashes annotating an unstructured stream of words. These dashes delineate thoughts rather than phrases. At moments of pause – for reflection or emphasis, or when there was a definite end to a subject on his mind or a start on a sudden new recollection – Clapperton marked a dash, or perhaps two or more. He treated breaks in and between sentences similarly. A full stop is rare, but is occasionally brought into play in place of a comma. Commas, when they occur, are usually written as dashes. Parentheses and quotation marks are sometimes included – and do not always close – but are at other times signified by a dash.

Clapperton's dashes have been retained, and where there was no punctuation at all, a spacing system has been adopted (three spaces for a full stop or colon, and two for a semi-colon or comma) to make a stream of prose readable without influencing content.

iv) Paragraphs, pagination and spaces. Clapperton's paragraphing follows no regular pattern. Course details were sometimes written on a line below, and often to the right of, the day's entry. On occasion a large space was left at the end of a day's entry, or a passage of text, presumably to allow for any additions. Wherever possible the lay-out of the original has been retained, or indicated, but for reasons of lack of space could not be systematically followed. On occasions new paragraphs have been created in massive blocks of text to facilitate reading. (Notation of original pagination has not been considered necessary.)

v) Deletions and insertions. Nearly all have been retained, if only to show absence of self-audit – the exceptions constituting very minor corrections, such as Clapperton's deletion of a repetition. Clapperton occasionally used asterisks (sometimes feint or ambiguous) to mark where passsages were to be inserted. These have also been retained.

vi) Indecipherable handwriting. Clapperton's sloping handwriting is irregular, especially at times of illness. Letters are often ill-formed in a speed-hand of his own. This can leave a run of letters, such as *i* (rarely dotted), *m, n, u, w, r, s, a* and *e,* indecipherable or ambiguous. Some numerals are similarly easily confused. Uncertainty or ambiguity has been indicated by the use of italics.

vii) General spelling. Clapperton's orthography was both idiosyncratic and casual, although not quite as wayward as it might seem to us today, belonging as it did to an age when a considerable degree of freedom in spelling was still perfectly acceptable. Some variations reflect contemporary practice; others are his own personal habits, or merely slips. Thus, for example, certain anomalies relate to particular sounds, usually vowels or dipthongs, e.g. *neuclus* ('nucleus'), *neally* ('nearly'), *smoaking* ('smoking'); *fowel* ('fowl'), and *bowel* ('bowl'); *carring* ('carrying'). Confusion appears over double letters, *pallace* ('palace'), or presence or not of the letter '*e*' as in *alternatly, squabbeling*. Inconsistencies, such as *watered/waterd/watred*, make it harder still to decide what is the norm and which the slip or exception. These forms and variations have been retained, with a few exceptions. Where spelling mistakes make for lack of clarity or could disturb the train of reading, the text has been annotated accordingly, by insertion, e.g., *of[f]*, or use of '[sic]'.

viii) Spelling of proper names. Names of places and people no longer identifiable are the most significant casualties of all these variations. Clapperton was often content to write down an approximation of what he heard, or what seemed appropriate, but he was not consistent. Like his companions, he sometimes adopted a French-based spelling form [*Kouka* for Kuka]. Where a name was evidently unclear to Clapperton and thus written down differently on different occasions, or where it is only partially legible and occurred more than once, extreme variants have been replaced by what seem to be the more usual forms – to avoid confusion, rather than for the sake of harmonization.

ix) Abbreviations. Clapperton was given to using abbreviations, not only at line- or page-ends where space was cramped, but regularly throughout his journals; such as *ob^d* (observed), *ac^a* (accompany), *st^d* (started). Some have naval derivations, e.g. *Isl^ds* (islands). Many, such as *n^o* (or *N^r*, *No-*, or, confusingly, *no* for 'number'), are shortened in several different ways. These short forms have been retained with annotation of the more obscure or potentially ambiguous.

x) Capital letters. Like most of his contemporaries, Clapperton deployed capital letters liberally, and often inconsistently, for a variety of purposes: for some, but not all, words of foreign derivation and some proper nouns, for instance animals; for emphasis; to start a quotation; or to mark a pause for thought. They can sometimes be likened to a drawing-in of breath; at other times they seem merely a habit of handwriting, for instance when the preceeding word finished with an upward stoke. These have been retained.

xi) Repetitions, duplications, simple slips and omissions. Minor errors of repetition (for example over a line- or page-end), have been corrected as appropriate for ease of reading, as have obvious slips or omissions making for ambiguity (such as *w[h]ere*, *the[y]* or *there* for *their*) .

The elements listed above fall into three broad categories. In some cases editorial guesses or alterations could have put accuracy at risk [e.g. i, ii, iii, v, vi, viii]; in a second group of cases there could be an argument for some editorial massaging of the text [vii, ix, xi]. In a third category [iv, x] editorial alteration is probably of little or no material significance, and a matter of style and personal preference, although here the argument in favour of keeping the flavour of the original applies, even if it may not be strictly necessary – as in the retention of both & and *and*[1].

---

[1] The antiquated ß, double 'ss', form used by Clapperton has not been retained.

A purist approach to transscription could make for absurdities but, equally, partial editorial massage risks error and inconsistencies, sometimes with a potentially cumulative effect. Words, particularly proper names, are unlikely to be retrieved once given the hallmark of published authority. The transscriber has therefore attempted to steer a course between openness and pedantry: to seek accuracy but to declare doubt, with the addition of any appropriate editorial comment or guess, for the sake of preservation of the original material.

BIBLIOGRAPHY

I   **Public Record Office, Kew, London**
i) Foreign Office Papers:
FO 76   (1756 – 1837))   Tripoli Consulate General and Vice-
FO 101 (1837 –   ))   Consulates at Benghhazi, Derna, Murzuq,
)   Ghadames and Misurata.
FO 160 (1752 – 1871)   Tripoli, Letter Books & Correspondence.

ii) Colonial Office Papers:
CO 2   Exploration: Original Correspondence, 1794 – 1844.

II   **British Parliamentary Papers**
Accounts and Papers (Annual)

III   **Royal Geographical Society, London**
Library Ms. file:
Mus. No. 403/3: two letters of Hugh Clapperton.
Mus. No. 408/7: four letters of Walter Oudney.
AR 64: The papers of Major, later Lieutenant Colonel, Dixon Denham.

IV   **Travellers' Accounts**
Barth, H. *Travels and Discoveries in North and Central Africa*, etc., (5 vols., London, 1857
or 3 vols., New York 1857-59, reproduced by Frank Cass of London, 1965).
Beechey, Capt. F. W. & H. W. Beechey, *Proceedings of the Expedition to Explore the
Northern Coast of Africa*. (London, 1828).
Bovill, E. W., (ed.), *Missions to the Niger* (4 Vols., Cambridge, 1964-66).
Caillié, R. *Travels through Central Africa to Timbuctu*, etc., (2 Vols., London, 1830).
Clapperton, H., *Journal of a Second Expedition into the Interior of Africa*, etc.,
(London, 1829).

351

Major Denham, Captain Clapperton and the late Dr. Oudney, *Narrative of Travels and Discoveries in Northern and Central Africa in the Years 1822, 1823 and 1824*, 1st. ed., with XXIV Appendices, (London, 1826).

Duveyrier, H., *Exploration du Sahara: les Touareg du Nord* (2 vols., Paris, 1864).

Ibn Battuta, (trans. H.A.K. Gibb), *Travels in Asia and Africa*, 1325-1354 (London, 1929).

Jackson, J. G., *An Account of the Empire of Morocco*, (London, 1820).

Lander, R., *Records of Captain Clapperton's Last Expedition to Africa* (2 vols., London, 1830).

Lockhart, J. R. B., (ed.),*Clapperton in Borno*, Westafrikanische Studien Bd. 12 (Cologne, 1996).

Lyon, G. F., *A Narrative of Travels in Northern Arica in the Years 1818, 1819 and 1820* (London, 1821).

Nachtigal, G., *Sahara and Sudan*, trans. and ed. A. G. B. Fisher and H. J. Fisher, (4 Vols., London, 1971-88).

Park, M., *Travels in the Interior Districts of Africa* (London, 1799).

Richardson, J., *Travels in the Great Desert of Sahara in the Years of 1845 and 1846.* (2 vols., London, 1848); repr. Frank Cass (London, 1966).

Richardson, J., *Narrative of a Mission to Central Africa*, etc., (2 vols., London, 1853); repr. Frank Cass, London, 1970).

Rohlfs, G., *Quer durch Afrika: Reise vom Mittelmeer nach dem Tschadsee und zum Golf von Guinea* (2 vols., Leipzig, 1874-5).

Vischer, H., *Across the Sahara from Tripoli to Bornu* (London, 1910).

V Contemporary Memoirs

Nelson, T., *A Biographical Memoir of the late Dr. Walter Oudney, Captain Hugh Clapperton and Major Gordon Laing* (Edinburgh, 1830)

Narrative of Ten Years' Residence at Tripoli (London, 1817); repr., S. Dearden, (ed.) (London 1957).

Smyth, W. H., *The Mediterranean: a Memoir Physical, Historical and Nautical* (London, 1854).

VI Reports from Societies

Proceedings of the Association for Promoting the discovery of the Interior Parts of Africa (2 vols., London, 1810).

VII Books

Agg-Alawjali, G: *Léxique (Awgalel) Touareg-Francais*, (Copenhagen, 1980).

Al-Hassan, A. Y., and D. R. Hill, *Islamic Technology: An Illustrated History* (Cambridge, 1987).

Al-Naqar, U., *The Pilgrimage Tradition in West Africa*, etc., (Khartum, 1972).

Baier, S., *A History of the Sahara in the Nineteenth Century* (Boston, 1978).

Baier, S., *An Economic History of Central Niger*. (Oxford, 1980).

Bates, O., *The Eastern Libyans: an Essay* (London, 1914).

Bellair, P., *Mission au Fezzan. Contributions à l'étude de l'Hydrogéologie de la cuvette Fezzanaise* (Tunis, 1953).

Boahen, A. A., *Britain, the Sahara and the Western Sudan, 1788-1861* (Oxford, 1964).

Bovill, E. W., *The Golden Trade of the Moors* (London, 1958).

Bovill, E. W., *The Niger Explored* (London, 1968).

Brenner, L., *The Shehus of Kukawa* (Oxford, 1973).

Briggs, L. C., *Living Races of the Sahara* (Cambridge, Mass., 1958).

Briggs, L. C., *Tribes of the Sahara* (Cambridge, Mass., 1960).

Brogan, D. and D. J. Smith, *Ghirza: A Libyan Settlement of the Roman Period* (London, 1984).

Bulliet, R. *The Camel and the Wheel* (Cambridge, Mass., 1975).

Cain, P. J. and A .G. Hopkins, *British Imperialism: Innovation and Expansion, 1688 – 1914* (London, 1993).

Capot-Rey, H. *Le Sahara français* (Paris, 1953).

Carbou, H., *La région du Tchad et du Ouadai*, Etudes ethnographiques, Vol. I – Dialecte toubou, (2 vols., Paris, 1912).

Chapelle, J., *Nomades noirs du Sahara: les Toubous* (Paris, 1982).

Clarke, P. B., *West Africa and Islam* (London, 1982).

Cline, W., *The Teda of Tibesti, Borku and Kawar in the Eastern Sahara*, General Series in Anthropology No.12 (Menasha, Wis., 1950).

Curtin, P. D., *The Image of Africa*, (2 vols., Madison, Wis., 1964).

Daniels, C., *The Garamantes of Southern Libya* (Stoughton, Wis., 1970).

Dearden, S., *A Nest of Corsairs: the Fighting Karamanlis of the Barbary Coast* (London, 1976).

Despois, J., *Mission scientifique du Fezzan 1944-45. III – Géographie humaine du Fezzan* (Algiers, 1946).

Droandi, I., *Notizie sul cammello* (Tripoli, 1915).

El-Hesnawi, H. W., *Fezzan under the rule of the Awlad Muhammad*, etc. (Sebha, 1990).

Fage, J. D., *A History of Africa* (London, 1978).

Fisher, A. G. B. and H. J. Fisher, *Slavery and Muslim Society in Africa*. (London, 1970).

Folayan, K., *Tripoli in the Reign of Yusuf Pasha Karamanli* (Ife Ife, 1979).

Fuchs, P., *Das Brot des Wüste: sozio-ökonomie der Sahara Kanuri von Fachi*, Studien zur Kulturkunde, 67 (Wiesbaden, 1983).

Gautier, E-F., *Le passé de l'Afrique du Nord: les Siècles obscurs* (Paris, 1952).

Gautier, E-F., *Sahara: The Great Desert* (New York, 1987).

Gladstone, P., *Travels of Alexine: Alexine Tinne (1835 – 1869)* (London, 1970).

Hallett, R., (ed.), *Records of the African Association, 1788-1831* (London, 1965).

Hallett, R., *The Penetration of Africa: European Enterprise and Exploration Principally in Northern and Western Africa up to 1830* (London, 1965).

Haltenorth, T. H. and H. Diller, *Säugetiere Afrikas und Madagaskars* (Munich, 1977).

Hanoteau, A., *Essai de Grammaire de la langue Tamachek* (2nd. ed., Algiers, 1896).

Haynes, D. E. L., *The Antiquities of Tripolitania* (Tripoli, 1965).

Herodotus, *The Histories* (trans. De Selincourt), (Harmondsworth, 1954).

Hopkins, A . G., *An Economic History of West Africa* (London, 1973).

Hourani, A., *Arabic Thought in the Liberal Age, 1798-1939* (Cambridge, 1983).

Khazanov, A. M., *Nomads and the Outside World* (Cambridge, 1983).

Knowles Middleton, W. E., *Invention of Meteorological Instruments* (Baltimore, 1969).

Last, D. M., *The Sokoto Caliphate* (London, 1971).

Le Coeur, Ch., *Dictionnaire ethnographique Téda.*, Memoires de l'Institut Francaise d'Afrique Noire, No. 9. (Paris, 1950).

Le Coeur, M., *Les Oasis du Kawar – une route, un pays: Vol I: le passé pré-colonial* (Paris, 1950).

Le Rouvreur, A., *Sahéliens et Sahariens du Tchad.* (Paris, 1962).

Lethielleux, J., *Le Fezzan: ses jardins., ses palmiers* (Tunis, 1948).

Levtzion, N. and J. F. Hopkins (eds.), *Corpus of Early Arabic Sources for West African History* (Cambridge, 1981).

Lhote, H., *The Search for the Tassili Frescoes* (London, 1959).

Lhote, H., *Les Chars rupestres sahariens des Syrtes au Niger par les pays des Garamantes et des Atlantes* (Toulouse, 1982).

Lovejoy, P. E., *Salt of the Desert Sun : Salt Production and Trade in Central Sudan.* (Cambridge, 1986).

Lukas, J., *Die Sprache der Tubu in der Zentralen Sahara* (Berlin, 1953).

Mackworth-Praed, C. W. and C. H. B. Grant, *Birds of West Central and Western Africa*, (2 Vols., London, 1970).

McBurney, C. B. M., *The Stone Age of Northern Africa.* (Harmondsworth 1960),

Merighi, A., *La Tripolitania Antica*, (2 Vols., Intra Verbania, 1940).

Micacchi, R., *La Tripolitania sotto il dominio dei Caramanli* (Intra, 1936).

Mori, A., *L'esplorazione geografica della Libia* (Florence, 1927)

Morsy, M., *North Africa 1800 – 1900: A Survey from the Nile Valley to the Atlantic* (London, 1984)

Nicolaisen, J., *Ecology and Culture of the Pastoral Tuareg* (Copenhagen, 1963).

Norris, H .T., *The Tuaregs: Their Islamic Legacy and its Diffusion in the Sahel* (Warminster, 1975).

Oliver, R., and Fage, J. D. *A Short History of Africa* (Harmondsworth, 1962).

Pennell, C. R., (ed.), *Piracy and Diplomacy in Seventeenth Century North Africa*, etc., (London, 1989).

Rodd, F. R., *People of the Veil*, etc. (London, 1926).

Rossi, E., *Storia di Tripoli e della Tripolitania dalla conquista Araba al 1911* (Rome, 1968).

Sahara Italiano, Il; Parte Prima – Fezzan e l'Oasi di Gat. Bollettino della Reale Società Geografica Italiana (Rome, 1937).

Savage, E., (ed.) *The Human Commodity – Perspectives on the Trans-Saharan Slave-Trade* (London, 1992).

Scarin, E., *Le Oasei del Fezzan, Ricerche ed osservazioni di geografia umana* (2 Vols., Bologna, 1934).

Scarin, E., *L'Insediamento umano della zona fezzanese di Gat* (Florence, 1937)

Scortecci, G., *Sahara* (Milan, 1945).

Taha, A. D., *The Muslim Conquest and Settlement of North Africa and Spain* (London, 1989).

Thiry, J., *Le Sahara Libyen dans l'Afrique du Nord Médiévale* (Leuven, 1995).

Todd, M. L. *Tripoli the Mysterious* (Boston, Mass., 1912).

Trimingham, J. S., *A History of Islam in West Africa* (Oxford, 1970).

Ward, P., *Touring Libya: The Southern Provinces* (London, 1968).

Wheeler, M., *Rome beyond the Imperial Frontiers* (Harmondsworth, 1954).

Wiet, G., *Configuration de la Terre* (Beirut and Paris, 1964).

Williams, E., *Capitalism and Slavery* (London, 1964).

Wright, J., *Libya*, (London, 1969).

Wright, J., *Libya, Chad and the Central Sahara* (London, 1989).

Zeltner, J. C., *Pages d'Histoire du Kanem, pays Tchadien* (Paris, 1980).

VIII Papers and Articles

Austen, R. A., The Trans-Saharan Slave Trade: a Tentative Census, in H. Gemery and J. Hogendorn (eds.), *The Uncommon Market: Essays in the Economic History of the Atlantic Slave Trade*, (New York, 1979), pp. 23-76.

Bovill, E. W., "Colonel Warrington" in *The Geographical Journal*, Vol. 131, Part 2, June 1965, pp. 161-166.

Brenner, L., "The North African trading commmunity", etc., in D. F. McCall and N .R. Bennett (eds.), *Aspects of West African Islam*, Boston University Papers on Africa, Vol. 5 (Boston, 1975) pp. 137-150.

Capot-Rey, H., "Le nomadisme des Toubous" in *Nomades et nomadisme du Sahara* (Paris, 1963) pp. 81-93.

Cauneille, A. "Le semi-nomadisme dans l'Ouest libyen (Fezzan, Tripolitaine)" in *Nomades et nomadisme du Sahara* (Paris, 1963) pp. 101-112.

Colvin, L. G., "The commerce of Hausaland 1780-1833" in D. F. McCall and N .R. Bennett (eds.) *Aspects of West African Islam* (Boston, 1971) pp.101-135.

Cordell, D. D., "The Awlad Sulayman of Libya and Chad: Power and Adaptation in the Sahara and Sahel" in *Canadian Journal of African Studies*, 1 , 2 (1985) pp. 319-343.

Fisher, H .J., "The Eastern Maghreb and the Central Sudan" in R. Oliver (ed.), *Cambridge History of Africa, Vol. 3, 1050-1600* (Cambridge, 1977).

Fisher, H. J., "The Horse in the Central Sudan" in *Journal of African History*, Part I, Vol. XIII, No. 3, (1972) pp. 367-388 ; Part II, Vol. XIV, No. 3 (1973) pp. 355-379.

Herzog, R., "Ein Beitrag zur Geschichte des nordafrikanischen Karavanenhandels" in *Die Welt des Islams*, Vol .VI. (1959-61) pp. 255-262.

Hume, L. J., "Preparation for civil war in Tripoli in the 1820s: Ali Karamanli, Hassuna D'Ghies and Jeremy Bentham" in *Journal of African History*, 21, 3 (1980) pp. 311-322.

Hunwick, J. O., "Black Slaves in the Mediterranean World: Introduction to a Neglected Aspect of the African Diaspora" in E. Savage, (ed.) *The Human Commodity*, (London, 1992) pp. 5 – 38.

Law, R. C .C., "The Garamantes and Trans-Saharan Enterprise in Classical Times" in *Journal of African History*, VII, 2 (1967) pp. 181-200.

Mahadi, A., The Aftermath of the Jihad in the Central Sahara as a Major Factor in the Trans-Saharan Slave Trade in the Nineteenth Century" in E. Savage (ed.) *The Human Commodity: Perspectives on the Trans-Saharan Slave Trade* (London, 1992) pp. 111-128.

Playfair, R. L., "Bibliography of the Barbary States. Part I. Tripoli and Cyrenaica". *Royal Geographical Society Supplementary Papers*, Vol. II. (London, 1889) pp. 557-614

Vikor, K. S., "The Desert-side salt trade of Kawar" in *African Economic History*, 1982, No. 11, pp. 115-144.

Zeltner, J-C., "Islam et sociétés au sud du Sahara: Tripolitaine et pays toubou au XIXe siècle" in *Cahiers annuels pluridisciplinaires*, No. 3 (Paris, 1989) pp. 90-105.

IX Ph.D. Thesis
Wright, J., "Nothing Else but Slaves": Britain and the Central Saharan Slave Trade in the Nineteenth Century (unpub. Ph.D. Thesis, London, 1998).

INDEX